Contents

Acknowledgments

Introduction: Taking Parts   v
in a Conversation About Leadership

Ingredients for Leadership

Chapter 1	**Leadership as Practical Wisdom:** **The Parable of Lincoln** Michael A. Leiserson	1
Chapter 2	**Rating the Presidents for Greatness:** **What Role Does Crisis Play?** Frank B. Costello, S.J.	29
Chapter 3	**Ignatius:** **Wisdom Through Discernment** Patrick B. O'Leary, S.J.	53
Chapter 4	**Perceval:** **From Naivete to Wisdom** Peter B. Ely, S.J.	75

Ingredients for Participation

Chapter 5	**"But Trusted Servants:"** **A Meditation on the A.A. Conception of Leadership** Thomas M. Jeannot	91
Chapter 6	**A Democratic Model of Leadership: Politics in an All Female Community** Eloise A. Buker	115
Chapter 7	**Italian/American Women Writers: Family Shapes Community** Mary Jo Bona	135
Chapter 8	**Learning to Lead** Jane A. Rinehart	151

Ingredients for Empowerment

Chapter 9	**Making School Real: Leadership in the Classroom** Julie Tammivaara	179
Chapter 10	**Careful Mutuality: Leadership and Friendship in the Workplace** Rose Mary Volbrecht	195
Chapter 11	**We Need Not Be Ruled By Leaders: The Early Town Meetings** Robert Waterman	215
Chapter 12	**A Lesson for Citizens** Blaine Garvin	233

About the Authors — 261

TAKING PARTS

Ingredients for Leadership, Participation, and Empowerment

Edited by
ELOISE A. BUKER
MICHAEL A. LEISERSON
JANE. A. RINEHART

Co-Authors
Mary Jo Bona, Eloise A. Buker,
Frank Costello, S.J., Peter B. Ely, S.J.,
Blaine Garvin, Thomas M. Jeannot,
Michael A. Leiserson, Patrick B. O'Leary, S.J.,
Jane A. Rinehart, Julie Tammivaara,
Rose Mary Volbrecht, Robert Waterman

UNIVERSITY
PRESS OF
AMERICA

Lanham • New York • London

Copyright © 1994 by
University Press of America,® Inc.
4720 Boston Way
Lanham, Maryland 20706

3 Henrietta Street
London WC2E 8LU England

All rights reserved
Printed in the United States of America
British Cataloging in Publication Information Available

Library of Congress Cataloging-in-Publication Data

Taking parts : ingredients for leadership, participation and
empowerment / edited by Eloise A. Buker, Michael A. Leiserson,
Jane A. Rinehart ; co-authors, Mary Jo Bona ... [et al.].
p. cm.
Includes bibliographical references.
1. Leadership. 2. Social participation. 3. Power (Social sciences)
I. Buker, Eloise A. II. Leiserson, Michael A. III. Rinehart, Jane A.
IV. Bona, Mary Jo.
HM141.T343 1993 303.3'4—dc20 93–45519 CIP

ISBN 0–8191–9396–8 (cloth : alk. paper)
ISBN 0–8191–9397–6 (pbk. : alk. paper)

 The paper used in this publication meets the minimum requirements of American National Standard for Information Sciences—Permanence of Paper for Printed Library Materials, ANSI Z39.48–1984.

Acknowledgments

This book is the result of a collaborative effort which is described in the Introduction. The editors appreciate each contributing author's patience, generosity, and hard work. We also want to thank a few individuals who made special contributions to this work: Bob Cahill and Kathie Yerion, for their help creating a much better title than the original one; Joanna Leiserson, for her expert assistance with the proofreading; and Sandy Hank, for her perseverance and good humor in preparing the manuscript for submission. Most of all, we are grateful to the students who have been both the real and imagined readers of these essays.

Introduction

Taking Parts in a Conversation about Leadership

This book is a contribution to the contemporary debate about how Americans can take an active part in shaping their lives and communities. In it we show some possibilities for meaningful social action at a time when many Americans seem disillusioned about their prospects for influencing events and policies. We write as teachers who have shared a conversation about leadership for the past several years. We came to that conversation from various academic disciplines, sharing some concerns and differing on others. We wanted to produce a work that would reveal what it is like to think seriously in collaboration with others, and that would invite readers into that work as partners.

Although each essay in the book was written by a single author, all of the contributors are responsible for the whole book. This does not mean that each of us agrees with everything that is written on these pages. What it means is that everything in the collection has been shaped by the readings and responses we have given to each other's work. Our individual essays echo the themes and concerns of the others, while also presenting a distinctive approach. For each of us, the topic of leadership has proved to be a vehicle for raising the issues of vision, character, communication, responsibility, and community. We see leadership as the task of helping life to flourish within groups, and we regard this as a task in which everyone can take part.

How The Book Came To Be

When we started work on this book, all the contributors were located at Gonzaga University in Spokane, Washington. Gonzaga is a Roman Catholic and Jesuit university with an enrollment of around four thousand students. It was founded in 1887 by Jesuit missionaries as a liberal arts college, and undergraduate teaching in the liberal arts is still the heart of what Gonzaga does. The Jesuit founders of Gonzaga had this in common with us: they believed, as we do, that excellent training in the liberal arts is the foundation not only for advanced studies, but also for better individual lives and communities. It matters that this book began at Gonzaga because Gonzaga provided this shared outlook as well as a shared setting.

Sharing an outlook does not mean, however, that we twelve authors are all alike. We are not all Catholics, let alone Jesuits; indeed, some of us are not religious believers. Most of us received our advanced degrees from non-Catholic universities, and have taught in places quite unlike Gonzaga. We are in different disciplines: education, literature, philosophy, political science, religious studies, sociology. Five of us are women. We each have strong philosophical or political passions not shared by everyone else involved in this project. We came to Gonzaga with different expectations, but once here we found an attractive meeting ground. On this ground, we came together and talked about important questions. Our differences from each other seem to have enlivened us, rather than threatening us into silence. We have respect and affection for one another and for our students. To put the point another way, we are enough alike that we could talk with each other, but not so much alike that our conversations would become mere variations on a single theme. In our conversations, we have assumed that differences can be appreciated and commonalties discovered.

We authors of this book have come to know and value one another not only in writing this book but in many kinds of conversations about our curriculum, teaching, public policy, and university governance. We recognize that our work as teachers, scholars, and citizens requires leadership skills. In this sense, we have experimented with the ideas expressed in our book, learning from both our successes and failures. We have found ways to question each other, and to be creative and positive about both our differences and our connections. We have found our conversations about leadership energizing, delightful, frustrating, and more. Sometimes the difficulties seemed overwhelming, but we kept coming back and discovered ways to listen and talk to each other that created this book.

Now we want you to regard the book as a conversation that requires your participation in order to continue. We hope that you will ask us many questions as you read--ideally, mail them to us--and that you will explore your questions with your own conversation partners.

This collection of essays is the culmination of a collaboration that began during the summer of 1987, although none of us realized that at the time. Some of the eventual authors of the book were invited by administrators to meet with a donor who wanted to establish a leadership center at Gonzaga. He said that money was no object; he just wanted the best leadership center Gonzaga could design. Not surprisingly, he

Introduction: a Conversation About Leadership

got our full attention, and the work of planning such a center began. Over the following eighteen months, we had an intense and spirited conversation that included seminars on leadership, meetings with people representing the academic and student life divisions of the university, writing essays on the meanings of leadership in the context of Gonzaga's identity and mission, and countless informal exchanges in the hallways and parking lots. Finally we produced a comprehensive proposal that included a curriculum, special programs, and a staffing plan for a leadership institute. But by the time our plan was ready, the donor who had sparked all this effort was no longer interested. The project was dropped. Many of us had spent months of extra hours working on this dream. Naturally, we were disappointed and discouraged.

So Eloise Buker and Mike Leiserson began to talk with each other about using what they had learned to write a book about leadership. They liked the idea of continuing to work with colleagues who had been engaged in the planning for the leadership institute. Leiserson hoped for a book that would show undergraduates what leadership is and how important it is in their lives. During the drafting of the leadership institute proposal, we had struggled to reach some shared understandings about leadership, and it seemed important to say what those were. Buker envisioned a book that would preserve some of the spirit of the good conversations that had taken place, and extend an invitation to readers to continue it with us. The two agreed that their goals might be combined, although the book seemed to be a risky prospect. It would require many hours of work, on top of heavy teaching loads and other university responsibilities. But they shared memories of exciting and enriching discussions about leadership that both wanted to continue.

These two invited other faculty members whose work they admired to an exploratory discussion about the possibility of producing a book that would reflect and deepen the thinking we had been doing about leadership. Involvement at this early stage was tentative because many of us wondered what we might have to say in a book about leadership. Most of us do not see ourselves as "experts" on leadership. We entered into this collaboration with good feelings about each other, anticipating stimulating discussions, but unsure about our individual contributions. We hoped that we might find our way together.

Sometimes that hope seemed misplaced, even foolish. When we each confronted the blank page and struggled to fill it with sage words, there were moments (often long ones!) of doubting our suitability for the task. Finally, we seem to have begun, each of us, with the question: "What do I really care about?" We began writing about things that touch us deeply, that stir us intellectually and emotionally. We wrote from our own experiences, reflecting on what we value. You might say that we wrote our way toward the topic of leadership by moving into our own stories and convictions. Instead of searching for the "right way" to discuss leadership, we discovered that there were many ways, that each of us had access to some truths about leadership. We saw that these truths were connected with what we already loved--our disciplines, certain books, key historical figures, forms of community, and the goodness in people. We surprised ourselves by finding our own voices and things we very much wanted to say about leadership. We were not foolish after all.

These were delightful surprises, but there was also an unpleasant one. We wanted each other's trust and support, but we learned that our relationships were fragile. Our conversations about our writing were often painful. Despite efforts to be tactful and encouraging, we uncovered some divisions among us, and we hurt each other's feelings. We found ourselves divided on what could and should be said about the different gifts of men and women, about the nature of American society and its prospects for good, and about the worth of western intellectual traditions. We also disagreed about how the chapters were related; some of us discerned common themes, while others were more aware of significant differences of perspective and emphasis. We missed opportunities to be thoughtful, to listen carefully, and to treat each other kindly. Often, we felt threatened and anxious. These feelings were made worse because we had not anticipated having them. There were times when our diversity seemed too burdensome, and our conversation was less than civil. We began to doubt that a book was possible.

But we kept trying to explain our positions to each other, and to be open to the differences among us. We continued to meet together, even though our conflicts were not minor and were not fully resolved, as they are not still. We kept searching for enough consensus each time to help us believe that it would make sense to meet again. We began to realize that negative criticism often helped us to articulate our own positions more clearly. We found ways to overcome the feelings we had of being marginalized and misunderstood, and to re-establish trust. Civility and concern for each other became necessary conditions for continuing our work. We came to depend on each other again. When one of us became frustrated to the point of exhaustion, someone else would step in and accomplish the next task.

This was especially apparent when we reached a point in the development of our project that required greater cohesiveness among the authors. Jane Rinehart agreed to join the editorial team, a move that made official her special contributions throughout our process. This change allowed us to work more effectively because it added her energy and particular gifts when we were facing several hard tasks: naming relationships among the chapters, describing our shared vision of the book, and negotiating editorial changes with several different authors. At that moment in our project, we needed to act on Rinehart's conviction that colleagues could help each other to think/write differently and better than any one of them might do alone, and that this process might serve as an example of how leadership can happen.

Introduction: a Conversation About Leadership

What We Learned About Leadership

Our struggles taught us about some of the things our chapters try to explain: practical wisdom, communal discernment, the habits of democratic citizenship, the contributions of feminism, the meaning of authority, failure as a step toward fulfillment, the role of friendship in forming good judgment, and the delicate task of building bridges across chasms of difference and estrangement. We shocked ourselves into living some of what we were writing about. So, we moved from the safe zone where leadership was only our topic to the dangerous zone where leadership was what we needed and had to provide each other in order to continue.

The book in your hand is proof that we found ways to meet that need for leadership. Our success in producing this book is evidence of one of its themes: leadership emerges in the midst of human relationships in ways that cannot be fully anticipated. When we decided to write this book, we agreed that all of us would be partners in the endeavor, even if a few were designated as editors. This decision turned out to be crucial for our experience of leadership. Leadership among equals, as we experienced it, turns out to have at least five distinctive features. First, it is not necessarily associated with "office." We editors usually presided at our meetings, but we were not the only ones who helped to bring these gatherings to successful conclusions. Second, leadership among equals is often spontaneous, arising suddenly from unexpected sources. At times, someone who had been mostly silent during a meeting would suddenly be the one to show the way forward. Third, leadership among equals is temporary. No single person always led. Fourth, leadership can engage "followers" more often than it upsets or alienates them. This tilt in favor of engagement was crucial to our process. Finally, leadership among equals affirms the sense of shared responsibility and mutual commitment, even though at times its task is to sharpen and clarify differences. This introduction contains the ideas of several contributing authors, and emerged from a lengthy series of discussions and drafts.

We developed a conversational experience of leadership, one in which there were many parts to play and real rewards for participation. We were attracted to working on the book by the prospect of being with each other, of having lively conversations. You might say we got more liveliness than we bargained for. But we also taught each other important lessons about what can emerge when the good for each individual and the good for the group are complementary. We came to realize that what really mattered in our project is not that we struggled with conflicts, but that we worked through them to insights about leadership. Often we had fun, and even the hard times we spent together have yielded the satisfaction that comes from persevering and the delight of finding a serendipitous unity in our questions, if not in our answers.

We had to learn to redefine our goals and expectations when the original ones got us into trouble. We never did come to a single definition of leadership. Nor did we find a way to make our book represent our conversations, although most of the authors do refer to each others' chapters. Still, these talks of ours, in large groups and in pairs, are implicitly present between the lines of every essay. And we share a common question that runs through all of our chapters even though we come from various disciplines and even love different things within shared disciplines. The question we discovered that we share is another of the surprises in our process, for we did not agree upon it in advance. We identified it near the end of our working sessions, with some relief and great pleasure. Our common question is this: *How do leaders act in ways that connect moral and ethical commitments with a solid, practical understanding of concrete situations?*

We also agree that this question is rooted in the activity we all share and love: teaching. Teaching involves preparing students to enter the practical world, but it happens in a sheltered place away from it. Everybody knows this, that school is somehow different from the rest of life. What not everyone appreciates is that teachers are always mindful of the need to connect what goes on in school with the world that students will enter. The authors of this book all care about public life, and yearn for ways to talk fruitfully among ourselves and with our students about values, virtues, ethics and moral conduct. Each of us hopes that our students will contribute to making the world better. Every day teachers have to work up the courage to do an audacious thing: to presume to show others what they need to know. As teachers and authors, we are entirely serious about teaching others what is right, while also acknowledging that the right thing is often elusive, difficult to name, and that claims about it are always open to question.

Glimpses of the Chapters

Talking about morality and ethics is risky. When teaching is heavy-handed or self-righteous, students may refuse to listen, and rightly so. Such clumsiness is common enough to have made students wary before they ever enter our classrooms. We hope that our teaching experiences have taught us a bit by now about genuine persuasion. We each want our chapters to catch our readers' attention gently and invite them to settle in for a good talk with the writer. As part of this effort to attract our readers' attention, we offer here a brief glimpse of each essay in the book. Like any brief glimpse, they miss more than they reveal; still, they highlight the choices we present to our readers about the meanings of leadership, participation, and empowerment. We hope these vignettes will entice the reader to go on. The italicized portion of each summary connects it with an adjacent one, in order to reveal some of the connections

Introduction: a Conversation About Leadership

among the chapters. What follows now will be like the storyboards movie directors assemble before shooting. From its parts, a story about how leadership joins the moral and the practical will be easy enough to see--only the lively characters, the action, the movement will be missing.

Bob Waterman:
The dignity of self-reliance and the sharing of group life can be combined. If there is a setting where ordinary people can state their interests, reach agreement with their neighbors, and share in governance, then this combination is assured. The group will continuously replenish the supply of leaders.

We needn't think of leadership in inflated terms. We can all lead and a good "ordinary" life affords us all respect and power, not just the leaders or those with official power.

Frank Costello:
Greatness in leaders seems to manifest itself when it is most needed, in moments of great crisis. Leaders who pull us through a crisis deserve acknowledgment and gratitude, but also emulation; they are shining models for future leaders. Of course, nothing guarantees that a crisis will draw forth a person of the right qualities.

However praiseworthy ordinary life is, extraordinary moments in a nation's life call for greatness. Leaders have--or can have--a specific gift of vision, a vision both moral and practical. This is why we follow and treasure the great ones.

Mike Leiserson:
Leaders are most helpful when they do what the label suggests--take followers to a good place they didn't know existed. A farsighted leader shows people how to overcome the difficulties standing in the way of doing the right thing. By contrast, bad leaders mouth fears and reinforce intransigence and immobility.

Lincoln was different from other great presidents. And the difference arises from the way he was ordinary.

Julie Tammivaara:
All important education has to do with making use of power. Confine education to the few and you create a powerful elite. Confine education to specialization and you create a narrow, generally ineffectual, specialist. Genuine education for leadership ought to reach many students, approaching each of them as worthy to take up leadership.

Talking about emulating great leaders is useful, but teachers cannot hope to raise new leaders if they don't recognize their students' gifts for leadership and take these seriously. They can't do this if they take a narrow "professional" approach to their work, instead of aiming at the education of the whole person.

Taking Parts: Leadership, Participation, Empowerment

Rose Mary Volbrecht:
Other opportunities for moral leadership are found close to home. In the workplace, for example, people must learn to combine the moral and the practical, a learning best brought about by a careful mutuality. Professionals teach fellow professionals in a sort of mutual apprenticeship.
In our everyday lives, demands for moral leadership are all around us. We would be lost if we had to depend on experts. Fortunately, we have each other to depend on, too.

Eloise Buker:
We like democracy and leadership among equals, but there is a tension between our desire for democracy and our longing for efficient societies where most people can afford to pay little attention to matters of governance. To build strong communities, it is important that we develop a model of leadership that can meet both of these desires.
A commitment to equality inside the home and outside at work can be surprisingly energizing. It's not the only way to do things, but it shows how our daily lives contain opportunities for democratic participation and decision-making, as well as time for fulfilling our individual responsibilities.

Mary Jo Bona:
The family can help. Close-knit, extended families with their distinct cultures provide many models for young people to follow as they try to become good and practical adults. But when the extended family migrates to a different culture, mediators are often needed to help young people preserve the older values and integrate these with newer ones.
It's true that character is shaped, first of all, at home. But the ambiguity of the world is easier to bear if help is available from others as well. Ethnic communities can produce leaders who serve their youth in unique ways, supplementing the family's and society's leadership.

Tom Jeannot:
We often think of the best leaders as self-contained and self-reliant. But this is not the only kind of leadership. A group of people who have come to terms with their powerlessness, who have surrendered self-absorption, can discover a new kind of leadership--"servant leadership."
With or without good families and neighborhoods, we ordinary mortals still often fall on our faces. This experience has much to teach us about leadership, especially by reminding us that we need each other's help to get off the ground and back to life.

Peter Ely:
You probably won't be a leader--not a true one--if there isn't a spiritual dimension to your life. You can discover this dimension if you are open to it. The discovery may well come when you're down, for "failure"

Introduction: a Conversation About Leadership

can be the opening to growth in the wisdom that leadership requires. Leaders must receive in order to give.
Sometimes even a knight in shining armor--and our modern versions of him, both male and female--has to fall on his face before he learns what is truly important.

Pat O'Leary:
Genuine leadership becomes possible for people who put away ambition born of self-centeredness. Being open to the mystery of creation and willing to follow a call to service can produce leadership qualities of a remarkably practical kind.
What you say about the knight is true. When he has learned his lesson and stood on his feet, watch out: Now you'll see what greatness looks like.

Jane Rinehart:
A moral preparation to deal with the world is not necessarily one that affirms the world as it is or its conceptions of greatness. Being open to seeing the world from a new perspective may make possible the creative energy that changes the world.
Leaders don't just show us a good place already obvious in our familiar world; they can lead us to new worlds. What was once practical and good may seem less so from the perspective of the new world.

Blaine Garvin:
If a good relationship between leaders and followers is to be maintained, then followers must avoid inflated expectations about what leaders can do, and learn to involve themselves in the group's shared life. Cynicism and inaction undermine freedom.
Leaders try to please as many people as possible, so don't be surprised when they disappoint you. Meanwhile, get busy yourself: get them to please you!

We invite you to revisit these chapter summaries when you are a seasoned veteran of the conversation this book represents. We think they might help you to think through once more the characters and actions we use to talk about leadership, and the part each of us has chosen to play in our shared enterprise. On the other hand, you might look at them again and smile, knowing how differently you would describe the lessons you have learned.

The Organization of the Book

We have grouped our twelve chapters into three sections. Each section corresponds to one of the themes of the book's sub-title. The three sections pose three questions about how people can take different parts in social life. The chapters in the first section discuss ingredients for good leadership and ask the question: What qualities do some leaders possess that set them apart as exceptionally worthy? The next section's essays focus on the ingredients of participation in various social communities. These chapters ask the question: How do leaders emerge from participation? The third section concentrates on the ingredients for empowerment, asking the question: What relationships and attitudes enable people to act as leaders within their everyday situations and responsibilities? Of course these divisions are not air-tight: many chapters address more than one question. The variety of answers illustrates more ways that leadership can be unconventional and surprising.

Ingredients for Good Leadership

What qualities help us to identify good leaders? In some ways, the most surprising thing we have discovered about leadership is that the "bottom line" is not success. It is only after there is general agreement that someone was a good leader that it seems obvious that leadership equals power used successfully. In the actual process of exercising leadership, good leaders display a complex mixture of success and failure, ordinariness and genius. The chapters in this section show that in order to understand the ingredients for good leadership, we must get past the habit of thinking that these ingredients may be thought of as a recipe: a series of simple and straightforward steps that guarantee success. With leadership as with cooking, more is involved than knowing a list of ingredients.

Mike Leiserson's chapter on Lincoln as a parable of leadership shows that a leader's practical wisdom includes vision, inspiration, and creative suffering. Lincoln inspired Americans to give their lives to preserve a free Union in which slavery would no longer exist. He gave Americans a vision of democracy that continues to inspire people throughout the world, as symbolized in the statue of liberty erected in Tienanmen Square and the demolition of the Berlin Wall. Leiserson reveals that Lincoln's practical wisdom required taking the risk of failure. He states that it may be in our capacity to know when it is worthwhile to fail that all of us can begin to practice being leaders. As Leiserson tells it, the story of Lincoln is not as different as we might expect from a story about how everyone can learn to lead.

Frank Costello's chapter focuses on the ingredient of vision. He says that what distinguishes great leaders is their capacity to persuade people to respond to a crisis by living out a shared vision. Not that the crisis itself makes the leader great. For every Franklin Roosevelt there is a Herbert Hoover, the one elevated by the same crisis that destroyed the other. Each of America's great presidents was guided by a vision and possessed the confidence to pursue it. Costello's portrait of the vision

Introduction: a Conversation About Leadership

that guided five great American presidents shows a family resemblance to pictures of the less famous leaders in later chapters, such as Volbrecht's characterization of the qualities of relationships that can foster leadership and Rinehart's portrait of leadership as a willingness to take risks in responding to the needs of the community.

Pat O'Leary looks at a different kind of leader, not a national president but the founder of a religious order. He emphasizes that good leadership involves inspiration. O'Leary presents the story of a leader who struggled throughout his life to learn ways of moving beyond his limits. When Ignatius of Loyola lived, the Jesuits were not the world-wide and influential group they are today. Ignatius imparted his vision to a small group of friends who took his conviction that God might be found in all things and applied it with great fervor to educational and missionary endeavors. Ignatius continues to inspire the efforts of his contemporary companions to work for social justice and spiritual growth. O'Leary's treatment of Ignatius presents interesting parallels to Jeannot's description of the "trusted servant" leader and to the leadership practiced in Buker's community of women.

It is perhaps familiar to consider practical wisdom, inspiration, and vision as ingredients of leadership. Peter Ely's characterization of leaders is more of a surprise: he tells us that leaders suffer. The tension between morality and power takes its toll on a leader. The leader is tested in its fire. A weak or evil leader will be revealed by how s/he avoids this test. A true leader will endure it in the way that a medieval knight would endure "trial by ordeal." Eventually, this process of creative suffering may bring a leader to a depth of spiritual awareness which few of us seek. Such a leader is one we can trust. This portrait of a leader resonates with Bona's mediators who provide leadership to ethnic communities and with Waterman's depiction of citizens struggling with each other to define goals and make decisions about their common life.

Ingredients for Participation

Leadership occurs in some surprising places and in exciting forms. In this section, four authors explore how leadership emerges in interactions among people who have a commitment to each other. In reading these chapters, it might be helpful to think of participation as the act of finding one's own voice, learning to play a part that is really right for oneself. The chapters in this section show some ways that this kind of participation-- active and authentic engagement with others--may foster leadership.

Tom Jeannot's chapter describes the type of leadership that emerges in groups of recovering alcoholics and in the organization of Alcoholics Anonymous. Among individuals who have admitted failure, leadership arises not from self-reliance and independence, but from service to others; not from an individual's strength, but from the group's discernment. Jeannot draws a striking contrast between would-be leaders who destroy themselves by clinging to dreams of self-sufficient greatness and leaders who discover in A.A.'s Twelve Steps and Traditions a way of life that requires dependence on others, shared responsibility, and mutual support. Jeannot's A.A. members learn that their powerlessness is a source of strength, echoing the lessons learned through failure by the knight in Ely's chapter.

Eloise Buker shows how a women's religious community practices a way of life in which connections to others and dedicated service foster democratic decision-making. Leadership among these sisters depends upon elements that we often overlook, such as the creation of supportive home environments and attention to matters of inclusion and consensus-building. The religious community displayed in Buker's essay has nurtured forms of participation that serve as a model for democratic leadership-leadership that engages and energizes the efforts of all the members of a group. Buker shows that it is not necessary to choose between effective action and full participation; she shows how shared responsibility can foster initiatives for change. She explains how her description is connected to themes in the chapters by Waterman, Jeannot, Volbrecht and Rinehart.

In Mary Jo Bona's chapter, novels by Italian-American women provide examples of how ethnic leaders recognize that the spiritual and aesthetic dimensions of a group's heritage may be valuable resources in its efforts to participate in a new society. The ethnic leaders whom Bona describes act as mediators between their group of immigrants and the world they are entering. These leaders reveal how the riches of the ethnic identity can be preserved and enhanced even as newcomers struggle to find ways of participating within a different culture. Bona says that the literary tradition of Italian/American women offers us an image of leaders who are imperfect and therefore approachable within their neighborhoods and communities. This image of the leader as mediator bears a striking resemblance to Waterman's portrait of citizens at a community meeting.

Jane Rinehart's chapter challenges those of us who feel unable to influence events in our world and who regard leadership as an identity and practice that is beyond their reach. She presents examples of ways to imagine ourselves as participating in transforming our world. Rinehart draws on her experiences with students in the introductory sociology course, her participation in feminist theorizing and education, and her understanding of teaching strategies that emphasize dialogue and active engagement to present an image of leadership open to all of us. Her chapter closes with the story of a student who discovered his capacity to respond creatively to desperate needs and thereby found a way to participate in making changes that matter.

Introduction: a Conversation About Leadership

Ingredients for Empowerment

What relationships and attitudes are needed for people to be able to take the lead within their everyday situations? How can groups and organizations nurture the development of these enabling conditions? We need to understand how leadership can be exercised by others than elected officials and bureaucratic supervisors. The four chapters in this section present challenges to a restricted notion of power, expanding our preconceptions of what leadership can look like and where it can be found. Each is concerned with empowerment as a process of connecting with others and gaining the ability to act constructively within our daily lives.

Julie Tammivaara's chapter on education shows how a person with official power (a teacher) can take steps to empower followers (students). She takes us back to the beginning of universities in the Middle Ages and forward through the development of the kind of university education we have today. Tammivaara's intention in this journey is to reveal past and present insights about the mission of the university that can serve as a basis for critical thinking about what we can hope for in university classrooms today. She invites faculty and students to establish conversations that affirm the active involvement of everyone in a process of understanding our choices and their consequences. Tammivaara urges us to teach and learn in ways that connect school with the real life tasks of deciding who we are and how we want to live.

Rose Mary Volbrecht's essay takes us to another site where people can empower themselves to shape their circumstances: the workplace. Based on her experiences working with mid-level managers and professionals to understand the practice of ethical decision-making, Volbrecht suggests that relationships are more important than rules. She shows that relationships characterized by "careful mutuality" can help people who work together to do for each other what we sometimes think it takes a powerful leader to accomplish. Volbrecht believes that we can learn ways of working together that foster the development of moral judgment through shared reflection. This can enhance both personal satisfaction in work and organizational success. The relational skills practiced in the workplace can carry over to community contexts such as those discussed by Rinehart and Waterman.

Bob Waterman demonstrates that it is still possible to put into practice the American ideal of self-governing communities. When most Americans lived in small towns, their town meetings created relationships among citizens that enabled them to lead. Waterman presents us with an attractive ingredient in America's political tradition: the commitment to local democratic decision-making. He analyzes how the town meetings worked and identifies the types of attitudes and relationships this form of politics required. His chapter closes with an example drawn from his own experience of how a similar kind of empowerment occurs today in community organizations. Waterman provides us a way to imagine dependence and independence, following and leading, differently. He suggests that this difference can help us to exercise power within our communities.

Blaine Garvin takes up the challenge of defining what we need most in order to be empowered for citizenship. Like Waterman, he does not pretend that America today matches all the conditions present in nineteenth-century town meetings. But he also shares with Waterman the conviction that citizens are still able to make a difference in American politics. Garvin argues that we need to do two things to practice citizenship: study the history that reveals how the United States meets the standard for a free and democratic society, and acquire the habits of civility that sustain political involvement in the midst of frustrations and disappointments. At the close of his chapter, Garvin expresses a desire shared by all of the contributors to this book: to encourage our readers to respond to what we have written here and to act.

Looking Backwards and Forward

Our experiences writing this book convinced us that leadership is an element of our daily lives, deeply connected with our most treasured convictions and commitments. They also showed us that leadership makes good things happen, though it does not save us from all bad things. Our book comes into your hands bearing the scars of our struggles to define for ourselves what it meant to write individually and collectively about leadership. We had many difficult conversations about the significance of gender in our thinking and relationships, how we define our work as teachers and scholars, and what we hope for in our world. These are general problems, ones that we share with many people. Our particular circumstances made it impossible to deny these points of genuine conflict, to pretend that we inhabit a utopia. Being forced to face them, we did our best to keep our disagreements from destroying our collective project. We sought ways to make sound practical judgments that could preserve both our conversations and our individual commitments. For us, the book bears the markings of our disharmonies and of our good fortune in integrating them. Our conversations have not been perfect, but we believe they have been fruitful. We invite our readers to join our conversation now and to make new discoveries. We hope that reading and conversing will bring you some of the pleasure we have found in talking and writing together about leadership.

E. A. B.
M. A. L.
J. A. R.

Chapter 1

Leadership as Practical Wisdom: The Parable of Lincoln

Michael A. Leiserson

What can the story of Abraham Lincoln leading the country to abolish slavery mean for Americans today? That this is a wonderful, exceptional country where "the system works" to produce justice and freedom for all? Or that this is a country (like any other) where the only choice is between kinds of injustice, like slavery and war, and progress like beauty is in the eye of the beholder?

This chapter suggests another answer. Lincoln shows how practical wisdom resolves problems of morals and politics. Lincoln was a practical politician who led Americans to confront and defeat the moral evil of slavery. And he did this starting not as president but as a defeated has-been without any political power. The practical wisdom he displayed shows how any person can find a way of action which is at once the most moral and the most practical course.

To explain this, I proceed as follows. Section One shows how morals and politics are different but connected. Section Two describes practical wisdom. Section Three explains how Lincoln's practical wisdom won the struggle against slavery. Section Four shows how Lincoln's practical wisdom provides a model for us to live by today.

I. Moral Innocence and Political Experience

Any child who visits the Lincoln Memorial in Washington, D.C., learns to look up to Lincoln--his statue is so tall. As a small boy growing up nearby, the Lincoln Memorial was my favorite public place. An early family photo shows me standing by the giant Lincoln statue. When I discovered that my birthday and his are on the same date, I felt almost as big as the statue. Then for one birthday my parents gave me *Abraham*

Lincoln's World.[1] This wonderful book with its pen-and-ink illustrations showed how everything that happened during Lincoln's life--from the Opium War in China and the Sepoy Mutiny in India to the European revolutions of 1848 and the English workers' and American women's struggles for their rights--was related to the stages of Lincoln's life and struggle against slavery. For my thirteenth birthday my father gave me a hardbound biography of Lincoln that was the handsomest book I'd ever held in my hands. I was so proud of it, I still have it.[2]

However, as I grew up another picture replaced the heroic Lincoln of my childhood. I first saw this other picture of Lincoln sketched in Richard Hofstadter's *American Political Tradition*.[3] Hofstadter's chapter on "Abraham Lincoln and the Self-Made Myth" made my boyhood's Lincoln seem painfully naive. According to this grown-up version, "deliberate and responsible opportunism ... was ... characteristic of his [Lincoln's] statecraft." He was just "a man of the atmosphere that surrounds him," who had to "'confess plainly that events have controlled me.'" His thinking was "not the philosophy of a reformer." He was "completely the politician ... looking for votes." Consequently he was "Never much troubled about the Negro," and his attitude toward slavery was at best "expediency tempered by justice."

In debunking my idol Lincoln this way, Hofstadter was not saying Lincoln was worse than other politicians, only the same: politicians have to be opportunists to succeed. This is simple common sense to most people. Politicians express it by the story of how the great Speaker of the House of Representatives, Sam Rayburn, advised a freshman Congressman, "If you want to get along, you've got to go along." Political scientists put it as a law of life: morals are for private life; politics works by different rules. To move from private life to politics we must give up moral innocence to gain political experience.[4]

For example, consider the Vietnam War. I opposed it, but my concern here is less the war than the difficulty of evaluating it. Some of its defenders used the same political common sense as Hofstadter had used to explain Lincoln. That defense went something like this.

> The American war in Vietnam is no worse than Lincoln's Civil War. Its goals are the same as Lincoln's: to abolish communism, which is tyranny, which is slavery. And Lincoln's war was just as unpopular, and was fought by just as "dirty hands" as this one. The war's critics are either naive (don't understand how war and politics work), or cynical politicians who are manipulating their naive followers.

If Hofstadter's picture of Lincoln were correct, this argument could make sense. A justification of the Civil War may well justify the American war in Vietnam. "The freedom fought for in both wars was good. The tactics in both wars were morally dubious. So either both wars were justifiable or neither were." Even some critics of the Vietnamese War admit this argument is persuasive.[5]

As this example shows, within the limits of the "moral innocence versus political experience" mindset, either everything seems justified or nothing does. And personally, during the Vietnam War, I was stuck, wanting to have my childhood-Lincoln's innocent morality along with my adult, Hofstadter-Lincoln's political experience. But the two were in painful conflict.

Here in this tension between moral innocence and practical experience, Americans who have other birthdays than Lincoln's--and Americans who did not oppose the war, or did not live through it--may be able to recognize some of their own experiences. This will happen if one's childhood was a time of innocence, where symbols or role-models like Lincoln directly connect one's innocent self with a good America. Of course Lincoln isn't everyone's symbol of America, but there are others; Lincoln was not my only one. Other chapters in this book show other things that symbolize, or connect to something positive about, America. Perhaps everyone who cares about being an American has some connector-symbol like Lincoln was for me. If identities were logical, the connection might go something like: "I love X. X shows what America is all about. Therefore, I love America." In this frame of mind, there is no conflict between our morals and our politics.

As we grow, however, that innocent self is compromised. The world of experience makes it seem childish, vulnerable, or inadequate. So we outgrow childhood and its loves, the way we outgrow Santa Claus, learning different stories about them. For me, Hofstadter's version of Lincoln was this sort of new story. For other Americans there will be other "Hofstadters" who debunk the childhood faith that America is good. Anyone who has experienced this sort of deflation but has not entirely given up childhood's symbols of America and her politics, has probably experienced the confusion I described above about the Vietnam War.[6]

A third stage of development can emerge out of the conflict between our innocent, childhood symbols of America and our growing-up experiences of America. This third stage may be despair about America, like losing faith in a church. Then America appears wicked; morality requires us to disown her. Or the third stage may maintain faith in America by denying the gap between child and adult experience of America. This saves America the Beautiful, but at a cost. Or the third stage may be muddling through, making a virtue out of the seeming necessity of living with the ambiguous tension between personal morality and political experience. The chapters in this book may perhaps be seen as definitions of this third stage.*

But I want to suggest another possibility for this third stage of our moral-political development.[7] Practical wisdom may resolve the tension

---

* It seems to me that *all* of my co-authors *might* so recognize their chapters, but I have not yet persuaded them of this!

between morality and politics by revealing a higher morality that is still politically effective.

II. Practical Wisdom: "Be Ye Wise as Serpents ..."[8]

Common sense tells us the words "practical" and "wisdom" refer to different things. College students looking for a major in something practical are not expecting courses with "wisdom" in their title. Students who want to study "the wisdom of the ages" are often afraid it isn't very practical.

But common sense also tells us that practical experience and wisdom can combine. When President Lyndon Johnson realized in 1968 he was in trouble about the Vietnamese War, he gathered successful lawyers, businessmen, bankers, generals, foundation presidents, and former Secretaries and Under Secretaries of State and Treasury to give him advice. This group became known among Washington insiders as "the Wise Men."[9]

By telling us opposite things about practical wisdom, common sense confuses us. This is the same common sense that caused the confusion between "Lincoln's America" and "Hofstadter's America"--between morals and politics--described above. We need to understand practical wisdom better than common sense does.

Lincoln liked to show the superiority of practical wisdom to common sense with a joke. In his first campaign for Congress, his opponent was a Methodist minister who tried to win votes by appealing to common sense. With Lincoln in his audience, the preacher asked all those to stand who expected to go to heaven. Then with most of his audience standing, he asked all those to stand who expected to go to hell. With all of his audience standing but Lincoln, he challenged Lincoln to explain why he was still seated--implying that Lincoln was indifferent to good and evil. Lincoln responded that he *might* be going to heaven and he *might* be going to hell but he *expected* to go to Congress. (Lincoln won the election.)

Lincoln first learned such practical wisdom from the Bible. "Only in the Bible did he find open discussion of such a tangle of sex, family, slavery, and violence."[10] To understand Lincoln's way of thinking about morality and practicality, we have to know the Biblical examples his thought was based on.

Of course education today does not use the Bible, as Tammivaara's chapter in this book shows. But Lincoln learned to read from it. Throughout his life, when he needed the right word at the right time, a Biblical phrase came to his mind. His image of America as a "house divided against itself," between freedom and slavery, which "shall not stand," came from the Bible (Matt. 12:25). When Lincoln heard that a rival had attracted only 400 men to a key meeting, he instantly reached for his Bible, flipped pages to 1 Samuel 22: 2, and read to his friends, "And everyone that was in distress, and everyone that was in debt, and everyone that was discontented, gathered themselves unto him; ... and there were with him about 400 men."

More seriously, debating his arch-rival Stephen A. Douglas, whose policy on slavery was to let the people in each state choose whether or not to have slavery, without the government in Washington deciding, Lincoln replied in a public debate:

> In the course of my main argument, Judge Douglas interrupted me to say, that the principle of [his policy] was very old; that it originated when God made man and placed good and evil before him [in the Garden of Eden], allowing him to choose for himself, being responsible for the choice he should make. At the time I thought this was merely playful; and I answered it accordingly. But in his reply to me he renewed it, as a serious argument. In seriousness then, the facts of this proposition are not as [Douglas] stated. God did not place good and evil before man, telling him to make his choice. On the contrary, he did tell him that there was one tree, of the fruit of which, he should not eat, upon pain of certain death. I should scarcely wish so strong a prohibition against slavery.[11]

Like Lincoln, in his day everyone knew the Biblical story of the practical wisdom of Solomon (I Kings 3:16-28). Two women came to King Solomon with a dispute. They lived in the same house and each had just given birth, but one baby had died in the night. No one besides the two women had been in the house. Each woman insisted she was the mother of the live baby. Solomon had to judge which woman was lying. He ordered his officials to divide the baby in two, giving each woman half. One of the two women cried out to stop this judgment from being carried out: "Give her the living child, and in no wise slay it." But the other woman said, "Let it be neither mine nor thine, but divide it." Now Solomon could judge. Since each woman had shown what she was, Solomon gave to the mother and to the liar what each one deserved.*

(There is a parallel between this story and Lincoln's, between this baby and America in the 1850s, between these two women and the claimants on 1850s-America's future. See Section Three, below.)

Another Biblical illustration of practical wisdom is the story of David and Bathsheba (2 Sam. 11-12), which was familiar to everyone in Lincoln's day. King David wanted Bathsheba, but she was married. So David arranged to have her husband killed so it looked accidental, and took Bathsheba into his house. To catch the King, the prophet Nathan asked him to judge a case like David's, but disguised so David didn't recognize

---

*   Peter Ely begins his chapter in this book on the development of Perceval's practical wisdom by quoting Solomon's prayer for it.

his own situation. In Nathan's case there were two men, one rich, one poor. The rich man had many sheep; the poor man had only a baby lamb which he loved. When the rich man wanted to have a feast, instead of taking a lamb from his own flock for food, he stole the poor man's lamb. Nathan asked David to judge the rich man. David said he was guilty under the law. Then Nathan showed David he had judged himself. David, condemned out of his own mouth, admitted his guilt.

To appreciate Nathan's practical wisdom here, remember that Biblical kings could kill people who criticized them. Nathan's practical wisdom found a way--like Solomon did with the two women--to get a person to admit the truth when he didn't want to. And Nathan did this in the face of King David's power. In a world where might makes right, such practical wisdom seems almost miraculous.

(There is a parallel between this story and Lincoln's use of the constitution to show the power-holders what was right and wrong when they didn't want to admit it, as Section Three explains.)

A final example of Biblical practical wisdom is the Parable of the Crafty Steward (Luke 16:1-8).[12] It needs to be reproduced in all its complex detail, because finding one's way through complex details is what this story's practical wisdom is all about.

> There was a rich man who had a steward
> and charges were brought to him
> that he was wasting his goods.
>
>> And he called him and said to him, "What's this I hear about you?
>> Turn in the account [book] of your stewardship
>> for you can no longer be steward."
>
>> And the steward said to himself, "What shall I do
>> because my master is taking the stewardship away from me?
>> I am not strong enough to farm and ashamed to beg.
>
>>> "I know what I will do
>>> so that when I am put out of the stewardship
>>> they may receive me into their own houses."
>
>> So summoning his master's debtors one by one he said to the first, "How much do you owe my master?"
>> And he said, "A hundred measures of olive oil."
>> And he said to him,
>>> "Take your bill and sit down quickly and write fifty."
>
>> Then he said to another, "And how much do you owe?
>> And he said, "A hundred measures of wheat."
>> And he said to him, "Take your bill and write eighty."
>
> Then the master commended the dishonest steward for his wisdom,[13]
> because the sons of this age are wiser
> than the sons of light in their own generation.

This is a story of a landed estate, run by a manager (the steward), where tenant farmers (the debtors) have signed contracts (the bills) to pay rent for the land they farm.[14] The manager's lack of response to the landlord's accusation in the second verse suggests he must indeed be guilty. Under the law at that time he would ordinarily be punished by a fine for the value of the missing goods. But the third verse shows the manager is an admirable person: an educated man (he can write), he still does not consider manual labor beneath him; too weak to work a farm, he still refuses to become a ward of the community (begging). So this man's guilt is not sheer wickedness. Rather, it reveals only the code of practical managers and politicians who live by the advice, "if you want to get along you've got to go along," who were symbolized in Section One by Hofstadter and Speaker Rayburn. In other words, Jesus' parable poses the question, "Since this is a man with practical wisdom, how does he exercise it?"

Notice that the parable does *not* say, as some might expect, "He repents his way of life, turns over a new leaf, and becomes a better person." Instead Jesus' story shows the steward's insight, at the center of the parable, is: I must do something so that "*they* [the tenant farmers on the rich man's farm] *may receive me into their houses.*" What does this mean? What insight has practical wisdom given him?

As this quote shows, whatever the manager is doing when he reduces the farmers' rents, he is not making a quick killing before moving on. This manager is not a modern, mobile individual planning how to take his cut before moving on to another town. His insight--his practical wisdom--involves seeing what to do in relation to the people he lives and does business with, so that they will welcome him into their homes. There is no suggestion he has any other world than this one. For him, this is the only game in town.

But he is fired. And the reduced rents will sooner or later be discovered as a fraud. So how can he even play, let alone win, in this game? Isn't he stuck? What can practical wisdom do?

Since the tenants don't yet know the Manager has been fired, if he acts quickly he can still appear to act with the landlord's authority. ("How much do you owe *my master*?") He gives the tenants the impression that he has talked the landlord into giving them a bonus, consisting of cuts in their rental contracts. Of course they accept. (The story suggests they see nothing criminal going on.) And out of their gratitude, naturally later on they may accept the Steward into their houses as a friend to whom they are indebted.

Following Bailey,[15] we may speculate the Steward's reasoning went somewhat as follows. "When the landlord sees the altered contracts in his renters' handwritings, he will know that they must have already begun to celebrate their good fortune, praising him as the opposite of the usual landlord who cares more about his rents than his renters. At this point the landlord will have to choose. He might go to the tenants and explain there was a mistake and demand that the original contracts be fulfilled, in which case my gamble fails. Or he might let his tenants keep their bonus and bask in their praise, in which case I will get away with my gamble. I think I'll take the gamble." And as Jesus tells the story, the steward's gamble pays off: the rich man "commends" him for his practical wisdom.

The Parable of the Wise Manager shows more clearly than the previous illustrations that practical wisdom needs to be understood in terms of its own cultural context. What can appear as immoral if we don't know its context--the Steward's changing the tenants' rent contracts--appears as almost miraculous practical wisdom when we understand the cultural context. And the Steward's story reinforces the stories of Solomon and Nathan: practical wisdom sees more possible good in the situation than most people can see. It is insight into a situation along a new dimension, when to common sense the situation appears as a one-dimensional flatland of anxiety, selfishness, and opposition between moral idealism and practical effectiveness. This extra dimension matters the same way that our third dimension of depth matters, keeping the world from being a desolate flatland of only length and width.*

III. Lincoln's Practical Wisdom

As Section Two noted, these Biblical illustrations of practical wisdom are similar to Lincoln's. Like the Steward, Lincoln was "so wrapped up in the world, so devoted to our own political advancement,"[16] that he had no choice but to save himself by helping others. Like Solomon, Lincoln had to expose which of two contending parties (abolitionists, slave-owners) really wanted justice and which was only pretending. Like Nathan, Lincoln had to find the right word to say to his political sovereign, the people, to lead them to repent of their injustice (if the murder of Bathsheba's husband can be equated with slavery).

But the connection between Lincoln's and the Bible's practical wisdom goes much deeper than mere analogies. Lincoln actually had the practical wisdom of these Bible stories. And he abolished slavery because of it. To see this, we need the kind of story for Lincoln we have for Solomon.

The Parable of the Practical Son

Once upon a time, in a far-off country, there were Freelands and Slavelands. In Freelands free people ruled themselves. In Slavelands

---

* For other ways of seeing this extra dimension, compare Mary Jo Bona, "Italian/American Women Writers"; Tom Jeannot, "But Trusted Servants"; Jane Rinehart, "Learning to Lead"; and Rose Mary Volbrecht, "Careful Mutuality."

free people ruled themselves and their slaves. The free people in each land liked their own way of life. Freelanders were dynamic and progressive; they wanted freedom, and a government to protect it. Slavelanders were elegant and cultivated; they valued their quality of life, and wanted government to protect it.

Despite their differences, Freelanders and Slavelanders signed a Contract to cooperate. Under this Contract each land agreed to send leaders to meet with the other lands' leaders in the country's capital. These leaders would decide jointly what the country would do. Never before had so many diverse people found a way to live together peaceably. Freelanders and Slavelanders were all proud of their country.

Now one year, one of the Freelands chose a handsome and strong leader named Stephen to go to the capital. Stephen had a vision. He knew the people wanted to go to the Land of Gold by the western ocean. But there was no road to take them there. Stephen wanted to build this road. And Stephen knew travellers on the road would bring back much gold to the land where the road started. So Stephen proposed to the other leaders, "Let us build a road to the Land of Gold. Let it start from my land."

But leaders from the Slavelands replied, "A road to the Land of Gold is a good idea. But why start it from your land? Why not ours? If you want the road to start from your land, let us build more Slavelands alongside the road. Both your land and ours will benefit. If you refuse, we will refuse to let the road start from your land."

Stephen talked with other Freeland leaders. Some said, "No! Slavelands are bad. We cannot agree to let them spread."

Stephen replied, "Truly Slavelands are bad. But refusing this compromise won't make a single Slaveland free. And if we compromise, we will have a road to the Land of Gold that starts from our land. Otherwise, there will be no road, or it will start from some Slaveland."

Stephen's words were powerful. Most of the leaders in the country's capital accepted the compromise.

When the people in Stephen's Freeland heard about Stephen's compromise, they held meetings to discuss it. At one of them a tall man stood up and spoke. He had once been a Freeland leader, and his name was Abraham.

"The Slavelands made this compromise with Stephen so they could build Slavelands west of us where they will compete with us. Have you ever tried to compete with Slavelands? They are not as productive as Freelands, but their labor costs are so low they can undersell Freelands anyway, and bankrupt them."

The Freeland people didn't like the sound of this. "Why would Stephen have made this compromise, if it's so bad?," they protested.

Abraham answered them and said, "The Slavelands are powerful. When they joined us to make one country, they made the Contract to allow them extra leaders. Today Slavelands have 20 more leaders than they would have if their people were counted equally with Freeland people. And Stephen's compromise was accepted by only 113 leaders; 100 voted against it. Without the Slavelands' extra 20 leaders the compromise would have failed. And now, with Stephen's compromise, there will be even more Slavelands with their leaders in the capital, and you will become even weaker."

When the Freeland people heard this, they hung their heads. They were proud of being dynamic, progressive and free. Abraham's words showed: not only had Stephen let Slavelands spread, he hadn't even made a good bargain. But Abraham comforted them and said, "Don't give up. It's not too late. You can still cancel Stephen's compromise and stop the Slavelands from spreading."

Then the people said, "You are right, Abraham. Stephen was wrong. We *will* stop the slave-towns from spreading. From now on we will choose only leaders who promise to do as you say. You should be our leader now. And after Freelands spread, we won't need help from the slave-towns to build the road to the Land of Gold and the western ocean." So they made Abraham and his followers their leaders.

This made the Slaveland people very angry. What they did, and what Abraham and the Freelands did about that, and how this all led to the end of the Slavelands, is told in another story.

The Parable Explained

This Parable dramatizes the history of the Kansas-Nebraska Act of 1854 which led directly to the Civil War. The lands in the Parable are the then barely-united states. The Contract is the Constitution. The leaders are the members of Congress. Stephen is Senator Stephen A. Douglas, a national leader of the Democratic Party; his Freeland is Illinois. The road to the Land of Gold is the transcontinental railroad to California. (1854 was five years after the gold rush began.) The land along the road is the Kansas-Nebraska Territory. The 113-100 vote is the actual vote in the national House of Representatives in 1854 on Douglas' bill. The Freeland people's decision at the end of the story represents the founding the Republican Party to stop the expansion of slavery, and Lincoln's election as president in 1860 on its platform.

The close similarity between the Parable's Abraham and the historical Lincoln appears easily from a comparison of Abraham's speech in the Parable with Lincoln's famous Peoria Address. The Peoria Address was Lincoln's response to the Kansas-Nebraska Act of 1854, just as the Parable's Abraham's speech was his response to Stephen's Compromise.[17] Lincoln's response, like the Steward's, must be understood in context: the role of slavery in American politics.

The Constitution gave the national government very little power to regulate slavery, and none to abolish it. No matter how much people cared about slavery, the key decisions about it were matters of state politics. The states north of the Ohio River and the Mason-Dixon line abolished slavery; the other states protected it. The only way the national government could abolish slavery was through Congress' power over new national territories and states. Under this power, Congress in 1820 prohibited slavery in the Louisiana Purchase (all the land west of the Mississippi not belonging to Spain or Britain) north of the southern boundary of Missouri except for Missouri itself. In the eyes of most Americans at the time, this Missouri Compromise of 1820 appeared as a "sacred pact:" it put slavery on the road to eventual extinction, since much more of the Louisiana Territory lay north of the Compromise line than south of it.[18]

In the next generation, however, Americans pursued their "manifest destiny" to expand across the continent into the Mexican and British land beyond the Louisiana Territory. War and diplomacy stimulated renewed congressional struggle over slavery, and even threats to secede from the Union. Eventually the Compromise of 1850 settled the questions raised by territorial expansion. (Slave-Texas and free-Oregon [including Washington and Idaho] had entered the Union a few years earlier, paired.) California came in free, but the rest of the Mexican Cession (what is now Arizona, New Mexico, Nevada, Utah, and Colorado) was organized as a U.S. territory which might allow slavery if the settlers chose it. Supporters as well as opponents of slavery were dissatisfied, and there were many of both, but moderates and compromisers provided the needed majorities. Lincoln himself supported the Compromise because it continued to apply the principles of the earlier Missouri Compromise. It did not treat slaves as if they were ordinary property. The extension of slavery was limited by the national government. Slavery was on the road to eventual extinction.

Then Senator Stephen A. Douglas (D-Illinois) took the great initiative of his career, the Kansas-Nebraska Act of 1854. With the Democrats already in control of the White House and Congress, Douglas united his party around the compromise described in the Parable. Southerners would vote to locate the proposed transcontinental railroad's eastern terminus in Chicago, in exchange for northerners' vote to let the settlers of Kansas (just west of slave Missouri) and a Nebraska territory including the present-day Dakotas, Wyoming, and Montana establish slavery if they wanted. The Act cemented Douglas' leadership of the Democratic Party. Southern Democrats appreciated the chance to extend slavery into Kansas. Northern Democrats liked having the transcontinental railroad go west from Chicago instead of New Orleans. And since the Democrats were the nation's majority party, Senator Douglas might ride the Kansas-Nebraska Act all the way into the White House.

Lincoln's response to the Kansas-Nebraska Act was his Peoria Address,[19] which corresponds to the Parable's speech by Abraham. The quote from this Address below shows Lincoln's attack on Douglas' defense of opening the Kansas-Nebraska Territory to slavery, namely, the "sacred right" of "popular sovereignty." According to this doctrine of Douglas', the meaning of democracy is: the people in their town meetings and states are the only ones with the right to decide whether slavery should exist where they live. So, Douglas argued, only the people of Kansas should decide whether slavery would exist in Kansas. To refute Douglas and suggest a better course of action, Lincoln observed (in what is about 10% of the speech):

> Whether slavery shall go into [Kansas-]Nebraska, or other new Territories, is not a matter of exclusive concern to the people who may go there. The whole nation is interested that the best use shall be made of these Territories. We want them for homes of free white people. This they cannot be, to any considerable extent, if slavery shall be planted within them. Slave States are places for poor white people to remove *from*; not to remove *to*. New free States are the places for poor people to go to, and better their condition. For this use the nation needs these Territories.
> Still further: there are constitutional relations between the slave and free States, which are degrading to the latter. ... [I]n the control of the government ... [the slave states] have greatly the advantage of us. By the Constitution each State has ... a number of Representatives in proportion to the number of its people ... But in ascertaining the number of the people for this purpose, five slaves are counted as being equal to three whites. The slaves do not vote; they are only counted and so used as to swell the influence of the white people's votes.
> The practical effect of this is more aptly shown by a comparison of the States of South Carolina and Maine; South Carolina has six representatives, and so has Maine. ... Thus in the control of the government, the two States are equals precisely. But how are they in the number of their white people? Maine has 581,813--while South Carolina has 274,567; Maine has *twice* as many as South Carolina, and 32,679 over. Thus, each white man in South Carolina is more than the double of any man in Maine. This is all because South Carolina, besides her free people, has 384,984 slaves.
> The [white] South Carolinian has precisely the same advantage over the white man in every other free State, as well as in Maine. He is more than the double of any one of us in this crowd. The same advantage, but not to the same extent, is held by all the citizens of the slave States, over those of the free; and it is an absolute truth, without an exception, that there is no voter in any slave State, but who has more legal power in the government than any voter in any free State. There is no instance of exact equality; and the disadvantage is against us the whole chapter through. This principle, in the aggregate, gives the slave States in the present Congress twenty additional representatives--being seven more than the whole majority by which they passed the [Kansas-]Nebraska bill.
> Now all this is manifestly unfair; yet I do not mention it to complain of it, insofar as it is already settled. It is in the Constitution; and I do not for that cause, or any other cause, propose to destroy, or alter, or disregard the Constitution. I stand to it, fairly, fully, and firmly.

But when I am told I must leave it altogether to other people to say whether new partners are to be bred up and brought into the firm, on the same degrading terms against me, I respectfully demur. [These "other people" would be the settlers in Kansas under Douglas' Kansas-Nebraska Act.--Ed.] I insist that whether I shall be a whole man, or only the half of one, in comparison with others, is a question in which I am somewhat concerned, and one which no other man can have a sacred right of deciding for me. If I am wrong in this--if it really be a sacred right of self-government, in the man who shall go to Nebraska to decide whether he will be the equal of me or the double of me, then, after he shall have exercised that right, and thereby shall have reduced me to a still smaller fraction of a man than I already am, I should like for some gentleman, deeply skilled in the mysteries of sacred rights, to provide himself with a microscope, and peep about, and find out, if he can, what has become of my sacred rights. They will surely be too small for detection with the naked eye.

In this quote and the rest of his Address at Peoria, Lincoln argues the way Abraham did in our Parable. He doesn't ask the free people of the north to choose *between* their own self-interest and justice for slaves. Rather, he finds a concrete way to show them how slavery is unjust, period--unfair to them as well as to slaves, and in precisely the same way, by denying the equal right of all people to the pursuit of legitimate self-interest.*

To see the practical wisdom of Lincoln's proposed course of action, it must be compared with the alternatives. There were three possibilities. **ABOLITIONISTS** would abolish slavery in the slave-states (which was unconstitutional). **APOLOGISTS** for the status quo defended the civilization which depended on slavery (and was protected by the Constitution). **REALISTS** knew some sort of compromise had to be made within the Constitution. *And before Lincoln spoke, common sense "knew" that the Constitution favored slavery.*

One way of seeing why this was so is to imagine Lincoln's and the other alternatives in 1854 as located on a map of the U.S. of that time. Distances east and west on the map show where people were located according to their attitudes about the Constitution: west was loyal, east was rebellious. Distances north and south on the map show where people were located according to their attitudes about slavery: north was anti-slavery, south was pro-slavery. People in the southwest on this map would be pro-slavery and pro-Constitution; in the 1850s realists like

---

* For other ways of explaining that goodness is *not* opposed to self interest, see Mary Jo Bona, "Italian American Writers"; Eloise Buker, "A Democratic Model of Leadership"; Blaine Garvin, "A Lesson For Citizens"; Tom Jeannot, "But Trusted Servants"; Pat O'Leary, "Ignatius"; Jane Rinehart, "Learning to Lead"; Rose Mary Volbrecht, "Careful Mutuality"; and Bob Waterman, "We Need Not be Ruled by Leaders."

Douglas (who owned a slave plantation in Mississippi, which was then the southwest) were located here on this map. People in the southeast on this map would be pro-slavery and anti-Constitution; apologists for slavery threatening secession, like South Carolina's Robert Barnwell Rhett, were located here. People in the northwest on this map would be anti-slavery and pro-Constitution, like Lincoln of Illinois. And people in the northeast on this map would be anti-slavery and anti-Constitution, like New England's abolitionists.

But in the early 1850s, abolitionists were burning copies of the Constitution as a "pact with the devil" (for its compromise with slavery) and refusing to obey the Fugitive Slave Law in the Compromise of 1850. This made it seem common sense that being anti-slavery meant opposing the Constitution. And most Americans, although they opposed slavery, were more strongly pro-Constitution than they were anti-slavery. Anti-slavery people were split into a small abolitionist minority ("northeasterners" on our map), and a much larger group whose support of the Constitution and opposition to abolitionist tactics made them feel more kinship with "southerners" on our map than with "northerners," making them vote as if they were neutral toward slavery (located in Kentucky or Tennessee instead of Illinois). And this guaranteed that Douglas and the slave-owners would win.

Lincoln's Peoria Address changed what common sense could see in this situation, just as Abraham's speech did in the Parable, by making it possible to take a stand against slavery but for the Constitution. For the people in the "northwest" on our map (opposed to slavery, loyal to the Constitution), Lincoln's alternative appeared as miraculously as the alternative of being able to eat your cake and still have it, too--what earned Solomon and Nathan the reputation of exercising divine practical wisdom.

Granted, Douglas displayed practical wisdom of a sort in his proposed deal. Douglas did just what Section One of this chapter showed we expect a normal, smart democratic politician to do. He compromised between ideological extremes, appealed to the broad, moderate political mainstream, promoted pragmatic material interests, and gained power in so doing. Though he violated the Missouri Compromise's prohibition of slavery north of the Missouri Compromise Line, he still said he believed in the eventual extinction of slavery. In short, *it is Douglas who epitomizes the type of opportunistic politician our experience makes us believe Lincoln must have been*, as Section One explained. *The real Lincoln showed a different kind of practical wisdom.* Compared to Douglas' plan to get the railroad, Lincoln's practical wisdom was almost a miracle-- the way Nathan's, Solomon's, and the Steward's practical wisdom was "divine" in comparison with the available alternatives.

The Parable of the Practical Son also explains what led to the abolition of slavery, although this might not be obvious without some more historical details. These can be organized under two heads: (1) Lincoln's opposition to the Kansas-Nebraska Act was the first step toward his election as president; (2) Lincoln's election as president caused the abolition of slavery. The rest of Section Three explains these achievements of Lincoln's practical wisdom.

How Lincoln Used Kansas-Nebraska To Become President*

Although separated by six years, Lincoln's Peoria Address (1854) and his election as president (1860) were actually one action-and-response. (This corresponds to the climax in the Parable, where the people respond to Abraham's speech.) Of course a lot of water flowed under the bridge between 1854 and 1860, and Lincoln's election was not inevitable. But six key features of the 1854-1860 period have been telescoped into the parable to maintain the dramatic unity of the story without distorting the historical record.

First, as the Parable says, in 1854 Lincoln was merely one of the people. He had held no political office since 1849, and was a member of a weak political party (the Whigs) which was disintegrating as its northern and southern wings fought over the Kansas-Nebraska Act. By 1860 the Whig Party was dead. So Lincoln could never have been elected president without his action opposing the Kansas-Nebraska Act in 1854, which gave him a new identity as a leader of the opposition to the Kansas-Nebraska Act.

Second, Americans' reaction to the Kansas-Nebraska Act was, as the Parable says, immediate and powerful. In the fall elections in 1854, Douglas' Democratic Party fell from 91 seats in the House of Representatives to 25, replaced by opponents who were anti-Nebraska (i.e., against the Kansas-Nebraska Act). The Democrats never recovered their strength in the north. In Illinois, Lincoln became the Whigs' choice for U.S. Senator. He lost only when the legislature deadlocked (in those days the states' legislatures chose Senators): 45 anti-Nebraska Whigs voted for Lincoln, five anti-Nebraska Democrats voted for an anti-Nebraska Democrat, and 41 pro-Nebraska Democrats voted for Douglas' candidate. But the 5 anti-Nebraska Democrats refused to vote for Lincoln, who was still a Whig. So Lincoln told his supporters to vote for the anti-Nebraska Democratic candidate, in order to elect an anti-Nebraska man. Most Illinois politicians of the day saw Lincoln's action as a self-sacrifice for the anti-Nebraska cause. Then, once the anti-Nebraska people united to form the new Republican party, Lincoln's sacrifice earned him the nomination for the Senate in the next Senatorial election, and the state's Republicans' support for the presidential nomination in 1860.[20]

Third, the Parable of the Practical Son gives an accurate picture of Lincoln's attitude toward slavery. As early as 1847 he voted to prohibit

---

* This and the next sub-section explain Frank Costello's claim in "Rating the Presidents For Greatness" that Lincoln's greatness rested on his "vision."

the expansion of slavery into the western territories. He always acknowledged that slavery was constitutional where it existed, but as early as 1837 he was one of six Illinois legislators who voted against a resolution approving slavery (77 were in favor), and published his minority report in the state legislature's Journal.[21]

Fourth, during 1854-60 events moved to a climax with the inexorability of a Greek tragedy, as if the actors were merely reading a script Lincoln had seen in 1854. Historians have noted Lincoln's uncanny ability to see in the passage of the Kansas-Nebraska Act what became visible for others only gradually.[22] Pro-slavery forces were not willing to allow slavery to be put at a permanent disadvantage. They were determined either to have the country opened to slavery or to secede. Three key events revealed for all to see what few but Lincoln had seen in 1854.

(1) Following passage of the Kansas-Nebraska Act, a vote was held in Kansas to organize the Territorial government and write a constitution. Pro-slavery Missourians crossed the border to vote in sufficient numbers to elect a pro-slavery legislature which met in Lecompton and drafted a constitution recognizing slavery, which was approved by Democratic President Buchanan.

(2) In its *Dred Scott* decision, the Supreme Court held unconstitutional the Missouri Compromise's prohibition of slavery in the Louisiana Territory north of 36°30." This ruling came after politicians of both national parties had acknowledged the Compromise was a "sacred compact" for 34 years, and amounted to holding that the new Republican Party should cease to exist just after it had won 33% of the votes in the 1856 presidential election.

(3) At the Democrats' national convention in 1860, when Douglas was nominated, most southern delegates withdrew and held their own convention, nominating a southern Democratic presidential candidate who ran against Douglas.

The struggle over "bleeding Kansas" and the fraudulent voting there for the Lecompton Constitution, the Democratic president's recognition of Lecompton, and the *Dred Scott* case, showed the pro-slavery forces' desire to open the country to slavery. The split in the Democratic Party in 1860 showed their impulse to secede if they could not open the country to slavery. All these provided evidence of what Lincoln had seen in 1854.

On the other hand, voting results in 1856 and 1860 confirmed the accuracy of Lincoln's 1854 perceptions of the minority strength of abolitionists within the anti-slavery movement. The abolitionist nominated by Republicans for president in 1856 (Fremont) won only in the northern tier of states (Wisconsin, Michigan, New York, New England). But to win nationally, the Republicans had to carry Pennsylvania and either Indiana and Illinois, or else carry all three of Illinois, Indiana, and New Jersey. So Lincoln could win the nomination by keeping the Illinois delegation solidly behind him and establishing a national reputation as a sincere but moderate anti-slavery man able to win the other key states.

This is what he did. Seward of New York was too northern, Chase was an abolitionist, and no other candidate had national standing in the anti-slavery cause. Within Illinois, Lincoln's situation was similar: Seward and Chase were unacceptable in the southern third of the state, candidates not known for their anti-slavery views were unacceptable in the northern third of the state, while Lincoln was acceptable to Republicans throughout the state.

Fifth, the famed Lincoln-Douglas debates in the 1858 Senate race in Illinois did not reveal any major new difference between the two men and what they stood for, beyond what was already visible in their debates in 1854 and in the Parable.[23] And Lincoln won the popular vote in his Senate race in 1858 against Douglas.[24] This showed the country Lincoln could win against the Democratic front-runner for the presidential nomination in 1860, even in Douglas' own state, and so transformed Lincoln from a local into a national figure. But it was the same Lincoln, against the same Douglas, as in 1854. Even the famous "House Divided" speech of 1858 was a revision of an earlier draft, which in turn drew upon 1854's ideas.[25]

Finally, Lincoln's election as president over Douglas was ensured when the southern Democrats split the Democratic party, and this was what Lincoln had seen coming in the vote on the Kansas-Nebraska Act in 1854, as the paragraphs numbered (1) - (3) above explained. In the Parable, Abraham's vote-counting corresponds to these electoral considerations.

How Lincoln's Election Abolished Slavery

As the Parable suggests, Lincoln was elected president on a platform to guarantee the eventual extinction of slavery by making all future states enter the Union without slavery. This platform was the immediate cause of the Civil War. The slave-states said before the election that if Lincoln were elected they would secede. After the election, they repeated their threat in the form of the Crittenden Compromise. If Lincoln would renounce his platform and let some western territory become slave states, the South would not secede; otherwise it would. To Lincoln and the Republicans, this was the same tactic the slave-states were always using: "If you don't give us what we want, we'll destroy us all." In the face of such terrorism, they believed, resistance was the only alternative to abject surrender. So Lincoln rejected the Compromise, and the South carried out their threat to secede.

Southerners claimed that the "right of rebellion" in the Declaration of Independence justified secession, so the Civil War was a Northern war of aggression, like England's war against American independence. In this view, the abolition of slavery was simply the result of international aggression, not constitutional politics as the Parable suggests. But this Southern apology assumes what must be shown. Was the Confederacy more loyal to the Declaration's "self-evident truths" than Lincoln's Union was? Was the South in truth asserting the ***Declaration's*** right to rebel ("to alter or abolish [existing government]"), or just a supposed "right" to do whatever one wants?

The answer is obvious. The Declaration asserts no right to rebel aside from the rest of its self-evident truths. The right to rebel is inseparable from the right to self-government which the Declaration asserts ALL people possess, not only white slave-owners.[26] So the South, determined to justify slavery, had to attack the Declaration's "all men are created equal" as a "self-evident lie," as one pro-slavery Congressman actually said.[27] There is no more doubt about which side in the Civil War was the real heir of the Declaration of Independence than there was about which woman before Solomon (Section Two) was the real mother of the baby he threatened to divide in half.

Then, with the South seceded and not voting in Congress, the Union became in political fact what Lincoln said in the Gettysburg Address it always had been, in principle: a "nation conceived in liberty, and dedicated to the proposition that all men are created equal ... government of the people, by the people, and for the people ... " If we remember this vision, we won't misunderstand (as his detractors do) Lincoln's statements during the War about being willing to save the Union without freeing the slaves.[28] Lincoln's Union was a place which denied slavery on principle, as he showed at Gettysburg by defining it in terms of "liberty," "equality," and the active consent of all the people. In Lincoln's Union, slavery existed only by a historical accident, and would cease to exist as soon as possible. The question for Lincoln after 1854 was: What shall we do to make that Union a reality?

His first step was to become president. The previous subsection explained how Lincoln's action in the Peoria Address led to his election. Then, once he was president, the rest was tactics. This does not mean it was easy. Opposition to the war in the North, and the necessity of keeping the slave-owning border states from joining the South, made Lincoln's tactics more cautious than abolitionists wanted. If he had freed the slaves in Maryland, for example, that state would have seceded, and the nation's capital in Washington would have been lost to the South, probably ending the war. But Lincoln succeeded in holding the Unionist coalition together and winning the war, which abolitionist tactics could not have done. The longer the war lasted, the closer Lincoln's Union came to being a reality. Lincoln repeatedly refused to settle the war on any terms--such as those proposed by rebel president Jefferson Davis in the spring of 1865--that would have delayed his Union from becoming a reality.

IV. Practical Wisdom: Knowing When Failure Is Success

This chapter began with the claim that Lincoln's practical wisdom combines morality and politics in a way that provides *a model for any person to find a way of action which is at once the most moral and the most practical course.* Now it is time to make good that promise. It will take just three steps. (But you must take the steps to get the help.)

Step 1: Accepting Lincoln as a Model

In my experience, the biggest obstacle to learning practical wisdom from Lincoln is that we reject him as a model.* "What does an old-fashioned, white-male, Republican president have to do with me and my life?"--everyone but George Bush might say. So the first step here is simply to get clear whether you--that is, each reader of this sentence--can accept Lincoln as a model of practical wisdom. Would you have voted for Lincoln in 1860? Do you judge Lincoln's stance on slavery in 1854 superior to the abolitionists' as well as to the slave-owners' and Stephen Douglas'? In terms of your own moral-political development (Section One), do you feel Lincoln shows you a positive third stage "beyond [your own] innocence and experience"?

You may well wonder. Lincoln's victory caused the Civil War. When he could have prevented war by accepting the Crittendon Compromise, he didn't, as Section Three explained. Who wants a Civil War? Americans in 1860 were so unsure of Lincoln that he got only 40% of the popular vote in 1860. (Douglas got 30%, the Southern Democrat got 18%, a border state compromiser got 12%. But Lincoln outpolled Douglas in almost every northern state, thus winning 173 Electoral College votes out of the total of 296, or 58%). Even in the North, in the middle of the War, just three months before his re-election in 1864, Lincoln himself thought it "exceedingly probable" he would lose. As one of his campaign workers wrote then from New York to Washington City, "There are no Lincoln men [i.e., people who will work for him] ... We do not know which way to turn."[29]

And on the other hand, although he was dangerous, Lincoln was a johnny-come-lately on the anti-slavery bandwagon. Abolitionists had been taking serious personal risks to oppose slavery for twenty years before Lincoln began to speak out. As late as the 1848 presidential election, when serious anti-slavery people banded together behind former President Martin Van Buren under the slogan, "Free Soil, Free Speech, Free Labor, and Free Men," Lincoln opposed them and campaigned as a Whig.

---

* Most of my co-authors have made clear that they do *not* accept Lincoln as a model!

Refuting Lincoln's Critics

(1) Northern capitalism *could* have reached an accommodation with southern slavery (as capitalism did with serfdom and feudalism in Germany, Russia, and Japan in the nineteenth century); it didn't need war.

(2) The pro-slavery coalition *forced* Douglas against his will to repeal the Missouri Compromise in the Kansas-Nebraska Act; they didn't know slavery was doomed! And even if slavery in agriculture was doomed, slavery was not, as its use for nonagricultural purposes in Nazi Germany, the Soviet Union, and China in the twentieth century shows.

(3) Lincoln admitted the Constitution did compromise with the fact of slavery (it did exist; to refuse to compromise would mean having no Union, without freeing any slaves), but argued it *opposed* the principle of slavery since slaves were never treated by the Constitution or federal law as ordinary property. E.g., federal law made the slave-trade a capital crime, which could not be done under the Constitution for the cranberry trade. (The validity of Lincoln's view is explained by Storing, note 31.) Lincoln was bound to uphold laws enacted persuant to that principle, even the Fugitive Slave Law.

(4) The rebels attacked the Union first, so Lincoln was fighting a war of self-defense, which just-war theory (see Walzer, note 5) admits is a just cause. (The text at notes 26-27 explains why the South was not asserting the Declaration of Independence's "right to rebel.") The blockade and war of attrition were not his first choice, but became the only alternative to losing the (just) war, so just-war theory allows them. Also, the Supreme Court upheld the constitutionality and international legality of the blockade in *The Prize Cases*.

(5) Yes: in fact, the conspiracy *did* split the Democrats in 1860, a propensity which Lincoln had discerned in 1854 by its determination and power to repeal the Missouri Compromise against Douglas' will. (See [2] above.)

(6) As the Parable of the Practical Son and the quoted section of Lincoln's Peoria Address showed, Lincoln did not act to free the slaves out of compassion for them anymore than for poor whites. He understood that slavery was incompatible with freedom regardless of who happened to be enslaved. So he always argued that the evil of slavery afflicted the *whole* body politic, not just its primary victims.

And on the third hand, Lincoln was Lincoln--an incomparable hero. A later president, Gerald Fold, asked if he felt qualified for the job, said, "I'm just a Ford, not a Lincoln." If even a president can't identify with Lincoln, how can we?

So, can *you* accept Lincoln as a model of both practicality and wisdom?

"No," say many people today. They ask questions like the six following. Only if these questions can be answered in Lincoln's favor, they say, can we be sure he represents practical wisdom for us. And they doubt it.

(1) What about other motives behind the Civil War? Wasn't it really a victory for northern capitalism rather than for African-Americans?

(2) Didn't geography and climate prevent slavery from expanding into Kansas? Wouldn't slavery have died out without any war?

(3) If Lincoln was really motivated by opposition to slavery, how could he have supported the Fugitive Slave Act? And why did he wait so long into the war to issue the Emancipation Proclamation?

(4) Didn't Lincoln's "war is hell" strategy--burning Atlanta, devastating Georgia and the Shenandoah Valley, seizing peaceful trading ships, fighting a war of attrition with hundreds of thousands of casualties--violate international law and morality, contradicting his claim to wisdom?

(5) Could Lincoln really have been so paranoid as to believe there was a conspiracy to expand slavery in 1854 which would split Douglas' party in 1860 and let him become president?

(6) Weren't Lincoln and almost all white Americans at the time actually racist in their attitudes? Didn't Lincoln want to send freed slaves off to another country? Was concern about the slaves' well-being really the reason for fighting the War?

If the criticisms implied by these questions were correct, then Lincoln must have been--far from a model of practical wisdom--an irresponsible demagogue for whipping up the voters to believe a danger existed when none did (and he didn't care about it anyway), and a warmonger for provoking a needless war. As long as we think this could be true, Lincoln can't help us learn practical wisdom.

But the criticisms implied by these questions are not true. They're not even new. They only repeat the same objections that were made against Lincoln while he was alive. Questions 1 and 4 were urged by **APOLOGISTS** for the South. Questions 2 and 5 were Douglas' **REALIST** argument. Questions 3 and 6 were used by **ABOLITIONISTS**.

These objections support different alternatives to Lincoln. One can't sensibly prefer all the alternatives to Lincoln at the same time. So all these objections can't possibly be valid. For example, if Lincoln provoked an unnecessary war (as realists believe), then it can't make sense to charge him with not doing enough to abolish slavery (as abolitionists charge). Once we grasp that such objections to Lincoln really consist in agreeing with abolitionists and Douglas and slave-owners all at once, we should be less readily taken in by them.

At any rate, specific answers to these six questions can be inferred from Section Three. They are summarized in the box on page 20. But whether or not they are as persuasive as I think Section Three shows them to be, a question remains: even if Lincoln represented practical wisdom for America in 1854-60 better than the alternatives to him did, how can this extraordinary hero be a model we ordinary people can identify with today? To answer this, you must take step two.

Step 2: Learning from Lincoln: Analogy, Concept, Quality

The second step in learning about practical wisdom from Lincoln is to see how you--each reader of this sentence--can re-live his example. There are three ways, in order of increasing relevance to ordinary people like you and me. The first is by analogy. We see an analogy between Lincoln and ourselves when we realize, for example, that his opponents still exist today. It is not only when we debate about the Civil War that abolitionists, realists, and apologists live again in us. When we talk politics, we sometimes play the roles of abolitionists, realists, and apologists--creating the opportunity for a new Lincoln to emerge as the original Lincoln emerged in 1854.

In foreign policy, for example, from the Vietnam War in 1968 to the Gulf War in 1991, Americans' attitudes fell into three rough categories.[30] People who supported the use of American force abroad were called conservatives or nationalists. They may be an analogy to the apologists of the 1850s. People who opposed the use of force abroad were called liberals or revisionists. They may be an analogy to the abolitionists of the 1850s. People who supported the use of force abroad but only up to a point, wanting a limited war like President Bush when he refused to topple the Iraqi government in the Gulf War, were called realists. They may be an analogy to Douglas' realism in the 1850s. Or, they may be an analogy to Lincoln's practical wisdom--and this is the trouble with analogies!

But it is no accident that the views of Americans today on our political issues can seem analogous to those of Lincoln's opponents. Disagreement on moral issues, such as slavery before the Civil War or abortion today, produces opposition between right and wrong: abolitionists vs. apologists for slavery before the Civil War; pro-life vs. pro-choice today. Such opposition structures a community into three groups: "extremists" on opposite sides, and "moderates" who stand between them. (Section One calls such "extremism" "innocence," and such "moderation" "experience.") On the slavery issue in the 1850s such moderates were the Douglas-realists. A majority of the American people today seem to be moderates on the abortion issue. Of course, there are many issues; people may be "extremists" on one and "realists" on another. But these are the three basic commonsense possibilities.

The practical wisdom of Lincoln transcends this commonsense, one-dimensional flatland by seeing/voicing/creating a possibility of more goodness than the three basic commonsense possibilities allow. Lincoln did not just "split the difference" between abolitionists and apologists, as Douglas did. He compromised, but in a way that maintained the principle (of the Declaration, the Constitution, and the Missouri Compromise) that slavery is an evil.[31]

To describe Lincoln's practical wisdom in this way, as an action which transcends the three commonsense possibilities,* shows us Lincoln's relevance for us today by means of general concepts rather than mere analogies. The description in the two previous paragraphs presents general concepts which you may apply to any situation you are or might be in. For example, suppose you wonder what you would have done if you were a Jew in first-century Palestine.[32] The key moral issue was to maintain fidelity to Yahweh in the face of the power of Greek culture and Roman armies. The ruling group of Sadducees were apologists for collaboration. Zealots rebelled violently against Roman oppression. Pharisees believed compromise was possible if strict rules were observed by Jews and Romans. Of course the situation is not precisely an analogy to Lincoln's. But by seeing how the situation was structured around an irrepressible conflict like slavery in the 1850s (Sadducees = apologists; Zealots = abolitionists; Pharisees = Douglas' realists), we can see how Jesus of Nazareth may have represented practical wisdom like Lincoln's. (This suggests that the "Lincoln Legend" and the "Christian Myth" have more in common than the accident of Lincoln's assassination falling on Good Friday, 1865.)[33]

Section Two used this concept of practical wisdom to show what Lincoln learned about it from the Bible. In a different educational system he could have learned the concept of practical wisdom from Aristotle or Confucius. For practical wisdom was known and taught by the ancient Chinese (as *shih*), Greeks (as *phronesis*), and Romans (as *prudentia*) as well as by the people of the Bible. It was one of the Five Constant Virtues of Chinese tradition, and one of the four Cardinal Virtues of western tradition.[34]

This is hardly the place for an analysis of *shih, phronesis, and prudentia*.** Each term grew up in its own unique cultural context, none of which was much like Lincoln's or our own. But the fact that vastly different societies have a concept which means roughly what we mean by practical wisdom is important in understanding Lincoln's relevance

---

* The other chapters in this section also stress the transcendent or transformative quality of leadership, as does Rinehart's "Learning To Lead."

** Mary Jo Bona's Italian-American leaders, and Rose Mary Volbrecht's "careful mutuality" illustrate key aspects of these concepts. (Pat O'Leary's criticism of Aristotle in "Ignatius" does not concern *phronesis*, I believe.)

for us, even if we are not politicians or nationally prominent. There is a concept of practical wisdom which is not limited to one culture or historical period, or to people in the government, but is a potential in any situation, including our own.

Moreover, these concepts show that practical wisdom is *not* primarily the ability to take the "correct" position, let alone a guarantee of success, but is more a quality of a person's personality. The Five Constant Virtues and the four Cardinal Virtues are desirable qualities of a person (like a sense of humor) rather than an ability to act well (like the ability to tell a joke). Because Lincoln's practical wisdom matches these concepts, it suggests that what we need to exercise practical wisdom is not elite status or power but rather to develop certain qualities in ourselves. Section One already suggested this, by showing how a naive child and conventional wisdom both fail to see the possibility of genuine practical wisdom, and asking if there is a more developed view. Sections Two and Three showed there is. But we must ourselves develop "beyond innocence and experience" if we want to see it for ourselves. This requires step three.

Step 3: When Failure Is Success

We are so success-oriented, and Lincoln was such a success, it is hard to see how his practical wisdom involved failure. Think back to Section Three: did you notice his failure? Probably not. Most people don't. But in fact he was a three-time loser. (His success only followed, and grew out of, his failures.) It turns out that the crux of his practical wisdom is simultaneously the quality in him which we ordinary people can all identify with: failure ... but in a certain way. To grasp this is the third and last step in learning practical wisdom from Lincoln.

First, let's review how much of a failure Lincoln was. After he dropped out of political office in 1848, he was just an ordinary good lawyer. He returned to politics in 1854 with his Peoria Address and campaign for the Senate, but he lost. He was still just a lawyer and has-been politician. He campaigned for the new Republican Party in the presidential race in 1856 but lost; Douglas' Democrats won the White House and majorities in both houses of Congress. He tried again, even harder, to win a Senate seat in 1858, campaigning against Douglas himself, but he lost.

The truth is, few of us have been such ***failures*** as Lincoln!* If we can't identify with him, it's more likely because we haven't risked ourselves as often and as passionately as he did, than because he was a hero and we are just regular folk. And after all, isn't this just the truth about

---

* Peter Ely's chapter on "Perceval" and Tom Jeannot's "But Trusted Servants" both emphasize the relevance of failure to leadership.

Lincoln which was summed up in the image of his humble, log cabin, rail-splitter origins? He *was* just ordinary folks.

How can such an ordinary failure have led the country to abolish slavery?

Our puzzle here arises from the mistaken way we keep thinking about practical wisdom. We think: wisdom chooses our goals, practical experience enables us to choose effective means to achieve those goals. Wisdom makes the goals good. Practical wisdom makes the means effective. Failure has nothing to do with it.

But Lincoln shows us otherwise. As Step 2 showed, the concept of practical wisdom points to a quality of a person, not to an ability to make correct choices.* In other words, practical wisdom concerns ends and means simultaneously, revealing the person and the action at one and the same time: "What shall we do, and who will we be if we do it?" It is a word, not a blow: its power is not "now I've got you, don't bother to squirm" but "now the truth is revealed."[35]

This is why even Lincoln's failures were successes. For example, even in defeat, his Peoria Address and Senatorial campaign in 1854 was meaningful. It "drew a line in the sand" which Douglas couldn't ignore. (By saying "the Kansas-Nebraska Act is a gift of free land to the slave-owners," Lincoln's speech required that Douglas either admit Lincoln was right, and lose all credibility in the North, or fight on Lincoln's side against the pro-slavery Lecompton Constitution approved by his own party's South-dominated president.) And when Lincoln threw his support to the anti-Nebraska Democratic candidate to defeat the Douglas Democrat (as Section Three explained), it was obvious to all that his devotion to the anti-slavery cause was stronger than his self-interest.

1858 was the same. Subjectively, the defeat felt (as Lincoln said) like a boy stubbing his toe: he was too big to cry but it hurt too much to laugh. But objectively, as Section Three explained, Lincoln's failure--the *way* he failed, showing who/what he represented in his speeches and debates to the people of Illinois and America--led the Republicans to nominate him and the voters to elect him president in 1860.

What is the difference between the naive martyr who makes a demonstration of his/her principles and the experienced realists whose conventional wisdom knows good guys finish last? Lincoln's practical wisdom.

And even if Lincoln hadn't been elected president? Then the light shining from his action would have lit up the darkness of the country and showed everyone the truth. Practical wisdom is acting in such a way that even if/when you fail, you learn the truth about yourself and your situation. At least, that's what Lincoln taught me.

---

* This emphasis on personal quality is central to the other chapters in this section, to Mary Jo Bona's, "Italian/American Women Writers," and to Tom Jeannot's "But Trusted Servants."

Notes

1. Genevieve Foster, *Abraham Lincoln's World* (NY: Scribner's, 1944).
2. Benjamin P. Thomas, *Abraham Lincoln* (NY: Knopf, 1952).
3. Richard Hofstadter, *The American Political Tradition and the Men Who Made It* (NY: Vintage Books, 1957), ch. 5. More balanced and thorough but still revisionist is Richard N. Current, *The Lincoln Nobody Knows* (NY: McGraw-Hill, 1958), ch. 9.
4. This lesson can be formulated in various ways: that personal ethics have no interpersonal meaning (Robert A. Dahl, *Modern Political Analysis* [Englewood Cliffs, NJ: Prentice-Hall, 1963], ch. 8); that human diversity requires different ethical standards for personal and public affairs (Stuart Hampshire, *Innocence and Experience* [Cambridge, MA: Harvard University Press, 1989]); or that the nature of politics simply requires "dirty hands" (Michael Walzer, "Political Action: The Problem of Dirty Hands," *Philosophy and Public Affairs* 1 (Winter, 1972), 160-80.
5. The best criticism of the ethics of the war, Michael Walzer's *Just and Unjust War* (New York: Basic Books, 1977), uses Sherman's "war is hell" tactics in the Civil War to illustrate what was wrong with the American "rules of engagement" in Vietnam.
6. Even in the 1950s, children of all social classes went through this sort of disillusionment between the fourth and eighth grades. Fred I. Greenstein, *Children and Politics* (New Haven: Yale University Press, 1965).
7. There are many studies of moral development, but few take seriously the complexities of politics. An exception is William K. Muir, *Police: Streetcorner Politicians* (Chicago: University of Chicago Press, 1979), especially chs. 10-12. The concept of practical wisdom is applied to modern politics in Harry V. Jaffa, *Crisis of the House Divided: An Interpretation of the Lincoln-Douglas Debates* (Seattle: University of Washington Press, 1959).
8. Matt. 10:16. In English-language Bibles the following stories of practical wisdom do not all use the words "practical wisdom." This is because the Hebrew and Greek words in the Bible that mean practical wisdom are translated into English by words like "sharp-wittedness," "shrewdness," "cleverness," "skill," and "astuteness," as well as by "practical wisdom." Which of these translations gets used depends on whether the translators think we should approve of the practical wisdom in a particular passage. The "shrewdness" of the Crafty Steward (Luke 16:8) and "wisdom" of the serpent recommended by Jesus (Matt. 10:16) both translate the same Greek word, *phronimos*. See *Eerdman's Analytical Concordance* (Grand Rapids, MI: Eerdmans, 1988), pp. 984, 1221.
9. On Johnson's Senior Advisory Group, see: The New York Times, *The Pentagon Papers* (New York: Dell, 1971), p. 609. See also Walter Isaacson and Evan Thomas, *The Wise Men: Six Friends and the World They Made* (New York: Simon & Schuster, 1986).
10. Taylor Branch, *Parting the Waters: America in the King Years, 1954-1963* (NY: Simon & Schuster, 1988), p. 8. (Branch is speaking of a forerunner of Martin Luther King, Jr., Vernon Johns, but the point applies as well to Lincoln.) Lincoln's biographers usually mention his learning to read by the Bible, but disagree

as to its significance for him. A balanced review of the controversy is Current's "The Instrument of God," ch. 3 of *The Lincoln Nobody Knows*, note 3 above.

11. Quoted in Jaffa, note 7 above, p. 305.

12. See note 8 above.

13. See note 8 above.

14. See Kenneth E. Bailey, *Poet and Peasant and Through Peasant Eyes: a Literary-Cultural Approach to the Parables in Luke* (Grand Rapids, MI: Eerdmans, 1983), pp. 86-110.

15. Ibid.

16. Lincoln's letter in commiseration to a former neighbor who had lost her son, describing himself, cited in Thomas, note 2 above, p. 481.

17. See, e.g., "A Railroad Promotion and Its Sequel," ch. 7 in *The Impending Crisis* by David M. Potter (NY: Harper & Row, 1976).

18. See Jaffa, note 7 above, chs. 5-8.

19. Historians (e.g. Thomas, note 2 above, pp. 148-52) recognize this remarkable speech as the turning point in Lincoln's career and in the formation of the new anti-slavery-expansion Republican Party. It is quoted here from John G. Nicolay and John Hay, eds., *Abraham Lincoln Complete Works*, 2 vols. (New York: Century, 1894), 1:197-198, emphasis added.

20. Don E. Fehrenbacher, *Prelude to Greatness* (Stanford: Stanford University Press, 1962), chs. 2, 3, 7.

21. For Lincoln's opposition to slavery in the Mexican Cession, see Stephen B. Oates, *With Malice Toward None* (NY: New American Library, 1977), pp. 84-91; for the 1837 resolution and minority report, pp. 38-42.

22. Jaffa, note 7 above, Part 4; Oates, ibid., pp. 116-133; Fehrenbacher, note 20 above, pp. 22-25. Historians less sympathetic to Lincoln, e.g., Potter, note 17 above, criticize Lincoln's belief in a plan to extend slavery, yet Potter admits that in the early 1850s "many southerners had come to believe that they faced a crucial choice: they must somehow stabilize their position in the Union, with safeguards to preserve the security of the slave system, or they must secede ..." (pp. 288ff., and 94).

23. See Paul M. Angle, ed., *Created Equal? The Complete Lincoln-Douglas Debates of 1858* (Chicago: Univ. of Chicago Press, 1958); also Fehrenbacher, note 20 above, pp. 106-112; Jaffa, note 7 above, Parts 3 and 4.

24. Malapportionment and holdover Senators in the state legislature turned a 125,430 to 121,609 (to 5,071 for the anti-Douglas Democrats) victory for the Republicans and Lincoln in the popular vote into a Douglas re-election victory in the legislature.

25. Fehrenbacher, note 20 above, ch. 4.

26. The Declaration's "right of rebellion" is carefully stated as follows: "that whenever any form of government becomes destructive of these ends, it is the right of the people to alter or to abolish it, and to institute new government, laying its foundation on such principles, and organizing its powers in such form, as to them shall seem most likely to effect their safety and happiness." The word "that" at the beginning of the clause shows that this right is one of the series of propositions whose truth is held to be self-evident at the beginning of the sentence. But the sentence begins, famously, "We hold these truths to be self-evident: That ALL men are created equal; that they [ALL] are endowed by their

Creator with certain unalienable rights; that among these [rights ALL people are endowed with by God] are life, liberty, and the pursuit of happiness; that, to secure these rights [which ALL are endowed with by God], governments are instituted among men, deriving their just powers from the consent of the governed; ..." Only then does the quoted "right of rebellion" occur. Obviously a rebellion whose immediate cause is to preserve slavery cannot be justified by the Declaration.

27. Cited in Jaffa, note 7 above, p. 314.

28. E.g., Hofstadter, note 3 above.

29. Thomas, note 2 above, p. 443.

30. Jerald A. Combs, *The History of American Foreign Policy* (NY: Knopf, 1986), Preface, chs. 15-21.

31. The Declaration's opposition to slavery is obvious on its face. The Constitution's compromises with slavery make its anti-slavery principle less obvious. For a good explanation, see Herbert Storing, "Slavery and the Moral Foundations of the American Republic," in Robert H. Horwitz, ed., *The Moral Foundations of the American Republic*, 2nd ed. (Charlottsville, VA: University Press of Virginia, 1979), pp. 214-225.

32. Information on the Jewish groups comes mainly from the first-century Jewish historian Josephus, and is accepted by historians even when they disagree about how to interpret it. Compare the accounts in, e.g., E. P. Sanders, *Jesus and Judaism* (Philadelphia: Fortress Press, 1985) and Marcus Borg, *Conflict, Holiness & Politics in the Teachings of Jesus* (Lampeter, UK: Edwin Mellen Press, 1984).

33. See Current, note 3 above, ch. 11.

34. *jen, i, li, chih, hsin* are translated as mutuality/human-heartedness, justice/righteousness, propriety or *savoir faire*, practical wisdom, and good faith [see, e.g., Fung Yu-lan, *A History of Chinese Philosophy* (Princeton: Princeton University Press, 2nd ed. 1952), vol. 1, p. 27]. The four Cardinal Virtues are practical wisdom, courage, justice, and temperance (a climate is "temperate" when it avoids extremes like equatorial and arctic).

35. This is why Confucius said practical wisdom issues in "non-action," and why Gandhi called it *satyagraha* or "truth-force" (usually mistranslated as nonviolent resistance). The best recent example of Lincoln's practical wisdom was probably the lunch-counter sit-ins in the Civil Rights Movement of the early 1960s; see Branch, note 10 above, ch. 7. The "Who ... and what ...?" quote is paraphrased from Hanna F. Pitkin, *Wittgenstein and Justice* (Berkeley, CA: University of California Press, 1972).

Chapter 2

Rating the Presidents for Greatness: What Role Does Crisis Play?

Frank B. Costello, S.J.

Nowhere in the following essay is the term greatness defined. A philosopher was once asked if he could define goodness and he answered, no, but he could identify a good person. Greatness may be as difficult to define as goodness, but I have found that a great person as well as a great political leader can be identified.

Of the five presidents who have achieved greatness, only two, Woodrow Wilson and Franklin Roosevelt, lived in this century. Wilson was out of office before I was born. However, the twelve years of Franklin Roosevelt's presidency are still very present to my memory. During those extraordinary times, I had the opportunity to observe a great president's effect on American society.

I can recall vividly that Saturday morning March 4, 1933 when, gathered with members of my family around a radio set for Franklin Roosevelt's first inaugural address, we heard him assure the nation that the only thing we had to fear was fear itself. Fear of the economic present and future was very real to our friends and neighbors. Though my father was employed that day, most of the heads of households in our area were out of work. Many families on our block and many families in the neighborhood did not have enough to eat, did not have the means to heat their homes.

Almost immediately after that day of inauguration, the mood in our neighborhood changed for the better. The banks reopened. Hope grew in us as we learned of the president's efforts to address the problems of unemployment and hunger. The blizzard of bills passed during the famous Hundred Days began to have its effect. We watched the young men from our neighborhood leave for the Civilian Conservation Corps (CCC) camps in the national forests, to earn their first paychecks ($30 a month) and to eat their first decent meal in a long time. Shortly after that, we watched the heads of households start to be employed by the Works Progress Administration (WPA), digging sewers and enlarging public works in the city. The recollection of my parents proudly displaying in the front window of our home the Blue Eagle of the National Recovery Administration (NRA) is for me an unfaded memory.

It was the leadership of Franklin Roosevelt which gave us hope and restored pride, confidence and dignity to the people around us. Without realizing it, I was watching one of the nation's great presidents at work. Fascinated by what I observed, I was led to a lifelong study of the American presidency and to this essay, which deals with the process by which great presidents can be identified. The crisis of the economic Depression allowed Franklin Roosevelt to demonstrate his great political leadership. I later discovered that other crises, earlier in our history, allowed for other presidents also to demonstrate their exceptional leadership qualities. This essay chronicles my search and discovery.

John W. Gardner has observed that most great leaders are the product of major emergencies or disasters. No doubt, he wrote, there are many born leaders, but it is generally only in times of trouble that their potentialities blossom into greatness. "Great leaders--Roosevelt, Churchill, DeGaulle in our time--appear when a society needs them desperately: only under such conditions are there likely to be both the mandate and the highly motivated followers that great leadership requires."[1]

It was President John F. Kennedy who reminded Americans that a nation reveals itself not only in the men and women it produces, but also in those it honors and those it remembers. This essay plans to review the history of five chief executives who have reached their niches in the pantheon of great presidents: Abraham Lincoln, George Washington, Franklin D. Roosevelt, Woodrow Wilson and Thomas Jefferson. The first part will chronicle the efforts of historians to identify these five great presidents, and identify what seems to have been common to all the presidents rated as great: a national crisis of major proportions. The second part will undertake to discover whether it was the crisis itself which produced the great president, or whether it was something else for which the crisis was but an essential condition in each of the president's administrations.

Historians Rate the Presidents

The major problem in rating the presidents for greatness is deciding on what criteria to use. Just four presidents--Washington, Jefferson, Lincoln and Theodore Roosevelt--have monuments in the nation's capital, though Roosevelt's is somewhat inconspicuous. These same presidents have their portraits carved on Mount Rushmore. Washington, Jefferson, James Madison, Andrew Jackson and Lincoln are the only presidents who have states or state capitals named for them. The number of counties named for presidents include thirty-one Washingtons, twenty-six Jeffersons, twenty-two Jacksons and sixteen Lincolns, to mention only the top four. There appears to be an inverse relationship between the face value of the United States currency and presidents' popular acclaim. Washington is on the one dollar bill, Lincoln on the five, while Ulysses S. Grant appears on the less frequently-seen fifty. Jefferson made it on the two dollar bill, but few ever see Wilson's portrait on the one hundred thousand dollar bill. Such norms as some of those mentioned above seem rather inadequate indicators of presidential greatness. Perhaps that is why historians have been asked to rank the presidents for their leadership qualities.[2]

Samuel Butler observed that God cannot alter the past, so God is obliged to connive at the existence of historians.[3] The evaluation of the presidents by historians is a relatively recent phenomenon. In 1948, fifty-five American historians were asked by Arthur M. Schlesinger, Sr. to rate the presidents using five categories: great, near great, average, below average, and failure. No specific guidelines were furnished for the poll. The results ranked all the presidents from Washington to F. Roosevelt, excluding William H. Harrison and James A. Garfield because of their brief tenure.[4] The six great presidents, in order, were Lincoln, Washington, F. Roosevelt, Wilson, Jefferson and Jackson.[5] Schlesinger asked himself if the results of his survey could reveal a common pattern. He found the following: (1) the great presidents were all identified with some crucial turning point in our history, (2) all of them took the side of progressivism and reform as understood in their day, (3) they all seemed politically ahead of their times, but not too far ahead, (4) all were party men, serving as party chief as well as chief executive, (5) all were strong moral leaders, (6) they were all expanders of executive power, (7) all were shrewd users of public opinion, and (8) nearly all were usually opposed by the press.[6]

In 1962, Arthur Schlesinger conducted another poll, increasing the number of historians to seventy-five and adding Harry Truman and Dwight D. Eisenhower to the list of those to be rated. The results were identical to the poll of 1948 except that Jackson was demoted to the rank of near greats. The great presidents in the 1962 poll were: Lincoln, Washington, F. Roosevelt, Wilson and Jefferson. Truman joined Jackson with the near greats, and Eisenhower was listed with the average chief executives. The presidents rated as great in both Schlesinger surveys appear in almost the same order in all subsequent evaluation attempts.

The Schlesinger polls provoked widespread comment and dissent.[7] One of the dissenters was Thomas A. Bailey of Stanford University. Bailey examined the possible prejudices in the Schlesinger polls and then outlined the criteria according to which presidents could be evaluated more extensively. At the end of his study, Bailey offered his own assessment of the presidents from Washington to Lyndon B. Johnson.

After all of Bailey's qualifying remarks, he ended up with three great presidents in Washington, Lincoln, and F. Roosevelt followed by three near greats in T. Roosevelt, Jefferson, and Wilson.[8]

Clinton Rossiter in *The American Presidency*, had earlier evaluated the presidents and arrived at a list of eight great presidents: Washington, Lincoln, Wilson, Jackson, T. Roosevelt, Jefferson, F. Roosevelt, and Truman.[9] In 1964 Eric Sokolsky published a book, *Our Seven Greatest Presidents*.[10] His list of seven in order was: Jefferson, Jackson, Lincoln, T. Roosevelt, Wilson, F. Roosevelt and Kennedy. There were two surprising ratings, the demotion of Washington from great to very good and the elevation of Kennedy to great. Though Sokolsky based his ratings on some explicitly stated criteria, at least one author suggested that Sokolsky's evaluation of Kennedy might not have been utterly objective.[11]

One of the more elaborate attempts to rate the presidents was undertaken by Gary M. Maranell in 1970. He involved not just fifty-five or seventy-five but five hundred and seventy-one historians and specified precisely the categories on which he wanted the presidents to be rated. There were seven distinct dimensions: (1) the general prestige of the president today, (2) the strength of action that he developed, (3) his presidential activeness in his administration, (4) the idealism of his official actions, (5) the flexibility of his approach, (6) the administration accomplishments, and (7) the amount of information the respondent possessed about the president.[12] The presidents were assigned precise scores on the seven dimensions. Maranell's poll covered the presidents from Washington through L. Johnson. The outcomes of Maranell's poll were strikingly similar to previous ratings. On the first dimension, general prestige, the six most favored presidents were: Lincoln, Washington, F. Roosevelt, Jefferson, T. Roosevelt, and Wilson.

The most recent and most ambitious survey was that which Robert K. Murray and Tim H. Blessing published in 1983. They studied results from eight hundred and forty-six respondents on presidential greatness. All who participated were Ph.D.-holding historians in American universities. Thirty-six presidents were evaluated from Washington to Jimmy Carter. Four presidents were considered great: Lincoln, F. Roosevelt, Washington and Jefferson.[13] Near greats were: T. Roosevelt, Wilson, Jackson and Truman. Murray and Blessing compared their results with two other recent polls. The first, by fifty-nine experts, appeared in the *Chicago Tribune Magazine* on January 10, 1982. That evaluation listed the ten best presidents: Lincoln, Washington, F. Roosevelt, T. Roosevelt, Jefferson, Wilson, Jackson, Truman, Eisenhower and James Polk. The second survey was an unpublished poll by forty-one experts conducted by David L. Porter. Among the all-time great presidents, the following were listed: Lincoln, Washington, F. Roosevelt, Jefferson and T. Roosevelt.[14]

Dean K. Simonton has studied the consensus reached by the historians on presidential ratings. He concluded that it is manifest that the rating of the presidents cannot be faulted for lack of consensus. He was convinced that the consensus was grounded so solidly that it reflected an objective reality rather than a subjective judgment.[15] In the following comparison of polls, the letter N indicates the number of persons participating in the poll.

A Comparison of Polls

Schlesinger 1948 (N = 55)	Rossiter 1956 (N = 1)	Schlesinger 1962 (N = 75)
Lincoln Washington F. Roosevelt Wilson Jefferson Jackson	Washington Lincoln Wilson Jackson T. Roosevelt Jefferson F. Roosevelt Truman	Lincoln Washington F. Roosevelt Wilson Jefferson
T. Roosevelt Grover Cleveland John Adams Polk		Jackson T. Roosevelt Polk Truman J. Adams Cleveland

Sokolsky 1964 (N = 1)	Bailey 1966 (N = 1)	Maranell 1970 (N = 571)
Jefferson Jackson Lincoln T. Roosevelt Wilson F. Roosevelt Kennedy	Washington Lincoln F. Roosevelt	Lincoln Washington F. Roosevelt Jefferson T. Roosevelt Wilson
	T. Roosevelt Jefferson Wilson	

Porter 1981 (N = 41)	Chicago Tribune 1982 (N = 49)	Murray- Blessing 1982 (N = 846)
Lincoln Washington F. Roosevelt Jefferson T. Roosevelt	Lincoln Washington F. Roosevelt Jefferson Wilson	Lincoln F. Roosevelt Washington Jefferson
Wilson Jackson Truman Polk J. Adams L. Johnson	Jackson Truman Eisenhower Polk	T. Roosevelt Wilson Jackson Truman

Common Aspects of the Great Presidents

Having demonstrated a remarkable consensus among historians about the greatest of our chief executives, it is time to attempt to identify any common aspects of their administrations.

As was mentioned above, Arthur M. Schlesinger, after his first survey concluded that all the great presidents were identified with some crucial turning point in American history.

> As our first President, Washington got the infant republic on its feet. Jefferson's Louisiana Purchase was our first territorial expansion, pushing the western boundary from the Mississippi to the Rockies . . . Lincoln preserved the union through four years of bloody civil war. Wilson's "New Freedom" and Roosevelt's "New Deal" introduced far reaching changes in the social and economic structure of the country, and both men led the U.S. to intervene in world wars and the making of international peace.[16]

Harold Laski in a perceptive study of the American presidency reached a similar conclusion:

> There have been five considerable crises in American history. There was the need to start the new republic adequately in 1789; it gave the American people its natural leader in George Washington. The crisis of 1800 brought Jefferson to the presidency; that of 1861 brought Abraham Lincoln. The war of 1914 found Wilson in office; the great depression resulted in the election of Franklin Roosevelt.[17]

More recently, Thomas A. Bailey observed that a great president is one lucky enough to serve in a crisis:

> All of the Big Five (Washington, Lincoln, F. Roosevelt, Jefferson, and Wilson) held office during a critical era. Three of them--Lincoln, Wilson and Franklin Roosevelt--got us into our three biggest wars. Perhaps one could more fairly say that these men occupied the White House when war erupted. The crisis in all three cases was not of their making, and by one line of argument each could have kept us out of the ensuing conflict--at least temporarily--if he had steered a different course. Both Abraham Lincoln and Franklin Roosevelt were accused of having diabolically goaded the enemy into attacking, the one at Fort Sumter, the other at Pearl Harbor.[18]

Though the crisis of war and/or depression may be the making of a great president, one might conclude that it was not merely the crisis but response to the crisis that constituted greatness in the chief executive. James Madison was in office when the war of 1812 began, but Madison's rating *as president* is average on both Schlesinger polls, the *Chicago Tribune* poll and the Porter survey. In a sense, James Buchanan confronted almost the same crisis as did Lincoln, but Buchanan was rated below average on both Schlesinger polls, and was listed as one of the ten worst in the *Chicago Tribune* poll. A similar observation could be made regarding Herbert Hoover, who experienced the Great Depression during most of his term in office yet ended up as an average president in both Schlesinger surveys, the *Chicago Tribune* survey, and the Porter survey.

If it was not merely the crisis itself which occasioned or caused the presidents to be great, it is time to review the administrations of the top five great presidents to consider each one's response to the crisis he confronted. A brief look at the presidencies of Lincoln, Washington, F. Roosevelt, Wilson and Jefferson will follow. Lincoln, Wilson, and F. Roosevelt will be considered first because the crises they confronted--war and depression--can be more easily identified. Washington and Jefferson will be looked at last because the turning points in American history with which they were associated are less easily identified, though no less important.

Lincoln

Of the five great presidents, Lincoln is the most paradoxical. From his family's economic background, he was the least likely to succeed. He was the quintessential born-in-a-log-cabin president who grew up poor. His parents were poor Kentuckians. His mother, who died in his youth, was an illegitimate child; his father was essentially illiterate. These circumstances are in striking contrast to the backgrounds of the other four. Washington, Jefferson, and F. Roosevelt were from wealthy families.

Wilson grew up in a Presbyterian minister's household of modest means. None except Lincoln had been poor.

Lincoln was also the least formally educated among the great five. He was largely self-taught. In contrast, George Washington had gone to school until he was nearly seventeen. Jefferson had earned a college degree and F. Roosevelt had attended college and law school. Wilson had not only a college degree but he had studied law at the University of Virginia and had earned a doctorate in political science at Johns Hopkins University.

Reviewing the political history of the five presidents, one would have to conclude that Lincoln came to presidency with the least experience as an administrator. With the exception of having served four terms in the Illinois state legislature and one term in Congress, Lincoln had no background in governmental administration before his inauguration. Both Jefferson and F. Roosevelt had not only served in their state legislatures but, in addition, had been governors of their respective states. Wilson had been president of Princeton University and governor of New Jersey. Washington, of course, had extensive administrative experience before he took the oath of office.

An examination of his writings on the role of the president before he took the oath of office would hardly have led any reader to conclude that Lincoln would be a strong executive. As a Whig member of Congress, Lincoln had written: "Were I President, I should desire the legislation of this country to rest with Congress, uninfluenced in its origin or progress and undisturbed by the veto unless in very special and clear cases."[19] After his election and on his journey to Washington, Lincoln made a speech at Pittsburgh in which he referred to certain "indirect" means by which a president may influence legislation:

> My political education strongly inclines me against a very free use of any of these means by the executive to control the legislation of the country. As a rule, I think it better that Congress should originate as well as perfect its measures without external bias.[20]

With all the negatives concerning his background and experience before he took the oath of office, Lincoln is still rated as the greatest of our chief executives. Some have said his reputation is due not so much for what he did as for what he endured. But endurance alone will not persuade the historians to rate him as the greatest leader among the American presidents. What was it in his administration that caused the historians to rate him so highly? There were two aspects of Lincoln's presidency that account for his greatness: his concept of energetic executive authority and his vision of the union.

In Number 70 of the *Federalist Papers*, Alexander Hamilton outlined the ideal of an energetic executive:

> Energy in the Executive is a leading character in the definition of good government. It is essential to the protection of the community against foreign attacks; it is not less essential to the steady administration of the laws; to the protection of property against those irregular and high-handed combinations which sometimes interrupt the ordinary cause of justice; the security of liberty against the enterprises and assaults of ambition, of faction, and anarchy.[21]

With almost uncanny foresight, Hamilton in the above passage seemed to anticipate the situation Lincoln faced in the early months of his administration. And it was Lincoln's energetic response to this crisis which is the first reason for his reputation as the greatest president.

Edward S. Corwin has observed that almost overnight, Lincoln caused the Commander-in-Chief clause of the Constitution to emerge as one of its most highly charged provisions. Lincoln chose to wed the "Commander-in-Chief" clause to the clause that makes it the duty of the president to "take care that the laws be faithfully executed."

> From these two clauses thus united Lincoln proceeded to derive what he termed the "war power," to justify the extraordinary measures he took between the fall of Fort Sumter and the convening of Congress in special session in July 4, 1861. During this period of ten weeks Lincoln amalgamated the available state militias into a ninety days volunteer force, called 40,000 volunteers for three years' service, added 23,000 men to the Regular Army and 18,000 to the Navy, paid out two million from unappropriated funds in the Treasury to persons unauthorized to receive it, closed the Post Office to "treasonable correspondence," subjected passengers to and from foreign countries to new passport regulations, proclaimed a blockade of the Southern ports, suspended the writ of habeas corpus in various places, and caused the arrest and military detention of persons "who were represented to him" as being engaged in or contemplating "treasonable practices"--*and all this for the most part without the least statutory authorization.*[22]

The secession crisis was only the first, though the most urgent, of the crises Lincoln faced. In August, 1862, when volunteers were in short supply, Lincoln initiated a military draft. In September of the same year, to dampen the protests that had grown in the Northern states, he proclaimed a nationwide suspension of the writ of habeas corpus, attempting to round up all persons "guilty of any disloyal practice." Such persons would be subject to trial and punishment of courts-martial and military commissions.[23]

Corwin concluded that some of these measures assert for the president, for the first time in our history, an initiative of indefinite scope in meeting the domestic aspects of a war emergency. Some authors, including Corwin, have even used the term "dictatorship" to describe Lincoln's energetic handling of the crises he faced.[24]

38 Taking Parts: Leadership, Participation, Empowerment

Sense of Vision

Robert E. DiClerico has argued that the one in the White House must have a vision. "After all, in order to lead a population *you* must know where you want to take them and you must be sure that *they* know also."[25] For Lincoln, his vision was the Union. His ideal had been expressed best by Daniel Webster's famous phrase: "Liberty and Union, now and forever, one and inseparable." Writing to Horace Greeley in 1862 Lincoln summed up his vision:

> My paramount object in this struggle *is* to save the Union, and it is *not* either to save or to destroy slavery. If I could save the Union without freeing *any* slave, I would do it; and if I could do it by freeing *all* the slaves, I would do it; and if I could save it by freeing some and leaving others alone, I would also do that.[26]

From Lincoln's vision of the Union that had to be preserved, he derived the strength to pursue that good unto the end. He never deviated from that ideal; unswervingly he pursued that quest. Six days after Appomattox, he had achieved the goal of the preservation of the Union at the terrible cost of six hundred thousand deaths, including his own.

Woodrow Wilson

Domestic Leader

In contrast to Lincoln and Franklin Roosevelt who confronted a major crisis as they entered the White House, Woodrow Wilson's greatest crisis--the entrance of United States into World War I--did not arrive until he had taken the oath of office for the second time. But one of the reasons Wilson is considered a great president is that his first administration had been a triumph for him in domestic achievements.

During the first four years of Wilson's administration, he was able to lead and guide a remarkable series of legislative enactments. Richard Hofstatder has observed that Wilson produced more positive legislative achievements than any administration since the days of Alexander Hamilton.[27] Lindsay Rogers further remarked that the ex-professor of political science "more than any of his predecessors...exerted an almost absolute authority over Congress."[28] The record of Wilson's first four years is impressive.

His was the first administration since the Civil War to secure a tariff revision downward. In the Federal Reserve Act he revamped the nation's banking and credit system. He got passed the Federal Farm Loan Act, the Clayton Anti-Trust Act, the Federal Trade Commission, the La Follette Seaman's Act. After the passage of these and other legislative achievements, Wilson took justifiable pride in a message to Congress:

> Our program with regard to the regulation of business is now complete. It has been put forth, as we intended as a whole, and leaves no conjecture as to what is to follow. The road at last lies clear and firm before business...the road to ungrudged, unclouded success.[29]

The planks in Wilson's electoral platform of 1912, outlining his major campaign promises which he called the "New Freedom," were almost all enacted into law by 1914. In contrast to Franklin Roosevelt, Wilson came into the presidency with an announced set of goals which he, with dynamic leadership, persuaded Congress to adopt. Not only did he have vision, he had the practical wisdom to ensure that his visionary goals were achieved.

As with Lincoln, Wilson's concept of presidential power, expressed in his earlier writings, was far from what he practiced in the White House. In 1879, Henry Cabot Lodge, the editor of the *International Review*, received and accepted a manuscript submitted by a young student of twenty-three, Woodrow Wilson. In the article Wilson identified radical defects in government:

> The President can seldom make himself recognized as a leader. He is merely the executor of the sovereign legislative will; his cabinet officers are little more than the chief clerks or superintendents in the executive departments who advise the President as to matters in most of which he has no power of action independently of the concurrence of the Senate.[30]

Yet it is this same Woodrow Wilson who as president has been evaluated by one of the most respected students of the American presidency, Clinton Rossiter. Of Wilson's first term he wrote: "Many historians think that the American Presidency, and with it our whole system of government, reached its highest peak of democracy, efficiency and morality in the first four years of Woodrow Wilson."[31]

Foreign Affairs Leader: World War I

In a lecture delivered at Columbia University in 1907, Wilson expressed his understanding of the president's obligation in foreign affairs.

> The president can never again be the mere domestic figure he has been throughout so large a part of our history. The nation has risen to the first rank in power and resources....Our president must always, henceforth, be one of the great powers of the world, whether he act greatly or wisely or not....We have but begun to see the presidential office in this light; but it is the light which will more and more beat upon it, and more and more determine its character and its effect upon the politics of the nation.[32]

Wilson's most severe crisis in foreign affairs came during World War I when for the first time a president was called upon to exercise executive power in a European conflict. In sober phrases, Wilson's message to

Congress in April 1917 asking for a declaration of war, conveyed his reluctance to end the neutrality of his nation in order to enter the European conflict. "It is a fearful thing to lead this great peaceful people into war, and into the most terrible and disastrous of all wars."[33]

The war placed new demands on the powers of the president. It required the mass production of complex weapons, the mobilization and deployment of troops at great distance from the United States. There was need to impose wartime economics and social controls on American society. Though he tried to seek explicit delegations of power from Congress, he did not hesitate to act when Congress failed to authorize him to arm merchant vessels. He went ahead and armed them anyway.[34]

The emergency powers that Wilson acquired during World War I were extraordinary. As Corwin has pointed out, the contrast between Wilson's and Lincoln's "dictatorship" was more of "method," not of "tenderness for customary constitutional constraints."[35]

Paul Von Riper has written that the expansion of executive power during the war planted a suggestive idea. During the Depression and the Second World War which was soon to follow, "these memories and the governmental mechanism and the administrative experience upon which they were in part based, were to return in new forms and under new auspices."[36]

It is ironic that Wilson, who Clinton Rossiter has called the "best prepared President, intellectually and morally, ever to come to the White House,"[37] was unable to implement his greatest intellectual and moral vision, the League of Nations. As Ernest R. May observed: "From the first day of the war to the last, all that Wilson sought was a peace that could be secured by the League of Nations, a peace that would make the world safe for democracy."[38] Like the defeat of Churchill's party in the House of Commons when World War II was about to end, Wilson's grand vision of the world safe for democracy, was blurred by the defeat of the Democratic party in Congress in the mid-term election of 1918. That election, a few days before the Armistice of November 11, gave control of Congress to the Republicans for the first time in eight years and placed Wilson's implacable foe, Henry Cabot Lodge, as chair of the Senate Foreign Relations Committee, which committee would approve or disapprove the treaty which would have the United States join the League of Nations. The story of Wilson's efforts to convince the American people to support the League is well known. He almost killed himself in the process. Unwilling to compromise, he faced defeat. The 1920 election, which Warren Harding won by an overwhelming popular vote, marked not only the end of United States' support of the League of Nations but also of much of Wilson's theory of presidential power in foreign affairs.

Wilson's concept of presidential leadership of Congress in domestic affairs established his position in the list of the greatest presidents. He exhibited in his first term Hamilton's ideal of energy in the executive. That his vision of the League of Nations failed, does not mean that he lacked the visionary gift necessary for a great president. He was but ahead of his time with an idea which would be eventually accepted in the United Nations. Speaking of the Versailles Treaty, Jan C. Smuts concluded that Wilson had not failed; it was the "human spirit" that had failed.[39]

Wilson's rating as one of the five great presidents seems secure. It may well be true as Arthur Link, Wilson's biographer, has written that historians a century hence will probably rate the expansion and perfection of the powers of the presidency as Wilson's most lasting contribution.[40]

Franklin D. Roosevelt

Domestic Crisis: The Depression

As Franklin Roosevelt was taking the oath of office on March 4, 1933, the country was experiencing the severest economic crisis in its history. The national income was less than half of what it had been four short years before. About one quarter of the labor force--nearly thirteen million Americans--was out of work. A few hours before, in the early morning of inauguration day, every bank in America had locked its doors.[41]

Four days later President Roosevelt called at the home of the retired Justice of the Supreme Court, Oliver Wendell Holmes, Jr.; the occasion was Justice Holmes' 92nd birthday. When the time came to leave, the President asked the Justice if he had any final advice for him. "Form your ranks and fight," the Civil War veteran urged. After the president and his party had departed, Justice Holmes eased himself into his favorite chair and evaluated his guest of the afternoon. "A second class intellect. But a first class temperament."[42]

In the light of Justice Holmes' evaluation of Roosevelt, it is interesting to note that the historian, Richard Hofstatder, has characterized the New Deal as being, at its heart, not a philosophy but a temperament.

> The essence of this temperament was Roosevelt's confidence that even when he was operating in unfamiliar territory, he could do no wrong. From the standpoint of an economic technician, this assurance seemed mad at times, for example when he tossed back his head, laughed, and said to a group of silver Senators: "I experimented with gold and that was a flop. Why shouldn't I experiment a little with silver?"[43]

James David Barber has classified recent presidential personalities into four types. He identified Franklin Roosevelt as a *positive-active* type defined as:

> Positive-active: self-confident; flexible; creates opportunities for action; enjoys the exercise of power; does not take himself too seriously; optimistic; emphasizes the 'rational mastery' of his environment.[44]

Roosevelt's response to the crises of the Depression was action and more action. In his inaugural address he promised just that: "This nation asks for action, and action now....We must act and act quickly."[45] Early in his administration he wrote: "The country needs, and unless I mistake its temper, the country demands bold, persistent experimentation. It is common sense to take a method and try it. If it fails, admit it frankly and try another. *But above all try something.*"[46]

It would be a mistake to conclude that Roosevelt's activity in the Hundred Days was the result of a well planned, grand design which he then implemented in orderly stages. Franklin Roosevelt had nothing comparable to Woodrow Wilson's expressed "New Freedom" to guide him in the early days of his presidency. Apart from acting from a broad concept that it was the "federal government's responsibility to guarantee the economic security of the people,"[47] Roosevelt often was not sure what his next move was to be.

At one of his earliest press conferences he compared himself to a quarterback in a football game. "The quarterback knows what the next play will be, but beyond that he cannot predict too rigidly because future plays depend on how the next one works."[48]

During the first Hundred Days of his administration, Roosevelt engineered a frantic series of pump-priming projects which resulted in a flood of legislation greater than in any comparable period in our history. Notable among this deluge were the Farm Relief Act, the Economy Bill, the Securities Act, the Federal Reserve Act, the Railroad Reorganization Act, the National Industrial Recovery Act, the Agriculture Adjustment Act, the Civilian Conservation Corps and the Banking Act. The latter was introduced and cleared by both houses of Congress in eight hours; forty-five minutes later, with photographers standing by, it arrived at the White House and was signed by the president.[49]

In addition to the flood of legislation during those Hundred Days, the first few weeks of Roosevelt's presidency marked an enduring change in the *spirit* of the country.

> In place of the despair and political paralysis of the Hoover years was an ebullient national mood and a refashioned executive which forged a vital link between the government and the people. In the past, one thousand pieces of mail a day had arrived at the White House. FDR's inauguration was greeted with 460,000 letters.[50]

It is astonishing to read of the changed attitude and mood of Washington, D.C. in those Hundred Days. Two weeks after the inauguration, Anne O'Hare McCormick described the temper of the nation's capital:

> The people are vivified by a strong undercurrent of wonder and excitement. You feel stir of movement, of adventure, of elation. You never saw before so much government, or so much animation in government. Everybody in the administration is having the time of his life. So they say and you

perceive as you watch the new officials...settling into the great business of national reconstruction. They dash from conference to conference, from hearing to hearing, brief cases bursting with plans and specifications. They are going someplace, that is plain.[51]

Franklin Roosevelt confronted the challenge of the Depression with Hamilton's ideal: energy in the executive. He confronted it with enthusiasm, with experimentation, with action. He conveyed to the American people a confidence that the problems which they faced could be resolved. Even though the Depression lingered on, there was hope that working as a nation their future was brighter, their economic issue could be resolved.

Foreign Affairs Crisis: World War II

In one sense, Franklin Roosevelt's responsibilities during wartime were similar to the obligations on the presidencies of both Lincoln and Wilson. The Commander-in-Chief Clause of the Constitution imposed heavy duties on all wartime presidents.

On the other hand, the differences between the obligations of Roosevelt compared to the other two were enormous. Though the conflict which Wilson directed has been called World War I, the designation of it as a *world* war was inaccurate. It was more a European-North Atlantic conflict, confined basically to that area. Lincoln, of course, directed the Union armies on American soil. But it was quite different for Franklin Roosevelt from 1941-1945. World War II was a global enterprise which involved positioning and directing American service men and women on the continents of Europe, Africa, Asia and Australia and coordinating the American plans with the Allies. At the time of Roosevelt's death there were twelve million American women and men in uniform. One historian has written:

> It must be borne in mind that President Franklin Roosevelt was the real and not merely a nominal Commander in Chief. Every president possessed the Constitutional power which that title indicates but few presidents have shared Mr. Roosevelt's readiness to exercise it in fact and in detail with such determination.[52]

In addition, Roosevelt insisted that the allied effort was to be directed from Washington and the center of information was to be in the White House. Roosevelt kept in close contact with the progress of events in the war, receiving daily and often hour-by-hour reports on the course of the campaigns.

Another aspect of Roosevelt's role in wartime was his choice of leaders for the armed forces. He found men who suited his needs and he kept them in his service. Their names are among the greatest war heroes in our history: General George C. Marshall, Admiral Ernest King, General

H.H. (Hap) Arnold, General Douglas MacArthur, General Dwight D. Eisenhower, Admiral Chester Nimitz, General Curtis LeMay.

To sustain the enormous powers he exercised, Franklin Roosevelt enlarged the concept of the Commander-in-Chief clause which Lincoln had first wed to the clause that the president "shall take care that the laws be faithfully executed." Perhaps the enlargement of that concept is best seen in a message to Congress on September 7, 1942, demanding that it repeal a certain provision of the Emergency Price Control Act. The following is a passage from that message:

> I ask the Congress to take this action by the first of October... In the event that the Congress shall fail to act, and act adequately, I shall accept the responsibility and I shall act... The President has the powers, under the Constitution and under Congressional Acts, to take measures to avert a disaster which would interfere with the winning of the war... The American people can be sure that I will use my powers with a full sense of my responsibility to the Constitution and to my country. The American people can also be sure that I shall not hesitate to use every power vested in me to accomplish the defeat of our enemies in any part of the world where our safety demands such defeat. When the war is won, the powers under which I act automatically revert to the people--to whom they belong.[53]

In effect, President Roosevelt said to Congress that unless it repealed a certain statutory provision, he would treat it as nevertheless repealed. The message of September 7, according to Corwin, can only be interpreted as a claim of power on the part of the president to suspend the Constitution in a situation deemed by him to make such a step necessary. This claim was not wholly without precedent, for Lincoln had implied as much in his message of July 4, 1861, when he asked with reference to his suspension of the writ of habeas corpus: "Are all laws *but one* to go unexecuted, and the government itself to go to pieces lest that one be violated?"[54]

In this case Franklin Roosevelt was proposing, however, not to set aside a particular clause of the Constitution, but its most fundamental characteristic, the division of power between Congress and the president, gathering into his own hands the combined powers of both.[55]

In the midst of his wartime duties, Roosevelt, with Wilson's failures in mind, excelled in planning for the post-war world. He deferred to the Senate in laying bipartisan groundwork for America's entrance into the United Nations. And in order to forestall angry dispute with a fallen enemy, he refrained from tying the United Nations Charter to a punitive treaty such as Versailles had been.[56]

As the war effort moved toward victory, Roosevelt was increasingly occupied with political issues which would have to be faced after the war was over. His death within a month of V.E. Day, marking the end of the Atlantic phase of the conflict, had been hastened by the superhuman demands on his strength. To be president of the United States in a major war is a killing job. The photographs of Lincoln taken year after year, as the shadows deepen, tell the story. The photographs of Franklin Roosevelt year after year, tell the same tale. During World War II, the *Harvard Alumni Bulletin* had the custom of publishing casualty lists of the university's graduates by rank: majors, so many; corporals, so many; generals, so many. The list for April 1945 was headed: Commander in Chief, 1.[57]

George Washington

Henry Lee's eulogy of George Washington in 1799 perhaps said it best: "First in war, first in peace, first in the hearts of his countrymen."[58]

Washington is ranked among the five greatest presidents not simply because he was first, but because he was the very best first president. The delegates to the Constitutional Convention, in drawing up Article II, had two key objects in mind: they wanted an executive strong enough to counter a runaway legislature and one not so strong as to become despotic. Many delegates, hoping that Washington would become the first president, fashioned the executive branch with him in mind.[59]

The new republic was extremely fortunate to have someone with Washington's qualities to choose from. As Seymour Martin Lipset has written, Washington was a classic example of what Max Weber called a charismatic leader, one "treated as endowed with supernatural, superhuman or at least specifically exceptional powers or qualities."[60] One historian has recorded that babies were being named after George Washington as early as 1775, and while he was still president, his countrymen paid to see him in waxwork effigy. "To his admirers, he was 'godlike Washington' and his detractors complained to one another that he was looked upon as a 'demigod' whom it was treasonous to criticize."[61]

It is not easy to imagine the consequences of the great gamble in constitutional government if George Washington had refused to accept his election to the presidency. Washington did the new republic mighty service by "promising that power can ennoble as well as corrupt and by fitting the presidency into the emerging pattern of American constitutionalism."[62]

The new president was keenly aware that because he was the first, his actions could establish enduring precedents. Early in his first term he wrote:

> Few who are not philosophical spectators can realize the difficult and delicate part which a man in my situation has to act... In our progress toward political happiness my situation is new; and, if I may use the expression, I walk on untrodden ground. There is scarcely any part of my conduct which may not hereafter be drawn into precedent.[63]

Clinton Rossiter has observed that Washington could have been king but he chose to be something more exalted: the first elected head of the first truly free government. In his inaugural address Washington made clear the solemnity of his mandate: "The preservation of the sacred fire of liberty and the destiny of the republican model of government are justly considered, perhaps, as *deeply*, as *finally*, staked on the experiment entrusted to the hands of the American people."[64]

Fifteen years after Washington's death, Thomas Jefferson, who knew him well, wrote a remarkable evaluation of the character of George Washington. He reflected that perhaps the strongest feature of his character was prudence. His integrity was pure, his justice inflexible. He was in every sense of the words, a wise, good and great man. On the whole, he wrote, his character was, in its mass, perfect, in nothing bad, in few points indifferent.

> It may truly be said that never did nature and fortune combine more perfectly to make a man great, and to place him in the same constellation with whatever worthies have merited from man an everlasting remembrance--For it was his singular destiny and merit...of conducting its councils through the birth of a government, new in its forms and principles, until it had settled down into a quiet and orderly train; and of scrupulously obeying the laws through the whole of his career, civil and military, of which the history of the world furnishes no other example.[65]

It is true that the crisis of the Neutrality Proclamation of 1793 and the crisis of the Whiskey Rebellion of 1794 were difficult periods in Washington's first two administrations. He is not however rated as one of the great presidents because of these. Rather he is considered great because "weathering times that were full of crisis, he left the republic stronger, more purposeful and more confident than when he began the task."[66]

Washington's place among the great presidents is secure. With his towering prestige, unfaltering leadership, and sterling character, he was the only figure able to command the confidence necessary to get the new ship of state off on an even keel. "He was perhaps the only man in the history of the presidency bigger than the government itself."[67]

Thomas Jefferson

If Abraham Lincoln's position among the five great presidents is the most paradoxical, Thomas Jefferson's place among them is the most problematical, not because the historians doubt his belonging there, but because it is more challenging and perhaps more difficult to arrive at reasons for his presence among the great.

The historians are in general agreement that Jefferson belongs among the five great presidents. In both Schlesinger polls and in Thomas Bailey's evaluation he ranks fifth. In the Maranell, Murray-Blessing, Porter and the *Chicago Tribune* polls, he was ranked fourth. The Sokolsky evaluation places him in first place while Rossiter gives him the sixth place.

To arrive at the reasons for their including Jefferson among the greats, the historians give different answers. Absent from their reasons are the types of crises which were identified with the administrations of Washington, Lincoln, Wilson and F. Roosevelt.

Jefferson's eight years as chief executive were relatively free of crisis of the magnitude that the other four presidents faced. The historians tend to cite two aspects of the Jefferson years to justify their assessments: the "Revolution of 1800" and the Louisiana Purchase.[68]

Jefferson himself styled the election of 1800 as a revolution but this is a misnomer. It should more accurately be called a readjustment or realignment in politics. Briefly, it was a triumph of the Democratic-Republican party in the congressional elections and the election of Jefferson to the presidency by a vote of the House of Representatives. In the presidential election, the seventy-three Democratic-Republican electors each cast two votes for Jefferson and Burr. (Apparently, one vote was to be withheld from Burr but this did not happen.) Since there was no majority as required by the Constitution, the election fell to the House of Representatives to choose between Jefferson and Burr. After thirty-five ballots, each state delegation having one vote, the House of Representatives elected Jefferson. Burr was chosen vice-president.

Jefferson's triumph in the election of 1800 and the triumph of his party marked the beginning of a critical realignment in American politics. His party became the nation's leading political party and remained so until 1828. In later life Jefferson wrote that the "revolution of 1800 was as real a revolution in the principles of government as that of 1776 was in its form."[69]

More significant in Jefferson's presidency was the Louisiana Purchase. In his first inaugural address Jefferson promised a party program of reform that included a strictly limited role for the national government and a support for state governments in all their rights. He advocated a frugal national government, dedicated to economy in public expenditure.[70]

In startling contrast to his views on the role of the federal government and the promise of frugality in his inaugural address, Jefferson in 1803 moved to purchase the vast tract of land known as Louisiana when Napoleon forced a weakened Spain to cede to France the entire territory. War with England dimmed Napoleon's dream of a vast overseas empire. He suddenly decided to sell the territory to the United States for fifteen million dollars, and a treaty to that effect was signed on April 30, 1803.[71]

Jefferson and his advisors, largely overcoming scruples about the constitutionality of acquiring new territory for the republic, had taken advantage of Napoleon's sudden decision. For Jefferson it was the major decision of his presidential career. Robert Ketcham has evaluated the Louisiana Purchase decision. Jefferson "in his own administration, despite lingering Whig biases for legislative supremacy, executive limitation and 'mild' government... provided vigorous leadership that has earned him a place on everyone's list of the half dozen most able American presidents. He understood, advocated, and practiced the art of active leadership."[72]

Webster's dictionary defines crisis as an unstable or crucial time or state of affairs whose outcome will make a decisive difference for better or worse. The decision of Jefferson to overcome his constitutional scruples and to take advantage of the French offer to sell Louisiana has made a decisive difference for the better in American history. It is probably true to say that no single act of any president has had such a positive, beneficial effect on the history of the American republic. The triumph of Jefferson's political party in the election of 1800 and the party's support for the purchase made it all possible. Jefferson's active, energetic leadership has assured him his place in the presidential hall of fame.

Conclusion

Five chief executives: Lincoln, Washington, F. Roosevelt, Wilson and Jefferson have been enshrined in the pantheon of presidential greatness. What is common to their histories is that they were in office at a time of a crucial crisis in American history. In each case it was not merely the emergency situation but the energetic response to the crisis that qualified them to be considered one of the five greatest presidents. Each of them seemed to have grasped the significance of Bismarck's observation: "A statesman has not to *make* history, but if ever in the events around him he hears the sweep of God's mantle he must jump up and catch at its hem."[73]

Notes

1. John W. Gardner, *Morale* (New York: Norton, 1978), 133.
2. For this portion of the paper the author relied on an excellent summary found in Dean Keith Simonton, *Why Presidents Succeed: A Political Psychology of Leadership* (New Haven: Yale University Press, 1987), 166-228.
3. Thomas A. Bailey, *Presidential Greatness: The Image and the Man from George Washington to the Present* (New York, Appleton-Century Crofts, 1966), 33.
4. In all subsequent polls mentioned in this paper, W.H. Harrison and Garfield will not be included in the rankings.
5. Arthur M. Schlesinger, "Historians Rate the U.S. Presidents," *Life* (1 November 1948), 65-66, 68, 73-74.
6. Ibid.
7. Arthur M. Schlesinger, "Our Presidents: A Rating by 75 Historians," *New York Times Magazine* (29 July 1962), 12-13, 40-41, 43. For a convenient listing of the literature about political biases and pitfalls in rating the presidents

see Jack E. Holmes and Robert E. Elder, Jr., "Our Best and Worst Presidents; Some Possible Reasons for Perceived Performance," *Presidential Studies Quarterly* 19 (Summer 1989): 548.

8. Bailey, *Presidential Greatness*, 262-335.

9. Clinton Rossiter, *The American Presidency*, 2nd ed. (New York: New American Library, 1962), 100.

10. Eric Sokolsky, *Our Seven Greatest Presidents* (New York: Exposition Press, 1964).

11. Tom Kynerd, "An Analysis of Presidential Greatness and 'President Ratings,'" *Southern Quarterly* 9 (1971), 309-29.

12. Gary M. Maranell, "The Evaluation of Presidents: An Extension of the Schlesinger Polls," *Journal of American History* 57 (1970), 104-113.

13. Robert K. Murray and Jim H. Blessing, "The Presidential Performance Study: A Progress Report," *Journal of American History* 70 (1983), 535-55.

14. The David L. Porter poll has not appeared in print but the participants in it received from Porter a full report of the results. See Murray and Blessing, "Presidential Performance Study," 536.

15. Simonton, *Why Presidents Succeed*, 185.

16. Schlesinger, *Life*, 68.

17. Harold Laski, *The American Presidency* (New York: Harper & Brothers Publishers, 1940), 52.

18. Bailey, *Presidential Greatness*, 98.

19. Edward S. Corwin, *The President: Office and Power, 1787-1957*, 4th ed. (New York: New York University Press, 1957), 324.

20. Ibid.

21. Alexander Hamilton, James Madison and John Jay, *The Federalist: Great Books of the Western World* ed. Robert M. Hutchins (Chicago: Encyclopedia Britannica Inc., 1952), Vol. 43, 210.

22. Corwin, *The President*, 229, emphasis added.

23. Ibid., 230.

24. Ibid., 232, 237.

25. Robert E. DiClerico, *The American President* (Engelwood Cliffs, N.J.: Prentice Hall, Inc., 1979), 357.

26. Quoted in Gabor S. Boritt, ed., *The Historian's Lincoln: Pseudohistory, Psychohistory and History* (Urbana and Chicago, University of Illinois Press, 1988), xv-xvi.

27. Richard Hofstadter, *The American Political Tradition and the Men Who Made It* (New York, Vintage Books, 1974), 334.

28. Ibid.

29. Ibid., 337.

30. W.E. Binkley, *The Powers of the President: Problems of American Democracy* (Gorden City, N.Y.: Doubleday, Doran & Company, Inc., 1937), 221-22.

31. Rossiter, *The American Presidency*, 99.

32. Woodrow Wilson, *Constitutional Government in the United States* (New York, Columbia University Press, 1980), 78.

50   *Taking Parts: Leadership, Participation, Empowerment*

33. Woodrow Wilson, *The Papers of Woodrow Wilson*, ed. Arthur S. Link (Princeton, N.J.: Princeton University Press, 1966-1985), 41: 526.

34. Sidney M. Milkis and Michael Nelson, *The American Presidency: Origins and Development, 1976-1990* (Washington, D.C.: C.L. Press, 1990), 231.

35. Corwin, *The President*, 237.

36. Paul Von Riper, *History of the United States Civil Service* (Evanston, IL: Ron Peterson, 1958), 282.

37. Rossiter, *The American Presidency*, 99.

38. Ernest R. May, "Wilson (1917-1918)" in *The Ultimate Decision: The President as Commander In Chief*, ed. Ernest R. May (New York: Braziller, 1960), 131.

39. Quoted in Bailey, *Presidential Greatness*, 311.

40. Arthur Link, *Wilson and the New Freedom* (Princeton, N.J.: Princeton University Press, 1956), 145.

41. Arthur M. Schlesinger, Jr., *The Coming of the New Deal* (Boston: Houghton Mufflin Company, 1959), 3.

42. Geoffrey C. Ward, *A First Class Temperament: The Emergence of Franklin Roosevelt* (New York: Harper and Row Publishers, 1989), xiii.

43. Hofstadter, *American Political Tradition*, 410.

44. Di Clerico, *The American President*, 267.

45. Schlesinger, *The Coming of the New Deal*, 1.

46. Hofstadter, *American Political Tradition*, 410.

47. Milkis and Nelson, *The American Presidency*, 255.

48. Hofstadter, *American Political Tradition*, 432.

49. Milkis and Nelson, *The American Presidency*, 262-263.

50. Ibid., 264.

51. Quoted in T.H. Watkins, *Righteous Pilgrim: The Life and Times of Harold Ickes* (New York, Henry Hold and Company, 1990), 325.

52. Eric Larrabee, *Commander in Chief: Franklin Delano Roosevelt, His Lieutenants, and their War* (New York: Harper & Row, Publishers, 1987), 1.

53. *The New York Times*, 8 September 1942.

54. Corwin, *The President*, 252.

55. Ibid.

56. Bailey, *Presidential Greatness*, 215.

57. Larrabee, *Commander in Chief*, 647.

58. Quoted in John Alexander Carroll and Mary Wells Ashworth, *First in Peace*, v. 7 of *George Washington, a biography*, ed. Douglas Southall Freeman (New York: Charles Scribner's Sons, 1957), 651.

59. Koeing, *The Chief Executive*, 27.

60. Seymour Martin Lipset, *The First New Nation* (New York: Basic Books, 1963), Chapter 1.

61. Marcus Cunliffe, *George Washington: Man and Monument* (New York: New American Library, 1958), 15.

62. Rossiter, *The American Presidency*, 88.

63. *The Writings of George Washington*, ed. John C. Fitzpatrick (Washington: Government Printing Office), 30:496.

64. Rossiter, *The American President*, 88.

65. *The Life and Selected Writings of Thomas Jefferson*, ed. and Introduction by Adrienne Koch and William Peden (New York: The Modern Library, 1944), 173-175.

66. Koening, *The Chief Executive*, 32.

67. Bailey, *Presidential Greatness*, 238.

68. Thomas Bailey has reservations about including Jefferson among the great presidents: "Though undeniably a great man and a giant among the Founding Fathers, Jefferson has more difficulty qualifying as a great president... In some respects he could more easily rank among the five greatest Americans of all times than among the five greatest Presidents." Bailey, *Presidential Greatness*, 271.

69. Quoted in Milkis and Nelson *The American Presidency*, 98.

70. Ibid., 99.

71. Koenig, *The Chief Executive*, 348.

72. Ralph Ketcham, "The Jefferson Presidency and Constitutional Beginnings" in *The Constitution and the American Presidency*, ed. by Martin Fausold and Alan Shank (Albany, N.Y.: State University of New York Press, 1991), 19.

73. Quoted in Alistair Horne's *Harold MacMillan, Vol. 1, 1894-1956* (New York: Viking, 1989), 454.

Chapter 3

Ignatius: Wisdom Through Discernment

Patrick B. O'Leary, S.J.

Many years ago during my theological studies, I chose as a topic for a major paper a key symbol of leadership in the Judeo-Christian scriptures, that of the shepherd. The image of the shepherd embodied the experience of God's abiding presence and providence. It belonged to God alone to shepherd the people he had chosen, to lead them from slavery into freedom, to bring them into a future that was the fruit of God's own initiative, creative love and fidelity.[1] From Abraham to Jesus there is an unmistakable affirmation that the leader is one anointed with the Spirit whose origin is in the heart of God.[2] The exercise of authentic leadership on any level has something sacred about it. Somehow it must embody the truth about our humanness before God. It must be grounded in a humility that lives a radical poverty. Leadership cannot be understood in a way that ignores the relationship that each person is called to have with God's own creative Spirit.[3]

In the symbol of the shepherd, Israel struggled to be faithful to this truth about leadership; the Christian sees in Jesus who leads us to salvation as the Good Shepherd the full embodiment of this sacramental sense of leadership.[4] Jesus can speak of his own leadership as characterized by a total dependence. He says of himself that he has nothing that he has not first received and can do nothing that he has not been empowered to do from on high.[5] Good leadership has something fundamental to do with a responsiveness to the creative Spirit. One who leads well follows well and is characterized by a discerning mind and heart.

In the conversation with the other authors of this book about leadership, I find I am still concerned with the deeper spiritual grounding of leadership. My concern seems to center on what validates a leadership that is faithful to what we are called to be as persons and communities who acknowledge God as Creator and Lord. In the stimulating exchange and interplay of ideas, intuitions, convictions, I can't help but look in new ways at the same question and try to integrate into my own perspective the insights I am hearing from others.

This exchange is a rich experience, but in many ways I find myself at the pre-integration stage. I am reminded of a sunny afternoon long ago when I was at a critical point in formulating my research on the scriptural approach to leadership. I had been working all day trying to organize my thoughts to get them on paper. Spread all around me were notes, partial outlines, quotations, books and all the familiar artifacts of high academe. At a certain point in mid-afternoon I felt stuck and remained so for some time.

When frustration seemed at the point of paralyzing the thinking process, the inspiration came to stop struggling and seek some help from the Jesuit Scripture professor who lived across the hall. I gathered up all kinds of notes and kept scanning them as I concentrated on how I would formulate my problem. After knocking about three times I finally looked up. I was knocking on the inside of my own door.

Finding the right door can be a rather important enterprise. There at the inside of my own door I felt foolish, but the experience rather graphically expressed my struggle that afternoon to put my own thoughts and convictions in a form that could be communicated to others. Dialogue and consultation are wonderful gifts but no substitute for that interior challenge of processing one's own experience, insights and reflective study in a way that integrates what is received from others. As the fruit of a wonderful exchange with respected colleagues, I have a sense of standing again before the door of my own perspective with fingers fanning an array of scribbled notes.

There is that jotting to follow up on Peter Ely's contribution on the education of the knight Percival toward spiritual wisdom; the note next to it on Michael Leiserson's analysis of practical wisdom in Abraham Lincoln. Both raise questions about the deeper origins of leadership. A few page references remind me that Tom Jeannot's rejection of a model of leadership grounded on self-reliance resonates deeply with my own convictions. The concern of Jane Rinehart with an approach to leadership that the ordinary person can identify with and that education can foster invites me to shape my sense of leadership along lines that are attentive to animating relationships that liberate the gifts of all. Rose Mary Volbrecht's reflections do much the same. Others probe as well the established perimeters of the more masculine models with the feminine considerations and possibilities that should find a place in any approach to leadership. The exploration into the various professions and into the political realm forces confrontation with the place of the spiritual dimension in the secular context. The many underlinings and marginal notes in others' texts indicate at least a hope that in some important ways my own reflections may be richer because of the exchange that has taken place with colleagues.

The fact that we authors are colleagues in a Jesuit institution of higher education and that our book is about leadership in itself gives a turn to the perspective on leadership that captures my attention. For four hundred and fifty years, the Society of Jesus has understood its mission in large part to be the formation of leaders. It was this vision that disposed the Jesuits to focus much of their energies in the area of education and to develop a system of education throughout Europe and in almost every region in the world. Jesuits today in full partnership with non-Jesuits share responsibility for this vision. It is as partners in this endeavor at Gonzaga University that we engage in a serious conversation about the meaning of leadership. This issue is not marginal to what we are about together and the vision of education that we shape and share.

The range of possibilities for exploring the subject of leadership as an animating principle in Jesuit education exceeds the boundaries of a simple essay. In an attempt to narrow the focus and yet address the vision of leadership itself and to capture something of its animating spirit, I would like to concentrate on the person of Ignatius of Loyola, the founder of the Jesuits. The profile of leadership that emerges will certainly express historical, cultural and gender limitations that will need interpretation and adaptation. Hopefully, in the concreteness of the Ignatian profile something of what is essential to the dynamics of leadership as such will emerge, that something that seeks to be embodied for each succeeding generation and age within the Jesuit educational tradition.

The essential element of this Ignatian profile of leadership is its grounding in a relationship to the Transcendent Other, God, whom Ignatius recognizes in faith as Creator and Lord. The spirituality of Ignatius explicitly expresses the Christian biblical sense of an intimate relationship of the human spirit to the Spirit of God. What keeps me absorbed, therefore, at the inward side of my own threshold is a desire to communicate with colleagues and readers who might not feel at home in such explicitly religious language. My conviction is that what I would like to present about Ignatius has something important to say about all leadership. My struggle is to identify the point of contact where the religious experience and language resonates with what is shared human experience.*

That place of contact I find in the broader notion today of spirituality. In writing about faith and feminism in the Catholic church, Sandra Schneiders highlights a contemporary usage of the term "spirituality" as embracing a non-religious and even anti-religious "life organizations"

---

* The reflection on William James' concept of religious experience in the chapter by Tom Jeannot addresses this same issue. See his "But Trusted Servants." The approach of Alcoholics Anonymous to the question of "God language" complements my own efforts to find a meeting point with those who might feel uncomfortable with the clearly God-centered character of the Ignatian concept of leadership.

as secular feminism and atheistic Marxism.[6] She draws upon her own definition from a previous article in defining spirituality as it is often used today. Some, she writes, locate the spiritual journey in "the experience of consciously striving to integrate one's life in terms not of isolation and self-absorption but of self-transcendence toward the ultimate value one perceives."[7] In this perception of self-transcendence toward ultimate value, this openness, as one colleague puts it, to the "holy mystery" that claims us all, there is, I would hope, a common meeting ground for understanding and appreciating the significance of Ignatius as leader. In order to prepare more fully for a fruitful meeting with the person of Ignatius it might be helpful to explore the concepts and terminology that are so much a part of the Ignatian understanding of leadership.

The Ignatian Language of Leadership

Magnanimity

The phrase constantly on the lips of Ignatius and scattered throughout his writings was "the greater glory of God."[8] It became the motto of the Society of Jesus he founded. It is in this sense of the "greater," the "more" of God's glory, that Ignatius will speak of the "great souledness," the magnanimity that should characterize the leader.[9] Magnanimity in the Ignatian sense implies an expansiveness and generosity that opens the soul to God's activity, an expectancy, an interior fire that reveals a readiness for what has not yet revealed itself. It is a fundamental disposition that enables a person to be stretched to a liberality and creativity that is more than self and that moves spontaneously toward action. It is the capacity as well to inspire by action and to articulate a vision in a way that engages others in what is essentially a response to what is of "ultimate value," the "more" that finds its origin in the Transcendent Other, God.[10] The link that Ignatius forges between magnanimity and the glory of God turns him dramatically away from the aristocratic characteristics of the Aristotelian notion of pride (*hubris*) and pride's quest for honor.[11] Humility, loving surrender and receptivity form the core of what is most characteristic of the "great souled" leader. Honor and glory belong to the one alone who is source of all, the one whom Jesus called Abba. The magnanimous person is not one who holds back on the one hand nor, on the other, is given to the *hubris* of self-sufficiency but one who lives generously in trustful reliance on and availability to the creative activity of God. Magnanimity as understood by Ignatius has much more in common with what Tom Jeannot espouses than what might be espoused by those intoxicated by the Greek aristocratic ideal.*

---

* Compare Tom Jeannot's chapter, "But Trusted Servants."

What is crucial to grasp in speaking of "the greater or the more" in the Ignatian sense is his understanding of God whom he addresses so frequently as "Creator and Lord." This way of speaking of and to God expresses for Ignatius not a sense of God being at a distance but of the intimacy and dynamism of God, Father, Son and Spirit, engaged in a process of co-creativity with us. The God of Ignatius is present to creation, empowering all things to that fullness that comes to be essentially as gift. The magnanimous leader is not drawn to *hubris*, to that which we might call an arrogant, self-sufficient pride, but to a sense of praise and reverence that arises from the experience of recognizing all as gift and embracing the radical poverty that implies. It is a stance of openness to an empowerment whose origin is from God. The "greater glory" is what God is free to accomplish in us when we are truly available to the divine initiative. The leader for Ignatius is one who has first learned the graced art of following, of listening and responding to the Spirit. He or she is one who has grasped this truth of radical dependence and is able to awaken others to this same empowering truth. We are dealing here with self-transcendence, with "ultimate value," with "holy mystery."

At the heart of magnanimity is a desire, even a passion, to be open to the "more" that transcends personal resources and experienced limits. The leader is captured by the "more" that is God's own creative presence and activity in his/her life and surrenders to it and is empowered by it. There is a humility that belongs to the truth of our humanity; genuine leadership must embody this truth. For Ignatius, radical availability to God's action is what animates the leader. Others may express this truth in terms of "ultimate values" or in some notion of a "holy mystery" that has a transcendent claim on each of us. Whatever the expression, the exercise of leadership is most powerful when it awakens in others an attentiveness to this transcendent "more" and draws to a surrender that becomes empowerment. Leadership is not imposing one's own truth on others but assisting others to discover how God (or one's ultimate values) is at work in their own minds and hearts and supporting them to respond generously.

The Ignatian sense of magnanimity looks toward the ordering of the passions of mind and heart to achieve union with the Spirit of God creatively at work here and now. The Spirit invites a response that stretches the leader's own creativity in such a way that what comes into being is decisively of God and yet is no less the fruit of human freedom and action. The creativity of the leader is a co-creativity with God.

A person like Ignatius whose approach to life was to find God in all things would be perplexed, no doubt, by the sharp division of the religious and the secular as though there were a realm where God as Creator and Lord could be banished. The point that we have made about different understandings of spirituality would be foreign to his mode of expression but not to his world affirming theological perspective. Great Presidents and responsible citizens, lawyers, doctors and educators faithfully contributing their gifts and skills, men and women living and working together in all that pertains to creation in process, our world in the making, Ignatius would find integral to his sense of what belongs to the greater glory of God.

The human spirit, in individuals, communities, peoples, in the whole human family is true to its deepest self when it is responsive to more than itself, to God and others in God. This fidelity to the truth of ourselves, however, may not find expression in explicitly religious language. But it is there in the longings and desires of mind and heart, in the values that guide our decisions and actions, in the concepts, symbols, images that express these values, or, perhaps, in a sensitivity beyond adequate expression. Even in the absence of religious language or the explicit expression of faith, there can be the presence of a spirituality. Leadership in the Ignatian sense is not relegated to the chosen few but it is a gift that finds expression in all in various ways and with decidedly different levels of power and intensity.

Magnanimity and Discernment

The Ignatian approach to leadership necessarily grapples with the profound ambiguities inherent in the exercise of leadership. We experience these ambiguities on the level of the day to day interaction of ordinary people, but the same dynamic is also written larger in more public figures and movements. This final decade of twentieth century offers many examples of leadership in action where light and darkness play in a way that raises serious questions about what is good and what is not, what is responsive to our deepest values and what is destructive of them, what is in God's Spirit and what is not.

The magnanimity of the Ignatian leader presupposes a purification from all that would hold one within the narrow bonds of the self, the confines of one's own self-centered interests and preoccupations. The leadership that we will see modeled by Ignatius follows the path of conversion and transformation that involves an ongoing surrender to the Spirit that leads us into the "more" of God that Ignatius identified with God's glory.

To journey on that path requires a discerning mind and heart to sift out what in the self and in one's experience and situation are in tension with authentic surrender to the "Holy Mystery," the source of those self-transcendent values that have a claim upon us in the name of what is good and true. There is a need to carefully distinguish what is of God and what embodies values that lead toward love and life from what is of contrary forces and powers, false and destructive idols, expressive of values contrary to love and destructive of life that can mold a leader into an instrument of devastating destruction.

Leadership has a problematic character, therefore, that requires of all and in every situation discerning minds and hearts. Ignatian leadership is characterized by magnanimity that grounds itself in humility, in an openness to conversion and transformation, in a fidelity to the arduous process of sifting experience to respond to what is true and good and to draw others into this same discerning experience. Ignatian leadership is about magnanimity and discernment.

I have a feeling that at this point, wrapped in my own abstractions, looking up, I am going to discover I am still standing on the inside of my own door. What I have sketched out may give a certain clarity but it lacks concreteness. For most of us, such a sketch comes alive when related to specific instances where the ideal is made real in lived experience. To do this I would like to call upon Ignatius' own story.[12] In his story, it seems to me, we can discover not just a trait peculiar to a particular leader but something essential to all authentic leadership. That "something" I have tried to gather within the frame of "magnanimity and discernment." In doing so, I am reminded, however, of the baroque painting on the ceiling of the Jesuit Church in Rome, the Gesu. The frame cannot hold the painting within its boundaries. The dynamics of leadership as exemplified by Ignatius can be framed in such concepts as "magnanimity and discernment" if we can allow for creative overspill.

Ignatius: Schooled for Leadership

A Passion for His Own Glory

The birth of Ignatius in 1491 coincided with two dramatic events that would shape the wider horizon of the early formation of Ignatius as a leader: the fall of Grenada, the last Moorish city in Spain, to the forces of Ferdinand and Isabella and the voyage of Columbus west toward the Indies. Ignatius' father and brother fought in the battle of Grenada; another brother would die years later in the Spanish conquest of the "New World." Ignatius, the thirteenth child and eighth son of Basque nobility, heard the stories and dreamed of exploits that he himself would accomplish. Surely with this in mind he entered into the king's service as a page when he was sixteen.

The personality of Ignatius resonated enthusiastically with the spirit of his age, the "golden age" of Spanish power and expansion. The mind and heart of the young Ignatius were largely insensitive to the dark side of those events that brought about the consolidation of Christian Spain and blind to the abuses that accompanied exploration and conquest. Within the horizon of the "glory" of Spain, the imagination of Ignatius was aflame with dreams of personal glory, of noble, heroic deeds, of outstanding service to his king that would gain for him his place among the powerful and influential leaders of the nation. The times and the place seemed to offer unlimited scope to a romantic, great spirited young hidalgo like Ignatius. One could describe the spirit of Ignatius as magnanimous but in the aristocratic, elitist sense with its stress on self-reliance and self-sufficiency.

Leadership emerges in the midst of events that stretch a person and test what lies within. In 1521 when Ignatius was serving under the Duke of Najera, Viceroy of Navarre, the king of France sent an army of 12,000 across the Pyrenees mountains to retake the town of Pamplona for the Navarese pretender. The local governor quickly retreated and the town surrendered. In the citadel a band of about a hundred men was persuaded by Ignatius that honor and loyalty demanded that they not surrender. The odds were overwhelmingly against the prospect of resistance, and yet, Ignatius, by force of his personal magnitude and persuasive words, rallied the small force to withstand the French. When a cannonball struck him down, shattering his leg, capitulation was immediate. The French treated the defeated with respect and gallantry, especially Ignatius, who was clearly their courageous leader.[13]

The cannonball that shattered Ignatius' leg halted at least for a time his pursuit of fame and glory. For the sake of vanity he had his poorly set leg broken again and reset; this determination to force his body into a full recovery brought him to a point where the doctors despaired of his life. The strong-willed Ignatius, who till now had ordered his life in the way of self-reliance and self sufficiency, experienced a power greater than his own, delivering him from death.

Months followed where Ignatius for hours on end struggled with the pain and weakness of a slow recovery and, stripped of the usual outlets for a man of action, experienced an openness he had not experienced before. His situation drew him into solitude. In this solitude he became vulnerable to a "more" that till now had not entered his consciousness in a manner that could really focus his desires, the deepest passions of his soul. This vulnerability opened his inner spirit more and more to a magnanimity grounded in the transcendent presence, power and love of God, Creator and Lord.

Awakened to the Greater Glory of God

Ignatius, like Percival,* found access to the spiritual at the point where the limits of human control and action appear, at the point where human resources fail. Faced with the long hours of solitude Ignatius sought to break his boredom with something to read, stories like that of Percival, popular medieval romances of his day. In the household of his pious sister-in-law there were only two books available, the life of Christ by Ludolf the Carthusian and another book on the saints. These proved a counterpoint to his ego-centered daydreams of knightly chivalry that had for so long captured his imagination. To his amazement his

---

* Compare Peter Ely's chapter, "Perceval: From Naivete to Wisdom."

reading gradually opened him to a glory beyond the narrow dimensions of self and purely human aspirations to what in the story of Percival is the deeper level of the spiritual. This movement oriented Ignatius to what would be the passion of his life, the greater glory of God.

This new horizon captured him completely and drew him with powerful affective, interior movements--an interior he had till now hardly adverted to--toward a realization of God's creative and saving activity in the world. This realization moved him to a wholehearted commitment to serve God in extending God's reign over all creation. The focus for Ignatius is the person and mission of Jesus, the embodiment of God's own transforming and saving love. The months of convalescence resulted in a transformation in Ignatius that was astounding to his family and, no doubt, to Ignatius himself. This radical conversion of mind and heart gave to the magnanimity of Ignatius a radically new focus. His own glory, previously so intertwined with the glory of Spain, ultimately yielded to a far more comprehensive vision.

This transformation that would be so central to the kind of leader Ignatius was to be was still incomplete in a critical way. His preoccupation at this stage was with what he would do for God. What fired his imagination was the glory that he would bring to God by deeds more illustrious than those of God's own heroes like Francis and Dominic. What they had done, he could do better. He awakened to the spiritual dimension with his concentration on action intact and his approach to action still solidly framed within the masculine, competitive framework of a Spanish hidalgo, confident in his self-reliance, self-sufficiency and capacity to keep control.

Even though the horizons of Ignatius had been expanded to embrace the whole of creation as the ambiance of "God's greater glory," he was still bound by a kind of Aristotelian *hubris*. What filled his soul was this preoccupation with what he, Ignatius, would do for God. The bent of his character made him competitive. This stage of the formation of Ignatius was characterized by a competitive self-confidence and self-reliance that took the form of a vying with the Saints themselves in the magnitude of great external deeds to be accomplished for God. Ignatius had not yet discovered the way of a truly discerning magnanimity of mind and heart, though his whole being was on fire with desire to serve God. There was, however, in Ignatius a graced, intuitive awareness that there was something deeper at stake in this service than what he had imagined in terms of knightly competition. What moved him more deeply than thoughts of great exploits for God was the desire not to lead but to follow. This attracted him powerfully toward a Jerusalem pilgrimage so that he might literally walk in the footsteps of Jesus and be schooled in discipleship. Francis of Assisi had done this; he would too. Ignatius was wholly focused on God and the service of God, but there was still an ambiguity as to what such a focus might mean for him and how he was to proceed in such a service.

His schooling did not wait for Jerusalem. A stopover for a few days at Manresa, a little village in the mountains near Barcelona, stretched into a year that Ignatius describes as an experience of "being taught by God like a school boy." A painful process of purification introduced him to interior dimensions that up to now had been hidden from his eyes. His desires to accomplish great deeds for God continued but his efforts began to flounder. He became confused and strangely powerless over forces that clashed within him. He was at a loss to comprehend, let alone control what he was experiencing. At one moment he felt strength, peace and a great capacity to serve God; then, the next moment, he was overwhelmed by dark, desolate thoughts and feelings that seriously called into question the whole direction his life was taking. On what basis, he wondered, was he to sift out the true from the false, what was of God and what was not.

A searing bout of agonizing scruples concerning his past transgressions brought him to a point of powerlessness and near despair. Again Ignatius experienced a situation where he could do nothing to save himself, not in this instance from the threat of death but from what seemed worse, his interior turmoil and confusion. Gradually, the failure of his own resources brought him to a painful process of letting go. There was for him an experience of being delivered by God from the paralyzing patterns his scruples inflicted on him. There was a powerful awakening to God's sovereign graciousness, the discovery of what had been the truth all along. It was not what he did for God that was crucial; it was rather what God would do in him and through him if he remained open and receptive to God's own creative Spirit.

In this transforming process, the spirit of Ignatius continued to be ordered toward action. What Michael Leiserson finds in the leadership of Lincoln is to be found also in Ignatius in his own way. Ignatius was a man of "spiritual wisdom" with a "practical" intent. The concerns of Ignatius were about the concrete dynamics by which the whole of creation comes to its fullness in God, and the active participation of men and women in that creative process. The wisdom of Ignatius consisted of more than the initial graced insight about God's continuing, active role as he experienced this truth in the intimacy of his own personal struggles. There were profound experiences of illumination, especially one experience on the heights above the river Cardoner where it runs deep in the gorge near Manresa. His understanding was opened to an intimate knowledge of God's creative activity in all things but most deeply in the saving mission of Jesus. Wisdom for Ignatius was the fruit of an on-going contemplation in the midst of action that would characterize his approach to life after Manresa. His "practical wisdom" was at the same time a "spiritual wisdom" grounded in an alertness to the presence and activity of God in persons and events, in situations that called for decisions, in actions that invited further reflection and, perhaps, new decisions in the light of new experiences.

In Service to God's Liberality and Love

Magnanimity would mean for Ignatius, therefore, a being stretched to embrace God's own liberality and love in a way that recognized and responded to the truth of the relationship of every human person to God who is and always will be Creator and Lord. To act in a way that gives glory to God presupposed in Ignatius a receptivity to the empowering Spirit of God. It is not surprising that his moments of vulnerability and powerlessness became special graces for him (as for Percival) that opened his spirit to his own inner truth. The desire in the heart of Ignatius to act for God's glory was already the initiative of the inspiring presence of God's own Spirit, the enlightenment and empowerment to act co-creatively with God. The key to Ignatius as a leader was his consciousness that the empowering initiative in every decision and action was to be looked for from God; in the same way it was God who ultimately sustained every work and brought it to completion. Human freedom and the leadership that engages human freedom was for him an exercise of the dignity for which every person is created, to be and to act freely in union with God to bring the whole of creation to the fullness to which it is called.

It is this conversion of mind, heart and imagination that demanded of Ignatius ongoing discernment. A discerning, listening, attentive mind and heart would be in him the handmaid of magnanimity. The leadership potential of Ignatius was doomed to be forever critically flawed so long as the empowering and motivating center was simply himself, what he would do for his own glory, or the glory of Spain or, even, the glory of God. Humility came slowly but sank deeply within his soul as an antidote to vanity against which he struggled all his life. At Manresa he was schooled in the truth that rooted the desires and endeavors of his mind and heart in the active presence of the Spirit of God. That Spirit worked a "greater glory" in Ignatius, a glory that was always God's own gift accomplished in his receptivity and surrender. Only through being humbled and schooled in the graced art of following a Spirit deeper than his own was Ignatius ready to lead others in a way harmonious to his own truth and to theirs.

The strength of Ignatius as a leader can be found in what he liked to call devotion, the capacity to find God in all things. This finding was accompanied by dispositions of loving surrender, reverence and humility[14] that kept him open and available to the active presence of God, the "Holy Mystery" that transcends the self and rightly orders all human endeavors. This devotion and these dispositions directed the path of Ignatius and shaped his character as a leader. Ignatius, like any leader, experienced the complexities of contrary forces that sought to direct his decisions, shape his commitments and animate his actions. The contemplative intimacy that he maintained with the One he recognized as Creator and Lord gave to his leadership a spiritual depth that clearly grounded his "practical wisdom."

Ignatius remained always a pilgrim, a man on a sacred journey whose beginning, middle and end was sustained and guided by that "greater glory" that was in him the work of God's gracious Spirit. This radical openness of Ignatius to reliance on God was not automatic. In every way he could, Ignatius sought to depend wholly on God in his pilgrimage to Jerusalem. He sought to really explore what it actually meant to live what he had discovered, this new, very concrete, practical, everyday reliance on someone other than self, the transcendent other, God. For this reason the poverty of the pilgrim took on a special meaning and importance since it enabled him to place his trust in the One who would provide. This singleness of purpose kept him on his way to Jerusalem a solitary pilgrim with God alone as his companion. Ignatius was to be thoroughly schooled in the graced art of listening and responding as the foundation for a leadership rightly ordered in God.[15]

This openness of Ignatius to God's guiding presence meant often enough for him a discovery that his grasp of what he was called to be and do was partial and incomplete and that the light given, more often than not, illuminated only the next step. The pull toward Jerusalem and the desire in Ignatius to remain there once he arrived did reveal in him what would be the passion of his life--to be placed with Jesus, the crucified, to walk in his footsteps, to follow his lead, to be his disciple. This was a genuine call but in a way that went far beyond the simplicity of Ignatius in identifying that following so literally with the homeland of Jesus. The attraction to Jerusalem held within it a truth that would be revealed only gradually in the years ahead. The Franciscan guardians of the holy places would not let him stay because of the tensions with the Moslems who governed the area. Years later a second attempt to find his way there together with the companions who had joined him, failed. His Jerusalem became Rome; his vision there was to embrace the whole world in a sense of mission that had matured from a focus on the historical Jesus to a dynamic union with the Risen Christ. It is clear in the case of Ignatius that the leader is one who is himself led. His decisions emerged within a process of discernment that recognized nothing as absolute but the passionate desires, wisdom and will of his Creator and Lord.

Magnanimity, Service and Leadership

The awareness in Ignatius of this intimate relationship with the guiding presence of God's own creative Spirit gave to his style of leadership a special sensitivity. The power and attractiveness of Ignatius that would make him an effective leader rested in large part on his respect for each individual person and the uniqueness of each one's own spiritual journey. Through attentiveness to his own experience, he found a way to open others to what was their own truth before God, their own call to surrender with loving reverence and humility to what was in them authentic responsiveness to the presence and power of God's own creative love. He did this through the instrumentality of disposing exercises, what he called *Spiritual Exercises* that led those who are moved by desire and generosity into an encounter with God similar to his own but unique for each one. In the mind of Ignatius, for those who lead and those who are led, there is one Spirit that guides all in all things.

In the years that followed his pilgrimage to Jerusalem, Ignatius responded to the lead of that Spirit in a long and arduous process of studies for ordination to the priesthood so that he might be able to help others as he so deeply desired and felt called to do. The wisdom that would always be the greatest gift of Ignatius was already his through the experiences of his own transformation, his schooling in the ways of God at Manresa, and the confirmation and further enlightenment that came from lived experience. His natural practicality helped him to realize quickly, however, that his lack of theological education and lay status would be an obstacle to the kind of service he had in mind. When he did invite others to enter into the dynamics of his *Spiritual Exercises*, he found himself not infrequently in trouble with Church authorities, investigated by the Inquisition, and even imprisoned. Ignatius trusted what he experienced in his own mind and heart and strove to be faithful to the call of the Spirit that he discerned within his own experience. He was respectful as well of the Spirit's presence within the community of the Church and the role of legitimate authority. The practical wisdom of Ignatius was sensitive to the human limitations within himself and within the community. The spiritual wisdom of Ignatius knew that "finding God in all things" and being united with God's creative Spirit in Jesus meant embracing the tension that would sometimes exist between the discernment of the individual and that of the community, the Church. His way of proceeding sought to be responsive to the Spirit of God, the same Spirit at work in his own experience and that of the Church. That fidelity led him in ways that otherwise he might not have gone.

As the conversion and transformation of Ignatius ordered his interior toward an openness and responsiveness to the dynamic presence and power of the "Holy Mystery" at work in our world, his attention became more centered on the mission to which he felt himself called. In the light of this mission that for him involved the "greater glory of God" Ignatius no longer aspired to be the solitary pilgrim. He desired companions who would share this vision and this total availability to the creative labor of God in the world as God's presence is most deeply experienced in the saving mission of Jesus. The instrument for drawing others to such an enterprise was not so much the persuasive articulation of this vision by Ignatius but the power of the *Spiritual Exercises* through which God alone drew the persons who entered them to what was each one's own truth and call.

Those who first joined with Ignatius in Spain and looked to him for leadership did not persevere. Efforts on his part to attract others to his way of life during his studies in Paris at first proved futile. Those who did make the Exercises were touched by God in transforming ways but were not led to cast their lot with Ignatius. When Ignatius let go of his own efforts to lead others into his way of life and concentrated on what he was called to do, his studies, God drew others to him who would be his companions for life and who would find in him a leader who could awaken and focus the deepest desires of their own hearts.

The instrument that forged the band of companions that would become the Society of Jesus, the Jesuits, was the *Spiritual Exercises*. There was also the spirited conversations of this small group of students in which they opened their minds and hearts to each other, spoke of their hopes and dreams, and came to realize how God was forming among them a common spirit and a shared commitment to service. Francis Xavier from Navarre, Diego Lainez, Alphonse Salmeron and Nicholas Bobadilla from Spain, Simon Rodrigues from Portugal, and Ignatius himself were pursuing degrees in theology at the University of Paris in preparation for ordination. Peter Faber from Savoy, the youngest of the group, had already been ordained. Three others, Claude Le Jay, Pachase Broet and Jean Codure would join the group at the close of their time in Paris. There was no structure of authority among them. Each spoke from his own experience and trusted that experience as integral to what they were together.

Leadership in the Service of Unity in Mission

The authority of Ignatius and his place as leader among them was something obvious to all. But his leadership was experienced in a way that involved the full participation and shared responsibility of all in interrelationships where experiences were vital to how the group as a whole was to understand its call together. A consensus that they would pilgrim together to Jerusalem like Ignatius had done reveals certainly the influence of his leadership. But their deliberations had led them to a further conclusion. Should for some reason passage to Jerusalem within a year's time prove impossible, they were agreed that they would then place themselves at the disposal of the Pope to be sent where they might best serve and be more effectively integrated into the mission of Christ mediated through the Church. In order to be more fully available for service, each took a vow of poverty and chastity; there was no commitment to obedience apart from the readiness of each one to respond to the Spirit and to the mission entrusted to them by the Pope should Jerusalem not be a possibility. The leadership of Ignatius was real but not exercised through any established authority structure within the body of companions themselves.[16]

Because of the dangerous situation that prevailed between the Muslims and Christian forces in the Mediterranean, no ships sailed for Palestine during the period of time the pilgrims had determined upon. The companions presented themselves to the Pope who, to their surprise, sent them not together but in pairs to various places throughout Europe. This precipitated a crisis of identity. What was the nature of their bonding? What hope might they have to sustain their union, dispersed as they would be in all directions? How were they to maintain this way of life to which they felt called if they were to be integrated too directly into the structures that prevailed within the Church? In the prayerful deliberations that this crisis precipitated, each was drawn easily into a sense of confirmation concerning the necessity of preserving the union that existed among them all. What so clearly had been brought together by God, should be preserved in God's name. But how to assure that preservation? Here there was strong disagreement.

The force of Ignatius' leadership is manifest in the way that the group drew from the *Spiritual Exercises* of Ignatius the principles that would guide their further discernment, Ignatius with the others. Great care was taken to acquire a sense of freedom and purity of heart, necessary dispositions for listening and responding to the Spirit. This particular discernment presupposes as guiding principles what has been discerned already, especially their shared commitment to all that pertains to the "*greater* glory of God." In weighing the advantages in terms of God's greater glory of one alternative over another, a method is devised by which all work together to surface the best reasons for each alternative. Then in prayer each one weighs these advantages and disadvantages with careful attention to the spiritual movements within that give a sense of confirmation from God. As each shares the fruit of prayer, a sense of the decision most in the Lord begins to emerge. Through this process the companions arrived at a consensus that they should take a vow of obedience to one of their number so that he might be a source of unity in their listening, responding and serving in the Lord together. For this structured role of leadership, all the companions turned to Ignatius who had to be persuaded to accept. When this process was confirmed by the Pope, the Society of Jesus came into being, and Ignatius lived out the rest of his life governing this new religious order and writing *The Constitutions of the Society of Jesus* that would guide its way of life.

The Qualities of the Magnanimous Leader

In the *Constitutions* Ignatius describes the kind of leadership he expected of anyone who would take up the office of Superior General within the companionship of the Society. It was what he lived himself. First and foremost, there must be a close union and intimacy in prayer and action with God. Only in and through this union and intimacy can there hope to be an authentic leadership that keeps the whole body of the Society living from the true source of its service, the gifts, graces, power and efficacy that comes from God's own gracious love and liberality. The *greater* glory is always for Ignatius what God is able to accomplish in those who remain available and responsive to God's initiative and creative power. The *glory* is not what we do for God but what God does in us and in our world through an intimacy with us that becomes co-creativity. Wise leadership keeps self and others focused on and faithful to what is fundamental.

Leadership is far more than articulation and exhortation. It is lived example and embodiment. Of primary importance are a profound love and genuine humility that make the one who animates and unites highly lovable, both to God and those whom he serves in the role of leader. Interiorly the one chosen for leadership is to be a person not governed by disordered passions but interiorly free and capable of sound judgment and exteriorly so composed as to be a source of edification to others.[17] He should manifest a capacity to challenge self and others to the *more* that is the fruit of God's transcendent presence and power while at the same time manifest a kindness and gentleness that is sensitive to limitations in self and in others. Constancy, courage and fortitude should characterize the magnanimous spirit in a way that enables the leader to bear the weakness of many, initiate great undertakings as called for in the pursuit of the *more* of God and the deepest human values. Such a leader is to have that kind of energy and diligence that can see through to the end great enterprises undertaken even in the face of contradictions and opposition. The magnanimous heart needs to be balanced with understanding, good judgment and prudence strengthened by learning. Of special importance is experience in discerning the interior movements of mind and heart and a discretion in dealing with others and in bringing decisions into action.

The structured role of leadership had as its purpose the strengthening of the companions in a unity in service that was responsive both individually and corporately to the transcendent yet intimately present and active power of God. The authority of Ignatius to elicit from each and all an obediential response of the whole person, and the total body of the companions was itself subject to the deliberations and decisions of all the companions gathered in their own version of a "Town Meeting"* what Ignatius called a General Congregation.[18] Various forms of consultation and communal discernment assured a style of leadership based on the *Spiritual Exercises*, a style respectful of the contribution of each person to the process of hearing and responding together and in union with the One who is Creator and Lord. The whole body of the Society was itself subject to the discernments of the wider community, the Church, according to the structure of authority and decision-making that characterized that body.

---

* Compare the discernment = decision process, and the qualities of leader-follower relations, of Ignatius' early companions in this chapter with those of American town meetings in Bob Waterman's chapter, "We Need Not Be Ruled By Leaders."

The Society of Jesus with Ignatius as unifying center would experience corporately tensions similar to the ones he had personally experienced from Church authorities. Had he and they together been confirmed in their Jesus-centered movement to the periphery, Jerusalem, their process of discernment toward service might have been spared much pain and trouble. The Spirit of Jesus, however, in a way similar to the experience of St. Paul,[19] prevented Ignatius from staying in Jerusalem and prevented him with his companions from even leaving Venice. The single-hearted desire of Ignatius to be placed with Jesus in God's saving presence and action in the world was to be realized from a different center, Rome.[20] Like the one whom he followed, Ignatius was to lead in the midst of the ambiguities of discerning and of authority structures that would be moved by various spirits, some grounded in God's own creative Spirit and some not. Mission for the companions would be in the midst of the community of the Risen Lord, the Church, where their faith recognized the risen Jesus as present in his service of salvation to the world. In Rome, Ignatius would have ample opportunity to exercise the "practical wisdom" that for him was animated by a spirituality ordered toward finding God in all things, a fidelity to the "Holy Mystery," the fruit of contemplation in the midst of action.

Ignatius as Leader: A Dialogue With Our Times

On the various levels of human interaction and in a rich diversity of ways there emerge among nations and in communities of people certain persons who embody and bring to realization a capacity to grasp possibilities and creatively animate others to bring such possibilities to realization. We call such persons leaders and look to them for leadership. One endowed with leadership qualities may move in very ordinary circles or have an impact on the wider community and even influence dramatically the course of human history. Some instances of leadership are more immediately obvious than others and more extensively recognized. In a very true sense, as Jane Rinehart points out, there is some potential for leadership in each person that needs to be nurtured and called forth. Styles of leadership differ and leadership itself is enriched when it draws upon the full range of human gifts in both men and women.* Success or failure may be the result of any enterprise; neither in themselves is a decisive measure necessarily of the quality of the leadership involved. An instance of leadership may be animated by a spirit that is good and may lead to good or the opposite. What makes the difference is the matrix of values and the perspectives of meaning and judgements of ultimate

---

* Compare the chapters by Rose Mary Volbrecht, Mary Jo Bona, Eloise Buker, Frank Costello, and Jane Rinehart in this book.

concern that guide decision and action. Here reason and faith guide the mind and the heart.

The startling succession of world events as we move toward the close of the twentieth century offers a collage of leadership in action. In Russia Mikhail Gorbachev and Boris Yeltsin, inheritors of an authoritarian ideology and of a stagnant bureaucracy of superpower proportions, vied with each other as leaders who struggled to move a nation to new possibilities and risked in ways that dramatically redefined the future of their people and our world. A shipyard worker and a Polish Pope forged a popular movement, *Solidarity*, into a power that gave voice and vigor to the aspirations of the Polish people. A poet and playwright, Vaclav Havel, with simple, persistent courage spoke out for truth and freedom and set in motion among the Czechoslovakians a spirit that would not be passive in the face of naked and continued aggression.

On the other side of the globe, a politically inexperienced widow of a slain opposition leader who became the rallying focus of nonviolent people power, Corazon Aquino, struggled to embody a leadership that could liberate her people from a history of corruption and injustice. The magnitude of the challenge allowed for only limited success. In Central America an archbishop, Oscar Romero, and six Jesuit University professors were murdered because they had become the voices of the poor and oppressed in the agonizing situation of El Salvador.

In other ways not so political there are examples of leadership that reveal profound sensitivity, compassion and creativity. We are blessed with models of service that opened us to a vision of new ways of being for and with each other. A Mother Teresa whose love could not pass by, unmoved and uninvolved, the dying abandoned on the streets of Calcutta, attracts others to join with her in a service to the most desolate and destitute of our world. Jean Vanier as a young intellectual from French Canada encountered in severely handicapped people a gift and a treasure that had been driven to the margins of human community. He created a network of communities, L'Arche, around the globe where these special children of God live with others who are not as handicapped as they are in ways of interrelating that enable the handicapped to share their own unique gifts. Those who were marginal become the animating center.

Concrete instances of leadership invite us to reflect upon the qualities and characteristics that seem to be essential to genuine leadership. The above examples from our own times and the examples of and approaches to leadership developed in presentations in this book exemplify the diversity of situations in which leadership happens and the still richer diversity of styles that manifests something of the uniqueness of each person as a leader.

Some of what we have said about Ignatius as a leader we appreciate simply as a part of who he was and of his historical situation and particular context. What characterized him as a leader most profoundly, however, has something essential to say about all leadership. What struck me many years ago about the Judeo-Christian image of the leader as Shepherd is the emphasis upon the sacred character of leadership. The authentic leader mediates the power and presence of God who is Shepherd of all humankind whom he creates and loves. Even a leader like Cyrus, ruler of Persia, is spoken of as the "anointed one." His right hand of power is grasped by Yahweh even though he does not know this God of Israel who, nevertheless, calls him by name.[21] What is said of Cyrus could be said as well of someone like Gorbachev or Yeltsin in our own day.

The leadership of Ignatius is exercised in profound consciousness of this sacred quality and of the humility and radical poverty that dispose the leader for that reliance upon God that orders all to a "greater glory." But there are leaders as well who serve that "greater glory" though they cannot name the source that animates their decisions and actions. Nevertheless, their leadership mediates a glory beyond themselves whenever it is ordered to a greater love and more fullness of life.

Ignatius rightfully centered his life and the life of the Society of Jesus in companionship with Jesus because he is the one who leads the whole of Creation into the fullness that God promised from the beginning. And this Jesus exercises leadership not as one who comes to lord it over his sisters and brothers but one who comes among us in the power of God's own Spirit as servant and friend.

In being available to be sent to go anywhere to do anything for the glory of God, Ignatius did not at first envision that his companions would be as engaged as they came to be in education. It happened that in the dynamics of incorporating companions into the Society in a way that shared his vision and spirituality but also involved a solid education similar to what the first companions experienced at Paris, Ignatius created something new. He integrated the best of the methods of the University of Paris with his own spiritual vision for the education and formation of leaders. The results were a system of education throughout Europe and in distant lands where the companions were sent as missionaries.

More than four hundred and fifty years later, I find myself as a companion of Ignatius on the threshold of the twenty-first century in a very different world than he knew and facing very different challenges with respect to the education of leaders. As Jesuits today listening to the Spirit within the experience of our own times, there has been an awakening to new ways of looking at the formation of leaders. There is certainly the perspective presented here of what will always be at the heart of the Ignatian sense of leadership. But there are characteristics and attitudes looked for in a leader today that might not have received the same emphasis in the time of Ignatius. He was profoundly a man of faith, his service embodied a commitment to justice and solidarity with the poor but not necessarily understood in terms of structural changes and social transformations that are a central dimension of today's consciousness. But Ignatius would not be at all surprised that the way of magnanimity and discernment and an openness to the Spirit might lead to new challenges and new possibilities.

Education for leadership in a Jesuit university today is the shared responsibility of teachers, Jesuit and non-Jesuit, and students in dialogue. It is easy enough to get closed behind the door of our own thoughts or so preoccupied with adjusting new possibilities to our own narrower perspective that we fail to catch the creative possibilities that open communication makes possible. I hope my own reflections have opened doors to a shared sense of leadership or, at least, contributed to the dialogue that is so necessary for the education and formation of leaders in our communities and for our world.

Notes

1. Ps. 23:1-4; 78:51-55.
2. Is. 63:10-13; Lk. 4:14-15; Jn. 10:14-15.
3. Ps. 100:3-5; Jn. 14:16-17, 26-27.
4. Jn. 10:17-18.
5. Jn. 5:19,30.
6. Sandra M Schneiders, *Beyond Patching* (Paulist Press, N.Y., 1991), p. 73.
7. Sandra M. Schneiders, "Theology and Spirituality: Strangers, Rivals, or Partners?" *Horizon* 13, p. 266.
8. This is especially true of the *Constitutions of the Society of Jesus* written by Ignatius but it is also evident from the focus of the *Spiritual Exercises*. George E. Ganss, S.J., *The Constitutions of the Society of Jesus* (St. Louis: The Institute of Jesuit Sources, 1970, #72, 258, 508); also, David L. Fleming, S.J., *The Spiritual Exercises* (St. Louis: Institute of Jesuit Sources, 1978), #179.185.
9. Ganss, *The Constitutions*, #728.
10. St. Thomas Aquinas in his *Summa Theologiae*, (Second Part of the Second Part, Question 129) speaks of magnanimity in terms of public recognition. Honor and recognition Ignatius turns away from himself toward God, the One who initiates and empowers him in all things. The magnanimous person, fully alive and co-creative with God, gives glory and honor to God. This is not the point that Thomas addresses but it is central to the spirituality of Ignatius.
11. What Aristotle has to say about pride and the proud man's concern for the "greater" and the "more" and the honors that come to the great ones would characterize the aristocratic magnanimity of the early Ignatius. Conversion and transformation led him to see things quite differently. Cf. Aristotle, *Ethics*, Book IV, #1123-1125 (New York: Dutton, Everyman's Library), pp. 78-83.
12. John C. Olin, ed., *The Autobiography of St. Ignatius of Loyola* (NY: Harper Torchbooks, 1974). Other works on Ignatius that might be helpful to the reader are: Philip Caraman, *Ignatius of Loyola* (London: Collins, 1990); Candido de Dalmases, *Ignatius of Loyola, Founder of the Jesuits: His life and Works* (St. Louis: Institute of Jesuit Sources, 1985); James Broderick, *Saint Ignatius Loyola: The Pilgrim Years* (NY: Farrar, Straus and Cudahy, 1956);

Joseph E Conwell, *Contemplation in Action: A Study in Ignatian Prayer* (Spokane: Gonzaga University, 1957). For an excellent bibliography on Ignatius and the spirituality of Ignatius, see Paul Begheyn, S.J. and Kenneth Bogart, S.J., "A Bibliography on St. Ignatius' *Spiritual Exercises*," *Studies in the Spirituality of Jesuits* (23/3), May 1991.

13. Olin, *The Autobiography of St. Ignatius*, 21. The next nine paragraphs are based on pp. 22-40 of this work.

14. *The Spiritual Diary of Ignatius*, #156-164; A translation of this work may be found in Antonio T. De Nicolas' *Ignatius De Loyola: Powers of Imagining* (Albany: State University of New York Press, 1986), pp. 175-238. My next eight paragraphs draw upon pp. 50-87 of this work.

15. Olin, *The Autobiography of Ignatius*, pp. 45-51.

16. Jules J. Toner, S.J., "The Deliberations that Started the Jesuits", *Studies in the Spirituality of Jesuits* (4/4), June 1974. My next two paragraph draw upon pp. 180-193 of this work.

17. Gauss, *Constitutions*, #726. The characteristics of Ignatian leadership described in the rest of this paragraph are found in #727-735.

18. Originally those who attended a General Congregation were all the Solemnly Professed members of the Society of Jesus. Such a body, gathered in Congregation, is the highest legislative body of the Society. *The Constitutions*, written by Ignatius, were submitted to the Congregation of the Professed Jesuits for approval. This structured "Town Meeting" still possesses the ultimate legislative power in the Society of Jesus. Because of the size of the Society it is a body of elected members who represent the wider companionship of the Society.

19. Acts of the Apostles, 16:1-10.

20. Olin, *Autobiography*, p. 89.

21. Isaiah, 45:1-7; 41:1-7.

Chapter 4

Perceval: From Naivete to Wisdom

Peter B. Ely, S.J.

> *And Solomon said [to God] ... "Give thy servant therefore an understanding mind to govern thy people, that I may discern between good and evil."*
> --I Kings 3:9

Chretien de Troyes' medieval romance, *Perceval*, is the story of a knight. In it I have found ingredients of leadership. One ingredient is the hero's exceptional naivete, which is clearly thematic in the story. Another is the movement from naivete to wisdom, a movement which, I believe, is the heart of the Perceval narrative. A third ingredient is the wisdom Perceval moves toward as he breaks through the limits of his young man's naivete. The interrelation of these three ingredients is the subject of this essay. I will argue that the movement from naivete to wisdom is not only the heart of the story of Perceval but an essential element in leadership.

The Story of Perceval

The story begins when the hero is young, before he has left his home and mother. One morning in the forest Perceval sees some knights on horseback. Dazzled by their appearance, he longs to be one of them and decides to leave home and mother to follow his ambition for chivalry. Perceval's mother is devastated. As he parts from her and passes through the front gate, she faints from grief and, as we find out later in the story, dies.

At first Perceval goes from success to success, overcoming older, more experienced knights and rescuing the maiden Blancheflor, whose realm had been besieged by an evil knight. Then, during a visit at a noble castle situated in a beautiful valley, Perceval encounters a challenge that is beyond him.

During the meeting between Perceval and the lord of the castle, a young man walks by carrying a lance from which runs a single drop of blood. Perceval is curious about what the lance means and where it is being carried. He does not turn his curiosity into a question, though, because he has been warned by his mentor, Gornemant, not to talk too much.

Then a young maiden carrying a bowl containing a communion host walks by the table. Again Perceval is curious but does not ask a question because he does not want to talk too much.[1] The lance and grail are carried in procession before the young man several times during the evening, but each time he lets the questions go unasked. (58-60) The meal ends and everyone retires for the night.

The next morning, surrounded by an ominous and unfriendly silence, Perceval leaves the castle, hoping to find some squires to question about the lance and the grail, for he is still curious. After proceeding a short distance from the castle, Perceval comes upon a maiden weeping under an oak tree for her love who has been killed. The maiden informs Perceval that the castle where he stayed the night before is the home of the Fisher King and that the King, maimed in battle, cannot move himself. Then the maiden asks Perceval if he had seen the lance that bled and the grail and questioned their significance.

When Perceval answers that he had seen the objects but asked no questions, the maiden tells him the consequences of his omission. Had he asked the questions, it seems, the maimed king would have been cured, recovered the use of his limbs, and been able to rule his lands with great benefit for the people. Now great misery will come upon Perceval and many others. The cause of his failure to ask the questions, the maiden informs Perceval, was the sin against his mother who died grieving him.

After recounting several more adventures, among them the visit to the court of King Arthur, the author tells us that "Perceval . . . had so lost his memory that he had forgotten God." (82) Then Perceval runs into a group of penitents observing the passion and death of Christ on Good Friday, joins them, and meets a priest, his mother's brother, to whom he confesses his sins. He tells the priest what happened at the castle of the Fisher King and is informed once more that his inability to ask the questions was connected in some way with the sorrow he caused his mother in leaving home.

Here the story ends without being completed. A closer look at the story of Perceval will reveal ingredients of leadership, naivete, wisdom, and the failure that leads from naivete to wisdom.

From Naivete to Wisdom

Most young people are marked by innocence and lack of guile. Perceval was more naive than most. Though edifying and inspiring at times, his naivete is merely ridiculous at others. At the beginning of the story Perceval insistently questions one of the knights he meets in the forest about his armor and weapons, refusing to answer the question the knight puts to him. Finally, the author tells us, "The boy who had little sense, said: 'Were you born like this?'" The knight is patient in his response: "Not at all, young sir, no one can be born like this." (13) But when the knight's companions rode up to ask him what he had learned from the youth, he says of Perceval: "He knows nothing of manners, so God help me, for he never properly answers any question I ask, but instead he asks the name of anything he sees and what it is good for." (12) This side of Perceval's naivete makes us want to laugh at him.

And after he had left home, Perceval developed the habit of announcing that he had heard certain things from his mother. When his mentor, Gornemant of Gohort, advises him to go to the church and "pray to him who made all things to have mercy on your soul and to keep you a good Christian in this earthly life," Perceval responds that this is what he had once heard from his mother. "Now, fair brother," responds Gornemant, "hereafter do not keep saying that your mother taught you this or that. Till now I do not blame you at all, but, begging your pardon, I ask that henceforth you correct yourself, for if you persist, you will be taken for a fool." (35) Because he is docile, Perceval accepts the advice. Perceval's docility too is part of his naivete. He is, in fact, literal minded in following advice. Because Gornemant of Gohort has warned him about talking too much and gossiping, Perceval says hardly anything when he meets the lovely Blancheflor whose realm he will rescue. "Then all the knights began to whisper among themselves. 'By God,' said each, 'I wonder if this knight is dumb; it would be a great pity, for never was so handsome a knight born of woman.'" (38) This naivete of Perceval's, in the form of mindless following of his mentor's advice, inhibits him from asking the questions about the lance and the grail.

But if Perceval's naivete is from one point of view a limitation, it has a positive side too. He may be literal minded in following the advice given to him, but he *is* open to advice and eager to learn. His naive wonder and desire to understand everything there is to know about chivalry is an ingredient of leadership. When his mentor, Gornemant, advises him to have mercy on those he overcomes in battle when they are unable to defend themselves, he accepts the advice and consistently puts it into practice. The very naivete which makes Perceval foolish also makes him teachable and, step by step, he moves from naivete to wisdom. Perceval's naivete is most complete and unchallenged when he is still in the protective atmosphere of his mother's home. Here he is truly innocent, inexperienced, untutored, and unformed. Perceval's passage from naivete to wisdom begins when he sees the vision of the knights in the forest. Through this vision he is awakened to the possibility of a greatness he did not know existed. Though he is still naive, Perceval is at least aware of a wonderful world that exists outside the protective atmosphere of his mother's home.

The movement from naivete continues with Perceval's separation from the protective atmosphere of home and mother and his setting out on the search for greatness. He develops physical courage, prowess, as it is called in the tradition of chivalry, and the code of ethics which comes through the advice given by Perceval's mother and his mentor, Gornemant. Perceval also learns from Gornemant the proper use of the equipment of chivalry and the techniques of battle. And, as we have seen above, Gornemant directly challenges Perceval's naive habit of referring to his mother's advice.

Up to this point, the path from naivete to wisdom has lead from one success to another. Then comes the moment of failure. Perceval does not ask the questions that occur to him when he sees the lance and the grail and thus misses the opportunity to bring about the healing of the Fisher King. Failure itself becomes Perceval's tutor, assisted by the women who reveal to Perceval the consequences of his not asking the questions. The full magnitude of the failure is first revealed to a very surprised and unsuspecting Perceval after he leaves the castle of the Fisher King. The revelation is repeated later at the court of King Arthur.

There follows the quest for understanding of his failure and repentance for the sin that caused it. Perceval joins the penitents in their spiritual quest and gains deeper understanding and peace in confessing his sins to the priest, his uncle. As a sign of his repentance, he received a penance. Though Chretien de Troyes' account of Perceval ends at this point without telling us what becomes of the hero, it seems Perceval has made a new beginning and discovered a spiritual dimension to his life. He is prepared to be a true knight in the fullest Christian sense of the word.

It seems that the very naivete which made Perceval foolish in the eyes of other knights contains a dynamism that moves him to a deeper level of existence. How this is true will be clearer as we look at the stages of Perceval's development.

Three Visions, Three Transformations

These, then, are the stages of Perceval's journey from naivete to wisdom: (1) the vision of greatness embodied in the knights he meets in the forest, (2) separation from his mother's house, (3) meeting a mentor who teaches him the arts of chivalry and its moral code, (4) the successful pursuit of a chivalric career including the liberation of the realm of Blancheflor, (5) the consistent practice of the moral code of chivalry,

(6) failure to ask questions about lance and grail, (7) the revelation of the failure, and (8) repentance and conversion.

Implicit in these stages of Perceval's journey are three visions and three corresponding transformations that move our hero from naivete to wisdom. Taken together, these visions and transformations mark the stages of Perceval's education as a leader, an education that occurs in two ways: through what he learns from others--the advice he receives from his mother, from his mentor, from the women who announce the consequences of his failure, and the priest who hears his confession--and through his own experience after leaving his mother's home and embarking on his career as a knight.

The first vision takes place at the beginning of Perceval's career. It is a young man's vision, full of naive wonder and ehthusiasm. Awakened in his encounter with the knights in the forest, Perceval is fascinated with each piece of their equipment. More than anything he wants to be like these angelic characters he has met and asks one question after another without even bothering to answer the questions put to him. He wants to know about the lance and its use. He asks about the shield and the coat of mail.

This is the vision of a profession, invested with all the wonder young people can experience. Perceval's mentor, Gornemant of Gohort, fills out the picture given by the knight in the forest by instructing Perceval in the use of arms and the skills necessary for a knight. And Gornemant advises Perceval, "Every profession demands effort, heart, and practice; every knowledge comes by these three." (32) From the beginning, Perceval is successful in realizing this vision. From the moment he slays the Red Knight just after his first visit to Arthur's court, through all the contests he wins against oppressing knights, Perceval manifests the courage and skill necessary for knighthood.

The second vision is ethical, not in a philosophical sense, but as practical wisdom about how to act nobly. It is expressed in the story through the advice given to Perceval by his mother and his mentor, Gornemant, and by his own conscientious following of that advice. From his mother Perceval learns that he is to aid maidens in distress if they ask for help. He may take a kiss from a maiden if she offers it, but nothing more; and if she gives him her ring, it will be proper for him to wear it. Perceval should never keep company long with someone before asking his or her name. Finally, and most important, he is to "enter church and monastery chapel and pray Our Lord to give you honor in this world and grant you so to act that you may come to a good end." (17)

From his mentor, Gornemant, Perceval learns that when he gains the upper hand against another knight in battle, and the other is not able to defend himself further, Perceval should have mercy on him and not kill him. He should also beware of talking too much and gossiping, advice which he was to follow too literally. If he finds a man or woman in distress and is able to help, he should do so. And, like Perceval's mother, Gornemant advises prayer: "Go to the monastery church and pray to Him who made all things, to have mercy on your soul and to keep you a good Christian in this earthly life." (35)

Except for the last piece of advice from his mother and his mentor, advice which is really spiritual rather than ethical, Perceval faithfully does everything he has been counselled to do. Each time he conquers a knight, he has mercy and sends the knight to Arthur's court. Several times he helps maidens in distress. After finishing his lessons with his mentor, he asks his name, just as his mother had told him to do. But Perceval does not pray and has, in fact, forgotten God during the five years since he left his mother's home, a fault he acknowledges when he confessess to his uncle.

In the professional realm and the ethical realm, Perceval is an outstanding success. And each of these successes moves Perceval further from naivete and closer to wisdom. For in the practice of his profession and the observance of its moral code, he is forced to abandon that absorption in self which naivete entails. And yet, Perceval's growing sophistication coexists with a deep naivete, which though not altogether negative, still holds him back from the achievement of wisdom.

The third vision has to do with the realm of sin, and suffering, and redemption, the realm of the spiritual, the realm of wisdom. Perceval does not easily enter this realm. His failure to enter is the core of the story. We have already seen that Perceval did not pray to God or even remember God. The full significance of Perceval's spiritual failure is revealed in the encounter with the Fisher King. Though his curiosity is aroused when the lance that bleeds and the grail pass before his eyes, he asks no questions. If he had, the Fisher King would have been healed and able to govern his realm with wonderful effects for all his people. By holding back from asking, Perceval misses an opportunity.

Why does Perceval hold back? The superficial reason he himself gives is that he has been told by his mentor not to talk too much. The real reason, as Perceval learns from the maiden who weeps under the oak tree and from the hermit-confessor, his uncle, is an unknown sin, the sorrow he caused his mother on leaving home. "Sin cut off your tongue," Perceval's uncle tells him, "when you saw before you the bleeding point which never has been stanched, and did not ask the reason. And great was your folly when you did not learn whom one served with the grail." (85)

Perceval's failure to enter easily into the third realm is all the more striking when contrasted to his success in the first two realms. Even though he had had no experience in the art of chivalry, he learned quickly: "Then the lord caused the youth to mount, and he began to carry lance and shield as adroitly as if he had passed all his days in tourneys and wars and had journeyed throughout the world seeking battle and adventure."

(32) And he was easily able to follow the ethical advice he had been given. But in the realm of the spirit, he seems to be at sea.

There is something mysterious in Perceval's failure, mysterious and catastrophic. The most bitter accusation against Perceval and the most eloquent recital of the evils which will result from his failure come from the loathsome damsel who rides into Arthur's court on her tawny horse.

The damsel's intervention comes at a moment of triumph for Perceval and of great joy for King Arthur and his court. For Perceval, whom Arthur has long sought, has just returned to the court. "Great was the joy," the author tells us, "which the King, the Queen, and the barons made over Perceval of Wales. They returned that evening with him to Caerleon, and the rejoicing lasted that night and through the morrow." (80) But then the damsel rides into court to deliver a grim message:

> On the third day they saw a damsel come riding on a tawny mule, with a scourge in her right hand. Her hair hung in two black twisted braids, and if the book describes her truly, never was there a creature so loathly save in hell. Her neck and hands were blacker than any iron ever seen, yet these were less ugly than the rest of her. Her eyes were two holes, as small as those of a rat; her nose was like that of a monkey or a cat; her lips were like those of an ass or an ox; her teeth resembled in color the yolk of an egg; she had a beard like a goat. In the middle of her chest rose a hump; her backbone was crooked; her hips and shoulders were well shaped for dancing! Her back was hunched, and her legs were twisted like two willow wands. Her figure was perfect for leading a dance. (80)

It is hard to imagine the dance for which this damsel was so well suited. Why does the author introduce such a ghastly character into this otherwise joyous scene? Probably because of the stark message which she is about to deliver to Perceval and, more to the point, because of the bleakness and waste that is left by Perceval's failure. After a general greeting to the King and his court, the loathly damsel addresses Perceval alone:

> Ah, Perceval, Fortune is bald behind, but has a forelock in front. A curse on him who greets or wishes you well, for you did not seize Fortune when you met her. You entered the dwelling of the Fisher King; you saw the lance which bleeds. Was it so painful to open your mouth that you could not ask why the drop of blood sprang from the white point of the lance? When you saw the grail, you did not inquire who was the rich man whom one served with it. (81)

The loathly damsel continues her bitter recital: "It was you, unfortunate man, who saw that the time and the place were right for speech, and yet remained mute. You had ample opportunity, but in an evil hour you kept silence." (81) If the question had been asked, according to the damsel, the king would have been completely cured and would have been able to rule his land in peace. Since he will never rule his land again and is not healed of his wound, "Ladies will lose their husbands, lands will be laid waste, maidens, helpless, will remain orphans, and many knights will die." (81) All these calamities, the damsel adds, will befall because of Perceval.

It is a stinging condemnation since the failure seems so trivial. Perceval certainly did not know that so much depended on whether or not he asked the questions that occurred to him. It does not seem fair to impute guilt to him and to be angry when he had no idea what was at stake. Yet the damsel is angry and she does judge him harshly, and we instinctively know there is truth in her judgment. We are, of course, in the realm of myth and symbol. Perceval's failure represents far more than the simple omission of a question about objects that pass in front of him. Perceval's deeply ingrained ignorance, rooted in naivete, is somehow culpable.

This hero, otherwise so admirable, noble, and successful, manifests a kind of blindness in the spiritual realm that keeps him from wisdom and leads him to miss the opportunity for healing the king and restoring his kingdom.[2]

But we should not overlook another aspect of Perceval's failure. With all its disastrous consequences, his omission is also the entrance into a realm of wisdom from which he had thus far been excluded. The story ends just at the point where Perceval's new life begins, and we do not know what sort of person he will become. But it is evident that the successful but naive hero has been profoundly transformed by what has happened. The nature of the transformation is indicated in Perceval's confession and in the prayer for repentance given to him by his uncle-priest to whom he confessed his failure.

Perceval begins his confession with the sweeping admission, "For five years I have not known where I was. I did not love God nor believe in Him, and I have done nothing but evil." (84) The admission is surprising because we have up to this point learned only of Perceval's failure to ask the questions about lance and grail. But now it seems Perceval sees his own life as a spiritual wasteland.

The penance assigned by Perceval's priest-uncle is intended to put Perceval on the path of spiritual renewal. It contains the last advice the hero will receive in the story. Every day Perceval is to go to the monastery church before any other place, when the bell rings, or earlier if he has already risen. If the Mass has begun, he is to stay until the priest has finished his prayers and chants. "If you choose to do so," his uncle adds, "you can still advance in worth and enjoy both honor and paradise." (86) Perceval's uncle concludes:

> Believe in God, love God, worship God. Honor good men and good women. Rise in the presence of a priest; it is a service which costs little and God in truth loves it because it comes from humility. If a maiden asks your help, or a widow or an orphan girl, give it, and yours will be the gain. Such service is the highest. Aid them, and on no account weaken in welldoing. This is what I would have you do to atone for your sins

and to recover all the graces which once were yours. Tell me now if you assent. (86)

And Perceval agrees "right gladly" to this traditional formula for Christian living which he receives from his mother's brother. What his life will actually be we can only imagine, for the story ends abruptly at this the beginning of Perceval's new life: "Thus Perceval learned how God was crucified and died on a Friday, and on Easter Day he received the communion. Of him the tale tells no more at this point." (87)

Some Generalizations About the Education of Leaders

I have interpreted the romance of *Perceval* as the story of a leader's education from naivete to spiritual wisdom and have indicated the stages of this transformation in Perceval's life. Now I want to generalize the movement contained in Chretien de Troyes' medieval story and propose that the transition from naivete to spiritual wisdom be taken as an essential ingredient of leadership.

I am aware of the risk in attempting this transition. Much of the power of a story lies in its concreteness and particularity. *Perceval* is the story of a leader, not an essay on leadership. But it is also a mythic story and invites us to go beyond its hero to reflect on human life. I am also aware, once again, that Perceval is the story of a man's education. Not all the lessons of his life are applicable to women. But it seems that the transition from naivete to wisdom takes place in women as in men, though in different ways, and thus transcends the difference between the sexes.[3]

The attempt to move from the particular case of Perceval to some more general principles about the education of leaders suggests some questions which will outline my argument. First, am I justified in saying that *Perceval* is the narrative of a leader's education? If not, it will be difficult to move from the lessons contained in his story to a statement of general principles of leadership. And what is meant by the spiritual wisdom I have said is the final stage of Perceval's journey? Why is it important for a leader? What is the connection between naivete and spiritual wisdom? Finally, in the education of a leader into spiritual wisdom, can one legitimately argue for the usefulness and even necessity of failure?

I believe *Perceval* is about the education of a leader. The point may be obvious but making the argument explicit will help develop more universal ideas about leadership from the example of Perceval. Some reasons exist for saying that Perceval is not really a leader. We never see him commanding an army or even a small band of soldiers. He travels alone and his conquests are individual. No one follows him. We do not know whether he is able to work with people and inspire them to achieve predetermined goals or not. We do not even know if he is able to formulate such goals and work out a scheme for achieving them. Most of the qualities I have listed enter into contemporary discussions of leadership.

But though Perceval may not manifest all the ingredients of commonly accepted definitions of leadership, he is essentially a leader. First, he is a hero, an idealized representative of the deepest human striving and an embodiment of the human being's efforts to achieve its deepest desires. Being such an embodiment is an element of leadership. Perceval's struggles have cosmic significance as do his successes and failures. Moreover, the profession Perceval chooses, chivalry, is not just one profession among others, like the cobbler's trade or the baker's. In medieval society, knights were leaders par excellence. And Perceval accomplishes some remarkable deeds in the public realm, the most important being the liberation of Belrepeire, the domain of the beautiful maiden, Blancheflor.

Though Perceval is a leader, he is not a fully mature leader. Chretien de Troyes' tells the story of Perceval's education and ends at a crucial point in the hero's development. Perceval is confronted with a challenge he does not understand. He fails to respond. The significance of his failure is revealed to him and a new realm is opened up, the way of spiritual wisdom.

If I am justified in saying that *Perceval* is the story of a leader, and that its hero moved from naivete toward wisdom, what is this wisdom he moved toward and what does it have to do with leadership? There is a wisdom that belongs to the professional sphere and a wisdom that belongs to the ethical sphere. I am concerned in this essay about a wisdom that is spiritual. Without it, all the other achievements of leaders will remain incomplete at best and possibly perverse and corrupt.

The easiest way to define the spiritual dimension is to contrast it with the professional and the ethical. The crucial point, I believe, is the sources of knowledge and action. In the technical or professional dimension, the sources of knowledge and action are conscious and controlled by the actor. Perceval, as we have seen, learned how to handle the lance and sword and, when the occasion arose, put into practice what he had learned. And being successful in his profession of knighthood took a kind of practical wisdom. The same was true in the moral realm. Perceval learned the ethical precepts of chivalry and put them into practice.

In the realm of spiritual wisdom, the source of knowledge and action is outside oneself, or at least outside the realm of consciousness. One is more acted upon than acting, more a receiver than a doer. Spiritual people are in tune with the deep forces which shape the worlds of nature and human life, including the unconscious energy of their own lives. The gardener presents a useful example. Gardeners operate in two dimensions: the professional or technical in knowing where and when and how to plant seeds and bulbs and how to care for them; and in the spiritual in recognizing that their planting and cultivating are useless without the growth that comes from forces beyond their control.

To live spiritually, people need more than to know and put into practice the rules and principles that govern activity. I could just as well say they need less, for what they need to be spiritual is both more and less than what they need to be professional and ethical. In terms of control and predictability of results, the spiritual realm demands less; in terms of contact with the deep forces that govern nature and human life, it demands more.

The spiritual realm has to do with fullness of life and fecundity. And the life and fecundity of leaders has an effect on those they lead. The health of the King in the story of Perceval is connected with the health of his entire kingdom. When the King is fecund, the whole kingdom thrives and grows. When he is wounded, the whole kingdom languishes.

Perceval's failure was spiritual. He did not perceive the relation between asking or not asking the questions that occurred to him and the consequences which would follow. A mysterious connection escaped him and probably escapes most readers of the legend. Perceval had not broken any rule, at least not any he knew about. Not asking the question was not a professional failure or an ethical failure. It would not have helped to learn more about the techniques of battle and the principles of ethics or to have worked harder at putting them into practice.[4] What Perceval did not know was how to follow the prompting of his own intense curiosity rooted in an unconscious intimation of causes and effects beyond normal human activity. He wanted to ask the question, even looked for squires from the Fisher King's castle after the opportunity had passed to ask about the lance and grail. But it was too late. The moment pregnant with possibility had passed.

One can argue that wisdom is the ideal fulfillment of the human person. But not every wise person is a leader. And a person can be a leader without being wise. What, then, is the connection between wisdom and leadership? Contemporary and past history are full of examples of unwise, unspiritual, and evil leaders. In fact, much of history chronicles the effects of lack of wisdom in leaders. Manfred Kets DeVries, a business consultant and educator, has written about the effects on institutions of leaders who fail because of some crippling defect in their character. The defects are always some kind of excess, some lack of wisdom and balance and perception of the deep inner connection of things. DeVries' two books, *Unstable at the Top*, and *Prisoners of Leadership*, give examples of men like Henry Ford and Edgar Hoover whose blind spots adversely affected their own performance and the organizations they served.[5] For leadership to reach its full flowering, wisdom is necessary.

I have been describing the spiritual wisdom which eluded Perceval, a wisdom which I believe is essential for true leadership. The theme of this essay has been that the movement from naivete to wisdom is at the heart of the story of Perceval. Can the connection between naivete and wisdom also be generalized beyond this story and made into a principle of leadership just as the necessity of wisdom was? Or is naivete just a characteristic of Perceval, interesting enough in Chretien de Troyes' medieval romance, but not relevant for a theory of leadership?

Paradoxical as it may seem, given the theme of this essay, I believe there is an intimate and necessary connection between naivete and wisdom. In calling Perceval's education a movement from naivete to wisdom, I have implied that wisdom is the opposite of naivete. But that is not the whole story. The relation between naivete and wisdom is complex because, as I mentioned earlier, naivete itself is an ambivalent quality; it can be limiting or enabling. And naivete admits of development. On the one hand, naivete is a kind of resistance to reality, a childish innocence that excludes the knowledge of good and evil, a stubborn belief that if one just obeys the rules one has learned as a child, all will be well. In this sense naivete is opposed to wisdom and is unspiritual.

But naivete has another side, a dynamism which propels toward wisdom. Naivete is wonder, openness to reality, willingness to learn and be influenced. These qualities, wonder, openness, and docility belong to wisdom and condition wisdom. Paul Ricoeur, in his book, *The Symbolism of Evil*, relates the two kinds of naivete.[6] The first level of naivete is precritical. The first naivete is followed by a stage of awakening to the reality of good and evil and is, at least for a time, swallowed up and lost in critical consciousness and even cynicism. The cycle is completed when naivete as wonder and openness to reality overcomes cynicism, giving way to wisdom.

This cycle of naivete is symbolized, it seems to me, in Perceval's relation to his mother. When Perceval was at home with his mother, before he had seen the vision of the knights in the forest, he was in the first level. As he moved toward the vision inspired by the knights in the forest and into his own career as a knight, he moved away from his mother and the simple naivete of this first relationship. But from the time he left home, the return to his mother becomes a quest for Perceval.

He will not agree to stay with Blancheflor and the people of Belrepeire until he has found his mother dead or alive. When, after leaving Belrepeire, Perceval comes to the stream with the boat and the two men, he exclaims, "Ah, Almighty God, if I could cross this stream, I believe I would find my mother, if she is still alive." (55) The quest which caused Perceval's restless movement from one place to another was not the quest for the grail--which is never mentioned in Chretien de Troyes' version of the story--but this quest for his mother. This is the second level of naivete, the mother rediscovered after the experience of leaving home and making one's own way. In leaving home and making his own way, Perceval lost his innocence, neglected God, and even forgot his own name. The shattering experience of the unasked questions put Perceval on the path back to mother, God, and self. The story of *Perceval* tells us, so it seems, that the way to wisdom is a circle that leads from naivete through achievement, through a loss of innocence, through failure, back to naivete. And the second naivete is wisdom.

I have taken the position that, for Perceval, at least, wisdom was achieved through failure. Should the idea of failure be included as a requisite in the education of leaders? At first glance the two ideas, leadership and failure, do not seem to belong together. Leaders fail, of course. But their failure does not seem to be a part of their leadership. Leadership leaves off, we are tempted to say, exactly where failure begins.

Failure is, I suggest, an integral part of leadership and of the education of leaders. I am not proposing that one seek failure hoping that wisdom might be just around the corner. But I think it is true to say that leaders can learn more from their failures than from any other source. For failure is a revelation of weakness, or misjudgment, or inexperience which opens up in a flash the realm one could have entered had it not been for the weakness or misjudgment or inexperience. And often no other key can unlock the possibilities revealed through failure. Perceval's failure was a missed opportunity, an opportunity he did not know existed; his failure was precisely failure to recognize the opportunity. When the failure was revealed, so was the opportunity. The door was opened and he could repent, learn from his mistake, and wait for the next opportunity. The disastrous omission contained in itself the seeds of renewal and of a deeper form of existence.

And it is not only a world outside one's self that is opened up through failure. Our hero, Perceval, it seems, discovers himself through missing the opportunity that was offered. After she has revealed to him the dimensions of his failure in not asking the questions about lance and grail, the maiden Perceval meets as he is leaving the Fisher King's castle asks him his name. "Then," we are told, "he who did not know his name divined it and said that his name was Perceval of Wales. He did not know whether he told the truth or not, but it was the truth though he did not know it." (64) Not knowing his name is part of his naivete. All his successes had not taught Perceval his name. He has learned it through his failure.

So, following my interpretation, the generalized theory of leadership which emerges from the story of Perceval goes something like this. Leadership has an active side and a receptive side. Leaders lead by taking charge, accomplishing things, achieving goals. They also lead by being led themselves, prompted by the deepest stirring of their own humanity, and by being in touch with the mysterious spiritual connections between things. The move from the creative self-exertion which characterizes the first stage to the receptivity which characterizes the second is not automatic or easy. Frequently it takes place through failure.*

---

* What I am describing here is expressed in different words in Tom Jeannot's chapter, "But Trusted Servants," and in Pat O'Leary's "Ignatius."

Conclusion

Perceval's education has taken him from naivete to wisdom, or at least to the threshold of wisdom. A world has opened up for him whose existence was unknown before his failure. What a long distance he has come from the haven of his mother's home. On the way, he has been liberated from his child's naivete by entering into and practicing a profession, by accepting and carrying out an ethical code, and by accepting a failure which opened the realm of spiritual wisdom.

At the end of his journey he has found his mother, not alive but dead from the sorrow he caused her in leaving home. He has learned that this sorrow had a crippling effect on him too, involved a rupture of some sort in him, was a sin. And this sin kept him from asking the questions about lance and grail. In repenting and accepting the penance imposed on him, he has been healed and has recovered the naivete that is proper to a man, not a child. He has discovered his own name, found God again, and entered a realm of wisdom whose existence he had not suspected before. Now he is ready to begin over again.

What will his life be now? How will the transformed Perceval act? Chretien de Troyes does not tell us. But he gives some clues from which we might sketch a conclusion. During the course of assigning Perceval his penance after confession, Perceval's uncle says: "If you choose to do so, you can still advance in worth and enjoy both honor and paradise." (86) Honor was a high ideal in the culture to which Perceval belonged. We are used to thinking and speaking of honor as something vain and empty, mere honor. Even people who really ambition honor do not readily admit their desire. But in the medieval world, dominated by chivalric ideals, honor was a worthy goal.

Honor was the respect and recognition accorded to successful people whose lives exemplified all that was worthy and noble. Though honor was a worldly good, not something monks and nuns would seek, it was something a Christian could ambition since it was the natural consequence of a virtuous life. Perceval will probably not become a monk. That does not seem to be his vocation. Perhaps he will find honor in returning to marry Blancheflor and serving as wise and compassionate master of her castle, Belrepeire, in ministering humbly to rich and poor, and in worshipping God.

Whatever he does, Perceval is now prepared to be a leader, having passed from naivete, through personal achievements and through failure, to wisdom. He now knows the difference between what he can do himself and what can be done through him.

Notes

1. Chretien de Troyes, "Perceval, or the Story of the Grail," from *Medieval Romances*, ed. Roger Sherman Loomis and Laura Hibbard Loomis, (NY: Random House, 1957), 59. Here the author inserts a note of warning: "I fear that harm will come from this, because I have heard say that one can be too silent as well as be too loquacious. But for better or for worse, the youth put no question." Chretien de Troyes' twelfth century version of the Perceval story is the oldest literary version. Page references in the text are to the Loomis edition.

2. We are told in the story only that the king was maimed by a javelin through the hips in such a way as to lose the use of his legs. Some commentators think it was a matter of emasculation and that the King had, in fact, lost his fecundity both physically and spiritually. Leonardo Olschki suggests that the King's mutilation and his prolonged martyrdom have a symbolic value and refer to the cause of man's damnation. "He [the King] is injured in his virility which lies at the root of all sin." *The Grail Castle and Its Mysteries* (Manchester: Manchester U.P., 1966), 34. Jessie L. Weston, *From Ritual to Romance* (NY: Doubleday Anchor, 1957), also takes the position that the Fisher King has somehow been wounded in his virility and that this wound affects his whole kingdom. "Now there can be no possible doubt here, the condition of the King is sympathetically reflected on the land, the loss of virility in the one brings about a suspension of the reproductive processes of Nature in the other." (23).

3. In his Jungian interpretation of the story of Perceval, Robert Johnson uses it to illustrate the development of the male personality. He also suggests that the story can be useful for women. Robert A. Johnson, *He: Understanding Masculine Psychology*, rev. ed. (NY: Harper Row, 1989), x.

4. Olschki discusses how the questions which Perceval should have asked would have cured the King. The questions would not have functioned, Olschki suggests, like a magic word found in folk tales but would rather have drawn some sort of confession from the King which would have freed him from his curse. See *The Grail Castle*, 32. However one interprets the King's wound or explains how the questions from Perceval would have healed the King, it seems evident from the story that, without knowing it, the naive Perceval has wandered into the realm of sin and redemption. He does not know where he is or what to do. And so he fails to act.

5. Manfred Kets de Vries and Danny Miller, *Unstable at the Top, Inside the Troubled Organization*, (NY: New American Library, 1987), Manfred Kets de Vries, *Prisoners of Leadership*, (NY: John Wiley and Sons, 1989).

6. Paul Ricoeur, *The Symbolism of Evil*, trans. Emerson Buchanan (Boston: Beacon Press, 1969). See especially "Conclusion: The Symbol Gives Rise to Thought," 347 ff. Ricoeur discusses first- and second-level naivete in relation to the interpretation of texts and not in terms of personality development. If mythic stories belong to the first level of naivete and are "demythologized" by critical interpretation, there needs to be a third stage, according to Ricoeur, in which these stories are recognized as life-giving for philosophy and for human living.

Chapter 5

"But Trusted Servants:" A Meditation on the A.A. Conception of Leadership[1]

Thomas M. Jeannot

> *"Aldous Huxley ... called Bill 'the greatest social architect of the century'."*[2]

In the reservoir of American experience, there are stories to tell about leadership that have a distinctive American taste. There are important reasons why these stories, as well as the theoretical accounts to which they give rise, are American rather than European. We have Lincoln, Roosevelt, and Kennedy, but we do not have the Sun King, the Czar, or Hitler. The stories that come from our experience are, in serious ways, our own. Our native sense of liberty and democracy, egalitarianism, the rule of law, the limits of government, checks and balances, is not quite paralleled in the historical experience of other peoples. Then again, neither are some of the myths most profoundly ingrained in our consciousness: Horatio Alger, the self-made man, the rugged individual.

If these myths animate so much of our thinking about civic and civil leadership, we also have lessons to learn about their limits. What we might call the idea of "self-constitution," the idea that as private individuals, we individually make ourselves the selves we will become, and that we bear the sole responsibility of self-creation individually on our shoulders, powerfully affects the notion we have of what a leader is. But for many of us, this idea has had mixed success at best. If, for example, the biography of Abraham Lincoln, rising up from the Illinois frontier, corroborates it, we also know that Lincoln was an *exceptional* man. At one and the same time, we are exhorted to "make something of ourselves," and also reminded that only some of us are able to succeed in "great" ways. And the stories of alcoholics are vivid reminders that some will miserably fail in this project.

Most alcoholics never recover from their disease, but a remarkable number do, and many of them do it by way of Alcoholics Anonymous (A.A.). Founded in 1935, A.A. has grown into an international movement. It has developed its own peculiar organizational structure with an eye toward preserving its grass roots character, and it has developed its own style of leadership, grounded in the experience of recovering alcoholics, who (since they are alcoholics after all!) insist on governing themselves.

The members of A.A. have had to find their way back to the world, and to responsible and useful citizenship, having been broken on the wheel of their alcoholic desperation. From their debilitating social isolation, they have had to learn anew how "to be one in a family, to be a friend among friends, to be a worker among workers, to be a useful member of society."[3] The meetings, the fellowship, and the service work of A.A. itself give its members practice in the art of living by restoring their sense of belonging, of social identification, and of cooperative work with others in pursuit of a self-transcending purpose.

But in order to work, A.A. must first of all be available, and in order to be available, it has had to find a way to perpetuate and institutionalize its message and program. By the late nineteen-forties, based on their collective experience to that point, the members of A.A. codified their structure, their method of self-government, and their philosophy of service in "Twelve Traditions." These traditions were formally adopted at A.A.'s first international convention in Cleveland, in July of 1950. The Second Tradition in particular summarizes A.A.'s basic conception of leadership as service: "For our group purpose, there is but one ultimate authority--a loving God as He may express Himself in our group conscience. Our leaders are but trusted servants; they do not govern."[4] In the following pages, my aim is to reflect on what I think is the fundamental implication of this way of thinking about what leadership is, the recognition that human beings are not gods, that "playing God"[5] is not an effective strategy for living well, and that therefore leadership does not consist in the apotheosis of a singular personality, but in the "group conscience" of a collective enterprise and shared responsibility.

As the members of A.A. conceive it, the method of the group conscience is a spiritual one, incorporating the best aspects of the American experiment in self-government. It is democratic and egalitarian, it respects dissent and minority opinion, it diffuses authority among the members themselves rather than concentrating it in an elite cadre of governors, and it takes its decisions from consensus rather than the individual will. As the pamphlet, "The A.A. Group," explains it, "The group conscience is the collective conscience of the group membership and thus represents substantial unanimity on an issue before definitive action is taken." Furthermore,

> On sensitive issues, the group works slowly--discouraging formal motions until a clear sense of its collective view emerges. Placing principles before personalities, the membership is wary of dominant opinions. Its voice

is heard when a well-informed group arrives at a decision. The result is more than a "yes" or "no" count--precisely because it is the spiritual expression of the group conscience.... The difference between a group conscience and a majority vote, or group opinion, is that one or more of the elements described above is missing.[6]

Respect for minority opinion and the insistence on consensus insure that no particular "power-driving" personality can succeed in imposing his own will or bright idea on the rest of the fellowship.

The best way to see how the rubber meets the road in the A.A. practice of leadership is to consider examples. Those drawn from the life of A.A.'s co-founder Bill Wilson (1895-1972) are especially apt, since Bill was an inveterate "power-driver" himself, liable to let his ego get the best of him, and he had to struggle throughout the course of his life in recovery from alcoholism to transcend his overweening ambition, to divest himself of his own personal authority, and to submit to the process of the informed group conscience he had been instrumental in designing. Two examples from A.A.'s early history, before the traditions were ratified, display the sort of group experience that led to their development.

The first of these is an incident from 1936, when A.A. was little more than two living room meetings--one at Bill's home in New York, the other in Akron, Ohio, where Dr. Bob Smith, A.A.'s other co-founder, was just beginning his own outreach to drunks like himself, in search of a way out of their private agonies. Bill and Dr. Bob had met in May, 1935, while Bill was on a business trip trying to salvage what remained of his shipwrecked career as a stockbroker. Their famous meeting happened in a moment of personal crisis for Bill, sorely tempted to drink again in the bar of an Akron hotel, when by one of those divine accidents, the thought occurred to him that if only he could talk to another drunk--tell a fellow alcoholic about how he managed to stay sober for several months running--he might well weather the storm of his present craving. His five-hour conversation with Dr. Bob (the day after he followed through on his inspiration by making several phone calls to churches listed in the hotel lobby's directory), which the movement dates as the birth of A.A., was wholly informal, one drunk talking to another, and it altered the destiny of both men. They had stumbled across a solution, one alcoholic sharing his "experience, strength and hope"[7] with another. After spending the summer in Akron, Bill returned to New York and immediately tried to reproduce the experience of his talk with Dr. Bob with other alcoholic prospects. As 1935 turned into 1936, several alcoholics were on the road to recovery in both cities, proving that Bill's and Dr. Bob's experience was not adventitious, but a formula that worked.

Meanwhile, through Dr. William Silkworth, a specialist in alcoholism who worked at Towns Hospital in New York, word reached Charles Towns that Bill had come up with something good. Silkworth himself had pronounced Wilson a hopeless alcoholic in the summer of 1934, and so he had reason to be impressed with Bill's remarkable recovery. Wilson was invited to join the staff of the hospital as a paid therapist. The setup looked ideal: Towns Hospital might get out of financial difficulty by offering a therapy for alcoholism that worked, and Bill, in addition to solving his own money problems, would have a forum to develop the new program of recovery. As Bill's authorized biography tells the story, Towns's offer seemed "verified by heavenly guidance: as [Bill] rode the subway home [from his meeting with Towns], the Biblical quote, 'The laborer is worthy of his hire' came to him. By the time he arrived home, he was convinced that it was his divine destiny to become a paid therapist."[8]

Bill's New York circle, however, was not convinced that it was a good idea to offer A.A. services for money. After some discussion, the group decided that the work they were just then beginning should be offered for free. The seed of what was to become the Eighth Tradition had been planted: "Alcoholics Anonymous should remain forever nonprofessional..." To professionalize its message and service, a collective wisdom counselled, would also be to distort it. Bill had been able to reach Dr. Bob precisely because he wasn't hawking a paid service, but simply reaching out to another alcoholic in similarly straitened circumstances, more to help himself than to save the latter; and it worked, as Chuck C. was later to express it, just because it was "for free and for fun."[9] Bill's New York group intuitively knew this, and so they greeted his claim of divine inspiration impassively. "When Bill described the incident later, he portrayed himself as the impulsive, self-seeking opportunist who would have wrecked the fledgling movement had it not been for the wise and timely advice of others. Both Bill and [his wife] Lois remembered the incident as an early example of the group conscience in action."[10] The nominal group leader had conceived a bright idea, but through the process of submitting to the group conscience, it became clear that it would be a grave mistake to professionalize A.A. Subsequent A.A. history has confirmed the wisdom of the group decision on this matter; and we also learn something about Bill and about leadership within A.A.

A second story from the early history also illustrates the group conscience at work. After some debate, both in Akron and in New York, it was decided that a book (*Alcoholics Anonymous*, known as the "Big Book") should be written to carry the A.A. message. It was clear that the new movement was spreading too fast for word of mouth to keep up. Bill assumed the task of primary author, but the writing and editing process was a collective one. Controversy and impassioned discussion abounded, especially on the touchy question of how to present the spiritual dimension of the A.A. program. In its early days, the movement was closely associated with the Oxford Group, a movement of spiritual renewal founded by Frank Buchman. But recovering alcoholics in both cities became increasingly uneasy with the association, among other reasons because the Oxford Group was so militantly religious. Everyone agreed that A.A. was a spiritual program, and that the newfound sobriety of the recovering alcoholic was the work of what they came to call a "Higher Power." But some were uncomfortable with too much talk of "God," and others who had recovered were self-consciously agnostic or atheist. They objected to affiliating the book with explicit Christian doctrines and Biblical terms.

Three factions emerged. Some insisted on emphasizing "God," others wanted any reference at all to "God" eliminated, and a middle group advocated soft-pedaling the spiritual aspects of the program. At the end of the debate, a group consensus emerged. Any time "God" was to be mentioned in the book, it was to be made clear that the reference should not be construed as designating the belief of any particular confession, but only to "God as we understood Him," leaving everyone free to choose his or her own interpretation of the spirituality of A.A., so that lack of belief would not pose a stumbling block to anyone in need of the message. Once more, the decades have shown the wisdom of this important decision against affiliation with any privileged doctrine or theology. A.A. members emphasize that theirs is a spiritual, but not a religious program; and the nondogmatic and pluralist character of the movement has opened the doors of recovery wide to all who seek it, regardless of the condition or degree of their belief or unbelief.

These two examples reveal how A.A. leadership works through the process of an informed group conscience, how minority views are respected and consensus shaped, and how leaders in A.A.--"trusted servants"--follow Bill's example of submitting their ideas, judgments, and decisions to a larger collective wisdom. My task now will be to attempt a reflection on the deeper philosophical underpinnings of the A.A. conception of leadership, although the characteristic A.A. reluctance to take up any position or orthodoxy as its own necessarily means that what follows can only be one person's view.

My thesis is that human beings, as much as they make themselves, are also made, creatures as well as creators. Our reflections on human nature may fix more on one aspect than on the other, on our creative power, or on our creaturehood. These different emphases may underwrite contrasting ideals of leadership. One emphasis may conceive of leadership more as an exercise of personal power, but the other will conceive it more as an exercise of service. One may locate the source of leadership in the character of outstanding individuals, whose nobility elevates them over their followership; but the other locates it within the community, a gathering of equals standing shoulder to shoulder on the level playing field of their common humanity. The former conception of leadership is essentially aristocratic; the latter, essentially egalitarian. The aristocratic conception seems closer to the culturally prevailing mode, even in America, where despite democratic ideals, the egalitarian conception is still countercultural.

American democracy betrays a peculiar ambivalence toward these counterpoised conceptions, reflected, for example, in the writings of Ralph Waldo Emerson, and in the tension between the Emersonian ideal of self-reliance and the breakdown of that ideal in the experience of people like Bill Wilson. The A.A. understanding of leadership as service paradoxically affirms personal "powerlessness" rather than power. Creaturehood and finitude are the stuff of which leadership is made. Humility is its cardinal virtue. The leader is a peer, rather than a "hero." The root experience from which the A.A. standard of leadership derives retrieves the profound etymological associations of humility, humanity, and humus.[11] In the end, we are mortal rather than divine, born of the earth and not of the sky.

Bill W.'s life presents an archetypal pattern of experience in which the members of A.A. see themselves as in a mirror. He was a man obsessed with power, but his alcoholism broke him by the time he was thirty-nine. Confined for the third time in Towns Hospital, he admitted he was hopeless. The creed of self-reliance had bitterly failed him. He was powerless over his condition. He experienced the full measure of what the psychiatrist Harry Tiebout called "ego reduction."[12] But apparently, this was a necessary ingredient of what came next. On December 11, 1934, he had a "vital spiritual experience"[13] that transformed his life. In May of 1935, he met Dr. Bob, and together they founded A.A. From then until November of 1950, when Dr. Bob died, the two men were more or less the personal stewards of their rapidly growing fellowship. But Bill was increasingly taxed by the problem of how their movement would survive after its founders were gone from the scene. His solution was the design of the Twelve Traditions, based on the movement's collective experience, adherence to which has assured A.A.'s continued vitality from the day Bill formally withdrew from personal leadership (July 3, 1955), when A.A. "came of age" at its twentieth anniversary convention in St. Louis.[14] The second tradition, quoted above, condenses the A.A. philosophy of leadership.

A.A. has become an enduring feature of the American landscape. Its members refer to it as a "fellowship,"[15] a term of spiritual resonance, but they insist that it is not a religion or a cult. Although it could be characterized as a "society" or an "association," its deliberately minimalist organizational structure defies comparison with professional societies such as the American Medical Association, or ministerial organizations such as the Society of Jesus (the Jesuits). In fact, insofar as A.A. has any organizational structure at all, its Twelve Traditions aim in part to insure against the prospect that it could ever become professionalized.[16]

Neither is A.A. a club, like the Elks Club or the Moose Lodge. There are no dues or fees for A.A. membership, no mandatory meetings, no formal rites of initiation, and no membership requirements other than "a desire to stop drinking."[17] Although A.A.'s "General Service Conference" has a registered trademark, and its publishing house, Alcoholics

Anonymous World Services, is incorporated, A.A. itself is not a corporation or a business. Finally, because A.A. is nonprofessional, it is not a type of group therapy or even a self-help group (like Weight Watchers), administered and overseen by professionals. Its members are not "clients."

A.A. is not an organized religion, not a professional society, not a club, not a business, and not a self-help group. Its ideal of democratic self-government verges on anarchy. And yet it has survived, and one cannot help but say flourished, for fifty-six years. Its members number in millions. It has spread worldwide. And by following its "suggestions,"[18] alcoholics around the world have been able to recover from alcoholism, adopt a new way of life, and become productive members of society again. How has this uniquely and essentially American institution managed to pull it off? The idea of leadership as service is an integral part of the explanation.

Perhaps the closest analogue to A.A.'s peculiar type of collectivity is the Third Order of Franciscans, an international organization of laypersons bound together by a common spirituality. Bill invited this comparison in a talk he gave at the convention in St. Louis. Explaining A.A.'s commitment to corporate poverty, he said:

> A big factor in our thinking at the time was the philosophy of St. Francis of Assisi. His also began as a lay movement, one man carrying the good news to the next. In his day it was common enough for individuals to pledge themselves to poverty. But it was unusual, if not unique, for a whole organization or fellowship to do the same thing. For the purpose of his society Francis thought corporate poverty to be fundamental. The less money and property they had to quarrel about, the less would be the diversion from their primary purpose. And just like A.A. today, his outfit did not need much money to accomplish its mission. Why be tempted and diverted when there was no need for it? Therefore A.A. adopted the wisdom of Francis as its own. Not only would we have the least possible service organization; we would use the least possible money.... It is in this sense that A.A. had declared for the principle of corporate poverty. It is a chief safeguard of our future.[19]

A.A. invites comparison, not only on the matter of corporate poverty, but in other ways too, with the Catholic spiritualities of St. Francis and St. Ignatius of Loyola, the founder of the Jesuits.[20] It is self-consciously a movement of spiritual renewal and transformation (which again serves to distinguish it from any form of secular therapy). But it is crucial not to overstate the similarities. Franciscan and Ignatian spiritualities are institutionally affiliated with and integrated into the ecclesiology, doctrines, and creeds of a particular confession, the Roman Catholic Church, whereas A.A. has no ecclesiology and no creed. In the same talk, Bill said, "A.A. is a society without organization, animated only by the spirit of service--a true fellowship."[21]

From an organizational perspective, then, A.A. is a spiritual movement that prefers anarchy to structure, personal liberty to hierarchy and institutionalized authority, pluralism to orthodoxy, and autonomy to the rule of law. In an article written for A.A.'s monthly journal, the *Grapevine*, in January, 1947, Bill posed the question, "Will A.A. ever have a personal government?" He replied, "The answer ... is almost surely 'no.' ... [The] only real authority to be found in A.A. is that of spiritual principle. It is never personal authority."[22] Despite his own native inclination to rule, Bill was struggling to divest himself of his own personal authority over the fellowship. The only recognized authority should be that of "spiritual principle."

The authority of "spiritual principle" seems more appropriate to the voluntary associations of friendship than to the requirements of an enduring international organization. Friendships are informal, noncontractual, governed only by personal choice, and cemented by personal bonds. In contemporary friendships, friends may counsel and even direct one another, but they thrive as friends only in the interstices of formal authority, outside the office, after work, during leisure time, in the pleasant interruptions of daily business, and in voluntary unremunerated collaborations. Your boss may also be your friend, but *as* your friend, she is not your boss. No partner in friendship is officially invested with authority over the other.

So how can the authority of "spiritual principle" serve as the basis for an association of persons otherwise strangers to each other, and one that stretches across generations? Furthermore, the problem is compounded by the principle of the first tradition, which states that "Our common welfare should come first; personal recovery depends upon A.A. unity." How can such a fellowship hang together without the usual accouterments of structure, discipline, and hierarchy? None of its members has authority to fire, expel, excommunicate, punish, fine, or sanction. No one in the fellowship is charged with personal rule over the others. Its organizational chart superficially resembles those of other collective enterprises,[23] except that at the top of the chart come the local "A.A. groups" themselves, rather than the General Service Conference located in New York. This constitutes a reversal of direction of the lines of authority mapped out in the standard organizational chart, where a board of directors, a company president, or a C.E.O. typically occupies the top position. Or if we think of the typical pyramid, in which authority trickles from the top down, in A.A. authority flows from the bottom up.

Bill was apparently delighted by the seeming contradiction of maximum unity based on minimum structure. He exploited it with relish in an article for the *Grapevine* of July, 1946. The first of A.A.'s traditions insists on "A.A. unity," while the third asserts that "The only requirement for A.A. membership is a desire to stop drinking." Bill wrote,

> Were the individual to yield nothing to the common welfare there could be no society at all ... anarchy in the worst sense of that word. Yet point three in our AA Tradition looks like a wide-open invitation to anarchy. Seemingly, it contradicts point one. It reads, "Our membership ought

to include all who suffer alcoholism. Hence *we may refuse none* who wish to recover. Nor ought AA membership *ever depend on money or conformity. Any two or three alcoholics* gathered together for sobriety *may call themselves an AA group."* This clearly implies that an alcoholic is a member if *he* says so; that we can't deny him membership; that we can't demand from him a cent; that we can't force our beliefs or practices upon him; that he may flout everything we stand for and still be a member. In fact, our Tradition carries the principle of independence for the individual to such an apparently fantastic length that, so long as there is the slightest interest in sobriety, the most unmoral, the most antisocial, the most critical alcoholic may gather about him a few kindred spirits and announce that a new Alcoholics Anonymous group has been formed. Anti-God, anti-medicine, anti-our recovery program, even anti-each other--these rampant individuals are still an AA group if *they think so*! Our nonalcoholic friends sometimes exclaim, "Did we hear you say that AA has a sound social structure? You must be joking. To us, your Tradition Three looks about as firmly grounded as the Tower of Babel.... Tell us, if you can, what holds AA together? Why doesn't AA tear apart, too? If each AA has personal liberty which can amount to license, why doesn't your AA Society blow up? It ought to, yet it doesn't."[24]

In the remainder of the article, Bill proceeds to resolve the contradiction by appealing to the lash of "John Barleycorn," the only real sanction the fellowship has: "we of AA must hang together or else hang separately. ... Could anyone imagine a more powerful restraint upon us than this?"[25]

The appeal to "John Barleycorn" is surely cogent, but it also falls short of a complete answer to the question so acutely posed: "Why doesn't your AA Society blow up?" If the answer consisted *only* in an appeal to the terror of alcoholic drinking, it would resemble Thomas Hobbes's explanation of the origin of government. Hobbes posed the question, What would human life be like if there were no sovereign authority to hold us in check? His answer consisted in an account of what he named the "state of nature": "In such condition," he wrote in a famous passage of the *Leviathan*, there is "continual fear, and danger of violent death; and the life of man, solitary, poor, nasty, brutish and short."[26] The inveterate egoism of human nature, left unchecked, would soon have us at each other's throats. Therefore, in Hobbes's argument, society requires a leviathan to bridle our selfish passions.

Although A.A. has no leviathan, the "Big Book's" depiction of alcoholics describes their character in terms reminiscent of Hobbes.

Whatever our protestations, are not most of us concerned with ourselves, our resentments, or our self-pity? Selfishness--self-centeredness! That, we think, is the root of our troubles. Driven by a hundred forms of fear, self-delusion, self-seeking, and self-pity, we step on the toes of our fellows and they retaliate. Sometimes they hurt us, seemingly without provocation, but we invariably find that at some time in the past we have made decisions based on self which later placed us in a position to be hurt. So our troubles, we think, are basically of our own making.... Above everything, we alcoholics must be rid of this selfishness. We must, or it kills us![27]

The self-understanding of the members of A.A. is virtually coincident with Hobbes's description of human selfishness. Hobbes apparently believed that, at least on a social scale, this egoism is incorrigible, and so he called for the police ("covenants, without the sword, are but words..."[28]). Police methods have been used to restrain alcoholics as well.[29] Prior to the advent of A.A., there was slender hope available for the reformation of the alcoholic character. But the A.A. assessment, which more than matches Hobbes's for its grim realism, cannot afford to be as sanguine about the prospects for human transformation. Without a radical transformation, the fate of alcoholics awaits them in prisons, asylums, and death. The amazing thing is that such transformation is possible. Capitalizing on this possibility, A.A. has developed a conception of authority that systematically contrasts with Hobbes's own.

Hobbes's solution was enlightened self-interest, but he was not the enemy of moral development, character, and virtue. He even claimed the golden and silver rules for his theory.[30] It was just that he did not expect us to be virtuous on our own, or in the aggregate. On the other hand, there are also theories of rule that *require* a degree of development of character in order for their proposals to be effective. One such theory is Emerson's.

Emerson's creed of self-reliance is deeply ingrained in the American ethos. Emerson celebrates the creative powers of the individual, the spark of divinity in each one of us, and nonconformists who have enough self-trust and courage to go their own way. In his most famous essay, "Self-Reliance," he tells us that there is a "divine idea which each of us represents," but that "God will not have his work made manifest by cowards."[31] Self-reliant people should aspire to their own unique greatness.

> Trust thyself.... Great men have always done so... And we are now men, ... and not minors and invalids in a protected corner, nor cowards fleeing before a revolution, but guides, redeemers, and benefactors, obeying the almighty effort, and advancing on Chaos and the Dark.

Emerson's brave conviction is that each of us can be guide, redeemer, and benefactor. Therefore, even though he criticizes the mediocrity and leveling trend of mass society, he is an American optimist rather than a European pessimist. "Society everywhere is in conspiracy against the manhood of every one of its members.... The virtue in most request is conformity. Self-reliance is its aversion.... Who so would be a man must be a nonconformist." However, since the self is divine, and each of us is in principle this self, we have it within ourselves to resist the leveling tide of conformity and the "foolish consistency" that "is the hobgoblin of little minds, adored by little statesmen and philosophers and divines," if only we are sufficiently self-relying and self-trusting. In America, the ordinary citizen can have a great soul. "When private men shall act with original views, the lustre will be transferred from the actions of kings to those of gentlemen." The one thing needful is only that we should learn to rely on ourselves.

Emerson's gospel sacralizes the self, fixing each personal star at the center of its own universe. It is vital to his doctrine that we should be "stars" rather than mud, our souls derived from the sky and not the earth. By Emerson's lights, America is the land wherein the temporal chains that bind us to the earth can be transcended. The dead weight of the past can be thrown off by a simple act of self-absolution. "Nothing is at last sacred but the integrity of your own mind. Absolve you to yourself, and you shall have the suffrage of the world." At bottom, "Self-Reliance" teaches the doctrine that we create ourselves, and not that we are creatures. This we do by willing ourselves to be, and by exercising personal power. Each of us can be ourselves a "planet," according to the measure of our self-sufficiency and self-reliance. "We must go alone.... But your isolation must not be mechanical, but spiritual, that is, must be elevation"--i.e., *self*-elevation.

In this vision of life, we are essentially on our own. But if we answer the call, we can become veritable gods.

> And truly it demands something godlike in him who has cast off the common motives of humanity, and has ventured to trust himself for a taskmaster. High be his heart, faithful his will, clear his sight, that he may in good earnest be doctrine, society, law to himself....

This hymn of self-aggrandizement verges toward elitism, but Emerson strains to democratize it. He engages the American myth. If some are "parlor soldiers" who "shun the rugged battle of fate, where strength is born," consider "A sturdy lad from New Hampshire or Vermont, who in turn tries all the professions, who *teams it, farms it, peddles*, keeps a school, preaches, edits a newspaper, goes to Congress, buys a township, and so forth, in successive years, and always, like a cat, falls on his feet..." This American image assures us "that with the exercise of self-trust, new powers shall appear..." And then Emerson finally says what his reader has suspected all along he wants to say, that each of us is a Christ: "a man is the word made flesh, born to shed healing to the nations..." Even discounting for his overheated prose, we find him captivated by the image of the self-made man, cut in the grain of American legend as much as Daniel Boone and John Wayne.

Emerson brings "Self-Reliance" to a close with this advice: "Insist on yourself; never imitate," but "be [your] own man," for "Society is a wave" and "Its unity is only phenomenal." "It is only as a man puts off all foreign support, and stands alone, that I see him to be strong and to prevail." The moral of Emerson's rhetoric seems to be that if we are having difficulty coping with life, it is because we have not been sufficiently self-reliant, self-trusting, and self-sufficient. If we have been defeated in life, we have no one but ourselves to blame. The recognition of powerlessness is only a capitulation to weakness of will.

There are certainly alcoholics (recovering and otherwise, in A.A. and out) who do wrong with bad intent, but alcoholics in general are not evil people (any more than human beings in general are), nor do they have weaker wills than the average human being. They have pummeled themselves, and they have gravely harmed the people who have crossed their tornado-like paths. Alcoholics Anonymous gives an account, in terms of moral psychology and spirituality, of why this is so. But that account pursues a strategy just the opposite of the aristocratic doctrine of self-reliance and self-sufficiency. It is precisely because self-reliance and self-sufficiency have not worked that a radically different strategy needs to be pursued. This is a strategy of humble submission to a power greater than the self. The A.A. conception of leadership is grounded in an experience of surrender. And the gesture of surrender to a power that is not oneself entails the idea that leadership is not an exercise of personal power at all. The individual will to power is forsaken. The locus of power shifts to "a loving God as He may express Himself in [the] group conscience."

So far, the argument has been that there is an aristocratic conception of leadership that can be democratic as well as elitist (for example, the one that can be gleaned from the writings of Emerson, as opposed to his English friend, Thomas Carlyle); that it runs deep in the American tradition; that it is based on an attitude toward human life that places the highest premium on self-reliance and self-sufficiency; that it tends toward self-apotheosis; and that it tends to blur the distinction between the human and divine orders, with the consequence of romanticizing the extent to which we make ourselves. Its principle of hierarchy is not the nakedly aggressive one of Hobbes's leviathan, because it subscribes to a nobler ideal than the modest aim of merely holding our darker impulses and baser passions in check by means of an externally imposed coercive power. It affirms human excellence, and contemporary readers of Emerson may strive to emulate the lofty model he portrays. In fact, it is hard to imagine a contemporary reader who identifies with "Self-Reliance" thinking of herself as too deeply flawed to aspire to the self-reliant end. But the portrait itself may be flawed if it draws only one side of the picture and fails to come to terms with the other side. We are challenged to make, regenerate, and transform ourselves through the continual exertion of will-power. In the aristocratic understanding of leadership, our leaders are the ones who light our paths. They have succeeded in exercising their own will to power. But the question persists, Is personal power the ultimate nexus of leadership? Our culture makes it extremely difficult not to answer yes.

As our brief consideration of Emerson showed, a certain type of humanism and individualism that celebrates our self-creative powers also tends to divinize the self. But once we have begun to tread this path, the question we must sooner or later face is whether the self is a worthy object of worship. If ordinary people who have not made a mess of their lives do not need to detain themselves long with this question, if it holds no urgency for them, if they have not been defeated by the overreaching vanity of their ambitions, if they are not tortured by their own hidden wish to be God, and if they rest contented and gracefully with the lot their lives have given them, then the experience of alcoholics, as narrated by the literature of Alcoholics Anonymous, dramatizes a pattern of human life in which it has become impossible to avoid calling the question on the sunny spirituality of the Emersonian creed.

For alcoholics, the only other alternative to surrender is a logic of denial, what Jack London calls the "White Logic" in his autobiography, *John Barleycorn.* He writes,

> How to describe this White Logic to those who have never experienced it? ... At once, O untraveled reader, you see how lunatic and blasphemous is the realm I am trying to describe to you in the language of John Barleycorn's tribe.... Alcohol tells truth, but its truth is not normal. What is normal is healthful. What is healthful tends towards life. Normal truth is a different order, and a lesser order, of truth.[32]

London drank himself to death. The self-defensive pride of his appeal to a greater order of truth betrays the hidden despair of failed self-reliance.

Alcoholics Anonymous did not exist when London wrote the tale of his own alcoholism in 1913. To admit the truth to himself that drinking had ruined his life was also to admit hopelessness. Still, in the last pages of his narrative, he cloaks his destitute misery and self-loathing in a self-justifying and implicitly self-aggrandizing testament to the uniqueness of his circumstances, and to the higher truth, inaccessible to mere mortals, of his "White Logic." He compares ordinary people to dray horses.

> Take a dray horse. Through all the vicissitudes of its life, from first to last, ... it must believe that life is good; that the drudgery in harness is good; that death, no matter how blind-instinctively apprehended, is a dread giant; ... that in the end, with fading life, it will not be knocked about and beaten and urged beyond its sprained and spavined best ... stumbling dizzily on through merciless servitude and slow disintegration to the end .... To the last stumble of its stumbling end this dray horse must abide by the mandates of the lesser truth that is the truth of life and makes it possible to persist.

London's sketch of the dray horse's miserable end betrays his characteristically alcoholic contempt for the mundane truths of common life. He only barely disguises what the reader can guess is his real view, that the "lesser truth" of daily life is a lie. Had he been able to find his way to A.A., there to sober up, and perhaps even to exercise an office of leadership as a "trusted servant," he might have been able also to learn about the redemptive hope there is in aspiring only to be a dray horse, a foot soldier, a common mortal, "a friend among friends, ... a worker among workers, ... a useful member of society."[33] But London could not detoxify, and therefore he could not accept the "lesser truth" of his own humanity.

London despises the dray horse precisely in virtue of its sanity and rationality, from which he finds himself debarred.

> This dray horse, ... like all other animals including man, is life-blinded and sense-struck. It will live, no matter what the price. The game of life is good, though all of life may be hurt, and though all lives lose the game in the end. This is the order of truth that obtains, not for the universe, but for the live things in it if they for a little space will endure ere they pass. This order of truth, no matter how erroneous it may be, is the sane and normal order of truth, the rational order of truth that life must believe in order to live.

The "White Logic" is based on the premise that the "lesser truth" that sane living requires is finally only the self-deception of the living. The ultimate truth for London addresses a universe unruled by a transcendent God. The "White Logic" whispers in London's ear through the succession of closing chapters, as he looks on the world with a "jaundiced eye." He cannot stand what he takes to be the universe's indifference to his being and having lived.

Toward the end of his story, London recounts a late afternoon's ride across his Sanoma ranch.

> Twilight is on, and the hunting-animals are out. I watch the piteous tragic play of life feeding on life. Here is no morality. Only in man is morality, and man created it--a code of action that makes toward living and that is of the lesser order of truth. Yet all this I knew before, in the weary days of my long sickness. These were the greater truths that I so successfully schooled myself to forget; the truths that were so serious that I refused to take them seriously...

The cognitive dissonance of this passage is almost palpable. London had aggrandized his despair by calling it the "White Logic" and proclaiming it a superior order of truth; but here, a note of honesty breaks into his denial. The truths of the lesser order, he begrudgingly admits, are really "greater truths" that he has "refused to take ... seriously." As an unrecovered alcoholic, he lived in defiance of the dray-horse morality, discontented with its ordinariness and sane humility, harboring secret dreams of becoming a god.

The question of the relationship between an author's life and what he writes is better left alone here, but London's alcoholic death is not irrelevant to the character of his "White Logic." Only months away from his early grave, he concludes his "alcoholic memoirs:"

> The White Logic now lies decently buried alongside the Long Sickness. Neither will afflict me again. It is many a year since I laid the Long Sickness away; his sleep is sound. And just as sound is the sleep of the White Logic. And yet, in conclusion, I can well say that I wish my forefathers had banished John Barleycorn before my time. I regret that John Barleycorn flourished everywhere in the system of society in which I was born, else I should not have made his acquaintance, and I was long trained in his acquaintance.[34]

Since London died of alcoholism, these lines, which seem to announce a kind of personal triumph and overcoming, are really a testament to the quietude of despair, the sort of calm we frequently hear overtakes the final hours of suicides, as they turn in their resignations from life. London's daughter, Joan, characterized her father's book as an exercise in "self-justification."[35] It also belongs to the literature of Kierkegaard's "sickness unto death," "despairingly willing to be oneself," to which "all despair can in the last analysis be reduced..."[36]

Kierkegaard expresses the alternative to despair this way:

> This then is the formula which describes the condition of the self when despair is completely eradicated: by relating itself to its own self and by willing to be itself the self is grounded transparently in the Power which posited it.[37]

According to Kierkegaard, the self that is not in despair is the one that recognizes that it is *not* self-constituting. In short, the way to despair is charted by way of a project of taking oneself for one's own creator; and the way to freedom from despair is charted by the frank recognition of one's creaturehood. One must have failed in the attempt toward self-reliance and self-sufficiency to grasp this election in so basic an antithesis.

In his presentation of "The Sick Soul" in Lectures VI and VII of *The Varieties of Religious Experience*, William James lays out the alternatives of the soul-sick in terms virtually identical to Kierkegaard's. James's book has had an incomparable influence on Alcoholics Anonymous, first of all because of its pluralism, its undogmatic openness to the vast array of human spiritual experiences. In the appendix on "Spiritual Experience" in the "Big Book," appeal is made to the authority of James to assure its membership that no one particular type of spiritual experience is canonical or necessary, to the exclusion of other types.[38]

One leitmotif of *The Varieties of Religious Experience* is a distinction James borrowed from Francis W. Newman and made famous, between the "once-born" "twice-born."[39] Whereas the "religion of healthy-mindedness" is more or less for the once-born, the soul-sick face a desperate alternative: either to despair, or to be reborn. Experiencing themselves as powerless over their condition, demoralized and hopeless, their well-being urgently depends on a conversion experience.

James defines "religion" experientially rather than ecclesiastically: it consists in "the feelings, acts, and experiences of individual [people] ... so far as they apprehend themselves to stand in relation to whatever they may consider the divine." Therefore, the Emersonian creed qualifies as a religion. James compares it to the atheism of Buddhism. "Modern transcendental idealism, Emersonianism, for instance, also seems to let God evaporate into abstract Ideality. Not a deity *in concreto*, ... but the immanent divinity in things, the essentially spiritual structure of the universe, is the object of the transcendentalist cult." James quotes at length from Emerson's 1838 Divinity College address, "which made Emerson famous," and which gave "frank expression" to the "worship of mere abstract laws..." In that address, Emerson claimed, "If a man is at heart just, then in so far is he God." He also claimed that the spiritual law of nature "is the beatitude of man. It makes him illimitable." After quoting him, James summarizes:

> Such is the Emersonian religion. The universe has a divine soul of order, which soul is moral, being also the soul within the soul of man. But whether this soul of the universe be a mere quality like the eye's brilliancy or the skin's softness, or whether it be a self-conscious life like the eye's seeing or the skin's feeling, is a decision that never unmistakably appears in Emerson's pages. It quivers on the boundary of these things, sometimes leaning one way, sometimes the other, to suit the literary rather than the philosophic need.

The once-born can afford this ambiguity; the soul-sick cannot. For the latter, the question whether a "Power greater than ourselves"[40] really exists is existentially urgent, calling for a basic decision that amounts to the difference between hope and despair.

Emerson's cult of the self lays the source of our difficulties squarely on our own backs. If self-reliance fails us, then we have simply failed to make connection with the latent divinity within. Like Emerson, A.A. also teaches that "our troubles ... are basically of our own making."[41] But it does not draw Emerson's inference that we are "begirt with laws which execute themselves."[42] Emerson believes we must willfully go out of our way to experience evil as a practical difficulty.[43] The inference implicitly follows that evil, suffering, tragedy, and weakness are voluntarily induced conditions brought on by a certain perversion of will that does not exert itself in the right way or to the right degree. The experience St. Paul recounts in the seventh chapter of his letter to the Romans--"What a wretched man I am! Who will rescue me from this body doomed to death?"[44]--lies beyond the grasp of Emerson's prose.

The experience of alcoholics confirms St. Paul rather than Emerson. Better self-knowledge and greater exertion of will prove insufficient to break the grip of their moral and spiritual malady. They require a conversion they find themselves incapable of achieving by their own power.

When James comes to the subject of conversion he distinguishes two modalities in which it may occur:

> There is thus a conscious and voluntary way and an involuntary and unconscious way in which mental results may get accomplished; and we find both ways exemplified in the history of conversion, giving us two types, ... the *volitional type* and the *type by self-surrender* respectively.

Although James does not say so, the creed of self-reliance and self-sufficiency belongs to the former type, while the spirituality of Alcoholics Anonymous is based on the latter.

> Even in the most voluntarily built-up sort of regeneration there are passages of partial self-surrender interposed; and in the great majority of all cases, when the will has done its uttermost towards bringing one close to the complete unification aspired after, it seems that the very last step must be left to other forces and performed without the help of its activity. In other words, self-surrender becomes then indispensable. "The personal will," says Dr. Starbuck, "must be given up. In many cases relief persistently refuses to come until the person ceases to resist, or to make an effort in the direction he desires to go."

James himself offers a quasi-physiological hypothesis to explain the well-documented and remarkable results of conversion by the "type of self-surrender:"

> "Man's extremity is God's opportunity" is the theological way of putting this fact of the need of self-surrender; whilst the physiological way of stating it would be, "Let one do all in one's power, and one's nervous system will do the rest." Both statements acknowledge the same fact.

James's epistemological and ontological pluralism intentionally leaves room for either kind of explanation, and his pragmatism makes him more interested in the fruits of conversion than in its origins. But self-surrender, which he claims to be "the vital turning-point of the religious life," is essentially the surrender of one's will to a power other than one's consciously conceived self. It is the experience that Tiebout called "ego reduction" and that members of A.A. describe as "hitting bottom." It is a necessary component of the recovery process A.A. delineates in its well-known "Twelve Steps."

James writes,

> So long as the egoistic worry of the sick soul guards the door, the expansive confidence of the soul of faith gains no presence. But let the former faint away, even but for a moment, and the latter can profit by the opportunity, and having once acquired possession, may retain it.

According to A.A.'s lay moral psychology, alcoholics exemplify an especially acute case of "the egoistic worry of the sick soul." As the "Big Book" puts it, "the alcoholic is an extreme example of self-will run riot."[45] Whatever the precise medical status of alcoholism, the "Big Book" insists, "Our liquor was but a symptom. So we had to get down to causes and conditions." It regards these causes and conditions as essentially spiritual in character.

In the chapter of the "Big Book" entitled, "There Is A Solution," A.A. members are told,

> Almost none of us liked the self-searching, the leveling of our pride, the confession of shortcomings which the process [of recovery through the twelve steps] requires for its successful consummation. But we saw that it really worked in others, and we had come to believe in the hopelessness and futility of life as we had been living it. When, therefore, we were approached by those in whom the problem had been solved, there was nothing left for us but to pick up the simple kit of spiritual tools laid at our feet.... The great fact is just this, and nothing less: That we have had deep and effective spiritual experiences which have revolutionized our whole attitude toward life, toward our fellows and toward God's universe. The central fact of our lives today is the absolute certainty that our Creator has entered into our hearts and lives in a way which is indeed miraculous. He has commenced to accomplish those things for us which we could never do by ourselves.[46]

The repeated message of A.A. to alcoholics is that their only alternatives are despair or conversion ("there is no middle-of-the-road solution"), that conversion requires self-surrender, and that the process of surrender requires "the leveling of our pride," or "ego reduction," in order to be effective. The millions who have recovered from their hopeless condition in this way are witnesses to its efficacy. But most of them were recalcitrant until they discovered in their own experience that the "volitional type" of moral and spiritual transformation would not work for them.

> Many of us had moral and philosophical convictions galore, but we could not live up to them even though we would have liked to. Neither could we reduce our self-centeredness much by wishing or trying on our own power. We had to have God's help.... First of all, we had to quit playing God. It didn't work.

Self-will, self-reliance, self-sufficiency, and volitional effort prove repeatedly to be of no avail, despite good intentions. Their failure is what authorizes the alcoholic to try a radically different tack.

Later in *The Varieties of Religious Experience*, James, who for the most part takes a position of descriptive neutrality, suggests a preference for the type of conversion that involves surrender of self rather than greater self-exertion. His bias is not overwhelming, but it surfaces in the margins of his text at least twice, both times in footnotes. Emerson explicitly figures in the first occasion, and implicitly in the second.[47] In these footnotes, James is careful not to inflate his point, but we can guess from his discussion of self-surrender that he believed the Emersonian creed of self-reliance to be deficient to the extent that it evades the question alcoholics sidestep only at their peril, namely, What happens when self-reliance fails? The "wider and completer"[48] view of human life, James suggests in the second of the footnotes, is one that is capable of coming to terms with our creaturehood and finitude as much as it celebrates the excellences and triumphs of our self-creative powers. This is the outlook in which humility is genuinely a virtue.

James argues that within human experience, there is a precariously balanced ideal of creative self-exertion and creaturely submission. Ralph Barton Perry, in his study of *The Thought and Character of William James*, credits James himself with having two kinds of faith, one corresponding to the efficacy of human will, the other to its limits. The former, "characteristic of *The Will to Believe*," is "the faith that springs from strength."[49] This is the faith of the once-born: volitional and virtually Emersonian. But:

> The second is the faith that springs from human weakness, and asks for refuge and security. In the fighting faith religion is a stimulant to the will; the comforting faith, on the other hand, is at the bottom of one's heart, relaxing. Though one may row with great earnestness, one is aware of being carried to port--safely, inexorably--by the very current in which one floats. The need for this sort of faith James understood both from his own periodic weariness and from his sympathy with that extremity and tragic plight which is the common lot of man. To this second faith, the comforting faith, James devoted special attention in the Gifford Lectures [i.e., *The Varieties of Religious Experience*].

Had James not suffered and known something of soul-sickness firsthand, he may not have been able to be "sympathetic with the morbid feelings of others." Perry writes that James's "own 'salvation' came through self-reliance and the idea of moral freedom, rather than through a sense of supporting grace," but he also had a keen ear and deep appreciation for the pattern of life that claims to be sustained by grace.

Once among the fellowship of other recovering alcoholics in A.A., its members characteristically report their own experience of "the comforting faith." They overcome their inner anarchy of spirit, their condition of "self-will run riot," by turning their lives over to the care of a "Power" greater than themselves, typically but not necessarily conceived as God. This act of surrender is what sustains them in their recovery. No particular canon of belief is required, except for the conviction, grounded in their own experience of having failed in the art of living, that they are not themselves the power to which they must submit.

The "Big Book" claims that "something like half" of the original members of A.A. "thought we were atheists or agnostics."[50] This occasions the appearance in the book of a chapter entitled "We Agnostics." But the chapter begins by addressing the alcoholic condition generally:

> If a mere code of morals or a better philosophy of life were sufficient to overcome alcoholism, many of us would have recovered long ago. But we found that such codes and philosophies did not save us, no matter how much we tried. We could wish to be moral, we would wish to be philosophically comforted, in fact, we could will these things with all our might, but the needed power wasn't there. Our human resources, as marshalled by the will, were not sufficient; they failed utterly. Lack of power, that was our dilemma. We had to find a power by which we could live, and it had to be a *Power greater than ourselves*. Obviously. But where and how were we to find this Power? Well, that's exactly what this book is about.[51]

The twelve steps of A.A.'s program of recovery have as their aim a "spiritual awakening" through which its members make "conscious contact" with that "Power."[52] The motives underlying this process of self-transformation have less to do with the desire to be good than with the dire straits of failed self-reliance.

The experience of personal powerlessness leads directly to the alternative conception of leadership adopted by A.A. Since its leaders are also members, they must learn to forsake the "strong man" ideal of the aristocratic conception of leadership. The locus of power lies not in the individual but in the group. The basic mechanism of government is the "informed group conscience" briefly portrayed in the opening pages of this essay. If Emerson's exuberant, "sturdy lad from New Hampshire or Vermont" is the protagonist of an American myth, then Jack London, living on the rim of the American west, is his alter ego. Bill Wilson, from Vermont, aspired to Emerson's ideal, to be his own man, to go his own way, to call his own shots. He would have suffered London's fate of hopelessness and despair, had it not been for the "vital spiritual experience" in late 1934. His own vocation to leadership arose from the transformation that saved his life, in no small part by stripping him of his desire to be God. A.A.'s second tradition, which summarizes A.A.'s conception of leadership as service, is grounded in this experience: self-government, shared responsibility, collective authority; a model that works, just to the extent that we gratefully recall our humanity.

Notes

1. The "Preamble" of Alcoholics Anonymous states that it "is not allied with any sect, denomination, politics, organization or institution; does not wish to engage in any controversy; neither endorses nor opposes any causes." This means, among other things, that there is no "canonical" or officially sanctioned view of what leadership is or implies within A.A. Therefore, the views expressed

in this essay are entirely my own. Where they are either controversial or erroneous, the fault is mine and should not be attributed to A.A.

2. Huxley is quoted in *'Pass It On': The Story of Bill Wilson and How the A.A. Message Reached the World* (New York: Alcoholics Anonymous World Services, Inc., 1984), p. 368. *'Pass It On'* is part of a body of "A.A. General Service Conference-approved literature," and as such we can regard it as Wilson's authorized biography. Another very good biography of Wilson is written by Robert Thomsen, *Bill W.* (New York: Harper and Row, 1975). For a good general history of A.A., see Ernest Kurtz, *A.A.: The Story* (San Francisco: Harper and Row, 1979, 1988).

3. *Twelve Steps and Twelve Traditions* (New York: Alcoholics Anonymous World Services, Inc., 1952), p. 53. In General Service Conference-approved literature, authors remain unnamed, in keeping with the A.A. practice of anonymity on the level of press, radio, films, and television. The author of this work is Wilson himself.

4. A.A.'s "Twelve Traditions" are published in several formats. One convenient place to find them listed is in the basic text of A.A., *Alcoholics Anonymous*, 3d ed. (New York: Alcoholics Anonymous World Services, Inc., 1976), p. 564. This work is commonly known as the "Big Book," which is how I will cite it below.

5. See the "Big Book," p. 62; and see also *Twelve Steps and Twelve Traditions*, p. 37. Here Bill summarizes his attitude toward the philosophy of self-sufficiency. "We are certain that our intelligence, backed by willpower, can rightly control our inner lives and guarantee us success in the world we live in. This brave philosophy, wherein each man plays God, sounds good in the speaking, but it still has to meet the acid test: how well does it actually work? One good look in the mirror ought to be answer enough for any alcoholic.... The philosophy of self-sufficiency is not paying off."

6. "The A.A. Group," revised (New York: Alcoholics Anonymous World Services, Inc., 1990), pp. 34-35.

7. This important formulation is cited from the "Preamble," quoted in n.1 above, printed in several forums including the inside cover of any A.A. pamphlet. Its copyright is held by A.A.'s monthly journal, The A.A. Grapevine, Inc. The "Preamble" states in its entirety: "Alcoholics Anonymous is a fellowship of men and women who share their experience, strength and hope with each other that they may solve their common problem and help others to recover from alcoholism. The only requirement for membership is a desire to stop drinking. There are no dues or fees for A.A. membership; we are self-supporting through our own contributions. A.A. is not allied with any sect, denomination, politics, organization or institution; does not wish to engage in any controversy; neither endorses nor opposes any causes. Our primary purpose is to stay sober and help other alcoholics to achieve sobriety."

8. *'Pass It On'*, p. 176.

9. Chuck "C," *A New Pair of Glasses* (Irvine, CA: New-Look Publ. Co., 1984), p. 44 *et passim*.

10. *'Pass It On'*, p. 177.

11. These three words derive from the same Indo-European root, denoting earth.

12. Tiebout was among the first psychiatrists to endorse the program of A.A. He first came into contact with the program through his patient, Marty Mann, who went on to found the National Council on Alcoholism. Tiebout wrote several papers on alcoholism in the nineteen-forties and fifties. One of them, originally delivered to the American Psychiatric Association in 1943, is included in *Alcoholics Anonymous Comes of Age: A Brief History of A.A.* (New York: Alcoholics Anonymous World Services, Inc., 1957), published to commemorate the event of A.A.'s twentieth anniversary convention in St. Louis, where Bill officially divested himself of the movement's leadership; see pp. 309-19 ("Therapeutic Mechanism of Alcoholics Anonymous"). Tiebout also gave a talk in St. Louis, published on pp. 245-51.

13. For one account, see "Bill's Story" in the "Big Book," pp. 1-16. And for a more detailed description of the experience itself, see *'Pass It On'*, pp. 120-21.

14. *A.A. Comes of Age* is, in effect, a documentary record of that convention.

15. Again, see A.A.'s "Preamble."

16. The traditions most directly addressing professionalization are the eighth and ninth.

17. This formulation appears in the "Preamble" and it is also the third tradition.

18. The "Big Book" refers to the twelve steps as "steps ... suggested as a program of recovery" when they are first presented to the reader on pp. 59-60. In keeping with the A.A. philosophy of authority, the steps could not be other than "suggested," even though members who have "worked" them will typically experience them as requirements, in order to achieve and maintain their sobriety.

19. *A.A. Comes of Age*, pp. 110-11.

20. With respect to St. Francis, mention should also be made of Bill's discussion of the eleventh step in *Twelve Steps and Twelve Traditions*. The eleventh step states that A.A. members "Sought through prayer and meditation to improve our conscious contact with God *as we understood Him*, praying only for knowledge of His will for us and the power to carry that out." In his chapter on the eleventh step, Bill offers advice on how to take it. There, he presents the Prayer of St. Francis as a model (see pp. 99-100), without mentioning Francis by name. He writes of the prayer, "Its author was a man who for several hundred years now has been rated as a saint. We won't be biased or scared off by that fact, because although he was not an alcoholic he did, like us, go through the emotional wringer. And as he came out the other side of that painful experience, this prayer was his expression of what he could then see, feel, and wish to become..." The prayer follows. Within A.A., it is known as the "eleventh step prayer." With respect to St. Ignatius, I should at least mention Fr. Ed Dowling, S.J., a Jesuit priest who befriended Wilson and acted as his spiritual director. Dowling had the conviction that the spirituality of A.A. was virtually identical with the spirituality of St. Ignatius's "spiritual exercises." Several accounts of Fr. Dowling's place in A.A. history are available; but see in particular Bill's introduction of his address to the St. Louis convention in *A.A. Comes of Age*, pp. 253-54.

21. *A.A. Comes of Age*, p. 120.

22. Bill's articles for the *Grapevine* are anthologized in *The Language of the Heart* (New York: Alcoholics Anonymous World Services, Inc., 1988); for this quotation, see p. 40.

23. For A.A.'s organizational chart, see *The A.A. Service Manual*, 1990-91 ed. (New York: Alcoholics Anonymous World Services, Inc., 1990), p. S23.

24. *The Language of the Heart*, pp. 32-34.

25. Ibid., p. 35.

26. Thomas Hobbes, "Leviathan," included in *The English Philosophers from Bacon to Mill* (New York: Random House, 1939), p. 161.

27. The "Big Book," p. 62.

28. Hobbes, "Leviathan," p. 174.

29. For an account of how western societies dealt with their alcoholics prior to the advent of A.A., see Bill Pittman, *A.A.: The Way It Began* (Seattle, WA: Glen Abbey Books, 1988), pp. 26-112; and for penal and punitive treatments in particular, see pp. 27-34.

30. See Hobbes, "Leviathan," pp. 164, 172.

31. Ralph Waldo Emerson, "Self-Reliance," in *The Collected Works of Ralph Waldo Emerson* II, ed. Joseph Slater, Alfred R. Ferguson, and Jean Ferguson Carr (Cambridge, MA: Harvard University Press, 1979), p. 28. Quotes in this and the next four paragraphs are from pp. 28-50 of this edition.

32. Jack London, *John Barleycorn: Alcoholic Memoirs* (Santa Cruz, CA: Western Tanager Press, 1981; orig. 1913), pp. 303-05. Quotes from London in the next four paragraphs are from pp. 305-15 of this edition.

33. See n.3 above.

34. London, *John Barleycorn*, p. 343. James B. Hall writes an "Afterword" to London's text (pp. 345-59) in which he examines the cause of London's death and makes it clear that it was alcoholism that killed him.

35. Quoted by Hall, ibid., p. 357.

36. Soren Kierkegaard, "The Sickness Unto Death," included in *"Fear and Trembling" and "The Sickness Unto Death,"* trans. Walter Lowrie (Princeton: Princeton University Press, 1954), p. 147.

37. Ibid., p. 147.

38. See the "Big Book," the second appendix on "Spiritual Experience," pp. 569-70. For James's influence on Wilson and Alcoholics Anonymous see *'Pass It On'*, pp. 124-25 ("[Bill] would later say that James, though long in his grave, had been a founder of Alcoholics Anonymous"), and pp. 197-99; in *A.A. Comes of Age*, see pp. 13, 64, 160 ("Most of the basic ideas [behind the twelve steps] had come from the Oxford Groups, William James, and Dr. Silkworth"), and 262-65, which includes quotation from the *Varieties* on the subject of "self-surrender"; and see also Pittman, *A.A.: The Way It Began*, pp. 170-73.

39. See William James, *The Varieties of Religious Experience* (New York: New American Library, 1958), pp. 77-78. Quotes from James in the next six paragraphs are from pp. 42-44 and 170-173 of this edition.

40. The second step is, "Came to believe that a Power greater than ourselves could restore us to sanity."

41. The "Big Book," p. 62.

42. Emerson, "Spiritual Laws," in Slater, et al., *The Collected Works* II, note 31 above, p. 79.

43. Ibid., see pp. 77-79: Emerson has many good things to say, and his optimism is fetching; it is just that his doctrine "that we miscreate our own evils"

is not an especially helpful solution to those whose experience falls outside the pale of his argument, the ones James calls the "soul-sick," who (perhaps only latently) *know* they have a problem, and *want* to do something about it, but who find that their best efforts are of no avail, and who have reached the situation in life that the "Big Book" describes as "pitiful and incomprehensible demoralization" (p. 30), a condition in which virtually all who come into A.A. find themselves.

44. Rom. 7:24.

45. The "Big Book," p. 62. The following quote is on p. 64.

46. Ibid., p. 25. The quotes in the next paragraph are on pp. 25 and 62.

47. James, *Varieties*, p. 193, n.6; and p. 369, n.2; the first of these notes quotes Emerson from "Spiritual Laws" (note 42 above, p. 78); in the second, James returns again to the distinction between the once-born and twice-born. There, he argues, quoting a "Dr. Channing," that "the outlook upon life of the twice-born--holding as it does more of the element of evil in solution--is the wider and completer.... Evil is not evaded, but sublated..."

48. Ibid.

49. Ralph Barton Perry, *The Thought and Character of William James* II (Boston: Little, Brown and Co., 1935), p. 324. Quotes in the rest of this paragraph are from this edition.

50. The "Big Book," p. 44.

51. Ibid., pp. 44-45.

52. The eleventh step encourages "conscious contact"; see n.20 above. The twelfth step asserts, "Having had a spiritual awakening as the result of these steps, we tried to carry this message to alcoholics, and to practice these principles in all our affairs."

Chapter 6

A Democratic Model of Leadership: Politics in an All Female Community

Eloise A. Buker

A Problem: Leading and Empowering Citizens

How much democracy is a good thing?[1] In our culture, many citizens experience a tension between their desire to be part of a democratic process in which they share in governance and their desire to live in smoothly operating societies in which they have to give very little attention to issues of governance. This tension occurs at all levels of government--in struggles between the Congress and Presidency, between state and county governments, between city councils and mayors. In governance in both public and private organizations the tension emerges--between democratic party officials and their members, between university faculties and their administrators, and between employers and their employees.

For our political leaders, this tension creates a particular difficulty. We want them to be heroes and heroines who charge ahead and energize us to follow, but we also want them to refrain from controlling or bossing us. As our leaders charge ahead, they may turn around and find us not only not following but complaining about the direction in which they are heading. This makes leading a very challenging task within our democratic context. Leaders embody authority and hierarchy while we ask them to create democratic, egalitarian relationships. Many women's organizations experience this problem intensely because of the high value women place on participation. This value may come about from women's more recent acquisition of credentials to participate in public life at all, since U. S. women got the vote only in 1920 and still comprise only about five percent of the Congress. Or it may be a result of women's socialization which emphasizes relationships over rules and principles of conduct.[2] Whatever the cause, this problem preoccupies various women's organizations, including those at the forefront of the women's movement. Because, historically, it is also a problem in American politics, some insights from the struggles and tensions within women's organizations can provide a model of leadership that will enable us to understand how U.S. leaders can work productively with this tension.

This essay reflects on women's organizations; it offers a model of leadership designed to respond to the problem of democratic leadership. Three experiences inform this model. First is the study of political science which sets out the basic issue. Central to political science is a perennial question: What is the best relationship between the citizen and the ruler, between the leader and the follower?[3] While we in America have chosen a democratic republic form of rule, we are not certain what that means in terms of the relationship between our citizens and our rulers. We want leaders to embody both democratic values that invite participation and hierarchical values that maximize efficiency and operational ease. Political science tells us that power can emerge from relationships and the bonds among group members as well as from hierarchical relationships in which rules control members. To the degree that we exercise our responsibilities of citizenship, we each act to shape our political environment.

My operating assumption is that all of us at various points in our lives take up the call to leadership as a part of our roles as citizens. My hope is that the democratic model of leadership that I am proposing will offer one practical way of responding to that call when it comes and that it will reveal something about each reader's own story and possibilities for leadership.

A second experience is the research on leadership which I conducted in an all-female organization which has been operating successfully for over one hundred years and so gives some insights into how to respond to this perennial question. The women of this organization are professionals who live together and share their income with each other. They are the Sisters of the Holy Names of Jesus and Mary, a Roman Catholic order, with a provincial headquarters in Spokane, Washington. These sisters are especially concerned about the tension between hierarchy and horizontal relationships because since the 1960's and Vatican II, they have been moving from a steep hierarchical structure to a more democratic one.[4] Perhaps these sisters' lives might be thought of as one of the "villages" to explore as we follow Jane Rinehart's story about the trip down the river.*

A third experience develops out of my own work in feminist organizations. This experience has alerted me to the problems involved in reconciling our desire for democratic participation and our desire to act effectively to achieve our goals. Feminist organizations have emphasized broad-based

---

* Jane A. Rinehart, "Learning to Lead."

political participation by members within horizontal networks of power as an alternative to simple hierarchical bureaucratic structures of governance. They encounter tensions working within bureaucratic structures while at the same time pressing for democratic participation. Hence, they seek a model of leadership that avoids oppressive, hierarchical control mechanisms of leadership, while retaining the capacity to exercise authority. In the abstract this may appear simple. However, in the reality of day-to-day decisions, our modern fast-paced American culture often leaves very little time or desire for consultation or reflection about decisions. The question political science raises here is: how can power be shared? The democratic model of leadership I propose is informed by this struggle.

Men and Women Readers

In the past, we have often "equated leadership with masculinity."[5] I hope that all readers--both men and women--will find ways to be leaders. As humans, it is our vocation to lead each other. Women are not naturally better leaders, nor are men. Our biology, our life in male or female bodies, does not determine our leadership style. Leadership is not determined by the shape of one's skin but depends on the quality of the relationships among members, and on their ethics, commitments, educations, and skills. However, while women are accustomed to taking male experiences and applying them to their own lives, men have had less opportunity for drawing upon the experiences of women. This essay suggests that men may apply to their own lives the lessons in leadership gleaned from women's experiences. Of course, the fact that I need to make this point underscores the ways in which female activities have been ignored, for studies of male groups do not often contain similar invitations to their female readers.

Developing a Democratic Model of Leadership

Because women's organizations struggle to find ways in which their leadership can emerge from the bonds among members rather than from a hierarchical pattern of authority, the model of leadership they use emphasizes relationships over rules and procedures. To explain the insights gleaned from these women's organizations, I shall present a model of leadership that emphasizes five qualities: responsive citizenship, connected cosmologies, mutual dependence, democratic decision-making, and companionship in home life.

Responsive Citizenship: Responsibility and American Politics

To develop a democratic model of leadership, it is necessary to begin with a model of citizenship. Because collaboration between "leaders" and "followers" requires an understanding of "followers" as active participants who shape the organization or community, active participation is what modern democratic thinkers call citizenship. In a democratic society that places civic responsibilities in the hands of all citizens and takes pride in disconnecting itself from old-world notions of royalty--kings, queens, lords, and ladies--the connection between leadership and citizenship is vital. As citizens, we cannot turn over the business of rule to others and withdraw from public life. We are all vital components in the American system, and the work of citizenship expected of us by our foremothers and forefathers goes far beyond simply casting a vote. For each of us, being called to serve as a leader is part of our cultural heritage. This understanding of citizenship as part of the fabric of our everyday life is very similar to the model of leadership presented in Jane Rinehart's notion of a web of relationships and in Bob Waterman's depiction of the town meeting.*

This part of our American heritage has its roots in Western culture, especially in the political philosophy of Plato and Aristotle. It was a guiding principle for Aristotle's work, even though he himself was highly suspicious of democratic processes. Aristotle defined a citizen as a "man" who rules and is ruled in turn to produce a good and just society.[6] Citizenship, as Aristotle saw it, is not simply residing in a locality. It involves responsibilities for ruling or leading, commitments to moving society closer to justice, and involvement in a set of relationships within a political community that encourages the practice of civic virtues. However, both Aristotle and our American founders explicitly excluded women from political leadership. So, my focus in this essay on women and leadership both draws from our heritage and invites us to rethink it.

In rethinking citizenship and leadership, the story of Sister Cathy Beckley, a Holy Names Sister, is helpful because she shows us how a citizen can act on her own initiative to make life better for deprived citizens. She does this on sharply limited budgets and without extensive organizational support, but she is still able to secure a place for herself and her group in Spokane's local civic life. Her leadership develops out of her own commitments to justice; and she relies upon a set of relationships and friendships in which commitment to civic virtue is taken for granted. Although she is not a man, she does exemplify Aristotle's model of the good citizen.

Sister Cathy has been a Holy Names Sister for about twenty years and has a masters degree in social work. She had been working as a counselor for a Catholic organization in Spokane for several years when she felt drawn to address the social needs of the city's street women.

---

* Rinehart, "Learning to Lead," and Bob Waterman, "We Need Not Be Ruled by Leaders."

First, she considered employment in already established institutions which had accepted some responsibility for addressing such needs. But nothing seemed right because the programs she encountered were not sufficiently directed toward *empowering* street women, although some were directed toward *helping* them. After talking with about 100 people whose work or other life patterns brought them in touch with street women, she formed the idea of founding a drop-in center for women in downtown Spokane near the bus station where many street people congregate. She then spent six months trying to find funding for such a center. She met many closed doors, but the more she talked to people, the more she saw the need for what she had in mind.

Finally a sister and friend said, "Cathy, you just have to do it. You are ready; do it." While trying to set up the center, she had been supporting herself by serving as a counselor to a few clients in her home. All sisters need to make sufficient funds to support themselves and contribute to the economy of the organization, which must be financially independent. Therefore, sisters do not have the luxury of working without pay. Sister Cathy decided to earn her income through private counseling. The flexible hours afforded her time to give to her drop-in project. She found a building owner willing to donate a street front area. Friends helped clean the place and refurbish the space and also donated funds for its operation. She opened her doors with $150 per month drawn from donations.

Sister Cathy describes her first three days as a "marathon." The women rushed to tell their stories, generating an intense nonstop conversation. She feared some would be turned off by this intensity, but she let the women determine the pace. She designed the center for all types of women. It brings together recovering middle-class women with working-class women. Their recovery includes overcoming problems with drugs, sexual abuse, poverty, homelessness, divorce, and other pains that threaten to break women's spirits. Relying on the AA twelve-step program for its approach and organizational structure, the center emphasizes honesty and mutual support. Many of the women involved in the center are friends of Sister Cathy's from a middle-class meditation group, including professional women and Catholic Sisters, but it remains a center for street women. Because the center operates as a peer support group, there is not much distinction between "clients" and "managers." Her friends make donations of time and money. There are various programs for recovering women that bring in the expertise of women doctors, potters, lawyers, academics. The center, a mix of brightly colored, newly made slipcovers and old torn furniture, is not fancy or spiffy; it is just comfortable, even plain. Sr. Cathy coordinates the work of the drop-in center with the work of another Sister who runs a home for battered women and women in transition. After four months of the center's operation, the local news media did several stories about the center, Catholic Services promised some funding for her salary, and the building's owners were seeking a grant to support the center. The street people, including the pimps, have accepted the center as a part of their lives. The center is not the target of malicious property destruction, which would indicate alienation and lack of support. Both street people and business people appreciate her work because the center provides a vital personal space for street women. Part of the reason it works has to do with Sr. Cathy's leadership approach. To her "clients" she explains that the center is "ours." To me she explained that there was more disclosure about personal life here than she had found in any other setting. She claims that she is as dependent upon the women as they are on her. Two women, who have worked with her from the beginning, serve informally as assistant managers and confidants. The women who use the center take responsibility for the conversation sessions, clean-up, and other tasks, but Sister Cathy is in charge. In overseeing the center, she has to pay attention to keeping it a safe place, since many of the neighbors experience severe stress. If there is a problem, she intervenes and sets limits. If outsiders threaten the center, the women themselves intervene. There is a punching bag for letting off steam and there are strict rules against violence. While some of these rules are necessary, what is significant about Sr. Cathy's leadership is its gentle but assertive tone and her ability to bring these women into active participation in the organization. These women are learning more than to recover from abuses; they are learning to affirm their own power and to become efficacious citizens. She describes her authority as a "leaven" that inspires others to act.

The center empowers each woman to be a more fully productive, creative citizen, and it gives Spokane a new forum for public life. Sr. Cathy has created an institutional structure that was not there before, and in this sense she is an example of a transformational leader.[7] Manifesting some of the old western frontier spirit of "can do," she did not wait for someone to solve the problem; she initiated the solution. In this spirit she found new territory by turning slum areas into productive spaces. But her case is different from many other downtown reconstruction projects because she does not turn out the poor to make room for middle-class citizens; nor does she simply fix up the poor. She is giving them an opportunity to organize themselves to obtain a voice in city life.

Who Are We? Cosmologies, Human Nature and Leading

To understand what makes this possible, it is necessary to move from our understanding of citizenship to a model of human nature. Each of us has a cosmology--a sense of how we as individual citizens fit into a community, the state, the universe. Citizenship is one piece of the puzzle, and cosmology is another piece. From my experiences with these sisters and feminist organizations, I have pieced together a cosmology that gives credit to and supports democratic leadership.

Every organizational structure is nested in a worldview or cosmology--an order of things, an explanation about how the world works--and a commitment to realizing certain goals. For example, a business is committed to making a profit and works from a model of how human nature is constituted in order to build an economy based upon product, labor, and profit. In some respects this fits with our liberal model of human beings as individuals, motivated by desires to improve our own situations.

Rose Mary Volbrecht contrasts a model of leadership that emphasizes hierarchy and technical learning with a model of leadership that emphasizes relationships and apprenticeship.* Tom Jeannot describes the liberal view of human nature which develops out of a notion of leadership that emphasizes autonomy, self-reliance and independence.** The liberal self-made person learns to rise above others and to be free of dependency. One can think of other examples within American society that emphasize independence and autonomy as a worldview--a cosmological scheme based on moving up the ladder of success, of "making" it on one's own. An inheritance of the great Enlightenment, this view of human nature places humans at its center and sees human reason as its divine force. This "secular humanism," as some have called it, delights when humans overcome adversity and win. It understands power as the exercise of control over other persons and over one's environment.

In contrast, the cosmology of the Holy Names Sisters does not emphasize individual independence or self-reliance. Rather than having humans as the power center, their power center is a mysterious force which might be called God, the Goddess, the Good, or Love or Justice. It manifests itself in the bonds of affection among members which transcend individuals. They are not self-made persons, but persons who are made through interactions with others. These interactions produce a shared vision, a value system, and rests on a shared commitment that they will spend their lives devoted to their relationships with each other and to their collective work. This means that their energy is devoted to working through difficulties since their commitment to each other and to their work is for life; they cannot simply move on if relationships are difficult or the work does not go well. In their situation, power is not a quality possessed by an individual but is the product of community interaction.[8] In this regard their cosmology is similar to that of many feminist organizations which emphasize sisterhood, mutual support, and bonding relationships. Furthermore, it resembles many of the values articulated by ecofeminism.[9] These philosophical approaches also fit with Western classical notions of the body politic developed by Rousseau, notions of community developed by Marx, and classical conservative notions of politics that emphasize our responsibility to and for others.

---

* Rose Mary Volbrecht, "Careful Mutuality."
** Tom Jeannot, "'But Trusted Servants'."

These sisters focus on the community as an interwoven set of relationships and elicit a cosmology that emphasizes the ways in which humans are connected to and responsible for each other. In that context, leadership has a relational quality that emphasizes these connections. Building on cosmological connections, the sisters emphasize mutual dependence* rather than independence. But it is not enough to simply say persons are connected. It is necessary to examine the nature of that connection in order to see how it might be possible to develop a democratic model of leadership.

Mutual Dependence

Mutual dependence is not mere need plus an exchange of commodities and services. Rather, it entails a community spirit which requires constant attention so that all citizens will identify themselves as both individuals and as members of the community. It might be helpful here to recall the discussion of mutuality by Bob Waterman** and his explanation of how mutuality supports good political relationships. The sisters' stories serve as an example of how a community spirit develops.

Making a Community

A common history binds the Holy Names sisters together and gives them a sense of unity. Their founding story comes readily to the lips of every member. The organization's founder, Eulalie Durocher, born in 1811 in Quebec, is now called Mother Marie Rose. She was born into a middle-class family and made herself known as a good student. In writing about these early childhood years, Sister Gertrude McLaughlin explains how Eulalie Durocher in her preteen years loved to learn and was skilled in serving as a housekeeper and hostess.[10] Education and home management were both important. These skills were further developed when she took over the management of the rectory where her brother served as a priest. Working with him, she developed a "special interest in the children and young women of the parish"[11] which is the mission of the Holy Names Sisters today. Durocher's own community began with bonding that developed out of her relationships with family and friends. In this sense, her personal life informed her professional relationships. Sister Gertrude McLaughlin describes Eulalie Durocher's leadership skills:

---

* Bob Waterman's development of mutuality is helpful here because many of the ways in which the sisters think about dependence is articulated by his notion of mutuality; see "We Need Not Be Ruled By Leaders" in this text.
** Ibid.

This innate gift of leadership was to grow with the years, so that even when she was a young girl, she was a source of inspiration to others.[12]

This reflection on their leader shows an appreciation for her ability to lead through inspiration, but equally important, by tracing their practices back to their foundress, the sisters build a common history that articulates shared values.

Early on in her work, Eulalie Durocher along with her long term friend and companion, Melodie Dufresne, made a private promise to live simply (articulated by the church as vows of poverty), to live a chaste virtuous life,[13] and to live a disciplined life (articulated as a vow of obedience).[14] These public promises forged their family bonds which made possible their primary work--to educate women so that they could make social changes.[15] The bishop, Ignace Bourget, helped Durocher to develop administrative skills which resulted in the founding of both the order and a school in 1843. A third woman was drawn to their work, and they signaled their new identities by new names: Sister Marie Rose, Sister Marie Agnes, and Sister Marie Madeleine. Others were drawn to join in a period of training which formed a small group of highly qualified women who lived and worked together in a home which served as a school. Only six years after the founding, Marie Rose died.

Two central values are important for understanding how leadership worked for these sisters. First, their founding was accomplished by three women with a common vision, even though their story emphasizes the special role of one woman. The Foundress herself lived only a short time after the founding, and if the community had depended upon her personality, it probably would not have survived. Instead, there was something about their relationship that made it work and that sustains the sisters today. In their stories they explain how each sister's work is a part of the work of the order--each one sees her own work as interwoven into the work of the others. Second, it is important to note that from the beginning the sisters integrated their home life, "family" life, with their other work. This will be discussed later.

Coming to Spokane

The Spokane sisters' story tells of a similar history. It begins with a small group of five sisters who came in 1888 to establish a school. In 1989, one hundred years later, their educational mission included the work of 29 teachers and other professionals, 16 administrators, 28 educational support staff, 13 musicians, 17 technical educational workers, 10 health care workers, 37 parish workers, and 29 in other types of service. In 1989 they had a convent which housed elderly sisters with an infirmary that was built dormitory-style; a second large dormitory style home for about 44 sisters was located near Gonzaga University; and scattered throughout Spokane were smaller homes where four to six sisters lived together.[16] Most of the sisters have bachelor degrees and beyond and work as professionals. They are mostly white middle-class women. While their activities are quite diverse and their political orientations may differ, they retain a communal life by sharing living spaces and economic resources.

Many feminist organizations also begin with a small band of five or so people working together. What is important is not so much their numbers but the strength of their bonds which gives energy to their work. While these programs do not involve shared living spaces or shared economic resources, there is a consistent desire to create authentic community. Community emerges in part through sharing a history about founding and building common values. While there is a desire for authentic relationships, there are tensions and differences. There is a suspicion of hierarchy and a fear that a leader will turn dictator. Mutual dependence which affirms egalitarian relationships can give way to bureaucratic organization, easing tensions but creating more distance in relationships. When this distance appears, the community is affirmed symbolically in the organizational *head*. Placing symbolic power in the head moves the organization toward hierarchy and away from democracy which can clash with founding values. If there is too little attention to internal community building and the egalitarian dimension of relationships, the original bonds grow weak and each person begins to operate as an individual rather than as a member of the community. The issue here is how to maintain the original mutual dependence while the organization both grows in size and responsibility and interacts with hierarchical structures which are not based upon mutual dependency.

Leading Is a Dependent Activity

Leaders *can* embody the original spirit while making use of bureaucratic structures that facilitate work. A perennial question that political scientists raise is how to develop an efficient bureaucratic structure that maintains a human face.[17] In the case of the Holy Names Sisters, the key is their relationship to the foundress. The foundress, Mother Marie Rose, is a "companion" to each sister. Her life exemplifies the values of the community--hard work, plain living, academic excellence, and service to others. But more than this, the spirit of Mother Marie Rose protects the sisters, even in Spokane today. Two stories illustrate this point.

In one case a fire broke out in a sitting room of one of the dormitory-style homes where a number of elderly sisters live. It was discovered in time and the fire department was able to extinguish it. The sisters explain that this early discovery had to do with their special connection to Mother Marie Rose. Their evidence was that the picture of Mother Marie Rose was left untouched, while it was in a room that was severely damaged.

On another occasion a large fire was raging in a field near the main school and convent. The fire fighters were unable to control it. As the brown grassy field went up in smoke, the wind was blowing the flames closer to the convent and school. The sisters called upon Mother Marie Rose to save their school. Some say a picture of her was taken to the fire's edge. Suddenly the wind shifted and the school and convent were saved. These two stories explain that Mother Marie Rose is not a person separate from their daily lives but is always present.

These are not tales of magic. They are stories that tell about the mysterious powers of relationships and the strength of friendship that goes beyond human explanations. As each sister bonds with Mother Marie Rose who protects them, they take up the task of protecting each other. Their own acts of courage and leadership begin with a focus on responding to the individual members of the community. Talking with the sisters, one cannot fail to notice how often they speak highly of each other's work. Even when there are deep philosophical and political differences, they will support, admire, and critique each other. One sister summarizes this by saying that leadership is a relationship between someone who gives care and one who receives care, rather than between a leader and a follower.[18]

From a feminist perspective, the role of Mother Marie Rose is interesting because these sisters do not turn to a man or group of men to protect them nor do they place their primary faith in the state.[19] If one were to apply this concept of "mutual dependence" to the state, it would mean that citizens not only depend on the state for goods, services, and protection but that the state depends upon its citizens for goods, service, and sustenance. Civic leadership, which places its faith in the state as the only organizing principle for public life, may well sustain a macho mentality that emphasizes controlling citizens through threats of punishment rather than encouraging good in citizens by means of education and affection. Finding one's final protection outside of a state system may be the very thing that makes full state citizenship possible because it frees citizens from fearing the state as a strange and sometimes monstrous Other.

Co-Mentoring

Mutual dependence makes possible a co-mentoring system. Sisters help each other develop themselves--professionally, personally, socially, and spiritually. This mentoring process includes honest assessment of each other's talents, the exchange of critical comments, and support for each other's interest. For example, one sister who is a computer science specialist was encouraged by her sisters to became an ice skating judge and photographer. However, equally important is the careful use of talents; those who are seen as unskilled in an area are discouraged from pursuing it. What this means practically is that when the sisters receive support and affirmation, they can take it to mean that others have made real and hard judgements about their talents.

A Democratic Organizational Power Structure

While citizenship is important, a connected cosmology is helpful, and mutual dependence is essential, the biggest piece in the democratic puzzle has to do with how decisions are made. It is important to avoid the alienation of hierarchies and bosses, but at the same time an orderly system that clearly allocates authority and responsibility is necessary. The Holy Names Sisters not only respond to an hierarchical order under the Vatican, but the Constitution for the Holy Names Sisters of the Washington Province reveals a typical hierarchical structure. In this province, the key officers include an executive head (called a provincial), a treasurer, a community director (who organizes local living situations), and a director of ministries (who handles professional work obligations). However, the organization is governed by the principle of subsidiary, which means that decisions are made at the lowest possible level. Before Vatican II, the sisters' organizational structure was a steep hierarchy with all decisions coming from the Provincial and all sisters understanding that their responsibility was cheerful obedience. As the order developed within the church organization, it changed from the original three friends to a large organization with international bases. As it did this, it became a steep hierarchy and fit its own structure into the general structure of other Roman Catholic religious orders. The sisters explained to us that before the 1960's, their daily lives were quite controlled. The house mother (called the superior) controlled many aspects of the women's lives. The sisters were required to ask permission of the house mother each time they wished to leave their homes in the evening. If they needed money, even for bus fare, they had to ask for it each time. Without consulting them, the administrative head told them where they would work, where they would live, and what type of work they would do.

The Vatican II Council produced a dramatic theological shift which changed internal governing practices, resulting in a movement away from this clear-cut hierarchy toward democratic processes. If these sisters, many of whom are undertaking this transformation in their later years, are able to do this, there is promise for the transformation of other organizations. While the sisters still are responsible to Rome and to the Pope, now their work and living assignments are arrived at by a system of consultation based upon the needs the community, the Church, and the individual sister. My research suggests that an individual who finds either her living arrangement or a work assignment unsatisfactory can find alternatives. Now, the sisters not only come and go as they wish and have their own individual annual budgets, but they all participate in establishing governing policies.

For example, a general policy meeting was called of all 287 member sisters (127 attended) in the Washington region in 1984.[20] A year earlier, all the sisters had met in small groups to discuss proposed policies. Many of these meetings took place in their living group, some were in special interest groups, and others were at special board meetings. All sisters could make policy proposals to a central committee. This committee compiled all the information and sent it out to all members for discussion in their homes. In this way, the agenda was generated from a bottom-up model rather than a top-down model. This dialogical process continued throughout the year, so that by the time of the meeting everyone had the opportunity of designing policies and responding to those designed by others.

Two facilitators conducted a general meeting which employed a consensus decision-making model. Votes were taken on controversial issues using a five-point scale--strongly agree, agree, can live with it either way, disagree, strongly disagree. Before a final vote was taken, those who strongly opposed the measure were invited to articulate their reservations on the premise of according respect to minority opinions. The sisters believe that good decisions require true understanding. Because in their view any voice could be the voice of truth, each person must be heard. If it appears that a vote will be close, they may table an issue for later consideration. About fifteen key policies were formed at this session, ranging from the structure of a religious retreat, to the disposition of retirement funds, to how to share a car. All policies were then written into a loose-leaf book to which each sister can refer in working out her daily decisions. By thus participating, the sisters not only share in making policies but also pledge themselves to carry them out. Each sister is responsible for implementing policies within her spheres of influence. In this way members gain a sense of responsibility for the life of the organization as well as a sense of efficacy in shaping it.

Hence each sister can see herself as a leader, even though one sister, the provincial, retains overall responsibilities for executing and implementing the group's general policies. This decision-making structure blends a hierarchical model of leading with a horizontal network of relationships, responsibilities, and commitments.

Leading Begins at Home

For many, leadership takes place solely in the public realm. Much of the political science literature on leadership focuses on public matters in ways that exclude considerations of the family.[21] However, feminist scholarship has shown us how public life depends upon the resources and strength of the family. This focus produces a different understanding of leadership.[22] The family makes public life possible, but the family has been given little real credit for its important public contributions to the welfare of the state. Women whose primary responsibilities have been in private family life have been given little recognition for the work they do in supporting the family through childrearing, family care, and community services. Women are taught to sacrifice their public goals, careers, and active citizenship to support their husbands, but the public has not been taught to recognize their contributions.

Carole Pateman argues that the social contract (which is our explanation of the way in which independent sovereign citizens give over some power to the state in return for protection by the state) rests on a prior sexual contract. In this sexual contract, women agree to be non-citizens in order to gain the protection provided by their place in the family.[23] This democratic process rests on the family in which one party serves another-- the woman serves the man in exchange for a type of protection. So here we have the old institution of monarchy preserved within a new modern democracy. But these sisters have found a solution to this contradiction. The last piece of the democratic leadership puzzle is the structure of home life.

Like others, these sisters have family-type commitments to each other and responsibilities for maintaining their households as well as their career obligations and civic duties. Because these women do not have children, their family circumstances may appear to be unlike those of other families, but it should be remembered that families now often contain two adults, both of whom work. Even for the idealized two-child family, only twenty years of the life of a family would be spent with children while the other thirty would be spent without children. Family life today is no longer focused on childrearing. While many families now include responsibilities for elderly care at home, these sisters have similar responsibilities for their elderly members.

The dormitory-style homes are managed by a combination of hired household staff and the sisters. It is important to note that all sisters--even those who are quite elderly--have household responsibilities. These are not retirement homes where people are warehoused but are active homes where sisters, even in their eighties and nineties, take over management responsibilities to free younger sisters to devote themselves to outside employment duties.

In the small household of two to six sisters, they do not hire outside help for cooking and cleaning. In many ways they resemble the American family. Most of them perform paid work outside the home. Each year the sisters plan household responsibilities that include sharing in cleaning, house and car maintenance, food preparation and other daily duties. They hold regular household meetings to tend to these matters which result in efficiency at minimum cost. Three aspects of their household management are important for understanding how it supports democratic leadership.

First, there is a commitment to a simple life. While basic standards of cleanliness are met, the households do not duplicate the "good housekeeping" look with such things as coordinated dishes, linens, towels. Money is not spent on acquiring and maintaining matching silverware and dishes. This is not a deprivation but an achievement, for they find beauty in simplicity. The household is functional and beautiful; cups don't leak and the accident of their diversity makes life interesting. This simplicity saves time, energy, money and worry. The appearance of their home is not for them an indication of their social worth--i.e. keeping up with the Joneses is not required. This does not mean, however, that no attention is paid to aesthetic values. But the art of homemaking is distinctly their own and largely untouched by the latest housekeeping fashions.

Second, the home serves as an environment for the support of critical reflection. A story illustrates this. One sister, a gifted musician, who was trained professionally to conduct symphonies was denied this opportunity because of her dress and appearance. Those in charge said that the sister's habit was inappropriate attire for the symphony. This echoes other situations in which women have been told they do not "look right" taking on a task traditionally held by men. This not only hurt her but deprived the area of this person's talents. She was able to sustain her own balance throughout this difficult situation. She was able to discuss this situation with her housemates and in that context to assess her own strengths and weaknesses. Her sisters affirmed her work. She knew that their reflections were genuine because these sisters consistently offer each other critical reflections; support is not defined as uncritical. They do not simply offer affirmations. Although she was unable to obtain the conducting position, a few years later she found a position conducting a youth symphony and since has become a professor of music in a nearby university. Because her home life gave her support for her public work, she was able to develop professionally even though she had experienced such raw discrimination. Her story is one of many such stories that show how reflective, critical conversations at home make possible wise, effective work in the public realm. Egalitarian relationships at home, in turn, make such conversations possible. When the work of the home turns some into permanent servants and others into the permanently served, such conversations become difficult, if not impossible.

The point here is not that women are gifted at making homes work. The point here is that the democratic model of leadership I am elaborating anticipates that both men and women participate in an egalitarian home life rather than in a division of labor based upon who can or does make the most money outside the home.

Third, home life includes activities designed to nurture the spiritual, emotional and physical needs of each member. While the sisters' prayer life is important to them, the focus here is on the evening meal which shows how a simple daily activity can minister to these three needs. In several homes, evening meals were prepared five times a week; breakfast and lunches were prepared by the individual sisters for themselves. Sisters are expected to make time for their evening meals together. Dinners are not a time for critical reflection, confession of errors, philosophical or personal disagreements but serve as a time for maintaining the "safe haven"[24] they have created for each other. There is power in knowing that each sister can provide her own food and feed others because each member is truly at home and expects to extend hospitality as well as receive it.

Hence the professional lives of these women are not sustained by women who focus on work inside the home. Each shares in the responsibilities for cleaning, maintaining clothing, making food, etc. No one has a quasi-body servant to perform these tasks so that they can be freed to do the "important" leadership work outside the home.

Making food for one another is not only a delight and a service but also holds symbolic power in that it reminds us of our mortality. Feminist scholars explain that women are sometimes devalued because their work, including food preparation, centers on caring for the physical body. This daily work reminds us of our own mortality and so we may prefer to focus on "immortal" types of work such as writing books and ruling nations. But democratic leadership may depend upon our valuing our mortality and having a daily experience of serving others at home as well as at work. We may need to give up the quest for an immortal place in human history--for eternal fame--and we may well need to serve those in our home to maintain our touch with the mundane. The paradox may be that our true spiritual immortality, whatever form it may take, depends upon our ability to focus on the daily mortal needs of the human beings who comprise our community.

Nevertheless, making strong and vital homes is as important as building a strong public community. This dual commitment was a basic element in the life of the foundress of the Holy Names Sisters. While homemaking is a part of the structure of daily life, it is not *women's* work nor is it merely instrumental labor.[25] It is work that is an end in itself in that it creates a daily atmosphere that articulates mutual dependence and affection. Households are not merely sites for taking care of physical needs[26] but serve as daily reminders that autocratic conduct can damage community bonds. The point here is that for leaders to create a blend of hierarchical and horizontal relationships in their public life, they may well need to experience democratic relationships at home.

Summary: A Democratic Model of Leadership

The democratic model of relationships that I propose for your consideration emphasizes five qualities. First is an understanding of citizenship in which the citizen both rules and is ruled. This means citizens have a commitment to make life better for each other and a willingness to take personal risks to fulfill this responsibility. Sister Cathy's work is an example of this quality. Second, democratic leadership depends upon a cosmology that articulates the connections among citizens and acknowledges that affection binds citizens together in ways that transcend human reason and explanation. Third, leadership is energized by members who see themselves as mutually dependent. Fourth, this model of democratic leadership calls for members to participate in making decisions, while authorizing particular leaders to act on their behalf. Fifth, it depends upon maintaining a commitment to an egalitarian home life that affords opportunities for serving others as well as being served. Such an environment supports reflections on the strengths and weaknesses of each member and demonstrates to us every day how our physical, emotional, and spiritual lives are interwoven.

Although these five qualities of democratic leadership are illustrated in the concrete situations of these sisters, this model is offered as a general guide for American citizens--both men and women. It is not offered as *the* model but as *a* model--one among many that may prove useful to citizens. Each of us will no doubt need to adapt, re-create, and even transform this model as we fit it to our own situations when the call to leadership comes to us.

Notes

1. For helpful discussions of earlier drafts of this paper, I would like to thank all the authors in this book as well as Robert Cahill, Jeff Hardy, and Joanna Leiserson.

2. For a documentation of this socialization in moral decision-making, see Carol Gilligan, *In a Different Voice* (Cambridge, Mass: Harvard University Press, 1982).

3. This is a theme in the work of political scientists, see James MacGregor Burns, *Leadership* (Harper & Row, 1978).

4. These interviews were conducted 1988-1991 and were funded by a research grant form Gonzaga University. The purpose was to understand how these sisters understood leadership in terms of their own living arrangements, professional duties, and community decisions. Both individual and group interviews were conducted with thirty-eight sisters. Marie Olson assisted in the interview process and served as a good conversational partner in developing my own understanding of the sisters' stories. Darleen Tipke worked to analyze some tapes and provided important insights into the sisters' lives.

5. This well-put phrase is from the former governor of Vermont, Madeleine Kunin, quoted by Christopher Graff, Associated Press, *The Salt Lake City Tribune*, July 21, 1991, A, 16.

6. Aristotle, *Politics*, Book 1, 1252a, 15, in *The Basic Works of Aristotle*, Richard McKeon, ed. (New York: Random House, 1941), 1127.

7. Burns, *Leadership*, 141-369, makes a distinction between transactional leaders who serve as power brokers and transformational leaders who generate new values and create new institutional structures.

8. Burns, ibid., 11, emphasizes the relational quality of leadership as well as the importance of seeing power not as a property but as a product of a relationship.

9. Ecofeminism argues that we are a part of our environment and that ecological concerns require us to be as responsive to our ecology as we are to the needs of humans. For discussions of this philosophical orientation and its policies, see Irene Diamond and Gloria Feman Orenstein, eds. *Reweaving the World: The Emergence of Ecofeminism* (San Francisco, Sierra Club Books, 1990).

10. Sister Gertrude McLaughlin, SNJM, "SNJM History Syllabus" (monograph produced by Holy Names Sisters, Otremont, 1979), 11.

11. Ibid., 16.

12. Ibid., 9-10.

13. The vow of chastity requires devoted love and depends upon a woman's genuine independence from secular commitments, including the demands of marriage. It is best understood as an institutional commitment to sisterhood rather than as sexual abstinence because sexual feelings and symbols are a part of this commitment even though genital sex is not.

14. Their pledge of obedience at this point is a promise to obey God not an individual person.

15. The Holy Names Sisters' Provincial Director, who serves as administrative head, emphasized to me that the expectation was that the women would use their education to create social change.

16. We talked with sisters in the two dormitory-style dwellings. One was located at the convent headquarters and included extended nursing care for the elderly, and the other was located close to Gonzaga University and housed a mix of retired sisters and sisters with paid employment. We also talked with sisters who were living in smaller homes. In some cases, we spoke with all the sisters in the home, while in others we spoke with only a few.

17. For a discussion of this see Kathy Ferguson, *The Feminist Case Against Bureaucracy* (Philadelphia: Temple University Press, 1984).

18. This language fits well with the model of care developed within feminist scholarship and articulated in the work of Nel Noddings, *Caring: A Feminine Approach to Ethics & Moral Education* (Berkeley: University of California Press, 1984), 104; Sara Ruddick, *Maternal Thinking* (Boston: Beacon Press, 1989); and the essays found in Joyce Trebilcot, ed. *Mothering: Essays in Feminist Theory* (Rowman & Allanheld, 1983).

19. Mother Marie Rose is a real force in their life. It may be important for those outside Catholicism to remember that this is not the same as worshipping God. This does not replace their faith in God, who is neither a human male nor female and in some sense is both male and female, nor is it to deny their faith in Jesus, who is both divine and human. But it is different to have a female founder who has such a continued presence in the life of an organization. At the time of this writing, a process has been initiated that would make Mother Marie Rose a Saint, which would give her this special standing throughout the Roman Catholic Church.

20. This is high attendance because many of the sisters are too elderly and frail to travel.

21. Glenn Paige, ed. *Political Leadership* (New York: Free Press, 1972), as an example and for an explanation see, Jean Bethke Elshtain, *Public Man, Private Woman* (New Jersey: Princeton University Press, 1981).

22. Helen S. Austin and Carole Leland, *Women of Influence, Women of Vision: A Cross-Generational Study of Leaders and Social Change* (San Francisco: Jossey-Bass Publishers, 1991).

23. Carole Pateman, *The Sexual Contract* (Stanford, California: Stanford University Press, 1988).

24. The home as a "safe haven" is an argument developed by Christopher Lasch, *Haven in a Heartless World* (New York: Basic Books, 1977). It is, of course, in many ways an ironical concept from a feminist perspective since the home for many women is a place where they put in four hours of work after an eight-hour job. For many women it might be more of a job site than a safe haven, because it is for many abused and battered women the most dangerous site rather than the safest.

25. Hannah Arendt makes a distinction between work and labor in which labor includes the necessities of life while work entails creative production in *The Human Condition* (Chicago: University of Chicago Press, 1958).

26. The web metaphor which is developed by Jane Rinehart, "Re-visioning Leadership with Feminists," paper delivered at the Northwest Women's Studies Association Conference, Pullman, Washington, 1991, can be useful in understanding how the sister's household is a web of relationships; each sister weaves new relationships into the web.

Chapter 7

Italian/American Women Writers: Family Shapes Community

Mary Jo Bona

Proverbs often encapsulate meaning in a few words. An Italian proverb useful to understanding Italian/American leadership says that "when you educate a man, you educate an individual. When you educate a woman, you educate a family."[1] Understanding the values of leadership in Italian/American literature requires knowledge about the family structure in which leadership skills are practiced. The kind of Italian/American leadership that I wish to explore has only tangential relation to actual political leaders of Italian/American extraction; leadership on well-known Italian/American politicians has been discussed fruitfully by historians.[2] Images of leadership in Italian/American fiction also can offer new insights into the meaning of leadership in twentieth-century America. Such images also offer students and citizens positive role models, that is, leaders within the family and surrounding community help young people make the right decisions about their future *and* encourage them to maintain family ties. The leaders depicted in the novels I wish to discuss are approachable, a quality unlike images of leaders discussed in history books.

My analysis of Italian/American women writers is influenced by my own ethnic background, but more importantly, I am inspired by the paradigm of cooperation I see working in many Italian/American novels. Students reading this essay might likewise be encouraged to emulate the nontraditional ways in which leadership is enacted in the fictional communities under consideration. To know how good leadership is facilitated by families and communities invites all of us to recall and value our own personal stories about the ways in which our families and neighborhoods have inspired the desire to lead judiciously and be led graciously.

A caveat is in order here, however. Leadership in Italian/American families has not always been effective, as I will demonstrate in my analysis of one of the novels. We can learn much about the causes of ineffective leadership by studying some of the characters and situations in the Italian/American women's literary tradition. Failed leadership often results from unabated physical and/or psychological suffering, for example, living in poverty, or having a mental illness. Nonetheless, people who are suffering are not inherently incapable of leading, and, in fact, particular forms of pain often *enable* families and communities to guide each other into a less disabling future.

The images of leadership Italian/American women writers incorporate in their texts I will qualify as *ethnic* leadership, a term historians use to define actual leaders in ethnic communities in late nineteenth and early twentieth-century America.[3] The following characteristics of ethnic leadership, drawn from studies of actual communities, complement the ways in which leadership has been fictionalized by Italian/American women writers.[4] I include the most representative features of ethnic leadership in southern and eastern Europe. Centrally important to the leaders of ethnic communities in America is the fact that leaders are not located in their native cultural milieu (their homeland country), but have immigrated to a new country (America) and have functioned to ease the process of adjustment for the community at large.

1. Very ordinary people assumed leadership in the villages of southern and eastern Europe in the late nineteenth century and as a result acquired the capacity to recreate vital communities in the cities of America.
2. Leaders focus on the consciousness of an ethnic group and clarify the group's identity through speaking to and writing about the group and modeling the behaviors intrinsic to them.
3. Leaders give to the culture they represent a dramatic rendition of the values it honors.[5]
4. Leaders feel and articulate the distinctive memories of villages in dissolution and the hope of urban communities in formation.[6]
5. Ethnic leaders function as interpreters of their culture's grievances, aspirations, and experiences. This position is uncomfortable, even agonizing.
6. Leaders occupy the critical marginal position of mediator between their own people and the American society outside.[7]

In focusing on the family and on women in the family, Italian/American women writers are able to expand our understanding of leadership qualities in Italian/American culture. To say there were no recognizable female pioneers of leadership (that is, early female immigrants who were leaders) in the nineteenth century,[8] would exclude consideration of the family and neighborhood--two principal areas wherein leadership was practiced. The family and neighborhood produced webs of relationships that anticipated voluntary associations (theatrical companies, labor unions), the principal social unit of mutual aid in the late nineteenth and early twentieth centuries in America.[9] Historians of ethnic leadership such as John Higham and

Josef J. Barton have recognized the influence of family life on the formation of connected networks of social relationships, including kin and *comari*,[10] the godparents who are given honorary membership within the family because of their function as guides and mentors for young people. Godparents assume tremendous importance in the fiction of Italian/American women. They not only occupy the critical marginal position of mediator between their godchildren and the sometimes hostile dominant culture, they often function to save Italian Americans from self-hatred and mental illness.

Two representative Italian/American novels that focus on the influence of the family and *comari* to aid in the emotional and spiritual development of young Italian Americans are Mari Tomasi's *Like Lesser Gods* and Octavia Waldo's *A Cup of the Sun*.[11] Each novel examines the ability of mentors to interpret the experience of feeling different (Italian) in a culture (American) that does not always celebrate difference. Moreover, each of the novels expresses an overwhelming concern with the family. The ability of young Italian Americans to grow into a healthy adulthood largely depends on their favorable relationship with the community mentor. The authors of the novels employ a mediator figure to give voice to the past, the culture of heritage, without overlooking the necessity of experiencing some form of accommodation to the new culture. In this way, mentors in each novel embody ethnic leadership by means of articulating the distinctive memories and customs of Italian villages and of reconstructing a tangible community identity based on shared aspirations and grievances.

Like Lesser Gods focuses on the first generation's response to America and incorporates a narrative structure suitable to immigrant novels, called the *bildungsroman*, or novel of development and education. Mari Tomasi's fictionalized Italian family adapts to the United States in the early decades of the twentieth century. Focusing on the coming-of-age of the Italian/American family in the United States, Tomasi dramatizes the struggle between the tug of the old culture and the lure of the new. Waldo's *A Cup of the Sun* similarly employs the narrative structure of the *bildungsroman*, but fully develops the second generation's response to their ethnic heritage and to American ideals. The struggle in this novel stems from the children's difficulty with adjusting to their parents' expectations; the conflict, then, is not just the struggle between old-and new-world cultures as in *Like Lesser Gods*, but also between parents and children who do not understand each other--whose silences confuse and complicate the processes of spiritual and emotional growth.

To understand the intensity of the conflicts between old-and new-world cultures and between first and second generation Italian Americans, an important distinction must be made between the Northern European concept of the American family and *l'ordine della famiglia*, the unwritten but uncompromising code of duties describing the Southern Italian family. Perhaps what makes adjustment so painful for Italian immigrants and their immediate descendants is the distinction between Italian and American definitions of self--the difference between the self as defined through group membership (*la famiglia*) and the self as an independent individual. The concept of family for twentieth-century middle-class Americans is understood to be relatively voluntary and emotional, especially after a person reaches adulthood. In contrast, the meaning of family in these novels and for Italian/American women especially has nothing to do with choice or feelings. Rather, the family always requires unquestioned loyalty and silence regarding the family's "secrets," those amorphous and most often innocuous family behaviors that remain private. Moreover, how one *feels* about being part of a family is often limited to the financially secure and fully Americanized members of families, who are no longer identifiably Italian American and who have the luxury to *choose* their ethnicity as a marker of identification.[12]

Tomasi's emphasis on the family is central to understanding the function of the leader in *Like Lesser Gods*. Tomasi incorporates a figure of mediation to reconcile the American emphasis on the quest for an individual identity with the Italian emphasis on identity through family membership. Two of the most apparent measures of maturity in the literature of Anglo Americans are separation from the family and personal autonomy.[13] In contrast, the Italian/American family's development depends upon family cohesion and support; the mediator ideally encourages reliance upon the family without depriving the developing character of an understanding of the values of Italian and American cultures.

Becoming an adult in the Italian/American novel does not require abandoning one's family; rather, maturation in *Like Lesser Gods* and *A Cup of the Sun* is indicated by the character's desire to maintain Italian/American customs *and* adopt some of the dominant culture's values (e.g., public education, freedom of speech, attainment of material comforts). Serving as mediators between inherited and adopted cultures, the leaders in both texts provide the young characters with practical guidance and encouragement for gradual adjustment to American culture. Moreover, as an interpreter of both cultures, the mentor has the ability to contextualize experience based on his or her larger understanding of both Italian and American cultures. Because of this, the leaders celebrate the qualities of the ethnic group by making its identity visible (through storytelling, cultural artifacts, literature, etc.) and by incorporating homeland virtues with the new world ethos (by sharing homeland rituals with non-Italians, by including other ethnic groups in Italian/American customs, by creating objects of art in America that symbolize and embrace, for example, the Madonna and the saints' lives).

The quintessential example of successful mentorship in Italian/American literature is dramatized by the fifty-five year old schoolmaster from Ibena (a village of the Piedmont), Michele Tiffone, in *Like Lesser Gods*. Mari Tomasi has created a character who embodies the qualities of a leader; in his role as a mediator, Tiffone articulates the needs of the ethnic community and eases their process of adjustment through his pragmatism, large-mindedness, and generosity. Deciding to move to America for the first time at the age of fifty-five demonstrates Tiffone's resiliency. *Like Lesser Gods* revolves around the working-class lives of Italians and other ethnic groups in Granitetown (a fictionalized Barre, Vermont), a stonecutting town filled with quarriers, craftsmen, and carvers. Michele Tiffone lives with an Italian stonecutting family, the Dallis, who welcome him as one of those selected outsiders who form part of the *comparatico* or *comparaggio* (godparenthood). In this capacity, Tiffone does not limit himself to the Dalli family, but interacts with other cultural groups (including Anglo Americans), who are influenced by his guidance.

Like Lesser Gods begins in 1924. Tomasi presents Michele Tiffone's intelligence, intuition, and empathy as he roams freely about the community, immersing himself in the thick of other people's interests and problems. His role as a teacher is never more evident than when he teaches the Dallis' two eldest children, Petra and Vetch, about the history of the stonecutting industry, by imaginatively reconstructing the migration of Italian cutters and carvers from the Como area, Carrara, into Granitetown at the end of the nineteenth century. In order to teach himself English, Tiffone avidly seeks literature pertaining to Granitetown's stonecutting industry. Practicing his English, Tiffone relates all the information he has gleaned from the public library to the Dalli children. Tomasi emphasizes three major ideas in this section of the novel. First, she compels a reevaluation of the processes of learning--they do not necessarily take place in the classroom and are not taught at a lectern with a figure of authority presiding. Tomasi, perhaps deliberately, stresses the fact that important learning, for the Dalli children, takes place "after school hours," and "before bedtime" when Tiffone works his magic by sharing all the new information he has learned in the library (30).

Second, learning is an activity that requires giving and receiving. Tiffone gives the children his new-found knowledge and receives from them their patience, attention, and enthusiasm as he practices his English. Tiffone understands the fundamental nature of leadership; it is an activity that paradoxically incorporates dependence and guidance for its effectiveness. The children are not only enthralled by the stories Tiffone relates, but they are led by his thirst for knowledge, of his love of stories, and of his obvious need to relate those stories to other hungry learners.

Finally, Tiffone occupies the position of a mediator, connecting his new knowledge of Granitetown to his understanding of the men of antiquity, "the ancient pyramid builders," and the stories of the "great Carrara quarries" (30). In this position, Tiffone functions as an interpreter of both cultures, ultimately linking the Douglas Hill of Granitetown (the quarry site) to hills of the ages: "Christ crucified on Calvary; Moses receiving the tablets of stone on Mt. Sinai; Noah's ark salvaged on the double peaks of Ararat; Rome built on its seven hills" (41). By employing a character like Michele Tiffone, Tomasi enlarges the reader's understanding and appreciation of Italian culture. Ethnic leaders articulate the aspirations of their own culture and the American society at large. Tiffone often transcends the category of mediator by his ability to embrace the larger *human* setting: the image of the crucified Christ on Calvary will recur in *Like Lesser Gods* as Tomasi makes apparent the stonecutter's role of using the chisel to memorialize the life that has gone. Thus the stonecutter functions like a lesser god, but in doing the work of stonecutting, he endangers his own life by breathing in noxious silica particles that eventually cause tuberculous-silicosis, or "stonecutters' T.B."[14]

Called the lifeblood of Granitetown, Douglas Hill occupies a central position in *Like Lesser Gods*: its hewers and carvers depend on the hill for their livelihood as Pietro Dalli does; its physical immensity dominates the landscape; its owners control the town's economy. It is no wonder Tomasi describes the huge bulk of the hill, pitted with quarries, as "open wounds" and "gigantic scars," for the author knows both the beauty and the danger inherent in the stonecutting industry. Her mediator, Tiffone, is able to articulate the experience of stonecutting, aware of the fact that "as long as beautiful stone was available, there would be men to work it" (41-42). In voicing the distinctive memories of the Carrara stonecutting districts, Tiffone gives the two oldest Dalli children a feeling of continuity with their culture of heritage. Moreover, when Vetch (the eldest boy) expresses his love for quarrying to his friend, Denny Douglas, who is the son of the quarry owners, Vetch teaches Denny that quarrying is one of the oldest, most important jobs in the world. When Denny skeptically wants to know which voice of authority made this declaration, Vetch responds "Mister Tiff" (the children's nickname for Tiffone). Accepting the quiet authority of Tiffone's knowledge, Denny responds in a complementary fashion, claiming that the art of carving, then, must be the second oldest job in the world (49). In giving the children this information, Tiffone gives them confidence in the laborious and honorable work of stonecutting, thus diminishing the difference between the owners and the workers.

Tomasi's mediator further diminishes the obvious class difference between the Anglo/American owners of the quarry, the Douglas's, and the workers, represented by the Dalli family. Even though Vetch inchoately perceives Denny to be of a different social class than he and his family, Denny is included in Tiffone's field trips to St. Michael's Catholic church. As a leader, Michele Tiffone welcomes all the neighborhood children who want to learn something about his patron saint, St. Michael. Huddling under the wings of the old-fashioned statue, the "grimy pilgrims" take part in Tiffone's invocation to the saint, as the *maestro* says the prayer in both Italian and English. Tiffone's recital of the Bible stories and legends of Saint Michael parallel his own role as a leader. Just as St. Michael safely leads the Israelites in their desert journey, Michele Tiffone gently leads the children to understand other cultures and, for the Dalli children, to make decisions about their future based on an acceptance of their dual heritage--Italian and American.

Tiffone's influence on Denny Douglas proves immeasurable, for in adulthood he embraces Petra's Catholicism and ethnicity because he remembers with great reverence his childhood trips with "Mister Tiff, his Michael, and those moments when [we] trooped with him into the church hot and grimy" (285). Tiffone's legacy to the children in the community will unify them in adulthood and serve as one of the compelling reasons for Petra's decision to marry Denny Douglas, whose ethnic, class, and religious affiliations are so different from her own.

Tiffone achieves the status of community advisor because he is not afraid of danger, of taking chances, or of using benevolent bribery to effect change for the good of the people. Thus in Book Two of *Like Lesser Gods*, Tiffone's role as mediator and guide assumes increasing importance because the Dalli children are in the process of making decisions about their futures. As in Book One, in Book Two, the people in the community gravitate toward Tiffone; they seek his advice on everything from recipes to romance. Tiffone successfully resolves the local political chief's illicit love affair; he encourages Gabbi Dalli (the youngest daughter) to accept her fiance's decision to work the stone, even though she wants her future husband to have white-collar status.

Gabbi Dalli's second-generation status puts her at odds with the Italian culture. To suggest the connection between immigrant parents and Italian/American children, Tomasi situates Maria Dalli (the immigrant mother) and Gabbi Dalli (the American daughter) in complementary positions. For the first-generation Maria, her husband working in closed sheds without proper health precautions (dust-removing machinery) will cause his death from occupational illness. To prevent this from happening, Maria goes so far as to destroy her husband's carving of a granite cross, hoping that he will be blamed and fired for the reprehensible deed. Her second-generation daughter, Gabbi, deliberately has pre-marital sex with Robbie, hoping that she can bribe her future husband into taking a white-collar job. Entrusting Tiffone with the knowledge that she is pregnant and unmarried allows Gabbi to come to the realization that her father's work was noble and beautiful, a life choice that she finally embraces in her own future husband. In both of these episodes, the women share with Tiffone deeds of passion and regret. Expressing his disapproval of their acts, Tiffone is neither judgmental nor angry; instead he articulates their struggle, which encourages them to make reparation. In this way, he functions much like the Catholic priest, who listens to confessions and forgives misdeeds.

Finally, and most significantly, Tiffone is instrumental in bringing together Petra Dalli and Denny Douglas, thus unifying Italian and Anglo/American cultures through the ceremony of marriage. Throughout his years in Granitetown, Tiffone has clarified the identity of Italian/Americans by connecting them to the Italian heritage of artists and artisans and by sharing the beliefs and values of their culture with other groups in the town. That he has functioned so successfully as a mediator between Italian and Anglo cultures is reflected in the way memories are recalled by the major Anglo/American character, Denny Douglas. Denny's love of Petra's culture is symbolized by his carving of a miniature replica of St. Michael and three smaller figures huddled under the angel's wings, an indelible memory of Tiffone as a spiritual guide. The fact that Denny preserves that union in stone suggests his acceptance of Petra's heritage and anticipates their relationship of equality in the future.

The Italian/American characters in *Like Lesser Gods* develop into mature, responsible citizens without separating from the family or denying their cultural background. Voicing the religious and historical homeland values, Michele Tiffone, like other ethnic leaders, gives to the community he represents a dramatic rendition of the values it honors: work, integrity, honesty, family, art, and literature. Entering with fluidity the quotidian lives of the workers in Granitetown, Tiffone educates them in the art of living, of overcoming difficulty, embitterment, and anger.

Like Lesser Gods certainly highlights successful leadership qualities within a small community, and in doing so, invites the reader to value and honor an older member of society, whose profession has nothing to do with material gain, but with teaching adults and children practical lessons in cooperation and compromise. While *A Cup of the Sun* ostensibly parallels *Like Lesser Gods* in its dedication to exploring the passions and needs of a small Italian/American community, it directly critiques the failures of the community itself (symbolized by parental-child relations and the Catholic church) for failing to clarify its purpose in raising children to become responsible, engaged adults. Waldo uses World War II as a backdrop to *A Cup of the Sun*, the effects of the war negatively influencing the Italian/American community, confusing its understanding of itself and heightening the already incendiary conflicts among children and parents. The leaders in this novel do not possess the foresight needed to protect the community as the ubiquitous Michele Tiffone so ably does in Granitetown. Though they try, these figures often fail to hear one another and lack the prescience to know when someone needs desperately to be saved from harm.

A Cup of the Sun revolves around the lives of Italian Americans in a small community around the outskirts of Philadelphia during the years 1941-1945. Like many other Italian/American writers, Waldo dedicates her narrative to exploring the development of the community, not just one particular individual; this narrative form contributes to what I call the ethnic or communal *bildungsroman*.[15] The narrative revolves around the lives of three Italian/American families, focusing primarily (though not exclusively) on the children: Andrea and Niobe Bartoli, whose parents are both living and whose father is a restorer of antiques; Laura and Pompeii Rossi, whose father never speaks and whose mother abandoned them in infancy; and Concetta and her mentally retarded brother, Romeo, a boy whose irrational behavior parallels the confusion of the community at large. Each of these families suffers in particular ways, and the only character who is able emotionally and spiritually to withstand her suffering is Niobe, named after the mythological goddess who was turned to stone. The three mentors who prevent Niobe from developing self-hatred and becoming ill are Giambelli, the major artist in the novel and a confirmed bachelor; Giovanna Bartoli, Niobe's mother, who does not understand her daughter, but intuits her pain; and Laura Rossi, Niobe's childhood girlfriend, who dies tragically at eighteen years of age.

Waldo, like Tomasi, makes clear that leadership figures can function as guides at any age and can be of either gender. While it is true that Tomasi's Michele Tiffone is the uncontestable spiritual and emotional guide in *Like Lesser Gods*, Maria Dalli, the mother, also functions as a leader, maintaining family solidarity after the death of her husband. My point is that both Tomasi and Waldo incorporate into their narratives strong female figures, who educate the family by example and by their acceptance and discernment of their children's needs. Godparents such as Michele Tiffone of *Like Lesser Gods* and Giambelli of *A Cup of the Sun* accept the importance of the family, but in their capacity as outsiders, they gain an awareness of the children's needs that the parents may not see. With regard to Niobe Bartoli's development in *A Cup of the Sun*, the three characters who try to guide her are concomitantly wounded by other forces affecting their lives, thus limiting their capacity to lead effectively.

All three characters are adversely affected by the onset of World War II. Mrs. Bartoli, unable to respond to the sexual advances of her husband, accounts for her unusual lack of desire by responding, "'The war's inside me...I cannot help myself'" (115). Mrs. Bartoli's response epitomizes the characters' behaviors, needs, and problems in *A Cup of the Sun*. Not only is the Italian/American community losing its sons to the war, but the parents are frightfully aware of the possibility of fratricide--one American son of Italian descent killing an Italian relative overseas in the booted country.

Like Michele Tiffone, Giambelli's sensitivity for people is very keen, yet he cannot order all the confusion in the community because so much of it is understated and silenced, depriving the artist of basic clues to the cause of such grief. As a sculptor, Giambelli functions like his mythological ancestor, Pygmalion, able to create and fall in love with beauty, but sometimes unable to see ugliness around the corner. Laura Rossi, Niobe's girlfriend, suffers tremendously from the fact that she is motherless and illegitimate, the daughter of a *puttana* (whore). As a result of this designation, Laura is limited by the community's narrow understanding of her. The community's legitimation of women as either celibate or married prevents them from perceiving Laura's pain. Like Mrs. Bartoli, Laura literally cannot help herself, for she has been wholly defined by her mother's putative sin and is not allowed to gain an identity outside her familial situation, a prerogative many children of immigrants in America have. All three of these characters, in pain themselves, help lead Niobe *away* from the community, not so she will leave it in despair and resignation, but so she will return to it a better leader in her own right: empowered to clarify the Italian/American identity and offer a rendition of the values it honors--some of them damaging and ineffectual in America.

Giambelli's relationship with Niobe changes as she grows into womanhood. Because he is a sculptor, Giambelli can see Niobe's beauty, but is unaware that her beauty may hurt her by arousing the passions of her older brother, Andrea. Waldo anticipates Niobe's experience of incest by describing an object of art--a sculpture of Leda, the figure in myth who was raped by Zeus in the form of a swan and "who never altered her stone embrace around a stone swan" (30). Giambelli is unable to prevent Niobe's incestuous experience with her brother, but he does detect that she acts unemotionally and is suffering. When Niobe is sixteen, she begins sitting as a model for Giambelli, the artist functioning as a mediator between the unstated problems in the Bartoli family and her own sexual confusion. Niobe is briefly granted a neutral space, where she can just *be* and privately sort out her confusions about herself and her future goals to be college educated. Unfortunately, Giambelli fails to maintain his position of facilitating Niobe's development of self-worth because he succumbs to his own desires and kisses her more than once. Unlike Tiffone of *Like Lesser Gods* whose celibacy gives him the freedom of hearing intimacies without engaging in them, Giambelli is cognizant of his own sexual needs and pulls away from Niobe, afraid of his own passional nature. Later in the narrative, when Niobe has fallen in love with Giambelli, the artist encourages Niobe to speak of the "something dark inside" her, but she refuses. At this time, Giambelli recalls his own youthful memory of being refused in marriage to the girl he loved. Instead of re-enacting the painful and violent drama of his past, Giambelli transcends his particular grievances in order to understand the propensity that *humanity* has for grief: "The indispensable aloneness of humanity was wounded in him; no mouth could tell it. ... There was only pain, and that he could feel and would feel" (202). As an artist, Giambelli is aware of his ineluctable position of interpreting and never denying suffering. While he does not know Niobe's actual form of pain, he is experienced enough to know that "life grew from it and sometimes because of it;" as a result, he is able to accept Niobe's suffering and reassure her that it will not negatively affect her future: "'It doesn't matter--not to anyone--not to anyone who loves you'" (203).

In hearing Giambelli's response, Niobe is able more fully to understand her earlier decision to leave the Church. In the confessional, Niobe had confessed her "sin" of having sex out of wedlock and with a relative. The priest's reaction to this admission is painfully disturbing--he both pointedly asks intimate questions about sexual acts and denounces such a sin in a verbal diatribe against the evils of the flesh. Beholden to Church doctrine and limited by his own vision, the Catholic priest in Waldo's text fails to guide Niobe; she leaves, hating her body, "its strength and grace" (73). In contrast, Giambelli's position as a mediator is uncomfortable, often agonizing, but ultimately helpful. In accepting Niobe's suffering, he recalls his own and the community's; in pushing her away from him, he gives her the freedom "to seek fulfillment among the young" (244), something that will be very difficult for Niobe, having had her body taken away (through incest) before it was her own.

Niobe's mother, Giovanna, does not understand her daughter, but she is perceptive enough to realize that Niobe is in love with Giambelli. Having learned from her daughter's silence that a mother cannot fulfill her needs through her children, Mrs. Bartoli warns Giambelli not to try to fulfill his own needs through loving Niobe. Mrs. Bartoli also functions to lead her daughter away from the community, realizing that Niobe will grow from her pain. Through her unequivocal acceptance of differences, Giovanna indirectly helps Niobe accept her confusions regarding her sexual and ethnic identity. In the first case, Mrs. Bartoli perceives her daughter's emotional distance to be the result of living in America, a culture that values individuality and thus countenances alienation. In trying to communicate with her reticent daughter, she learns that Niobe is reading *Death in Venice*, a novella about the love between an old and young man. Mrs. Bartoli's responses to the text will ultimately compel Niobe to re-evaluate the afternoon in which she and her brother had sex. Just when Niobe relates that she has never known the love between men to have happened, Mrs. Bartoli responds, "'Still, it happens. Right around us; if we could look into all these houses whenever we wanted to, we'd probably see stranger things than that'" (122). Niobe is not yet able to unify her divided self, but her mother's comments contribute to her reintegration of body and soul.

Second, Mrs. Bartoli contextualizes her daughter's experience of being a second-generation Italian American through a conversation that Niobe recalls her mother having had with Andrea, her brother. To emphasize the fact that Niobe is distanced from her family, Waldo has Niobe recall her mother's words in a memory, while she is swimming in the ocean. The water imagery is key to Niobe's feeling of purgation; she is not annihilated by the ocean, but rather, as an expert swimmer, she has *control* over her body's movements. During her swim, Niobe recalls her mother's belief in difference as a valuable attribute: "You live in a world that would deny you differences. Yet that is all your Mamma can give you" (140). Elsewhere in the text, Mrs. Bartoli is described sitting on the beach looking like a "tremendous sphinx;" though she is unable to solve the riddle that is Niobe, she gives her daughter lessons in interpretation--not just for Mann's *Death in Venice*, but for the text of her community in which different patterns of confusion are woven.

Unable completely to accept her stature as an Italian American, Niobe receives the practical wisdom of her girlfriend, Laura Rossi, whose own pain far exceeds all the others in *A Cup of the Sun*. Dying from infection brought on by a self-inflicted abortion, Laura's last words to Niobe resound with the honesty and large-spirited nature of which Laura is greatly capable. While she encourages her friend to go away and grow--"because you're the only one of us who can do it"--Laura warns Niobe not to relinquish her Italian/American heritage, not to keep it secret, and not to be ashamed of who she is.

Niobe is led by the three characters to accept her difference, to love her cultural heritage, and to believe in her capacity to love. Each of the leaders in *A Cup of the Sun* renounces something of her or his own needs to give guidance to Niobe, the character who leaves for college at the end of the novel. What Niobe takes with her is her pain, nurtured by the unsettling experiences of World War II and her own losses. Living in a disordered community will prepare Niobe for the larger social arena; her reasons for leaving her neighborhood in Philadelphia stem less from her need to escape than from her desire to return and finally understand the community which helped to formulate her identity. Niobe's education truly parallels the proverbial words that began this paper: When you educate a man, you educate an individual; when you educate a woman, you educate a family.

Several of the characters in *Like Lesser Gods* and *A Cup of the Sun* are educated to understand their role in the community and family; this neither undercuts their roles as individual Italian Americans nor as members of American culture. What their education does is to prepare them to meet the goals of ethnic leadership, modeling the behaviors basic to a pattern of leading that stems from the interaction between two cultures, in this case, Italian and American. Italian/American leaders clarify their culture's traditions by speaking to and writing about their heritage. As they occupy the position between two cultures, they learn the art of mediation, which requires vigilant adjustment to changes in one's culture without relinquishing one's ethnic heritage.

In her chapter in this book, Jane Rinehart writes, "the wisdom and strength associated with women, but manifested also by men, is the foundation for an image of leadership as humble, respectful of differences, relational and patient."* The Italian/American women's literary tradition offers images of leadership that embrace differences and challenge the traditional assumption that views leaders as famous, wealthy, and inaccessible. In contrast, ethnic leaders understand their role in the context of relationship and with an awareness of their own needs and deficiencies. They are able to guide young citizens in their quest to adjust to their communities and the larger American social context. They model the

---

* Jane Rinehart, "Learning to Lead," in this book.

behaviors intrinsic to the Italian/American community, emphasizing a love of art and culture, and a respect for work and home. The African/American poet and writer, Maya Angelou, once said that to know and not to do is not to know. From the Italian/American women's perspective, leadership depends on knowing and doing, learning from pain and suffering and guiding others to do the same.

Notes

1. Aileen Riotto-Sirey, "A Culture of Matriarchs," in Linda Brandi Cateura, *Growing Up Italian* (NY: William Morrow, 1987), 119.

2. Three Italian Congresswomen of the 1980s--Marge Roukema, Connie Morella, and Nancy Pelosi are actively involved in community service and raising families. All three attribute their interest in public service to the experience of being raised in close-knit Italian/American families. Pelosi and Morella name their mothers as the outstanding role models in their formative years. While it is not the purpose of this essay to explore the formation of political leaders of Italian/American extraction, I find it more than coincidental that *actual political leaders and fictional depictions of leadership by Italian/American women writers share the same thoughts on the efficacy of the family in producing leadership qualities in its children.* See *National Italian American Foundation Quarterly* (Winter, 1989-1990): 5-9. For information on Italians in the political arena see Salvatore J. La Gumina, "The Political Profession: Big City Italian American Mayors" and Peter F. Pugliese, "Americans of Italian Descent in the Judiciary of Pennsylvania," in *Italian Americans in the Professions*, ed. Remigio U. Pane (Staten Island, NY: The Italian American Historical Association, 1983), 77-110, 111-126.

3. John Higham, ed., *Ethnic Leadership in America* (Baltimore: The Johns Hopkins University Press, 1978). I also align myself with anthropological ethnic theory in defining the terms *ethnic* and *ethnicity* in this paper. See Werner Sollors, ed., *The Invention of Ethnicity* (New York: Oxford University Press, 1989), ix-xx. Typically based on a contrast, ethnic like racial or national identifications "rest on antithesis, on negativity." (Sollors, 288). By calling ethnicity, that is, belonging to and being perceived by others as belonging to an ethnic group, an *invention*, one challenges the notion that ethnic groups are relatively fixed, or self-evident categories. George Devereux warns of the danger in clinging to one's ethnic identity too insistently or obsessively, thus revealing a "flaw in one's self-conception as a unique multidimensional entity." George Devereux, "Ethnic Identity: Its Logical Foundations and Its Dysfunctions," *Ethnic Identity: Cultural Continuities and Change*, George de Vos and Lola Romanucci-Ross, eds. (Chicago: University of Chicago Press, 1982), 67. As a term for literary study, moreover, ethnicity "largely evokes the accumulation of cultural bits that demonstrate the original creativity, emotive cohesion, and temporal depth of a particular collectivity, especially in a situation of emergence--be it from obscurity, suppression, embattlement, dependence, diaspora, or previous membership in a larger grouping." Werner Sollors, "Ethnicity," *Critical Terms For Literary Study*, Frank Lentricchia and Thomas McLaughlin, eds. (Chicago: University of Chicago Press, 1990), 290. Being "Italian American" is a fairly recent phenomenon, based on a historical

occurrence of migration primarily during the late nineteenth and early twentieth centuries. What it means to be Italian American in the 1990s will have a different meaning, and will have to be reinvented for Italian/American writers of the late twentieth century. The writers examined in this paper, Tomasi and Waldo, both emerge from the particular experience of migration and settlement of ethnic enclaves in the new world. Thus their stories will share a kind of "emotive cohesion" based on the collective experience of finding comfort and a sense of self in America.

4. The following list is culled from Higham, *Ethnic Leadership in America*, and Victor Greene, *American Immigrant Leaders 1800-1910: Marginality and Identity* (Baltimore: The Johns Hopkins University Press, 1987).

5. Higham, "Introduction: The Forms of Ethnic Leadership," in Higham, *Ethnic Leadership in America*, 1-18.

6. Josef J. Barton, "Eastern and Southern Europeans," in Higham, *Ethnic Leadership in America*, 150-175.

7. Greene, *American Immigrant Leaders*, 11, 123.

8. So Greene contends, ibid.

9. Barton, "Eastern and Southern Europeans," 150-175. Voluntary associations were created in the peasant villages in Southern and Eastern Europe as a way to defend themselves against the agricultural modernization that threatened and eventually dismantled the household industry. What this caused was a steady pattern of population movement in which small land-holding peasants and day-laborers migrated seasonally for money to buy tools or seed. This disaggregation of community life was felt most severely in the household. Families dealt with the imposition of an external economy by (1) engaging in an enlarged network of kinship ties outside the household, and (2) forming volunteer associations to "insure for illness and death, to supervise education, to form agricultural and artisan organizations, to pursue political aims." (154) The voluntary associations established in the new world were, thus, in part a "reconstruction of old models of order and in part an accommodation to the life of the city." (156) In these new urban settlements, voluntary associations became the characteristic social unit that created "a matrix within which the group organized its policing devices, family life, marriage, churches, educational system, and association for cultural and social ends." (160)

10. See notes 3 and 6 above. My colleague Julie Tammivaara reminded me that in anthropological terms, godparents are considered "fictive kin," which appropriately corresponds to those fictional characters who are not consanguineously related, but are accepted as part of the family network. The Italian term for such relationships is *comparaggio*: a system of relationships whereby men or women were included as members of a family upon their assuming the role of godfathers or godmothers to a child of whom they were sponsors at baptism or confirmation. See Leonard Covello, *The Social Background of the Italo-American School Child* (Leiden: E.J. Brill, 1967), Appendix A.

11. Milwaukee: The Bruce Publishing Company, 1949; New York: Harcourt, Brace & World, 1961. Page-citations to these two novels in the rest of this chapter refer to these editions.

Several novels in the Italian/American tradition focus primarily on the family's ability to nurture its children, thus contributing to their development in America. To be sure, not all of the families are successful. A selective sampling of novels is: Helen Barolini, *Umbertina* (New York: Seaview Books, 1979); Dorothy Bryant, *Miss Giardino* (Berkeley: Ata Books, 1978); Tina de Rosa, *Paper Fish* (Chicago: The Wine Press, 1980); Rachel Guido de Vries, *Tender Warriors* (Ithaca, New York: Firebrand Books, 1986); Pietro di Donato, *Christ in Concrete* (Indianapolis: The Bobbs-Merrill Company, 1939); Josephine Gattuso-Hendin, *The Right Thing to Do* (Boston: David R. Godine, 1988); Jerre Mangione, *Mount Allegro* (Boston: Houghton Mifflin Company, 1943); Jo Pagano, *Golden Wedding* (New York: Random House, 1943); Mario Puzo, *The Fortunate Pilgrim* (New York: Atheneum Publishers, 1964); Julia Savarese, *The Weak and the Strong* (New York: G. Putnam's Sons, 1952).

12. Herbert J. Gans describes third-and fourth-generation ethnics who experience their cultural heritage as engaging in "symbolic ethnicity." "People may even sincerely desire to 'return' to these imagined pasts, which are conveniently cleansed of the complexities that accompanied them in the real past." "Symbolic Ethnicity: The Future of Ethnic Groups and Cultures in America," in *On the Making of Americans: Essays in Honor of David Riesman*, ed. Herbert J. Gans, et. al (Philadelphia: University of Pennsylvania Press, 1979), 193-220, at 205.

13. The narrative of the young man, leaving the home to find his way in the world, did not originate in Anglo/American literature. The seminal novel of formation, or *bildungsroman*, was Goethe's *Wilhelm Meister's Apprenticeship*, in eighteenth-century Germany. Other well-known novels of education include Dickens's *Great Expectations* and Joyce's *The Portrait of an Artist as a Young Man*.

14. Alfred F. Rosa, "The Novels of Mari Tomasi," *Italian Americana*, vol. 2 (1975): 66-78, at 72.

15. See my articles, "Mari Tomasi's *Like Lesser Gods* and the Making of an Ethnic *Bildungsroman*," in *VIA: Voices in Italian Americana* 1 (1990): 15-34; and "Coming of Age Novel: Italian/American," in *New Ethnic American Literature and Arts: An Encyclopedia* (New York: Garland Press, forthcoming).

Chapter 8

Learning to Lead

Jane A. Rinehart

Introduction

We live within a story about leadership the way one might ride upon a raft in a gently flowing river on a beautiful sunny day. On such a raft trip one would be comfortable, at ease with the surroundings, perhaps even blissfully unaware of anything other than the pleasant motion. The current would bear us along; no effort or attention would be necessary for long periods of time. Occasionally we might come upon an unusual sight--a differently shaped tree or rock, for instance--but mostly the trip would be uneventful. Frequent trips would assimilate even the unusual into the overall vista, defining them within its limits.

Living within our leadership story is like this. We are comfortable with it; its narrative carries us along, bringing us past sights which are mostly familiar and reassuring. The occasional odd character in the story-- e.g., Empress Catherine of Russia or St. Joan of Arc who led the French army--lends interest and color, but does not disrupt its stately pace or alter its course. The story about leadership allows us to float gracefully, perhaps asking a question here or there, but fundamentally accepting the narrative's direction, tone, and cast of characters. The traditional story about leadership in Euro-American culture is, for the most part, a description of the activities and character of a few great individuals, usually males, operating in the public realm of politics, military campaigns and business enterprise.

What might happen to disrupt such a peaceful ride? Let's imagine that we are floating on the river and we glimpse a settlement, a collection of buildings and people, not too far from the riverbank. We are filled with wonder as we realize that we have not noticed this before, although we have made the same trip many times. We are too curious to simply float on by, so we bring our raft to the shore and climb the path which leads to the village; as we come closer to it, we see that it is much larger and busier than we had thought.

Strangely enough, nothing about the place suggests that it is new; instead it looks and feels like a place we know well. The people we meet there act friendly and glad to have us; they also seem very familiar. We decide to stay with them for a while. During this visit we listen to other kinds of stories, quite different from the ones we tell and hear on our river journeys. We can see that the river is still there, but we also learn that it isn't all there is, its stories the only good ones. We begin to appreciate the significance of location for the stories we tell, the things we believe in.

This chapter is an example of how choosing certain locations can shift our perspective, and provide us with some stories about leadership that may be unsettling. I want to raise some questions, for myself and for the reader, about what we might say about leadership if we left the river, eased ourselves out of the dominant narrative. I hope to present some ways in which we might think together about the meaning of "education for leadership." Before we gather around the village common to share these tales, however, I want to take a few moments to describe how I see our activity. Let me begin by talking about what I think I am going to be doing in these pages, and later move into a consideration of your role as reader.

I want to use this chapter to say some things about leadership. Obviously, I think they are important, but this is not the same as thinking that they are all that could or should be said about this topic. That is one of the joys of presenting my ideas as one part of a collaborative project among several teachers and writers. The themes in my chapter are echoed in the writings of several other contributors, most notably in Mary Jo Bona's discussion of leadership figures in some novels by Italian-American women, in Eloise Buker's presentation of the connections between the community life and apostolic work of Holy Names Sisters, in Rose Mary Volbrecht's emphasis upon friendship and colleagueship as resources for the development and nurturance of leaders, in Blaine Garvin's and Bob Waterman's descriptions of how citizenship can be gratifying and effective, and in Tom Jeannot's account of the servant-leadership model in Alcoholics Anonymous. I want to be understood as offering a way to conceptualize leadership which I find intriguing and attractive. I hope my discussion of leadership produces some similar responses in its readers. But I am not claiming that mine is the only or best way to view leadership; rather I am more intent upon showing its possibility, indicating its benefits, and inviting readers to consider for themselves what promise it might hold.

I hope the pages which follow will make clear my avoidance of the "voice of authority," or what has been called the "view from nowhere": a disembodied, free-floating insight into Reality, a knowing without knowers which seeks certainty and power.¹ I believe that seeking this kind of knowledge is dangerous because it enjoins us to forget that all of our efforts to know, to answer the questions we have about who we are, what life is like, how our world looks and how it might be changed, bear the imprint of our context and choices. As knowers we are always somewhere, and so human story-making is necessarily "located, limited, inescapably partial, and *always* personally invested."²

Having left the river which represents the western tradition's grand narrative about leadership, we are nevertheless still situated some place. Even if there is something new about our location, it is also familiar and we have brought to it all our experiences as river-travelers. In leaving the river, we take it with us; we carry our tradition in the language we speak, the customs we have learned about how to relate and understand. So, we are never completely removed from the river, but our position on the land next to it should give us some different ways of using what we have learned while we were borne along by its current. We can strive to look at and appreciate the river--our traditional story about leadership--in a different way, to be more reflective about its contours now that we are able to regard it as something less than everything.

Such striving is essential when the subject of our story is leadership, because we have such a frequent, close, and long-standing relationship with this theme. When we ask ourselves what is meant by "leadership", an answer will come readily to our lips or pens. Our answers derive from all the images of leaders presented in folktales, myths and legends, formal histories, novels, poems, newspaper accounts, movies and television programs. It will be difficult to refuse the seductiveness of the familiar here. It is foolish to presume a clean beginning in this chapter, to believe that we can put aside all we have learned. What I hope we can do instead is to have a conversation with what is already available to us as images of leadership, to raise some questions about what we know, to be willing to let this conversation take us by surprise.

What follows, then, is a record of my conversations with some people and texts which tells a story about education for leadership. In the telling, I am trying to uncover the sources of my thinking and I hope that this effort invites you to do the same. My essay argues that responsible knowing and acting, both conceived as communal enterprises dependent upon the participation of many people, are key dimensions of leadership and the learning which prepares us for it. I want to coax the reader away from an understanding of leadership as something s/he cannot do, and ground it instead in everyday practices. I believe that we can create a conversation here--in my writing and your reading--which is a shared process of discovery. The conversations we enjoy, remember and wish to continue are experiences of mutuality, creativity, and openness to the new. That is the sort of conversation I am seeking, so I am asking for an active, engaged reading, one which recognizes that the written text is just a beginning and that its writer and reader form a partnership in creating its meanings. I regard this approach as one way of representing the desires and activities I associate with leadership.

I begin with a focus and two assumptions. The focus is showing how education for leadership may be formulated as education for social and individual change. Conceived in this way, education for leadership includes:
1. developing and deepening an awareness of the structural dimensions of social problems, the crises that appear to demand leadership;
2. gaining a knowledge of the feminist movement and the scholarship it has inspired as manifesting the possibility that consciousness and organizations can be transformed; and
3. participating in an educational process that gives priority to critical reflection on social structures and cultural values, and nurtures this kind of analysis within a collaborative, empowering conversation.

The earliest source of this focus is the uneasiness I experienced on my own river raft ride. While I could sometimes be seduced by the pleasures of the journey, there was always an insistent inner voice challenging me to question the effects of the ride. I was bothered--unsure about whether I wanted to take this sort of trip, about the kind of forgetfulness it seemed to require. I have spent years trying to understand my discomfort and seeking alternatives to a life of ease upon the river. I knew that I could not accommodate myself to the route, the sights, the stories. I felt betrayed somehow because the more that I learned about my tradition and its definitions of power, success, leadership, the more I felt like a missing person. So, the focus of this essay is rooted in my experience of the negative effects of familiar ways of speaking about leadership and my discovery of other possibilities.

My assumptions are prompted by this statement made by the contemporary theologian, David Tracy: "What conversation is to the life of understanding, solidarity must be to the life of action."[3] What I will be saying about leadership is an elaboration upon these connections among conversation, understanding, solidarity and action. I want to show that these communal images of knowing and doing are essential for an image of leadership which overcomes the feelings of powerlessness and despair produced by identifying leadership with extraordinary individuals and their highly specialized activities. In place of this very common image, my starting point assumes that leadership is grounded in the social practices of knowing and acting upon what we know, and that the way we think about these practices has a significant influence on the kind of leadership we produce.

Learning and Teaching Sociology

The discipline called sociology has always had a knack for disturbing the status quo. Marx, Weber, Durkheim, and others during the mid-nineteenth to early twentieth century period are regarded as the creators of sociology's classical tradition. For these thinkers, sociology means

> engagement with the pain, misery and confusion, as much as with the achievements of the spirit, that exist in society. It assesses the character of a social order, asks how it originated, where it is going, and where it could go with the contribution of a clear and humane vision.[4]

Sociology, then, has claimed some big questions from its beginning. Sociologists encourage us to examine the embeddedness of our individual lives in social structures and culture, to seek to understand the relationships between what we have learned to distinguish as the private and public spheres. This is the capacity which C. Wright Mills called "the sociological imagination."[5]

Each year, thousands of American college students read Mills' characterization of sociology and learn the benefits of interpreting our personal experiences within the context of our time and place. When I was a college student during the 1960's, Mills' idea seemed liberating to many of us; we took it to mean that we were not stuck within the confines of our immediate routines, that we could practice a way of thinking which enlarged our experience without denying it, and supplied us with tools for changing what seemed wrong about it. It has been my experience as a teacher that fewer students are inclined to give sociology this meaning today.

Recently, Norman Denzin has written a critique of Mills' formulation of what is most distinctive about sociology.[6] Denzin's approach clarifies what is at stake in our understanding of sociology and how this is connected with views of leadership. Denzin begins by characterizing *The Sociological Imagination* as the text which captured the imagination of newcomers to the field of sociology during the 1960's. While he does not deny that the work still speaks to many sociologists today, he clearly wishes that this was not the case. In Denzin's interpretation, Mills' text contributes to the death of the social by failing to give voice to ordinary people and their stories--the stuff of social life--and substituting instead the master theories of "great sociologists." Denzin offers a way of seeing sociology both as contributing to the negative effects of the dominant narrative about leadership and as presenting an alternative to it.

Introducing college students to the discipline of sociology is difficult since this is a field with "multiple paradigms," a phrase which can often seem like a fancy cover for confusion and incoherence. I suspect that this is why so many of us who teach it have found Mills' idea about a unifying special task so appealing. Nevertheless, I have puzzled over the difficulties students and I have had in meeting each other through

Mills' text, and I think these struggles teach us something important about the differences between stories told upon the river journey and those we hear in the villages along its edge. Mills claims that the sociological imagination is a form of consciousness which allows us to grasp the intersection of biography and history, to relate personal troubles to public issues and so find an illuminating knowledge which contributes to purposeful social action. Denzin argues that this promise goes unfulfilled in Mills' own work and that of many other sociologists. In the terms of the river metaphor, he is saying that the story of the sociological imagination pleases the raft riders, but looks dangerous to those who watch from the riverbank.

The occupants of the raft go on telling one another this story--that sociologists can supply readings of the world which are powerfully explanatory. What Denzin sees, watching from the shore, is that ordinary women and men "find history going on behind their backs." The "behind their backs" image expresses his belief that the cultural tools for interpretation, for making sense of our lives, are not useful. In Denzin's analysis, this experience of the inadequacy of the reigning stories is the central theme within postmodern societies; it is an experience he hears in the stories told by members of those societies to one another. This sort of listening is what sociologists should be doing, and it can happen only if we forsake the lulling rhythm of the established stories. Denzin asks that we "bury social theory" and put in its place stories which stay as close as possible to those narrated by ordinary people. He calls upon sociologists to give expression to these efforts to understand as a way of intervening against the writings of experts. This is Denzin's fundamental objection to allowing Mills to have the definitive word on what sociology is all about: Mills identifies himself and other sociologists who use his "imagination" as virtuoso readers of the signs of the time.[7]

Ah ha! Now I have some better words for expressing my confusion. In relation to the students in my Soc 101 classes, I have often been at a loss to explain their resistance to using sociological perspectives. I am inclined now to relate it to this problem of virtuosos arrayed against the unenlightened, raft riders too deeply attached to their own conversations with the great thinkers to pay attention to the homier tales being shaped in the hidden villages where most folks live. "Homier" does not mean simple or uninformed; it refers instead to the rootedness of these stories in daily experiences. I think Denzin is right when he asserts that sociology's stories should be anchored in the villages, and that the telling of these stories can contribute to empowerment. Translating his argument into the terms of this chapter, Denzin supplies us with a way of showing that sociology can be an education in leadership by inviting us toward new ways of living within our own stories.

Let's consider, as an example of this invitation, the work of Alvin Gouldner on leadership. Gouldner's collection of *Studies in Leadership* was published forty years ago. In his introduction Gouldner argues that popular concern about leadership arises when existent social problems become urgent but when prevalent conceptual tools, the leading ideas of the time, fail to make intelligible the institutional roots of the problems. These tensions are then defined as possible of solution by changes in leading personnel.[8]

Gouldner asserts that this tendency to respond to social problems as requiring new and better leaders has been fostered by the American cultural values of individualism and mastery of the environment. Our heritage is full of images of self-made men, hardy pioneers, and wise founding fathers which are used to demonstrate that our social arrangements are basically fine (at times even called the best in the world) and that individuals can make an enormous difference when they are motivated, brave and responsible.

I don't think that Gouldner is declaring this heritage worthless or evil. By inviting us to stand apart from it for a moment and to act like strangers who find it curious, I think he is showing us that it is possible to take off the cultural assumptions we usually wear so comfortably and look at them with a fresh eye. Gouldner wants to suggest ways that our traditions can make us too comfortable by diverting our attention from structural forces which need to be studied critically and modified if our social problems are to be addressed. Gouldner is making the argument that training better leaders to operate within unchanged structures and assumptions is a misunderstanding of the kind of leadership a democratic society needs.

His discussion alerts us to a profound contradiction at the heart of the concern with leadership which is no less present today than it was in 1950: we perceive a state of crisis in our society, know that some things need to be changed, and then deny the necessity for real change by imagining that all we have to do is to find or educate more capable leaders. Sociological perspectives such as Gouldner's highlight the ways in which our organized social practices create social problems, and remind us about how this connection is hidden by the attention we pay to individual leaders. This serves to divert the energies of citizens from social analysis and efforts to transform the status quo, thus preserving vested interests in its continuance.

Gouldner's work on leadership, then, can be read as an intervention or a wedge between the tales told by experts and the resources present in our own storytelling. Gouldner serves us by showing the gap between stories of democratic participation in movements for social change and myths of great men providing vision and solutions. For Gouldner, the "crisis in leadership" is a cover story; he tells us we are spending too much time gazing at the river and yearning for its adventures. The articles in his book may be read as encouragement to appreciate the thrills of village life, the hard work of building a life with other people through the stories we tell.

There is, at present, a widespread consensus that America's leadership in the world is declining. Our sense of America as destined for lasting greatness because of the demonstrated superiority of its economy and political system is eroding in response to accumulating evidence of stagnation, incompetence, greed, and corruption. Our sense of America as a land of opportunity for all, as a place where leaders emerge in each generation who have vision of the common good and the skills to make that vision a reality, is giving way to a suspicion of confusion, self-aggrandizement, and wasted potential. My students readily express agreement with some of the most scathing indictments of American institutions: they believe that there is a power elite running this country which is more protective of its own special interests than the general welfare; they acknowledge the operation of extreme bias in the administration of justice which gives more and lengthier prison terms to convicted criminals who are poor and non-white than it does to their opposites; they regard homelessness less as the fault of those who make do with cardboard beds over subway grates and more as the result of government policies and priorities. In this sense, they are very open to Gouldner's case that leadership is better viewed in terms of a democratic process of critique and reform of social structures than as changing the faces at the top of existing hierarchies.

But the students also pull back from the full implications of this position. I think they do this because it is very difficult for them to imagine how structures can be transformed, and what role they might play in that. It appears to me that my students do not regard themselves as having, or as likely to obtain, any significant public power. They seem mystified by what it means to be "a public," unless this term refers to the readings of opinion rendered by pollsters. So, they make what appears to be a sensible decision to concentrate upon their own education as a step in the achievement of a clearly defined personal reward, such as qualifying for management training in a successful corporation.

Sociological analysis brings into plain view the gap between our suspicion that a fundamental shift of direction is required and our avoidance of asking what impact this might have upon our personal goals. And it does this in a particular way, by locating the sources of our reactions in social structures and cultural understandings rather than in character flaws. It is crucial that this context of our desire to translate education for leadership into training for economic success be developed and examined; otherwise, sociological knowledge becomes dismal and destructive because it seems irrelevant to students' genuine fears about jobs and money and can seem to condemn them for having these anxieties.

The liberating potential of sociology can be buried under contempt for the real hardships faced by students, but it does not have to be. Instead, the discipline's emphasis upon social institutions can help us to free ourselves from their spell and teach us alternative ways of arranging our world. Sociological work can provide us with tools for resisting the prevalent view of leadership as the activity of individuals who occupy the uppermost positions in the most powerful social institutions. It can help us to question the identification of leadership with a few individuals who have succeeded within the established structures. Sociology can give us an awareness of the relationships between the social rules and understandings we take for granted and the social problems which appear intractable. It can do this by helping us back into our own storytelling, giving us ways of celebrating what we are able to produce together when we resist the repressive view from the river. Even the saddest of the stories told amidst the routines of life in the villages has more potential for fostering leadership than the escapist tales of glory told from the distant raft.

Currently, "homelessness" is a social problem which seems to cry out for more effective leadership. Sociological analysis can help to identify the numerous sources of this condition including American values and beliefs; the impact of business interests upon government policy-making; the way in which so-called "welfare" provisions deny participation and power to their recipients; the absence of accountability of elected officials, program administrators, and business leaders to the poor; and the practice of making decisions about specific matters without regard for their connections and reverberating effects on other areas. Homelessness is then revealed as having deeper roots than the ineptitude, shortsightedness, or callousness of any particular leaders; its possibility is shaped within institutionalized assumptions and methods of acting. These also influence the perception that ordinary members of society cannot expect to be able to do anything about "the homeless" we see on our streets. The streets they inhabit are not, in effect, really *ours*; they are someone else's responsibility. Sociology can help us to understand how this has happened, how so many have learned to feel helpless and confused while others lack what most would judge to be basic necessities.

So, I think sociology offers a helpful alternative to the common view in our society which associates leadership with occupancy of top positions, assumes the basic rightness of our social goals and the organizations charged with realizing them, and presumes that a college education can impart at least some of the skills necessary for acquiring power and prestige within these arrangements. Many sociologists incline toward Gouldner's more critical stance, regarding talk about leadership as an avoidance of the task of naming the injustices in our established practices and finding methods for correcting them that promote a democratic process of social change. There is another way to talk about leadership which begins with questions about why the sidewalks and streets seem no longer to be ours and how this might be changed. This sort of beginning can originate in a movement toward the creation of narratives in sociology classrooms which allow us to turn around and discover ways of entering history.

An example of this approach is an opening-day exercise I have used with my last two Sociology 101 classes. I asked each student to make two headings on a blank sheet of paper: "leadership" and "social analysis." For the next ten minutes, they listed characteristics they associate with these words. Then we had a general discussion and the class produced a shared response to the exercise which I recorded as two lists on the blackboard. We took some time to look these over, searching for similarities and differences. Both classes created characterizations of leadership and social analysis which I found intriguing. The most significant move the students made was to recast the terms I had given them into social roles for individuals. Rather than treating leadership and social analysis as activities which might be carried out by groups, they transformed the words into "leader" and "social analyst," and proceeded to show that these roles require different forms of expertise, are likely to attract different personalities, and ideally work as a partnership: the leader draws upon the expertise of the analyst in making decisions.

On the second day of the semester, we began to explore what these two roles might have to do with ourselves, both in the present and in the future. These conversations were much more awkward than the opening exercise. What emerged clearly enough amidst their hesitations was an inability to see themselves in either role; to identify with leadership, they seemed to find it necessary to trim it down to mean occupying a position in the middle to upper levels of a specific hierarchy (e.g., I hope to become a marketing manager, a personnel director). No one was willing to declare a wish to lead society, to assume a major responsibility for shaping its destiny. They seemed to find it difficult to associate the practice of social analysis with specific careers, and this mitigated against identifying themselves with it at all. I heard them saying that they see their education as an investment in becoming qualified for some of the better occupations, that this is the meaning which leadership has for them.

A few days later, I gave these classes an essay to read on the importance of humanities, and asked them to consider that education might be an adventure in discovering a vision for their community or honing the skills of citizenship. They were honest enough to express the opinion that they could not afford this type of education; what they saw themselves as needing was job preparation. If sociology is about formulating a social vision and becoming better citizens, many seemed certain it would be a frustrating waste of their time.

So this is where we started, moving into our own stories about what seems possible, about the choices we are making, and the reasons we give for them. During the semester, we added other stories to our repertoire and tried to become more and more aware of how we listen and assimilate these accounts to what we know. We worked hard to produce a safe space for challenging each other and using that space for recomposing the narratives we shared. It has been my experience that this way of learning sociology--using it to gain access to the many stories our society has to tell and allowing that multiplicity to enlarge our own--can transform a mysterious "system" into a set of possibilities for participation which include more than simply taking up a specific occupation.

Facilitating that transformation is my self-chosen job description. I have faith in this type of learning, the inspiring effect of watching new sociologists at work figuring out what is going on in our society and what needs to be done. My faith has been strengthened by what these same students, initially so doubtful and intimidated, produced by the end of the semester. They developed together an experience of talking seriously about their society which revealed to them different ways of understanding leadership, ones which have to do with changing how we live. In addition, their conversations appeared to empower them by showing leadership to be a group enterprise of uncovering problems, discovering solutions and simultaneously revealing their own talents for this. I characterize this as an exercise in Denzin's revised sociological imagination which holds the promise of preserving the liveliness of the social and the leadership potential it holds. This does not mean that every day of class was a splendid, uplifting occasion; we made lots of mistakes and found the going tough. But what comes with these efforts seems worth the struggle.

Feminist Knowing and Acting

I am not sure where the students got the nerve to attempt such things, but I have acquired this sort of courage from my participation in the feminist movement. Feminism has taught me the best of what I know. It brought me back to teaching and scholarship when I was keenly disappointed in both, and it has kept me intellectually and emotionally on the edge. Feminist thought is a vast provocation--it leaves nothing untouched and is relentlessly unforgiving of my laziness and yearnings for approval. Feminist writers, artists, teachers and friends--this community and its conversation--embody the notion of leadership and articulate the critique of other models that I have come to claim as my own.

Feminism is the recognition that women have been denied full membership and participation in culture and society, and the conviction that this must be changed. Feminists have displayed ways of thinking and acting together beyond the constraints of the known which I take to be the essence of leadership. Feminists have revealed the lie in traditional presentations of leadership as a highly individualized and acutely rarefied enterprise. They have also demonstrated that leadership need not be confined within our present models; it can be fashioned in distinctly different ways within emerging groups that are committed to changing the status quo.

This insight makes a great deal of difference to me when I ask myself who I am, who I think my students are, and what our work might have to do with leadership. Feminists have been doing social analysis and becoming a group that leads, moves toward something better than what we have already. When I read and talk about feminism, I have an experience of being empowered, and I can see that this experience is transferable. I also know that the obstacles to sustaining it are not as formidable as I once thought. There is a lot less to fear from leadership in application to ourselves if we associate it more with questioning than having answers, with process and struggle rather than safe arrival at certainty, with membership in groups and all that entails--shared joys and sorrows, support, a multiplicity of gifts--rather than a position on the mountaintop. I think that the understanding of leadership which feminist activists and theorists are continuing to develop is more inviting than intimidating, and that acting upon it brings an immediate enjoyment which is self-perpetuating. Let me discuss a few examples of what I mean.

Bettina Aptheker's *Tapestries Of Life*[9] is a testimony to the change that occurs when we put women at the center of our thinking, especially when we take that to mean paying attention to the "dailiness of women's lives." Aptheker explores various kinds of writing that reveal the everyday experiences of women from diverse class, racial and ethnic categories. She does not deny that these differences matter, that they have significant effects on women's lives. She is not seeking unity, but rather allowing truth to be multiple and choices numerous. She wants to show how women often resist and escape from the dichotomies that limit our visions and resources. Aptheker believes that in ignoring women's lives, we have deprived ourselves of the tools we need to create more just and peaceful ways of living together. She finds within the small and ordinary practices of women insights for a new kind of politics. Aptheker says: "The point is to change the values and the rules and to change the process by which they are established and enforced." (253-4)

These two tasks, changing the rules and the process of creating rules, constitute a large agenda; this is the program of feminist scholarship, pedagogy and social action. Realizing these goals depends upon a continuing effort to grasp what happens when we admit that our knowing and doing have been unnecessarily limited, and we strive to push their boundaries outward by bringing people previously considered insignificant into our conversations. As Aptheker constructs them, women's ways of knowing and living make what seem to be "problems" into "strengths." The daily strategies that women have devised for resisting powerlessness and erasure transform paradox and ambiguity into pathways toward greater knowledge and more inclusive action. When we acknowledge that truth has many sides, we are more likely to design social action as requiring the participation of many and an openness to change. We are more ready to accept that all of our categories must be re-thought again and again, and that our plans should be humble and responsive to critique. It is not Aptheker's intention to set women's ways of knowing and acting in opposition to men's; rather she wants to uncover a possibility which has the power to resist such tendencies toward exclusion and denial.

In the final chapter of her book, Aptheker performs a reading of Ursula LeGuin's *Always Coming Home*, presenting it as an example of how contemporary women novelists are creating alternative ways of thinking by imagining cultures very different from the modern industrialized world. Aptheker uses LeGuin's book to speak about the dimensions of women's culture: the values, beliefs, and practices rooted in women's routines. She interprets LeGuin as demonstrating that women's experiences and consciousness, values and knowledge offer a basis for a viable ordering of the world. (234-5)

It is important that LeGuin and Aptheker both acknowledge that everyone inhabits two cultures, learns two possible ways of life. Sex is not fate here; it does not consign us to separate worlds, either one of which must dominate the other. The naming of the two cultures as "mother's" and "father's" does not express an immutable natural given; on the contrary, these names point to the human construction of the division and separation of these possibilities in human living. Since we are the creators of these two distinct worlds, we might also choose to undo what we have made; the thinking and imagining associated with this project is a major task of feminist inquiry and art.

Let's explore what Aptheker means by her usage of home and mother, and how she relates these to a concept of politics and leadership. In her reading, LeGuin's novel is emphatically not an invitation to escape into an alternative world. She interprets it instead as calling us to our own ground. "Home" is the everyday world of our own making, a world in which survival and growth are treasured. The warrior society is definitely not home, and the gift of LeGuin's novel is how it reminds the reader of this, while also revealing the persistence of another world that we all can recognize. LeGuin's vision is empowering because what is necessary for change, even revolutionary change, in the established orders of culture and society is named as already there, waiting to be excavated from the places it has been hidden by official accounts of the real. Aptheker says that *Always Coming Home* beckons us to inhabit this familiar world of our own making, to believe in its viability, to manifest our belief by living its values every day, "no matter how hard this is and how 'impractical' we are told that it is to be this way in the 'real' world." (239-40)

While LeGuin and Aptheker relate this notion of home to women, Aptheker emphasizes that this relationship should not be taken as an instance of dichotomizing thought:

> This is not to say that only women have or express these ideas and values.
> ... It is not to say that all mothers personally nurture, or nurture adequately.
> ... Women are not "essentially" virtuous, or more nurturing than men, or more loving, more caring, or "closer to nature." (246-7)

Aptheker's analysis points to the nature of women's labors and the conditions under which they are enacted as forming a particular form of consciousness. Her work contradicts efforts to delineate a "woman's nature," focusing instead on women's experiences as *socially organized*. Women do housework, cooking and child care, and appear to have learned from this doing a wisdom and strength which has been overlooked in standard images of leadership.

Let me try to identify some dimensions of this wisdom and strength. Josephine Donovan has elaborated upon what she terms the "new feminist moral vision."[10] Donovan asserts that the structures of women's lives, not a female essence but particular activities and relationships, have contributed to the formation of a distinctive epistemology and ethic. The roots of this have been women's experience of political oppression, assignment to the domestic sphere of housekeeping and mothering, performance of the economic function of production for use, and the various aspects of the female reproductive role. As a result, Donovan argues that women's knowing is characterized by respect for the concrete context, a willingness to accept the validity of many perspectives, the recognition that humans are not "in control," the need for patient waiting rather than imposing solutions, and an openness to change as both necessary and good.

Like Aptheker, Donovan does not identify these capacities solely with women; she does not construct "Woman"--a timeless, faceless, universal essence of humility and care. She draws upon the works of Keller, Gilligan, Ruddick,[11] and others to suggest that it is the social division of tasks among women and men that has facilitated the emergence of different propensities for thinking, feeling and acting. Even when the division of labor by sex has an obviously biological foundation, the meaningfulness of the biological "facts" is socially endowed. We need to recognize and understand these differences, while at the same time avoiding the temptations to honor one side and denigrate the other and to establish the distinction between them as fixed and final. Donovan does not deny that women and men may and do cross into each other's territories. The wisdom and strength associated with women, but manifested also by men, is the foundation for an image of leadership as humble, respectful of differences, relational, and patient. These adjectives describe the actions of leading, not the gender of leaders. A politics grounded in this type of acting would be non-hierarchical, cooperative, modest, sensitive, and practical.

What is most important in Aptheker, LeGuin and Donovan's delineation of "women's" and "men's" cultures is not the relationship between these signs and observable behaviors (who does what, who has which traits), but rather what these words signify for both men and women. In dividing the world into separate spheres for females and males and speaking of these as "feminine" and "masculine," we have made differences, given them significance, and used them to legitimate numerous decisions. The culturally defined distance between the worlds of women and men, and the identification of leadership with the world of men, has made it difficult for us to imagine what women's work and gifts might have to do with leadership. When feminist theorists and artists such as the ones discussed here attempt to reveal this as error, they begin with the available signs and their effects. So, they do discuss women's ways of knowing, women's experience, etc., and they do point out that these have qualities which contrast with what is likely to appear under the sign of "men" or "masculine." But it is crucial that their work not be regarded as blessing these divisions because this would contradict their purpose, which is to rescue valuable ways of being from the neglected side of an artificial and destructive dichotomy.[12]

When we give attention to the world of home and family, and refuse to relegate these to the shadows of a private realm which is mistakenly viewed as disconnected from communal decision-making, we reconstitute the conversation about leadership. We resist the tendency to exclude many important aspects of our human experience as "too personal and individual." The exclusion has been based upon the assumption that the private sphere is characterized by qualities which make it unsuitable for incorporation into serious public debates about policy. This is part of the false dichotomy which assigns to women a propensity for bias and irrationality, and associates men with the capacity for detachment and reasoned judgment. The potential for distortion and confusion is always present in human affairs; it is minimized not by excluding women or what have been defined as "women's interests" but by representing as much diversity as possible in our conversations.

Cognition is a human practice; knowing is a social process with rules and standards that derive from membership in a community. Many structures and experiences shape what we know; our access to the world is given through our theories, methods, and language. Knowledge is created by the practical judgments of a community of fallible inquirers. It is an illusion to believe that it is possible to assume a position or orientation that "can eradicate all confusion, conflict and contradiction."[13] In my interpretation, the recovery of the experiences of women, carried out with respect for the ways in which these have been significantly shaped by social class, race, and ethnicity, can make a vital contribution to our understanding of leadership. But this contribution does not rest upon a belief that women are better than men, have a special access to the "Truth," and can save us from the present crises in our society and world.

I am using feminist scholarship to say something quite different. I believe it is necessary to discard the categories which have cut up experience and knowledge into separate fragments and give one set of these a privileged position in our image of what it takes to know, to choose, to lead. I think we have a distorted view of leadership based upon an impoverished concept of who is able to speak meaningfully about matters of common concern. This concept, founded upon an incorrect version of expert knowledge and skills, has denied the participation of too many. Feminists have demonstrated that we can have a better public conversation when it is more inclusive and more exploratory. This kind of conversation presumes less and therefore allows more to emerge; most importantly, it enables its participants to experience themselves as having the capacities otherwise identified only with a few "leader-types."

Contrasting metaphors, borrowed from the authors of *Women's Ways Of Knowing*, may help us to focus this understanding:

> In the complexity of a web, no one position dominates over all the rest. Each person--no matter how small--has some potential for power; each is always subject to the actions of others ... In contrast, the self premised in autonomy sees individuals relating through bonds of agreements, such as contracts, laws, and the like. Their metaphors for suggesting the world are more often images of pyramids and mountains. On the metaphorical mountain the few at the top dominate the many at the bottom. Those near the base must move the whole mountain to affect those near the apex; in the image of the net, even the least can affect all others by the slightest pull on the gossamer thread.[14]

The metaphors we use become self-fulfilling prophecies. If we have a "king of the mountain" image of leadership, if we regard hierarchy and competitive striving between autonomous selves as unavoidable, if we begin with a model which identifies change with "lifting the mountain," then it is difficult to conceive of politics as joy-filled, mutual, empowering, and inclusive. In other words, it is difficult to imagine ourselves as participating, as leading. The project of giving expression to the alternative metaphor, to revealing the net and the possibilities that recognizing it creates, has been a task assumed by feminist thinkers and activists.

Even in movements for social change, leadership and participation have often been compromised by the limits of shared metaphors. The discovery of this by women in the student, civil rights, and anti-war groups of the 1960's was an important source of contemporary American feminism and its efforts to re-think leadership. Women participants in movements committed to liberation have often discovered that this ideal does not apply to them, that they are still excluded from leadership and relegated to supporting roles as secretary, housekeeper and hostess. For some women, changing this has meant opening traditional leadership roles-- making speeches, writing policy papers, organizing demonstrations--to women. But another understanding has also been developing during the past twenty-five years which asks for incorporation of women's traditional jobs into the image of leadership.[15]

This argument denies the hierarchical ordering of leader/follower, thinker/coffee-maker. It asserts that those who have been in the background--running the mimeograph machines, cleaning up the debris of all-night meetings, going from door to door soliciting support--have knowledge and skills which are essential to a conception of what it means to lead. It claims that the things that are learned in the performance of these tasks, through membership in the group which is assigned to them, are valuable pieces of the perspective needed by leaders. This explicit concern with the ways in which leadership is defined and exercised has enabled American feminists to enlarge and enrich our conversation about leadership. Feminists have experimented with styles of leadership that seek to eliminate its mystique, to shift it away from identification with rare, charismatic individuals and toward a genuinely democratic process. Efforts to divide and rotate standard leadership responsibilities, serious attention to communication patterns and rules and the adoption of strategies to minimize dominance, as well as the decision to privilege women's insights and gifts, have contributed to the creation of alternative models of action for change.

Too much of our knowledge about leadership and social change has left out the awareness and participation of women and non-elites. When we bring these excluded materials in, leadership and the possibilities it shapes for a different world look very different. The major difference is that other kinds of activities and people are seen as part of what leadership means. The willingness to distinguish between "important individuals and big matters" (the stuff of leadership) and the choices made by all of us in our everyday routines is decreased, and replaced by an awareness that so-called small things matter (the personal is political). Feminists are teaching us that the rigidity of the distinctions between the private and the public, and the way in which this division is employed to keep most of us stuck in the private sphere of individual "lifestyle choices," serve to diminish our society's leadership resources. Feminists are showing that it is possible and desirable for all of us to seek opportunities to have an impact upon our common life. A different story about leadership is being told and it is one which minimizes competition and domination and stresses cooperation and conversation instead.

In order to enter this story, we have to unlearn the disdain for ourselves--our ideas and abilities--which we have acquired from our culture's focus upon special forms of expertise. We have to discover capacities for knowing and acting together which can give us the confidence to become leaders: people of vision and initiative. I think such a discovery is more likely within a certain kind of educational experience, one which brings together critical reflection on society and culture and feminism's ideas about how to create genuinely participatory conversations and organizations.

The Relationship Between Leading and Learning

The picture of a college classroom is odd, isn't it? Typically, the roles of the student and the teacher present themselves in our imagination as extreme contrasts: the teacher may choose whether to sit or stand, expects to speak without interruption and to have everyone's attention, gives directions to everyone else, decides the topic for discussion, evaluates the success of everyone's performance; and the student may do none of these things. The standard classroom rules give permission for activity to the professor and passivity to the student. Even when individual instructors choose to substitute a different set of rules, we recognize this as a choice and as theirs to make.

The Brazilian educator, Paulo Freire, along with several American collaborators, has developed a marvelous analysis of classroom rules and has indicated the key qualities of positive alternatives.[16] Freire and his associates have managed the rare feat of combining trenchant criticism of what is with profound faith in the possibilities of what can be.[17] I want to use this section of the chapter to discuss two prominent themes in Freire's work and show their connections to the way I have been talking about leadership. These themes are "problematizing" and "dialogical, situated pedagogy."

The activity of problematizing is central in Freire's model of knowing. He presents it as the antithesis of technocratic "problem-solving." In that mode of knowing, an expert assumes some distance from a problem, breaks it into its component parts, suggests what would be the most efficient means for solving its difficulties, and develops a policy based on these criteria. Freire regards this sort of activity as reductionist and elitist. It removes problems from their context and declares that the people closest to them have nothing worthwhile to say about them.[18]

Freire contrasts this with "problematizing" which is a group exercise, a conversation in which nothing is sacred except the freedom to question and the dignity of all the participants. Problematizing assumes that problems have a context, that knowledge is relational, and that enabling relationships and conversations is crucial; waiting for and depending upon "experts" is part of the problem rather than a step towards its solution. Education is important because it can be a place where many people learn how to participate in the activity of problematizing and become empowered by that.

Freire's vision of this potential is an antidote to two common forms of escapism from responsibility:

1. He refuses to identify leadership with experts who are detached from the situations they analyze, who set themselves apart by their special competencies and narrow approaches to defining what is at stake, and who deliver momentous pronouncements on what needs to be done from within their isolation and disinterest.
2. He does not succumb to the cynicism and despair which befalls social critics whose judgments about what is wrong with existing arrangements are often stated with a certitude about the futility of trying to correct them.

Freire could not be more different from both experts and cynics. He is deeply optimistic and his optimism is grounded in his conviction that ordinary people can overcome domination and learn to act together for a new society.

Freire's commitment to problematizing is expressed in his contrast of liberating and domesticating forms of education. Liberating education is anchored in and expressive of values; it identifies teachers and students as co-learners, and all learners as subjects; it views education as an activity of creating knowledge, not simply transferring it; it expects that educational activity will transform its participants and their situations; it continually reflects upon its sources; and it is open to correction. Liberating education is comfortable with ambiguities and provisional, multiple forms of understanding; it welcomes difference, newness, and lack of closure. Domesticating education, on the other hand, seeks order and certainty and finds these in conformity to established ways of thinking.[19]

Liberatory education does not mean that educators disappear, or that "anything goes." Freire does not suggest that teachers stop being present, but that we stop being "the presence itself."[20] He sees the teacher as one who gives direction to the process of knowing, but this process also belongs to the students. This view has been stated by one of Freire's associates in these terms:

> . . .the openness of the dialogical educator to his or her own relearning gives dialogue a democratic character. . .liberatory learning is a social activity which by itself remakes authority. These challenges demystify the teacher's power, open it up to change. They impose humility upon the existing order. They invite the students to exercise their own powers of reconstruction.[21]

The last four sentences of this quotation are especially important because they point to the connections between this educational philosophy/practice and leadership. Freire and his colleagues are interested in revealing the non-necessary nature of existing power structures and versions of social order. They seek to accomplish this by developing classroom environments in which participants may discover and use their ability to fashion new ways of seeing the world. In this pedagogy, learning is a cooperative enterprise which draws out and rewards the creativity of all the participants. This form of learning resists hierarchy and promotes exchange. It expresses the conviction that a classroom should not be an environment in which students are continually reminded of what they lack; instead, it should be a place where they are reminded of what they have.

What seems most important in Freire's model of liberating education is not an equality between the students and the teacher, but the quality of their relationships with each other and with their subject matter. Education is the practice of knowing and this practice must always be mutual, responsible and non-controlling. The leadership offered by the teacher shapes the possibility that these qualities will characterize a particular learning situation. When that happens, the class is an experience of shared responsibility which contains many opportunities for engaging in leadership. In the classes envisioned by Freire, leadership is dispersed. While there are significant differences in the tasks of teachers and students, these do not foster a situation in which control equals leadership and all control belongs to the teacher.

Freire explicitly accepts the political nature of education. He strongly criticizes the conventions which invite us to pretend that organizing classroom discourse, designing syllabi, and posing questions are value-free acts which have nothing to do with our beliefs and commitments. He is willing to identify the teacher as a political leader, and to describe ways in which this leadership may emerge as tyrannical or collaborative: "We must say to the students how we think and why. My role is not to be silent. I have to convince students of my dreams, but not conquer them for my own plans." (157) As a leader, the teacher does not conquer, but enables.

Freire's discussion of the political nature of education also deals with the relationship between what happens in classrooms and the rest of social life. Freire does not wish to be understood as arguing that there is no distinction between changing classrooms and changing society: "Only political action in society can make social transformation, not critical study in the classroom." (175) Nevertheless, there is a connection between how education is shaped and whether we can find within ourselves capacities for imagining changes and acting to achieve them.

Classrooms can be spaces in which a different social reality is created and experienced. A pedagogy for liberation presents opportunities to have conversations and insists upon the radical nature of this activity. Its proponents believe that present distortions in our culture and social organizations are directly linked to the suppression of conversation in favor of silence or rote repetition of ideals which protect the status quo. Liberatory educators reveal that we have been encouraged to deny and forget our human potential to name our own experience and to play with possible futures. They do this not by telling us that this has happened, but by presenting chances to discover it for ourselves in the midst of a lively, genuine conversation.

The excitement and truthfulness of these conversations depend upon a sharing of power, respectful giving of direction, and an explicit articulation of values which neither forces agreement nor hides behind a facade of impersonal "facts." They also depend upon the students and teacher finding ways to situate their discourse in matters of real concern to them. The leadership which Freire has shown to be feasible in learning environments, and profoundly transformative of its participants, is a leadership grounded in location. Freire has criticized readers who interpret his ideas as universally applicable directives; for him, everything entails translation and interpretation. We cannot hope to discover fixed and certain principles; rather, we should aim to know where we are and to figure out what this means. This harkens back to what I said in the introduction about developing the "view from here."

Social transformation cannot happen if people do not *show up*, are not invited to be present to themselves and others. In order to show up, we have to be able to explore where we are, what we know, what we are saying and doing. This means we are given permission to be in our situation in new ways, with a greater awareness of what it contains and what it denies. And this is empowering. Freire and Shor believe that empowerment has been wrongly identified with individual "notions of getting ahead." They argue, on the contrary, that there is no such thing as personal empowerment; we discover, use and develop power in social groups. Power is for others: just as we cannot have power without relationships, conversations and actions in solidarity, we also cannot separate individual liberation from social transformation.[22]

Freire and his colleagues help us to see why so many of our educational experiences are dispiriting for both students and teachers. Freire supplies us with some tools for grasping why an education for leadership in society entails a new design for pedagogy. His work allows us to show that the insights of sociology and feminism are best revealed through conversations in which truth is sought but not captured.

Pulling It Together (Somewhat)

Let me see if I can gather these thoughts together into some statements about leadership. What I mean to accomplish in this final section is not a closing but an opening, to put forth some suggestions about where we have been in this essay and what the next steps might be. The image that guides my thinking and writing at this point is "dancing at the edge of the world," which is the title of another book by Ursula LeGuin. She has borrowed the figure from a line in a dancing song composed long ago by California Indians.[23]

I am attracted to this metaphor for describing what I have been doing in this chapter for several reasons. I like what happens what we imagine thinking, writing, and conversing as dancing. When we dance, we use our bodies as well as our minds; we move in graceful, disciplined ways capable of expressing many things at once. Dance happens in the moment and reveals the riskiness of bringing one's talent and preparations together in an offering that may or may not "work." The dance does not give us a place to hide from these risks; to dance is to take them on and keep on doing so. Dancing speaks of being fully alive and present.

Dancing may appear to be a crazy way to behave at the edge of the world. In the Indian song, this word "edge" is translated as "brink." Both words may be used to refer to a point near the beginning or the end, but either one often connotes danger--as in being on the threshold of disaster or the top of a cliff. To be "on edge" is to be anxious. We know ourselves to be on a round ball of a planet, but we need these words, "edge" and "brink," to speak of a sort of knowing in which it does indeed seem possible to fall off the world. We have experiences on steep cliffs that tell us it is possible to go to the limits of safety and to tremble at the chance we might lose our footing. We have something like this fear when we move to the limits of the words and ideas we have constructed. When we approach these, it takes some nerve not to turn back or grasp at anything within reach. It is difficult to imagine dancing on a precipice, whether it exists in the terrain of our thoughts or in nature. It becomes more possible if we believe that dancing on the edge is perhaps the only way to find new words and ideas. This seems to be LeGuin's point when she remarks that:

> To make a new world you start with an old one, certainly. To find a world maybe you have to have lost one. Maybe you have to be lost. The dance of renewal, the dance that made the world, was always danced at the edge of things, on the brink, on the foggy coast.[24]

I think we have lost a world in which it is helpful (if it ever was) to talk about leadership as role to be played by an outstanding few, matching a particular type, in a limited set of places--the White House, the Capitol, the executive suite at corporate headquarters. We need more leaders, not fewer, and in order to get them we have to find ways of talking together which nurture a sense of responsibility, giftedness, and hopeful action in everyone. We also need leaders who are different; that is, we need to allow other characters who are already present in the story but silenced by its selective attention, to reveal themselves as actors and be heard. We have a narrative about leadership in which the critique of our social institutions by sociologists, the stories told by women's lives, and the possibilities created by dialogues about things that really matter to all of us have too often been left out.

When we bring these in, the story we tell about leadership changes. It is not enough to supplement our version of leadership as the elite at the top with a discussion of leadership in the middle of the same pyramids-- the manager as leader. This is so because managers are not expected to shape visions, to think beyond the requirements of their organizations. If we identify leadership with training people to occupy managerial positions, we lose too much of what leadership has traditionally meant in terms of the ability to meet great challenges and to be willing to risk asking radical questions. We need to hold onto these special qualities of leadership while at the same time believing that they are not reserved for a limited number of individuals. We need to learn them instead as practices of groups; such learning is unlikely when we have a model of learning as ideally "value-free:"

> ...in schools and colleges, science, engineering, technology, business and many social science courses generally present knowledge as value-free, free of ideology or politics. If not value-free, then these subjects are presented from an establishment point of view. Students are trained to be workers and professionals who leave politics to the official policy-makers at the top. These falsely neutral curricula train students to observe things

without judging, to see the world from the official consensus, to carry out orders without questioning, as if the given society is fixed and fine.[25]

Leadership is the activity of questioning the job. It takes us toward the possible society which waits within our existing set of practices and arrangements.[26] Sociologists, feminists and liberatory educators make it plain that this leadership is within our reach. They show us that we do not have to remain on the river raft. We can move off into our villages, other conversations. This does not mean that we must erase the traditional stories about leadership by deciding that they have nothing to teach us. Choosing to create other stories is a constructive, rather than destructive, act.

Michael Kirwan's story[27] of how he came to be involved in providing hospitality for homeless individuals is an example of the kind of leadership story this chapter is inviting its readers to enter. In 1978, Kirwan was beginning graduate studies in sociology at George Washington University in Washington, D.C. and working as an account clerk at the University Hospital. One very cold night when he was walking near his apartment building, a man asked him for a dollar to buy some soup. Kirwan describes himself as "very irritated and annoyed that he had disturbed my peace." He was sure that the man actually wanted the money in order to buy a drink, and, to spite him, he went up to his apartment, fixed some soup, brought it down to the man on the street and walked away.

Because doing this made him feel pretty good, he fixed soup, tea, and sandwiches the next night, brought them down to some men hanging out near his home, and walked away without talking to any of them. He says he was too afraid and embarrassed to say anything. He kept doing this for several nights, and the soup container got bigger and bigger. On one of those nights, a man in the group picked up the jug of soup and broke it over Kirwan's head. Kirwan's first words to these people he was feeding were to ask his attacker why he had done that. The man replied that Kirwan was feeding them like pets, setting the food down and walking away; he asked Kirwan to stay and visit with them.

That was the real beginning of relationships between Kirwan and the people congregated around the heating vent. He stopped to listen and talk, and began to fill small requests--for a bus token, a bar of soap, a razor. His assumptions about street people were challenged: these were people who cared about how they looked, who kept searching for work, who weren't always after money to get a fix. But he was still afraid, and when one man asked him if he could come up to his apartment to shower and shave in preparation for a job the next day, Kirwan realized that he wasn't ready to take this risk. He lied and said he wasn't allowed to invite people who did not already live in the building, but the man persisted.

A few days later, Kirwan relented and even allowed the man to stay overnight in the apartment. He took an even greater risk the next day when he left to go to class and allowed the man to stay there without him. That man stayed for thirty days, and by the end of the month, fifteen people were living in Kirwan's apartment: "at the time I thought of them as nothing more than friends." At the request of a nun who had heard he was taking homeless people into his apartment, Kirwan gave his own room to a man evicted by his landlady because he was dying of cancer. He arranged for a visiting nurse to come in every day. When the sick man died, Kirwan's secret was revealed and he was ordered by university officials to get rid of all his house guests. But he didn't; they went on as before and a year passed. Then a young man died of a drug overdose after coming up to shower, and the university took Kirwan to court. A sympathetic judge gave him three months to find another place to live, and he located a small boarded-up house that he could afford on his hospital salary. Within a few months, there were forty people living there and the house had become the "Llewelleyn Scott Catholic Worker House of Hospitality." Now there is a farm in Virginia with a house for men and one for women and children, as well as the house in Washington.

Michael Kirwan refuses to see himself as *special*---crazy or holy or both. He describes what he does in very simple terms: "I give hungry people a meal or floor space so that they won't have to sleep on the streets." He questions the images we have of homeless people as dangerous and unworthy:

> Problems are everywhere, and we are no exception, yet somehow this works and my only explanation still is that it is based on mutual trust and respect. It's a remarkable event, six days a week, to give meals, clothes and assistance to upwards of 300 people a day. It goes on with people in charge whom, under other circumstances, most people would avoid, discriminate against, judge, be intimidated by; because, just as I once did, we look at a person in terms of what they are wearing or the conditions under which we find them. If we take these same people out of those surroundings, they are transformed; we are transformed; it cannot be otherwise. They are no different than you and I when all of their situations are addressed rationally and realistically. We must stop shifting the blame for the circumstances others find themselves in, and look at ourselves and our preconceived notions, which are often means of escape or avoidance.

Michael Kirwan is telling us a story about leadership in the choices he has made about how to live. His story is not about power, success, and fame as these are defined by many people in our society, including many writers on leadership. He did not set out to become a leader and does not see himself as organizing a social movement. Kirwan has responded to suffering in his neighborhood in a very direct way; he has acted with poor people to create some possibilities for community and mutual help. Michael Kirwan's story shows that we need not feel powerless and despairing or wait to be rescued by an extraordinary leader. Instead, we can allow ourselves to discover what needs to be done and then to act in the ways that seem open to us in our own situations and within our own limitations. I think his is a story about leadership that is worth telling and that in its telling we can find an embodiment of the messages communicated by the sociologists, feminists and dialogical educators discussed in this chapter.

Entering these stories about leadership requires just this step: we simply have to remember together, over and over again that we share the responsibility for creating and renewing our world. This cannot happen without us, while we wait for leaders to emerge or believe that we are training to become them by learning professional roles. Leading is playing another kind of part. It is declaring our desires to help one another see those things that the routines of membership in society render obscure, and to act together to change whatever seems wrong and unjust. Why not dance on the foggy coast?

Notes

1. Susan Bordo, "Feminism, Postmodernism, and Gender Skepticism," in *Feminism/Postmodernism*, ed. Linda J. Nicholson (New York: Routledge, 1990), 133-156.

2. Ibid., 144. Emphasis in the original.

3. David Tracy, *Plurality and Ambiguity: Hermeneutics, Religion, and Hope* (San Francisco: Harper and Row, 1989), 113. First published in 1987.

4. John Walton, *Sociology and Critical Inquiry: The Work, Tradition, and Purpose* (Chicago: The Dorsey Press, 1986), 62.

5. C. Wright Mills, *The Sociological Imagination* (New York: Oxford University Press, 1959).

6. Norman Denzin, "The Sociological Imagination Revisited," *The Sociological Quarterly*, 31 (1990): 1-22.

7. Ibid., 6 and 15.

8. Alvin W. Gouldner, *Studies in Leadership* (New York: Basic Books, 1950), 9.

9. Bettina Aptheker, *Tapestries of Life: Women's Work, Women's Consciousness, and the Meaning of Daily Experience* (Amherst: University of Massachusetts Press, 1989). Quotes in the following paragraphs are from this edition.

10. Josephine Donovan, *Feminist Theory: The Intellectual Traditions of American Feminism* (New York: The Ungar Publishing Co., 1987), 172-178.

11. Evelyn Fox Keller, "Gender and Science," in *Discovering Reality: Feminist Perspectives on Epistemology, Metaphysics, Methodology, and Philosophy of Science*, ed. Sandra Harding and Merrill B. Hintikka (AA Dordrecht, Holland: D. Reidel Publishing Co., 1983), 187-205; Carol Gilligan, *In a Different Voice* (Cambridge: Harvard University Press, 1982); and Sara Ruddick, "Maternal Thinking," *Feminist Studies* 6 (1980): 342-367.

12. That dichotomy has been generalized beyond the categories of masculine and feminine. Sandra Harding has shown its presence in the contrasts drawn between the European and African world views. In her formulation, both the feminist and the Africanist models view the self as dependent upon community

and embedded in nature, and regard knowing as a contextual, tentative enterprise which unites manual, mental, and emotional operations. In this kind of knowing, the knower is always part of the known. European and masculine models exhibit the opposing tendencies to define the self as autonomous, isolated from others and from nature. These models idealize knowledge which is produced by detached knowers who control their subject matter. Each side of this dichotomy reveres the sort of acting which complements its version of knowing so each has implications for models of leadership. See Sandra Harding, "The Curious Coincidence of Feminine and African Moralities: Challenges for Feminist Theory," in *Women and Moral Theory*, ed. Eva Feder Kittay and Diana T. Meyers (Totowa: Rowman and Littlefield, 1987), 296-315.

   13. M. E. Hawkesworth, *Beyond Oppression: Feminist Theory and Political Strategy* (New York: The Continuum Publishing Co., 1990), 137.

   14. Mary Field Belenky et al., *Women's Ways of Knowing: The Development of Self, Voice, and Mind* (New York: Basic Books, Inc., 1986), 179.

   15. Sara Evans, *Personal Politics: The Roots of Women's Liberation in the Civil Rights Movement and the New Left* (New York: Random House, 1980). First published in 1979.

   16. There are significant connections between the feminist ideas elaborated in the preceding section and the pedagogical philosophy of Paulo Freire. The interested reader can consult these two anthologies for examples of how feminist educators have appropriated Freire's methods: Charlotte Bunch and Sandra Pollack, eds., *Learning Our Way: Essays in Feminist Education* (Trumansburg: Crossing Press, 1983) and Margo Culley and Catherine Portuges, eds., *Gendered Subjects: The Dynamics of Feminist Teaching* (Boston: Routledge and Kegan Paul, 1985).

   17. Henry A. Giroux, "Introduction," in Paulo Freire, *The Politics of Education: Culture, Power, and Liberation*, trans. Donaldo Macedo (New York: Bergin and Garvey Publishers, 1985).

   18. Dennis Goulet, "Introduction," in Paulo Freire, *Education for Critical Consciousness* (New York: Seabury Press, 1973), ix.

   19. Freire, *The Politics of Education*, 101-103 and 114-116.

   20. Ibid., 105.

   21. Ira Shor and Paulo Freire, *A Pedagogy for Liberation: Dialogues on Transforming Education* (New York: Bergin and Garvey Publishers, 1987), 101. The quotes in the next six paragraphs are from this edition.

   22. This can be related to Nancy Hartsock's discussion of Hannah Arendt's re-theorization of power. In Hartsock's interpretation, Arendt rejected the identification of power with domination and redefined it as action in concert. Hartsock maintains that Arendt shifts the ancient concept of heroic action away from individuals competing for dominance and toward action with others to address shared concerns. For a fuller discussion of Arendt's re-working of the Greek political tradition, see Nancy Hartsock, *Money, Sex, and Power: Toward a Feminist Historical Materialism* (Boston: Northeastern University Press, 1985), 211-222. Echoes of this conceptualization can be found in Elizabeth Kamarck Minnich's reminiscence about Arendt in which she asserts that Arendt viewed power as "something which springs up between people, that only increases with being shared," and which is dependent upon speech and persuasion. See Elizabeth Kamarck Minnich, "Hannah Arendt: Thinking As We Are," in *Between Women: Biographers, Novelists, Critics, Teachers and Artists Write about Their Work*

on Women, ed. Carol Ascher, Louise DeSalvo, and Sara Ruddick (Boston: Beacon Press, 1984), 177.

23. Ursula LeGuin, *Dancing at the Edge of the World* (New York: Grove Press, 1989), 48.

24. Ibid.

25. Shor and Freire, *Pedagogy for Liberation*, 12-13.

26. For an elaboration of this notion of a possible society and how it is the task of social theorizing to reveal it, see Alan Blum, "Theorizing," in *Understanding Everyday Life*, ed. Jack Douglas (Chicago: Aldine Publishing Co., 1970), 305-319.

27. Michael Kirwan, "Hospitality is Mutual Trust and Respect," *The Catholic Worker*, LVIII, 6 (September): 1, 4, and 7. Quotes in the following paragraphs are from this source.

Chapter 9

Making School Real: Leadership in the Classroom

Julie Tammivaara

> *Every life is a viewpoint on the universe.*
> José Ortega y Gasset

Carolyn Heilbrun has defined power as "the ability to take one's place in whatever discourse is essential to action and the right to have one's part matter."[1] If this be power, I would like to suggest that leadership is the ability to involve others in conversation that is essential to action and to affirm the significance of the others' contributions to that conversation. In the essay that follows, I focus upon leadership in the university classroom. Beginning with a description of the European medieval university and how teaching practices were connected with university purposes, I next move to a discussion of present American university practices and how they relate to present higher educational aims. I shall argue that while some features of the medieval university survive in contemporary institutions of higher education, at least one aspect has been lost and should be restored: the university's mission to connect students with a general system of ideas that will enable them to lead meaningful lives. By failing to do this, the university fails to involve students in conversations important to action, that is, to empower them. The European medieval mission is then extended to incorporate the specific circumstances prevailing in contemporary society.

I

The higher education that predates the Middle Ages was not organized as permanent institutions of learning; there were no diplomas, faculties, courses of study, examinations, commencement exercises, or academic degrees. Higher education in Europe was in the hands of the Church, either in monastic or cathedral schools or available from 'wandering scholars' who succeeded to the extent that they could attract paying students.[2] The university as we know it today has its roots in medieval Italy. Late in the eleventh century, there appeared in Bologna a student class consisting of hundreds of scholars not only from Italy but from countries beyond the Alps. Removed from the protection of their feudal estates, these students were vulnerable to the harassments of townspeople and inconvenienced in a variety of ways. Merchants and landlords with an eye for profits charged exorbitant rates for food and lodging. For protection, the students united along the lines of the guilds common in Italian cities. By forming a union (hence the term "university"), students were able to bring costs under control. Merchants who did not please the students could be brought into line through threats of a boycott. This organization of local and foreign students was the beginning both of the university and of "town and gown" antipathies.[3]

With the taste of victory over the merchants still fresh, students turned next to their "other enemy," the professors.[4] Since professors earned their keep through students' fees, the organized scholars were able to extend the threat of a boycott to bring professors under their rein. One set of Bolognese statutes (1317) specified that the professor might not be absent without leave for even a single day, and if he desired to leave town he had to make a deposit to ensure his return. If he failed to secure an audience of five for a regular lecture, he was fined as if absent.... He must begin with the bell and quit within one minute of the next bell. He was not allowed to skip a chapter of his commentary or postpone a difficulty to the end of the hour, and he was obliged to cover ground systematically, so much in each specific term of the year.[5]

To counter the growing power of the "universities" of students, professors eventually united by forming guilds or "colleges" of their own. Entry into a college could be made only by consent of its members; this consent eventually took the form of a license that permitted its bearer to teach. The course of study offered at the medieval universities could be completed in six years, at which time students could sit for a fixed exam and, if successful, were awarded a degree or license that would permit them to teach anywhere. In time, the term "university" came to denote a society of masters and scholars.

Haskins notes that we can detect in the medieval universities four features present in modern universities: first, the corporation of scholars and masters as mutually engaged in a life of learning; second, the idea of a set curriculum leading to examinations and the granting of degrees;

third, the organization of faculties in colleges or schools with deans and other, higher offices; and, fourth, the idea that teaching in a university is a profession supported by tuition-paying students. These four features of the medieval university are unmistakably present in today's universities.

II

Although professional training in the law and medicine also has its roots in medieval times, the central concern of the universities at that time was not, as it is today, professional training and scientific investigation; rather, the central concern was the transmission of what the Spanish philosopher Ortega y Gasset called "general culture," that is, the system of ideas concerning the world and humanity which people of that time possessed. "Life is chaos," he states, "a tangled and confused jungle in which man is lost." The ideas with which medieval students grappled enabled them to develop a "repertory of convictions which became the effective guide" to their existence.[6] This, Ortega argues, was the mission of the medieval university.

Life in the Middle Ages in Europe was a very different proposition than it is today. In his City of God, Augustine had bid good riddance to the Roman Empire and argued that the world was not worth bothering about so there was no point in trying. Heaven was what mattered and what we knew of heaven was contained in old texts written by holy Fathers. The knowledge needed to grasp matters of faith was also old, residing as it did in ancient Greek texts. Everything worth knowing was old.

The system of ideas, or curriculum, of the medieval universities consisted of the seven liberal arts that had been written into a single book in A.D. 600 by the Cartheginian lawyer, Martianus Capella. The seven liberal arts consisted of the trivium, instructing one on how to use facts, and the quadrivium, containing the facts one needed to know. The trivium, which constituted the curriculum for the Bachelor of Arts degree, encompassed grammar necessary for getting the spoken word right, rhetoric for putting words into texts, and logic which enabled one to explain things clearly. For the advanced degree of Master of Arts, the curriculum consisted of the quadrivium comprised of music or the theory needed to sing hymns, geometry so one could measure things, arithmetic to add things up, and astronomy for knowing what day it was.

The texts studied by medieval students and professors were few in number and laboriously copied or manually printed. Until Johann Gutenberg's invention of printing presses with moveable type in the mid-fifteenth century, manuscripts were produced in copying rooms (scriptoria) and stored in the libraries (armaria) of monasteries. Monastic libraries included the Holy Scriptures, the writings of Church Fathers, and commentaries on them. Larger collections included as well the works of Bede, Augustine, Albertus Magnus, Aquinas, Roger Bacon, and secular works by Virgil, Horace, Cicero, Plato, Aristotle, and Galen. Students who had studied at Bologna, Paris, or other European university centers would bring back to their monastic libraries their lecture notes consisting of transcriptions and the latest interpretations of both sacred and secular classics.

The laboriously copied texts embodied in monastic libraries were limited by orthodoxy and dogma. While there was much more known in the world than what medieval scholars studied, the combination of lack of contact (with the Chinese and Arab worlds, for example) and a point of view that treasured preservation of the old above creation of the new ensured a highly circumscribed definition of knowledge.

III

Because medieval universities emphasized the preservation of existing knowledge over the production of new knowledge, students did not expect nor were they expected to be independent and creative learners. Since what mattered was not the world but heaven, scholarly work focused on discovery and remediation of errors of faith. "Classes" consisted of lectures, commentaries, and disputations in Latin. Students' insistence that professors stick to their texts is consistent with their desire to be accurately informed of the known. The lecture (from the Latin lectio, "a reading") was the most sensible method by which to transmit accurately the otherwise unavailable texts. Professors also read commentaries or "glosses" consisting of brief explanations of technical or difficult points. These commentaries usually appeared as marginal notes in the professors' texts. Disputations, introduced early in the twelfth century, had a more conversational tone than lectures or commentaries; they consisted of the lecturer posing a problem to students and attempting to resolve its difficulties through questions and answers. Professors conducted disputations using the logic of Aristotle and appeals to authority to form orderly arguments for and against specific theses. While disputations could be presented in a manner that was entertaining, bold, original, and "able to move to laughter the serious minds of men," as was said of Peter Abelard,[7] arguments were inevitably cast in a polemical yes or no form, such as, are there one or three Almighties, and if there are three, can God beget himself? This form of argument left no room for intermediate positions where, many would argue today, truth is to be found.

The heart of the medieval university consisted of the seven liberal arts. The curriculum consisted of clear, relatively firm ideas about the universe and the nature of things. Universities taught the system of ideas known to Europe at that time. Scholars did not engage in research nor was the preparation of professionals central to their mission. The emphasis was on becoming educated by building on the past (lectures) and reflecting on the present (commentaries) through a form of reason (disputations).

The university, then, is some 900 years old and a brief look at its form demonstrates a degree of continuity across time and space. These, however, are not the Middle Ages; it is appropriate to ask to what extent the missions of the medieval university and the modern university coincide and, given a very different cultural context, what might be the implications for schooling practices today.

IV

The medieval university's emphasis on the transmission of knowledge through what might appear to the modern student to be fairly rigid and limited means, that is, lecturing and controlled argument, is clear. More difficult to grasp, at least for me, is the fact that all of what could be learned in the cathedral and monastery schools and in the European medieval universities was well within the grasp of the ordinary student.[8] Professors, therefore, did not have to make decisions about what to include in the curriculum, how to adapt their teaching presentations to meet particular student needs, or to wonder how their activities connected with larger social structures. In medieval universities, what was defined as worth knowing could be known by all who participated.

In the intervening years since the Middle Ages, the mission of the university and the social context within which universities function have changed. In most North American universities, the mission is twofold: to train professionals (lawyers, physicians, educators, engineers, entrepreneurs, etc.) and to engage in research and train future investigators. The liberal arts which in the past connected individual scholars with a system of ideas have dwindled in importance, although students are often required to take something of a general nature, some history, say, or philosophy. At the postgraduate level, professional schools offer a greater variety of advanced degrees and overall enjoy higher student enrollments than postgraduate studies in the liberal arts. Their professors are also more adequately compensated for their labors.[9] Far from being the core of the university, the liberal arts, not addressing as they do either professionalism or research as it is commonly defined, are on the verge of becoming vestigial, if they are not so already.[10] "The university today," Ortega noted in 1930, "is a tropical underbrush of subject matters."[11] The mission of the university has shifted from one of enabling students to connect with ideas that will help them to live a meaningful life to one of enabling students to earn a living. This is reflected in the fact that the most serious (and seriously taken) American critiques of the university today are made by the business and (speaking on behalf of business) political sectors.[12] These critics do not assail educational institutions for failing to nurture humane and moral citizens but for failing to graduate students able to reverse the loss of competitive edge once enjoyed by American business.

The "professionalization" of the university's mission has been facilitated by the exponential explosion of knowledge during the past 300 or so years. It is no longer possible to expect that either professors or students can learn all there is to know. As a result, knowledge and, hence, courses of study, have become specialized and segmented. Professional fields are marked by ideas, but these ideas refer to the doing of particular kinds of work, not the living of life in general. A degree in education, medicine, the law, engineering, business, and so forth might equip students with the wherewithal to make a living but not necessarily to live a more thoughtful and meaningful life.

The increase in knowledge has another consequence important to the argument here: the development of pedagogy. In small, relatively isolated societies where what one can or must know can be learned in a reasonable amount of time, teaching is not a problematic activity. In such a society (as was the case in Europe in the Middle Ages) one listens, observes, and practices until one gets the hang of things. The anthropologist Edward T. Hall has identified three kinds of learning, the first two of which are germane to the kind of learning dominant in the early universities. Learning by precept and admonition ("Not 'goed'! Went!") is called formal learning. Underlying formal learning is the assumption that there is one right way to do things. The 'teacher' knows this way and communicates such to the learner through a series of corrective moves. A second mode of learning is accomplished through modeling. The teacher asks that learners observe others doing whatever is at issue until they master it. Here, again, there is the implication that there is an acceptable form of knowledge and with time learners will become skillful.[13]

These two modes of learning are adequate when what must be learned is within the grasp of the learner, and there is sufficient time in which to learn. Teaching under these circumstances evokes few practical methodological debates. For example, all infants must tackle the complex and difficult task of learning their native language. Barring profound mental disability, all children acquire language from the people closest to them. The parents, siblings, and friends who teach children language do not require training in linguistics or pedagogy. Teaching language comes "naturally" and learning language is well within the bounds of a child's capability. If what can be learned exceeds the grasp of the learner, however, then teaching becomes problematic; that is, choices must be made. This had become evident by the mid-eighteenth century, and thus it is no surprise that the concept of pedagogy made its appearance then. Unable to transmit all knowledge, scholars began to ponder where the teacher's emphasis should focus. Whereas the medieval focus was on transmitting a set body of knowledge, later thinkers--Rousseau, Pestalozzi, Froebel, and, later, Montessori--suggested that the focus should be the student. They argued that it is to learners and their characteristics that teachers should look to determine instructional decisions and make something organic of education. Thus, in shifting the focus from relatively simple transmission of knowledge to issues of what should be taught and how, the modern profession of teaching was given birth.

V

While the development of the idea of pedagogy was spurred by the rapid proliferation of knowledge, the realization of "serving students" today has an unabashedly technical concern. Educational discourse[14] is underlain with the hidden (and sometimes not-so-hidden) assumption that serving students means conceptualizing schools as businesses that produce students who will meet the nation's industrial needs and assist students in contributing to its economic productivity. What any nation is, the argument goes, depends on the quality of its workers. What any reasonable student desires, the argument continues, is to make a living. Thus, universities can best serve students by preparing them to be good workers which, in turn, benefits the national economy.

With this concern, professorial and administrative discourse centers on what subjects should be taught, what forms of instruction should be used, what objectives should be developed, and how objectives can be matched with standard forms of evaluation.[15] This discourse is pursued in professional journals, in conjunction with agencies of general and specialized accreditation, at faculty meetings, and between administrators and faculty during performance reviews. Educational goals become consumer goals; they are rationalized technically. Educational leaders focus on how to attain goals (back to the basics, longer school terms, more standardized testing, etc.) rather than on developing a mutual inquiry into why certain goals are pursued and thence to choosing and owning them.

In my view, students should be the central focus of what universities do, but the mission of the university should not be primarily professional preparation (although that is important) nor scientific inquiry (although that too is important). As in medieval times, the central focus should be to prepare students to live their lives by connecting them with ideas that locate them (the students) in their time and with the ideas of their time. Given a very different sociocultural context, however, fulfillment of this mission requires the development of classroom practices very different from medieval times.

VI

For humans, life is given as unorganized and chaotic. We do not have the finely developed instincts that make it possible for other forms of life to secure their niche and flourish. Humans must make their world. They must find the roads; they must make their way through the forest.

They do so through systems of ideas; ideas enable us to make meaning and meaningful lives.

One way of reducing the chaos into which each of us is born entails selectivity. Older, more experienced persons in our environment indicate those things to which we should attend and, tacitly, those things we should ignore. By so doing, the buzz and boom of our environment is diminished, at least some of the time, and we can make sense of the world. In a similar vein, societies are structured to lessen the ambiguity of the social and natural worlds by defining rules of behavior and explaining laws of nature. Of course, there is wide variation in the forms these rules take and variation, as well, in the extent to which limitations are successfully imposed.

In medieval Europe, the limitations were (as far as we know) relatively strong. That is, the range of appropriate beliefs and behaviors, by contemporary standards, was narrow. Daniel Boorstin notes: "Writers of original texts were reluctant to take the credit, or risk the more likely blame, for innovation. In the great age of manuscript books, anonymity was dictated by technology, orthodoxy, and prudence."[16] Whereas the professorial task then was to connect individual scholars with a system of ideas and, given the tenor of the times, the best way to do that was through lecture, commentary, and disputation, the task today entails connecting students with multiple systems of ideas with a completely different technological repertoire.

What this means is that while it is important to train professionals and also to make scientific discoveries, universities and the professorate need to raise ideological questions about the curricular and pedagogical choices they are making. These questions allow students to grapple not only with what to do to be a teacher or a lawyer or a physician or an engineer or a scientist but also, and more significantly, with the question of what is their idea of a teacher, a lawyer, a physician, an engineer, a scientist. To grasp the "idea" of one's professional (or other) group is to examine how one's own views of knowledge, values and society are mediated through common sense assumptions one uses to construct an identity as a member of that group.

If the student is central to what a university is, and what is central to students is "doing" life, then professors can only meet students' needs by reconceptualizing their specialized subject matters to include vital systems of ideas and to connect these with individual student ideas in all of the courses they teach. Unlike the social context of the medieval university, the present social context (at least in American universities) is far more varied and complex. While it may have been reasonable in feudal times to educate a select group of people toward a fairly coherent set of ideas, today's university does not consist of such a select group nor are the available and legitimized ideas so unitary. In the midst of this complexity, people need not only the ability to grasp a limited set of ideas, but also the ability to analyze critically and choose among many available ideas. In a society where knowledge is relatively certain, the lecture, the commentary, and disputations are appropriate teaching practices. In societies where knowledge is recognized as uncertain and complex, the ability to inquire critically is more important than the mastery of selected bits of knowledge. If this is the case, the pedagogical implications are several.

VII

There are three aspects of the educational endeavor that are largely ignored in the current, dominant conception of schooling at all levels. First, there is the fact that knowledge is always socially produced by particular people who have particular interests in producing it and who infuse (knowingly or not) such knowledge with their own values. Second, schooling happens in the company of others, a teacher and other students, and thus the relationships of the classroom participants is problematic. Finally, what happens in the classroom is imbedded in schools with particular organizational structures. Each of these will be discussed in turn.

Knowledge

In the hallways and lounges of universities, one hears students and professors talk of "material" to be covered in courses. "I just don't know how I'm going to get all the material covered this term in my 353 class. Here we are almost halfway through the semester and we're only on chapter six," says a professor. "I am thinking of taking five classes next term, Dr. Jones. How much material would I be responsible for in your 353?" asks a student. In these remarks we see the content of courses seen as "out there," quantities with an almost physical dimension that are to be presented, consumed, and then measured. Lost in this discourse is the idea that in producing the cited knowledge, somebody (or, more accurately, several somebodies) produced the knowledge through a process in the service of specific values. Written texts are accounts by particular people wherein discoveries imbedded in points of view are offered. Writing the text is not a singular, objective act but a process. The process begins with the author who possesses a point of view or frame of reference on the world. Next, the author selects a subject or topic, gathers information, develops an organizing idea, and uses evidence. Each of these elements is problematic; that is, at each point in the process, choices are made to include some things and exclude other things. The message and shape of the text depends entirely on what choices the author makes. For example, suppose an author wanted to discuss the relationship of ethnicity to school achievement. It is well known that as a group, Asians and northern European-Americans outperform other ethnic groups on standardized tests of knowledge in American schools.[17] If one's frame of reference were a version of social Darwinism, one would attribute differences in achievement to genes and go on to argue that achievement differences were a matter of inheritance and there is nothing that can change the way things are. Taking a psychological stance, one would attribute the differences to patterns of child development and, if equality were a goal, prescribe early intervention in patterns of family life. If one were sociologically oriented, one might look to the schools and how they are organized to value certain ways of doing things while neglecting other ways and locate the problem in the educational institution.

Depending upon which of these frames of reference is chosen, what information one gathers is determined, the possible organizing ideas are limited, and the appropriate rules of evidence are restricted. It is seldom evident that each step is problematic and requires choices; neither is it evident that a particular choice implies a limited and specific array of possibilities for choices in succeeding steps. Since an author is most often interested in expressing her own point of view, she will write as if hers were the only point of view. Knowledge is treated as if it were objective, that is, external to students, and it therefore can be imposed on them. Selected knowledge is thus treated as if it has an authority beyond question, analysis, and negotiation. Once knowledge is conceptualized as independent from its human producers, the student's purpose becomes one of accumulation and categorization.[18] In this way, knowledge is not seen as doubtable, analyzable, or negotiable. As Giroux has noted, "knowledge is removed from the self-formative process of generating one's own set of meanings, a process that involves an interpretive relationship between the knower and the known."[19] By separating knowledge from its producers, it becomes knowledge "about" the external world; lost is the idea that knowledge should also be "of" the world. Knowledge of the world implies a subject's participation in critical understanding.

To bring students into the larger society as vital participants, professors need to help them understand the processes whereby the knowledge they strive to grasp was made. If students are to participate critically and with self-awareness in producing knowledge, they need to learn how to do it. Teachers as leaders need to engage their students in a discourse that not only considers the message of the text but also permits a critique of the process that produced the text.

Professors can invite students into this dimension of knowledge by infusing classroom encounters with the problematic nature of knowledge production. What is the knowledge being presented here? By what process did the author(s) arrive at this form of knowledge? What other forms are possible? Whose interests are served by this form? What larger sociopolitical context renders this account sensible? How do the experiences and issues of individual students' lives intersect with the larger context?

As noted above, at the point when what was available to be learned exceeded an individual's ability to learn, curricular choices had to be made. Philosophy professors had to decide which philosophies to examine in their courses, theologians had to decide what theologies to teach, astronomers had to decide which theories of the universe to cover, and so forth. The necessary selection, organization, and distribution of knowledge in a given classroom, department, or school in a university implies assumptions about truth and legitimacy. By selecting one set of philosophers and ignoring others, a professor says in effect, "These people are worth your time and effort in this class, and the others are not (or, at least, are less so)." Through this process, students' conceptions of the world are structured.

If students are not given the opportunity to question the particular selection, organization, and distribution of knowledge offered in courses, then they learn to value conformity above critical inquiry. They learn that whatever their own perspectives on the ideas presented, what counts in terms of grades and degrees is mastery of the professor-selected material. To nurture critical inquiry, professors must raise as problematic the selections they have made and made explicit the reasons for those selections. By doing so, they acknowledge and legitimate the existence of alternative points of view and alternative purposes. For many professors this is not an easy thing to do. If a professor cares very much about a particular point of view, he or she will find it difficult to introduce competing points of view. Such a professor may forget that students do not necessarily share his or her life experiences or, even worse, may operate under the illusion that students do not have their own life experiences that have contributed to their own legitimate points of view. Acknowledging student perspectives and admitting (if not embracing) competing points of view affects what students do in the classroom. The task of the student shifts from one of "giving the teacher what he wants" to entering into a dialogue wherein the student can practice making his or her own way toward a considered point of view. This point of view, then, can become the basis for the student's life guide.

Classroom Relations

In American universities, education at all degree levels typically occurs in classrooms with a set of students and at least one professor. Whether it be a small seminar or a large lecture course, people come together to learn, and there are a variety of ways in which they can relate together to do this learning. Curricula that are conceptualized as objective and external to students' experience lead to an idea of the classroom that considers participants as individual consumers with some unifying characteristics and varying abilities to ingest and metabolize the "material." Professors who structure their classes according to this view focus on attempting to connect students with the subject matter and ignore developing connections between themselves and students and among the students.

The practice of stating goals, defining objectives, designing course activities to fit the goals and objectives and then evaluating courses on how well these fit facilitates and highlights the dispassionate and disembodied character of such classrooms. What has this to do with the living of one's life which, presumably, occurs in the company of and in connection with others?

If we accept that knowledge is constructed and reconstructed by people who are attempting to make life meaningful, then why should students who are also involved in this process of making meaning leave this important task outside the classroom door? It is my contention that they should not.

In a classic study of the classroom, Philip Jackson noted that teacher-student encounters are permeated by the ideas of crowds, praise, and power.[20] That is, relative to students' experiences of the family, classrooms consist of relatively large groups of students under the tutelage of a single adult. The consequence for students is that they must learn to wait their turn to be recognized; gratification must be delayed. In waiting their turn, students learn to be patient. This is not a patience, Giroux notes, born of reflective discipline, but one rooted in "unwarranted submission to authority."[21] The student further learns that the classroom is a forum in which evaluation is important. Students are praised for doing well, chastised for doing poorly, and these assessments are often carried out in public. Beyond the day-to-day oral praise and blame attached to students by their teachers and classmates, evaluation is received in written form at the end of school terms. Finally, students become aware of their unequal status vis-a-vis teachers. While students will, on occasion, evaluate one another, what counts in the classroom is the teacher's evaluation. That student evaluations rest on more than intellectual achievement is well known; proper demeanor is important as well.

In raising classroom relations as problematic, I do not intend to suggest that students should not outnumber professors, that evaluation should not occur, nor that students should be as powerful as professors although an argument could be made for each of these suggestions. My intention is, rather, to suggest that the way students relate to one another and to the professor should be explicitly raised in classroom situations by the professor, and that the alternatives and their implications be considered. As students should become part of the conversation about what counts as knowledge, I am suggesting that students be brought into the discussion about how social relationships in the classroom can or should be realized. The ways in which we learn to relate to others in the schoolroom inevitably become part of the repertoire of ways we know to relate to people more generally. Students who only see authorities (professors) exploit and devalue them as underlings are likely, when they assume authoritative positions, to exploit and devalue those over whom they have power.

Universities as Organizations

All classrooms of students and their professors are situated in an organization that itself is located in a larger social order. Professors, then, are not only in a relationship with students but in a relationship with several layers of authority above them. In American education, administrators and professors have become divided: administrators issue policies and professors assume the technical role of carrying them out. This is not to imply that administrators can wield their authority freely; on the contrary, they often feel bound by constraints they perceive issuing from even higher levels, for example, the church or state. They may, at times, feel as powerless as professors.

What is missing in many administrator-professor relationships is parallel to what is missing from professor-student relationships. That is, there is an absence of a language and, hence, a discourse to permit them to focus on issues of power, educational philosophy and theory, and politics.

The present university structure separates students from professors and professors from administrators by centering the discussion on technical matters (teaching summarized numerically, number of publications, number of committees served, variety of teaching strategies employed, and so forth); this very separation forecloses discussion on issues that undergird the reasons why many professors chose to teach in the first place. Many chose this profession because of a strong commitment to justice and freedom and a belief that whatever benefits they may have been fortunate enough to have derived in their lives should be benefits shared by all.

VIII

In a time when there is no compelling and widely shared world view in our universities, let alone the society as a whole, the ability to detect alternative models of doing life and to critically examine them from some moral perspective is essential to a meaningful life. To develop an appropriate language to engage in such a discourse, we need not only professors who will let students in on the politics of teaching, but administrators who will let professors in on the politics of higher education. Administrators, professors, and students alike need to engage in conversations (not "sharing," but real conversations) about the meaning of society, school, and freedom. Conversation is rendered meaningful by its link to action; that is, the conversation is realized in the concrete doings of the classroom as situated by the professor as a leader.

Dialogue about important issues is, of necessity, not only intellectually charged but emotional as well. To ensure that the conversation continues, then, participants must feel safe. Individual and collective exploration of meaning and the link between the two entail risk. Many would not be inclined to take such a risk if they felt they might flunk a course or lose their source of livelihood for doing so. The evaluative premise would need to shift from the current one, which measures the value of someone or something, to one more in line with an earlier definition of evaluation which meant to empower or strengthen. In other words, evaluative activity should focus not on who fails and who succeeds, but on how I (as student, professor, or administrator) can better serve my co-members at the university.

Returning to Heilbrun's definition of leadership at the beginning of this essay, the central question should be: How can I as a professor further involve others (students, other professors, administrators) in the discourse that is essential to action and affirm the significance of their contributions to the conversation?

If the purpose or mission of a university ought to focus on preparing students to lead meaningful lives, one way this can be accomplished is by establishing the classroom as a place where professors and students grapple with more than the visible, explicit curriculum. Our world presents us with more knowledge than we can master and a multiplicity of points of view to interpret it. As such, choices must be made and with those choices, commitments are effected. Professors as leaders fulfill this mission by inviting those with whom they are organizationally tied to make their choices explicit and discover through critical inquiry what ideologies underlie the various options. By thus connecting individual biographies with those who produced the ideas examined in a course and by articulating the relationships among classroom and organizational participants, schooling becomes an opportunity to engage in the discourse essential to action. By ensuring that each voice matters, all are empowered.

Notes

1. Carolyn Heilbrun, *Writing a Woman's Life* (New York: Columbia University Press, 1989), 18.

2. Peter Abelard, *Historia calamitatum*, translated by Betty Radice (London: Penguin Books, 1974). Abelard notes, "When it became apparent that God had granted me the gift for interpreting the Scriptures as well as secular literature, the numbers in my school began to increase for both subjects while elsewhere they diminished rapidly. This roused the envy and hatred of the other heads of schools against me; . . . two of them especially were always attacking me behind my back for occupying myself with secular literature in manner totally unsuitable to my monastic calling, and for presuming to set up as a teacher of sacred learning when I had had no teacher myself" (p. 78). Abelard's tormentors questioned his credentials, an early reference to a matter dear to the hearts of modern academics.

3. Charles Homer Haskins, *The Rise of Universities* (Ithaca, NY: Cornell University Press, 1923/1990).

4. Ibid, 9.

5. Ibid, 10. While this description of a professor's obligations does not generally hold true today, Princeton University, among others, still requires that faculty receive their dean's permission if they are to be absent for more than one day.

6. José Ortega y Gasset, *Mission of the University* (New York: W. W. Norton & Company, 1966), 37.

7. Betty Radice, *Introduction to The Letters of Abelard and Heloise* (London: Penguin Books, 1974), 40.

8. As noted earlier, the knowledge available to medieval European scholars did not represent all that was then known to the world.

9. The College and University Personnel Association (CUPA) annually conducts a faculty salary survey. During the academic year 1990-1991 salaries for faculty in departments of letters were exceeded by curriculum and instruction (school of education) faculty salaries by 21% in private institutions and 27% in public institutions. Business and management faculty averaged 24% and 43% more, while engineering faculty averaged 51% and 62% more. College and University Personnel Association, *1990-1991 National Faculty Salary Survey by Discipline and Rank in Private Colleges and Universities and 1990-1991 National Faculty Salary in State Colleges and Universities by Discipline and Rank* (Washington, D.C., 1991).

10. An argument could be made that the liberal arts have become or are becoming "professionalized" as Gerald Graff has done for English in *Professing Literature: An institutional history* (Chicago: University of Chicago Press, 1987).

11. Ortega y Gasset, *Mission of the University*, 53.

12. Several critics of American education have cited a link between school and the economy, notably the Carnegie Forum on Education and the Economy in its 1986 publication, *A Nation Prepared: Teachers for the 21st century* and the 1983 report of the National Commission on Excellence in Education, *A Nation at Risk: The imperative of educational reform*. According to Papagiannis, Easton, and Owens, "Most commentators agree that the impetus for the (restructuring of education) movement springs in large part from sources outside the educational system itself." George J. Papagiannis, Peter Easton, and J. Thomas Owens, *The School Restructuring Movement in the United States: An analysis of major issues and policy implications* (Paris: International Institute for Educational Planning, 1991), 20. Prominent among these sources are politicians, notably President Bush and many governors, and representatives of the business sector.

13. Edward T. Hall, *The Silent Language* (Garden City, NY: Anchor Books, 1981).

14. "Discourse" as used in this text refers not to what is being said but the ways in which things are said. When people come together to discuss issues that are important to them, they do so using a shared language, e.g., English, French, Chinese, and so forth. Equally importantly, members of a discourse community share ways of thinking about what they are discussing--the assumptions they make, the points of view that are considered legitimate, and so forth. Discourse is a concept that "signals the inescapably political contexts in which we speak and work." Michael Appel, "Series Editor Introduction," in Patti Lather, *Getting Smart* (London: Routledge, 1991). Thus, for example, biologists who ascribe to an evolutionary perspective with regard to life on earth belong to one discourse community, while those who hold a scientific creationist point of view

belong to another. The assumptions and theories of a given discourse community both enable fruitful communication within the group and constrain productive communication with another discourse community.

15. Andrew Gitlin and John Smyth, *Teacher Evaluation: Educative alternatives* (New York: The Falmer Press, 1989).

16. Daniel Boorstin, *The Discoverers* (New York: Vintage Books, 1985), 493.

17. James S. Coleman, *Equality and Achievement* (New York: Westview Press, 1990).

18. Henry Giroux, *Teachers as Intellectuals: Toward a critical pedagogy of learning* (Granby, MA: Bergin & Garvey Publishers, Inc., 1988).

19. Ibid., 14.

20. Philip Jackson, *Life in Classrooms* (New York: Holt, Rinehart and Winston, 1968).

21. Giroux, *Teachers as Intellectuals*, 32-33.

Chapter 10

Careful Mutuality: Leadership and Friendship in the Workplace[1]

Rose Mary Volbrecht

Introduction

We all live our lives in organizations. But until I got my first "real job"--a job in my chosen career that I hoped to keep for some time--I really did not think much about organizations. As a student, I moved in and out of several university organizations. I was a very active member of several church organizations. Along the way, I had jobs in a supermarket, a hospital, a cafeteria, doctor's office, and a library. These were temporary, in-between jobs. They were a means to an end--earning money to pay for my education.

When I began teaching, ten years ago, I thought of the university organization which hired me as merely a place for doing what I wanted to do. The university was like a classroom: it was the place where I went to teach and which I left at the end of the class. Someone made sure the room had chairs, desks, blackboards, and chalk. Similarly, I expected other people to run the university and I would show up to teach. But very quickly the life of this organization began intruding on my teaching life. There were meetings and debates about curriculum, policies, procedures, and university priorities. In the first year or two, I regarded all of this as annoying distractions or interruptions from my "real" work of teaching. Gradually, however, this sharp distinction between my real work and this other work became more blurred. I began to see the organization as a complex network of relationships with particular people rather than simply a place. I am part of this network now. These relationships are important to me. I am now part of a community of people engaged in a common project. Without this community, I would feel very isolated and lonely in my work.

Meetings still sometimes feel like interruptions of my work, but they are part of the ongoing conversation about who we are at Gonzaga University and about the values and standards which define and guide us. I participate in these meetings because it matters to me who we are now and what we will be five or ten years from now. But I also participate in these organizational conversations because I have discovered that working with others who share my work context is itself a positive experience. The experiences of organizing, planning, solving problems, and learning how to be effective are themselves empowering and affirming. In short, I have discovered that being part of an organization is not merely a necessary means to my ends of teaching and research. It is a worthwhile end in itself.

My reflection on organizational life took another turn five years ago when I began teaching a graduate course called Organizational Ethics. The students in this course are mostly middle level managers of a variety of profit and non-profit organizations. This course has provided an opportunity for me to think about moral decision-making in work organizations. My views have been shaped significantly by my ongoing conversation with these managers.

Numerous events in the past twenty years, from Watergate to Boesky, have created a crisis of values in American culture. My students are acutely aware that social expectations for work organizations are changing. There are increased expectations for profit and non-profit organizations to be responsible participants in their local and regional communities. Changing gender roles in our society generate new moral issues concerning the relations between work and family and issues such as sexual harassment within the work environment itself. Consumers and clients are increasingly better educated and more articulate about products and services they purchase and use.

These social changes have called into question the past assumptions that organizations can rely simply upon the personal values of managers as the only resources needed for making ethical decisions in the workplace and for modeling such standards for their employees. Managers increasingly are searching out ethics workshops, ethics courses, and ethics consultants to help them through the current shifting expectations and values. In many cases, they are seeking a ready-made formula for resolving complex and, often, ambiguous ethical issues.

In this paper, I will question both the practical adequacy of this formula approach to ethical decision-making and the conceptual adequacy of the ethical theory which this model assumes. I will present an alternative model of ethical decision-making in organizations. This model builds upon my experience and growing understanding of organizations as a community of people engaged in a common project--rather than merely a means to other ends. The model of ethical decision-making and moral leadership presented here focuses on the ongoing development of moral judgment through mentoring relationships in organizations.

I invite students, as you read this paper, to consider your own participation in the organizations you presently inhabit. Perhaps, as I did, you see yourselves as simply passing through your university, and workplace, or your club. I encourage you to consider whether these organizational experiences might also be shared projects worth doing in themselves. How do these projects shape who you are and how you perceive your world? How do the collaborative relationships you are developing in these organizations contribute to your skills in making moral judgments? How might these collaborative skills which you are developing now foster good moral decision-making in your future workplace?

Critique of the Rule-Oriented Model

Many ethics seminars and workshops are available for managers of all sorts of organizations. Let's consider what these workshops aim to do. The goal in numerous current ethics workshops and seminars is to present a short manageable list of ethical principles and then to teach seminar participants how to apply these principles to particular cases which are relevant to the participants' organizational contexts. The ethical principles may be summed up, for instance, as principles of equality, justice, truth, and freedom[2] or as principles of utility, rights, and justice[3]. The rule-oriented model of ethical decision-making assumes that all moral considerations can be summed up in a finite number of rules and that all ethical decisions can be adequately resolved by applying these rules to the relevant case.

The simplicity and logical clarity of this rule-oriented approach is very seductive for both seminar participants and instructors. I have conducted many of these kinds of workshops and seminars for health care professionals and business managers. Articulating and explaining some of the fundamental values that inform the work of various organizations can illuminate for managers and professionals the ethical foundations of their work. Likewise, discussion of cases involving ethical dilemmas and participant involvement in the analysis of these cases using the basic ethical principles can provide the seminar participants with practical skills that are transferable to similar cases in their organizations.

Of course, a workshop or seminar, whether two hours or two days in length, will necessarily present a simplified and limited account of the rule-oriented model of ethics which generally is being assumed. My concern about these ethics workshops and seminars is not that they are necessarily simplified accounts of a process of ethical decision-making. That is, I am not that concerned about the encapsulation of weeks of a typical university ethics course, which methodically outlines the multiple axioms and corollaries of two or three major theories of ethics, into four or five pithy principles. Some such encapsulation is obviously required by the workshop/seminar format. My concern is much more foundational:

I believe that the rule-oriented model of ethical decision-making is a conceptually flawed and practically inadequate account of ethical decision-making.

The rule-oriented model attempts to codify ethical decision-making in order to eliminate the need for experience, character, and judgment. Such an approach is particularly attractive to organizations caught in the press between accelerated social and technological change and escalating public demands for social responsibility. Advertising for ethics workshops and seminars suggests that with a few hours of expert instruction and a few hours practice at case analysis, managers can acquire the basic skills which they will need to resolve the ethical dilemmas of their organizations. Of course, we all recognize--as do the seminar participants-- that seminar brochures and video demo ads contain a certain amount of sales hype. Again, this is not my primary concern. My concern is that the "instant competence" promised in these glossy brochures is merely a simplified, mass-marketed version of the current orthodox philosophical view of the nature and process of ethical decision-making.

This current orthodox view is rooted in the Enlightenment tradition of the social contract, the tradition of Hobbes, Locke, and Kant. In this contractual model, the social order is made possible and sustained by a social contract among all free and equal moral agents, which establishes the rights, privileges, and obligations of various members of the social order.[4] The task of moral philosophy is, then, the delineation of these duties and obligations; the task of applied ethics is the application of these abstract, universal principles to particular cases. Edmund Pincoffs notes that the social contract theory of morality rightly assumes that some moral rules are socially essential, but then falsely assumes that rule responsibility is the essence of morality.[5] This assumption is not accidental or unexamined. It reflects the Enlightenment rejection of moral authority based upon privilege due to birth, inheritance of wealth, or social position. The modern passion for the codification of moral judgment reflects the democratic desire of the Enlightenment tradition to make ethics equally accessible to all by mitigating the uneven advantages we derive from our family and social backgrounds, or from our access to good schools and good teachers, or even from the accidents of our personal history and experience and our luck in companions. The rule-oriented model regards all moral agents as on equal footing with regard to moral judgment.

I do not want to argue that some persons' moral judgments should be privileged simply because they occupy positions of power or authority. I would agree that some areas of moral judgment do lend themselves, like the practice of cooking, to fairly satisfactory codification. Rules such as "do not kill innocent persons" or "do not intentionally deceive competent adults" are general moral principles (rules) that have emerged from our communal reflection on our shared human experience over time. These principles are usually reliable guides for action. However, I will argue that experience, character, and contextual judgment cannot and should not be eliminated from the process of ethical decision-making. Even in areas where we find that the rules are relatively adequate as guides for action, this codification is a substitute over good judgment. Even thoroughly tested recipes are not a complete substitute for the judgment of an experienced cook. Moral rules, like recipes, are merely approximations of good judgment. Furthermore, rules will not adequately cover all cases and the process of codification and revision is too slow to keep pace with the constant and rapid social and technological developments which impact today's organizations.

My critique of the rule-oriented model of ethical decision making and the alternative approach which I will present are shaped by recent work in both virtue ethics and feminist ethics. The current virtue ethics movement has criticized the Enlightenment tradition's focus in ethics on individuality, impartiality, and abstract reason. Virtue ethics encourages an appreciation of the moral significance of community in the development of moral character and in the exercise of moral judgment. Moreover, this perspective regards one's particular role in a community, one's relation to others as friend, spouse, or citizen, and one's particular location in time and place as potential moral assets rather than as moral liabilities which must always be escaped.[6]

There is no one theory or approach which represents feminist ethics; there is a great diversity among philosophers engaged in this project. Nevertheless there are two shared assumptions of this common project: (1) that the past and present subordination of women is morally wrong, and (2) that the moral experience of women which has been ignored and denigrated by traditional ethics is morally worthy of respect. Feminists, consequently, work to expose the male bias in traditional ethics and to critically examine the moral experience of women. Feminist ethics shares with virtue ethics the conviction that relationships are essential to our moral development. We develop as we interact and our agency is affected by our interaction with others. But feminists insist that we pay attention to the ways in which the dominance of men in a patriarchal society affects our relationships to one another.

Feminists, like virtue ethicists, also emphasize the moral importance of the context of moral judgments. Women are socialized in most cultures to attend to the concrete particulars of relationships and of their home, work, and community environment. The ability to provide care and nurturance critically depends upon these skills of attending to details. Women's experiences provide models for contextualizing moral judgment. Attending to the emotions of others and ourselves is another part of this socialization. Feminists have criticized the exclusion of emotion from most androcentric patriarchal traditions of ethics, noting that emotions often reveal the moral dimensions of our relationships with other persons and projects.[7]

Virtue ethics and feminist ethics draw our attention, then, to aspects of the moral life that are neglected or excluded by the rule-oriented approach, but which are essential in understanding the development of moral character and the exercise of moral judgment. These include the moral significance of relationships and community, of the particular context of moral judgments, and of emotions and concrete experience. Much of the time we must make moral judgments in situations where rules or regulations simply do not tell us what we should do. In these situations, ethical decision-making requires more than the logical application of rules: it requires good moral judgment. We need to look to other contexts which recognize the need for the development of good judgment and which provide appropriate contexts and programs for this process. We will find these in programs involving an apprenticeship or a mentoring process whose goal is the development of professional judgment. These programs have two important features. (1) Learning is contextual, involving a process of imitation of good models and communal reflection on experience. Consequently, it is not primarily rule-governed. (2) They involve an ongoing collaborative process that is institutionalized and extends beyond the formal training program. Before we turn to this alternative model for the development of good moral judgment, I want to present two cases that call for moral judgments which go beyond the application of moral rules or principles.

Cases Requiring Moral Judgment

The first case concerns the responsibility of employers to provide health care benefits for their employees. In the U.S., access to health care is primarily through insurance. If you are in good health and have a well-paying job with a medium to large firm, you probably have insurance and your employer pays for it. Yet one out of nine American working families, a total of 37 million people, has no health insurance at all.[8] Most of the uninsured work for small companies that do not offer such coverage. Firms with fewer than 100 workers employ one-third of the work force in the U.S., but only about half of these offer health insurance to their employees. Medicaid is supposed to cover the medical expenses for those who cannot pay for coverage. But in 1990 Medicaid covered only 38 percent of these people.[9]

The cost of health care in America is out of control. The health insurance system stitched together in the past 50 years is now unraveling. Americans spend more than $2 billion a day on medical care which accounts for 12.3 percent of the gross national product. While inflation is currently 5 percent, health care costs are increasing 8 percent annually. Health care has become a crippling expense for corporate America.[10]

Facing a projected 30 percent increase in health care costs next year, many employers are cutting their work force, reducing health benefits, or increasing the workers' share of premiums or treatment costs. In 1990 the Service Employees International Union, whose members are hospital workers, janitors, and government employees, reported that 48 percent of its low-wage members turned down their health insurance benefits because they could not afford the premiums.[11]

Employers are increasingly taking steps to control costs by imposing greater control on their health care plans. Workers may be forced to choose physicians from designated Preferred Provider Organizations or from Health Maintenance Organizations. In some cases, employees must get approval for many hospital procedures from their employer while more outpatient care is mandated also. Many employers have instituted wellness programs to increase employee health, and some corporations have even set up their own medical clinics.[12]

Working Americans have often taken health care for granted. But the current health care crisis has raised many important employee concerns about cost-cutting strategies. Companies are pressing for collectivization of medicine, challenging the right of patients to choose their doctors. The reduction or restriction of benefits amounts to a pay cut. Employees question the competence of business people to make judgments about the quality of medical care provided by PPO's and HMO's.

Ultimately, employers and workers will need to ask even more fundamental questions. Why have we made the workplace the gateway to medical coverage? What responsibility do workplace organizations have for the health of their employees and for their families? What role should corporations play in the public American dialogue about solutions to our healthcare crisis? Should they take a leadership role in this dialogue? Would corporations lose anything if government assumed responsibility for health care insurance?

The answers to these questions cannot be deduced from ethical principles or rules. A conversation between managers, owners, workers, and their communities is needed. Collective critical reflection is needed on the nature of workplace organizations and their relation to their employees and to the communities in which they operate. Employee benefits packages should be a concrete reflection of these relationships. Particular judgments about health care plans should only be made in the context of a conversation and consensus about these larger issues.

The second case is drawn from my own experience as a professor in a private, small (4,000 students), liberal arts university with five professional schools. This university has always emphasized teaching as the first priority and obligation of its faculty. In recent years, increasing weight has been given to professional development, including research, in tenure and promotion decisions. The two other areas of faculty responsibility, student advising and academic citizenship, are outlined in the *Faculty Handbook* as criteria for evaluation of faculty. Service to one's department and to the university is part of the obligation of academic citizenship. The handbook states that "[a faculty member] accepts his share of faculty responsibilities for the governance of his institution."[13]

Steven Cahn includes this obligation in his discussion of the responsibilities of college faculty in his *Saints and Scamps: Ethics in Academia*:

> An additional professorial duty is to take on a share of the sundry, day-to-day tasks that are an inescapable part of departmental life. Failure to join in this work is unfair to colleagues, overburdening them and weakening that cooperative spirit on which the success of a department depends. Indeed, trouble is on the horizon when those who have been volunteering their services suddenly realize that, as a former colleague of mine once put it, "There are more people in the boat than are rowing."[14]

Although Cahn speaks here of departmental obligations, the same concerns apply to service in the broader university community.

College professors have multiple areas of responsibility; teaching in a classroom is only a small part of a teacher's duties. Like all professionals, college professors must make judgments every day about how they will structure their day or spend their time, about how they should fulfill their professional duties. Few particular guidelines or requirements are established by the university or by the profession. What makes the area of university service a particularly difficult area of moral judgment, at my university, is that very few rewards for service and almost no sanctions for failure to serve have been institutionalized. Service carries little weight in either tenure and promotion decisions or in salary decisions. Yet service is like the academic lawn and garden work of a university. It profoundly affects what kind of workplace an institution will be as well as what kind of academic curriculum and standards will grow there.

Consequently, individual faculty must make frequent judgments setting priorities for their professional duties, making trade-offs between the daily tasks of teaching, the ongoing responsibility and need for professional growth, and the hoeing, weeding, and watering tasks of university service. If no one does the latter tasks on a regular basis, we will all be choked out by weeds. But, as Cahn's colleague notes, it is possible for individuals to share the produce without working the soil. Prioritizing decisions cannot be made by simply following the rules outlined by the University or the profession. They require judgments informed by experience, dialogue with colleagues, and personal character.

These two cases illustrate the need for ethical decision-making skills which go beyond the ability to apply general moral principles to cases. I will argue that what managers, professionals, and workers need to learn is a process of ethical decision-making which involves collaborative, ongoing reflection on how basic values can be embodied in individual judgments and how they can be institutionalized in their organizations. In this model, the conscience of an organization will be located in an ongoing dialogue among all stakeholders, representing the various functions in the organization, rather than simply among those at the top of the organizational hierarchy.

A Model for Development of Judgment

In order to learn how to make moral judgments that go beyond the application of rules, it is useful to look at other contexts in which people are trained to make judgments that go beyond applying rules. The training of professionals is one such context.

One of the characteristics of professionals is that they face numerous discretionary judgments--judgments in areas where decisions cannot be deduced from relevant rules or regulations. A professional is expected to use his or her special training and professional experience to make an informed judgment. Professional training and education frequently include a program of apprenticeship designed to develop such judgment. Such an apprenticeship program exhibits the two features noted earlier: (1) it is not primarily rule-governed, but involves a process of imitation and reflection; and (2) it involves a continuous collaborative process with peers which extends beyond the formal training program.

The medical internship is a familiar professional apprenticeship. Medical interns are immersed in the diagnostic context along with good models/good practitioners. The intern must learn to imitate the senior physician by seeing as this mentor sees, hearing as she or he hears, feeling what she or he feels in order to really understand and recognize, in the future, the similarities and differences of particular cases. It is not enough to know a clinical definition of jaundice: one must actually be able to identify a particular face as jaundiced. The intern must feel the tumor that the senior physician feels, smell the diabetic's breath, and hear the congenital heart irregularity of the neonate. At one time, interns also had to develop the ability to taste the sugar in a diabetic's urine. (Generations of interns have been grateful for the pharmaceutical technology which no longer makes this necessary.) The intern must understand the point of the various considerations that go into a diagnosis and observe how the senior physician determines the proper weight to be given to each factor in particular cases. One cannot learn these skills of judgment by simply learning the rules. The intern must practice these skills with the guidance and correction of the senior mentor. Through this process of apprenticeship, the intern develops the practical knowledge and skills of practical reasoning which are particular to the practice of medicine.

Professional training involves not only the development of practical judgment, but also the embodiment of professional values. Professionals enjoy a great deal of autonomy in their jobs, which is a necessary correlate of the demand in their jobs for extensive discretionary or professional judgment. Society permits professionals, for the most part, to judge for themselves how they will exercise this professional judgment. Consequently, professionals enter into a trust relationship with their clients and with society at large.[15] Professionals are granted a great deal of autonomy to exercise their professional judgment for the sake of their patients/clients and for the sake of the communities they serve. When patients place themselves in the care of a physician, they expect their privacy to be protected and their well-being to be promoted. The training of a physician, like the training of all professionals, requires then, not simply the acquisition of specialized information and skills, but also the embodiment of professional values and the cultivation of professional integrity. Patients count on professionals to embody these professional values when they place themselves in their care both individually and collectively.

Developing judgment and embodying the values and traits of the profession needs to continue even after an intern becomes a practicing professional. Professionals need to continue to look to the practice and judgment of other professionals for guidance, continue to reflect critically on the practical adequacy of their judgments, and continue to reassess the values of their tradition and their embodiment in the current practice. This is institutionalized in such formal procedures as postmortems required in most hospitals, formal professional consultations on particular cases, and peer review and publication of particular cases in professional journals. It may continue more informally in daily discussions with peers. There are often a few practitioners who will be particularly revered for their wisdom and experience, but much of the continuing development of professional integrity and judgment takes place with peers in the give-and-take of everyday practice. In the course of resolving new cases, the characteristic ways of thinking about analogous cases and the understanding of what constitutes good medical practice may themselves be modified. In this way, professional standards of practice may be revised.

Unfortunately, many medical professionals feel that their apprenticeship is ended when their formal residency requirements are completed. Some physicians retreat entirely to the privacy of the one-on-one relationship with their patients. They resent any attempts to make these private decisions more collaborative with peers or with other health care professionals. Physicians have done a notoriously poor job of monitoring one another's practice and of disciplining practitioners who have made poor medical or moral judgments. They have vigorously resisted efforts by hospitals, nurses, and social workers to develop a team approach to decision-making in health care. Nurses have become the primary advocates and practitioners of this more collaborative approach. Rampant litigation reflects the current lack of public trust in the medical profession's self-regulation. Professionals are in a much better position to evaluate their own professional judgments, but if they do not do it, the courts or the legislature will. However, whether physicians continue to mentor one another after their initial training or not, the tradition of medical education provides us with a useful model for the development of practical judgment.

Development of Moral Judgment

Just as the professional judgments of an oncologist or of a criminal lawyer cannot be reduced to a list of rules, neither can the judgments needed in ethical decision-making be reduced to or codified in a list of ethical principles or rules. We must apprentice, immersing ourselves with good models in the various activities and projects of our communal lives. This does not commit us to the idea that human living is an activity with just one point or purpose similar to the functions of medicine or law. As James Wallace explains,

> The notion that living itself is like a craft in that it has a certain point or purpose is replaced by the idea that the considerations we consult in practical reasoning have points analogous to the points of crafts. That is, both moral considerations and crafts involve accumulations of practical knowledge developed in response to quite specific problems for specific purposes.[16]

Moral considerations involve ways of thinking about problems we face in living and working individually and together. Each moral consideration has a point. The point of justice, for instance, is to ensure that persons receive their due. Addressing particular moral problems will involve determining which moral considerations are relevant and then, by means of analogous reasoning from past similar cases, working toward a solution to the current case.

Managers, professionals, and workers in all organizations must develop the skills of practical moral reasoning as well as embody the dispositions, values, and commitments which make good judgment in particular cases possible. This returns us to our initial question, how can this knowledge be learned? Can this sort of moral judgment be acquired in weekend workshops and all-day seminars? Can it be learned in semester length courses in ethics? As a matter of fact, all of us do develop this knowledge to some degree in the process of socialization and education in a civilized society. It can be further cultivated, I argue, in adult life with the help of mentors, peers, and friends, and also in formal educational contexts.

A significant part of our moral education, in which we develop character and judgment, comes through our observation and imitation of early role models. Through this early apprenticeship, we begin to develop our character, embodying values, dispositions, and commitments of the models and traditions within which we are socialized. In our homes, in our schools, and in our religious and community organizations, we begin to learn the point of such moral considerations as fairness, courage, benevolence, accountability and responsibility, friendship and loyalty, faithfulness, promise-keeping, consequences, and respect for others. We also develop some ability to give weight to these considerations in our decisions. Of course, some of our socialization and models are negative, as well.

As adolescents and young adults we experience the challenges of sustaining commitments and intimate relationships, of making career and life choices, of balancing diverse commitments and projects, of maintaining individual integrity, and of balancing the dispositions of critical reflection and creative imagination.* Adult models and mentors continue to play a critical role at this stage, while the counsel of peers and friends gains importance. Young adults entering college or the workplace may find their basic assumptions about human nature, relationships, and moral values challenged by others with alternative conceptions and diverse experiences. At this stage, young adults must develop a personal practice of critical reflection and begin to embody the dispositions and skills which will enable them to participate, facilitate, and sustain debate on controversial issues. Modeling is essential.

What then of adults? Is an apprenticeship model still appropriate to describe our moral education as adults? A moment's reflection will confirm that our character and our moral judgment, as adults, continue to be shaped by the company we keep. Some people consistently draw out the worst in us, while the company of others enables and inspires us to become better people. Feminists, especially, have pointed to the contributions of care and of friendship to our moral development as well as to the ways in which our participation in relationships based on the exploitation, degradation or disadvantage of others disfigures our character.[17] Our personal morality is embedded in and is constituted through a web of dynamic relations with various persons, groups, and organizations.

It is in the context of these relationships that we live our lives, share common experiences, and collaborate in work and play. These relationships provide essential contexts for ongoing critical reflection about who we are, about what our values and commitments are, and about how we can live out these basic values in our daily decisions and actions. A diversity of relationships with people from a variety of backgrounds, races, religions, and lifestyles can provide important perspective and checks against our individual and group biases.[18] Among these relationships there need to be close friends with whom we share details of our lives, whom we trust enough to examine our motives, intentions, doubts ánd struggles.[19]

Ethics courses, workshops, and seminars can play an important role in our adult moral education, also. Courses provide a systematic study

---

* Mary Jo Bona explores the important role which a mentor figure plays in the lives of adolescents who are second-generation Italian-Americans. The mentor assists these young adults as they appropriate the diverse commitments and values of Italian and American cultures. The mentor's concrete experience in both cultures and her or his intimate connection to these young adults as extended family members are critical to the mentor's success in this role. See Bona's essay, "Italian/American Women Writers: Family Shapes Community," in this volume.

of a variety of moral considerations and of their histories: what sort of problems they originally addressed, how they have been modified and adapted to function in different circumstances to solve new but analogous problems. Such courses will also consider a variety of ethical theories which provide alternate accounts of the relation between different moral considerations and of the relative weight of each consideration. Courses in applied ethics provide opportunities to consider particular issues in the relevant applied area. However, they provide more than simply occasions for the applications of ethical theories (and rules) to cases. The study of applied areas of ethics generates new moral considerations which the unique circumstances of these areas require. This leads to new insights or revisions of old moral considerations. Workshops and seminars can provide significant opportunities for us to learn about and to reflect on the moral considerations and issues which are most relevant to our own work or they may provide a general introduction to the study of ethics. The development of moral judgment is then an ongoing process in our adult lives. Although the formal study of ethics can play a critical role, our most important resource is one another. Organizations must take this into account if they want the best possible moral leadership.

Organizations and Moral Judgment

Co-workers can help each other make and review their moral judgments. Together they can provide moral leadership in their organizations. Organizations should be structured in ways which will support this process of co-mentoring. The first critical step is to institutionalize a commitment from the top to give weight to ethical issues in the bottom-line decision-making of the organization. A person's job security must not be threatened by raising an ethical issue. In addition, the evaluation of job performance must include an evaluation of this person's consideration of ethical issues. Attention to ethical issues relevant to the organization must be positively linked to organizational rewards and sanctions.[20]

Robert Jackall notes both the essential role which top management plays in the institutionalization of values in an organization and the difficulty of this task.

> [T]o sustain the links between the corporation, the individual [within the organization], and the common good over the long haul, important conditions must obtain within an organization. Specifically, the ideology incorporating certain values must be continuously and forcefully articulated by key authorities who are ostensibly committed to its premises, and, at the same time, the ideological links between the good of the corporation and the common weal in particular must be plausible both to managers and to important external publics. As it happens, both conditions are difficult to meet. Day-to-day exigencies, the personnel transitions of large organizations, the endless circulation of new rhetoric of innovation among

top managers, the entrenched cynicism of middle managers on whose backs the burdens for any such policies will fall, and of course, the "take the money and run" ethos, make it difficult to sustain organizational commitment to goals defined as socially important.[21]

Developing some working consensus about the meaning of organizational social responsibility will require an ongoing collaboration involving top management, relevant external stakeholders in this organization (customers, suppliers, stockholders, local and broader communities), and all internal stakeholders (employees). In this way, the conscience of an organization will be located within this ongoing dialogue among all organizational stakeholders, rather than in the hearts and minds of top management alone. This vision of corporate responsibility can only have effect if, as Jackall notes, top management continually and forcefully articulates it and institutionalizes this vision. But the input of those who are closest to the concrete work of creating and delivering the organization's particular services or products is also essential. Those who are immersed in the contexts of particular problems often develop practical skills of judgment, including moral judgment, in these areas.

Further contexts are needed for ongoing reflection and critique of the moral judgments made in day-to-day organizational life. Informal and formal mentor relationships need to be encouraged and supported. Opportunities, again both informal and formal, for "post-mortems" of significant value decisions must be supported and institutionalized. This requires a willingness to accept responsibility for decisions and to allow individuals to learn from the critical evaluation of these decisions. This may threaten some implicit assumptions of the complex and multiple alliances managers and professionals consider essential to organizational survival and success.[22] The more bureaucratic the organization, the more complex and necessary such alliances become. These alliances are based upon shared interests, shared work, and shared experiences with similar problems. They also enable us to get things done or to exert influence in an organization. Moreover, such alliances are constructed to counter other alliances in an organization. Inclusion in an alliance carries with it some expectations of loyalty and of confidentiality among members of the alliance. These commitments of loyalty and trust are precisely the qualities which are necessary for the mutual development of moral judgment.

However, the collaborative alliances can only provide a supportive environment for critical reflection on moral judgments if the ethos of these alliances permits the discussion of these concerns. Frequently, managers and professionals alike expect that members of their alliances will "cover" for one another, protecting their cohorts. If a collective action of the alliance goes awry, there may be an expectation of collective amnesia in order to protect the group. Alliances based only upon such collective self-interest cannot provide the appropriate context for collaborative reflection upon moral judgment and support for actions based upon moral values. Commitment from the top can help to create an organizational ethos in which acceptance of responsibility for one's actions and shared reflection on moral judgment become the norm.

One of our most fruitful contexts for continued development of our moral judgment will be with individual friends and trusted colleagues. These are people with whom we share the details of our daily lives: they are immersed with us in the contexts of our judgments. They know us well. They know details of our personal histories, they know strengths and weaknesses of our character, they know our ambitions. We have a relationship of sufficient trust and respect that we can discuss our failures, our near-misses, and our doubts. The cultivation and maintenance of these personal relationships will run counter to much traditional wisdom about organizational life which tends to encourage personal isolation of decision-makers as they move to the top. But those with increasing responsibilities need to surround themselves with friends and colleagues with whom they can risk critical reflection on their values and judgments.

One last detail which should not be neglected in the institutionalization of ethics in an organization is the provision of physical space and of time for these processes of collaborative reflection. A good deal of our mutual review of decisions and actions takes place in lounges, dining rooms, and even restrooms. Accessible gathering spaces which allow for both open and private conversations should not be regarded as dispensable luxuries, but as essential. They are necessary for the process of collaborative reflection on the value commitments of an organization and on the embodiment of these values in individual and organizational decisions.

It is worth noting what the "organizational hero" will look like if this model is institutionalized. Persons who are regarded as successful in these organizations will be persons who build community, attend to feelings and educated intuitions, engage in mutual critique, and recognize the positive value of mistakes as learning opportunities. This, of course, flies in the face of traditional models of organizational success which praise individualism and yet demand a self-effacing homogeneity in managerial ranks.[23] Individual judgment and critical assessment are submerged in order to promote and support the ideas of one's boss or of the organization. Furthermore, mistakes are regarded as occasions for blaming, damage control, and cover-up. Such a climate of "watching one's back" does not promote the commitments of trust, loyalty, and friendship which are necessary for the mutual development of moral judgment and neither does the traditional expectation of frequent moves by managers.

Such a model of management regards management as a technique which can be mastered and applied independent of a thorough understanding of the context and personal relationships in which this technique is applied. It is not surprising then that managers trained in this way, similarly, will regard moral judgment as a technique rather than as a lived practice which is concrete and connected to others. George Eliot noted this need for experience and character over a century ago:

> The man of maxims is the popular representative of the minds that are guided in their moral judgment solely by general rules, thinking that these will lead them to justice by a ready-made patent method, without the trouble of exerting patience, discrimination, impartiality, without any care to assure themselves whether they have the insight that comes from a hardly earned estimate of temptation, or from a life vivid and intense enough to have created a wide fellow-feeling with all that is human.[24]

It is often the workers who are closest to the actual production of products or delivery of services who have developed this sort of insight and judgment. Their work experiences are vivid with detail, intense with day-to-day experiences, and connected to the processes and persons which constitute an organization's activity. These are the caretakers whose skills of attending to and nurturing the various processes, transactions, and tasks of the organization have been honed by a daily practice of shared activity, problem-solving and cultivation of cooperative relationships with co-workers, suppliers, and clients.

These habits of attention to the context and dynamics of the workplace are essential to the practice of moral judgment, as well. The rule-oriented model of moral decision-making has devalued these virtues of attending and nurturing since they are more typically associated with caretaking functions performed by those with less power--mothers,[25] wives, nurses, clerks, and blue-collar workers. If moral judgment is to be a lived practice rather than a mere technique, every member of an organization must cultivate these virtues and collaborate with other workers and stakeholders to share the insights and experience which arise from each area of expertise.

Creating an organizational ethos in which shared reflection on moral judgments is the norm requires commitment from the top and from the bottom. But what can we do if we find ourselves in organizations which lack this sort of commitment at the top? The traditional hierarchical structure attempts to give persons at the top credit for organizational successes and control over blame for mistakes and failures. To those who have made it to the top through personal sacrifice, hard work, and well-timed luck, the collaborative model of decision-making will seem to them as an increase of accountability and liability in return for a loss of control. It is not surprising then that many will resist such change.

But, even in organizations which lack commitment from the top, individuals can find support for ethical reflection and action in the context of carefully gathered alliances with other workers. All workers have some areas of responsibility in which they have some freedom to determine how decisions will be made. By collaborating with other workers to share decision-making and expertise, these areas may be expanded. In most organizations, there are also areas or issues in which individuals and groups can have some input if they take the initiative to organize and to be heard.

Of course, we have all experienced resistance to these sorts of efforts. Repeated resistance and failure can be discouraging and exhausting. Why bother? The most basic answer, I think, is that most human beings enjoy the experience of working with others on a common project. We are empowered by the experience of organizing, planning, learning how to be politically successful--cultivating allies, addressing opponents, persuading fence-sitters. Even when we fail, the process of working together with others who share our life situations is itself a positive experience. Being heard by others who respect our experience and our judgment is affirming; developing our understanding of our work context by sharing information and experience is valuable; collectively discerning possible solutions to value-oriented problems can be empowering. All of these activities affirm the value of each of our experiences and provide the context for developing knowledge of one another and our work which is necessary for building trust.

Readers of this anthology will note that this rationale for active collaboration in the workplace echoes the argument Bob Waterman makes for active participation in community groups. Workplace organizations are one of the most obvious contexts for the development of the good citizenship habits he describes. Workplace collaboration measures up to Waterman's town-meeting benchmark insofar as workers develop and exercise good habits of community citizenship, learn that they are powerful with others in an important area of public life, and gain the self-respect which comes from thinking for themselves.*

Also in this anthology, Jane Rinehart reminds us that if we take seriously the claim that our character and our agency are affected by our interaction with others, then each person has some potential for power and each person is affected by the actions of others. Change in organizations does not require moving the people at the top so that they can move others. Our complex connections to others, Rinehart notes, gives each of us the capacity for affecting others and for shifting the structures which hold us. She suggests that we invest less energy in trying to move the organizational pyramids of power, and focus more on cultivating our connections to others.[26]

These collaborative organizational projects potentially will improve the ability of workers to do their work efficiently and knowledgeably. They also benefit the larger organization by encouraging workers to think about and care about the interests of a group rather than simply their own self-interests. These benefits may encourage others in the organization, particularly supervisors, to more openly consider collaborative

---

* Bob Waterman, "We Need Not Be Ruled By Leaders: The Early Town Meetings," in this volume.

decision-making. But even if such efforts fail to facilitate such structural change in the organization, most persons will find work which involves some collaboration more satisfying than work which involves none. Of course, we must all be open to the possibility that a particular workplace is simply too repressive, too lacking in respect for individuals, and that one should look for other job opportunities. In any case, we each need to accept some responsibility for the quality of our workplace and for the quality of our ethical decision-making in our organizations. We should not relinquish all responsibility or all of our autonomy to those at the top of our organizational hierarchies.

Conclusion

Organizations need to recognize that there are no quick fixes for the current crisis of values which they face. Their leaders need to learn that the need for experience, character, and judgment cannot be eliminated from ethical decision-making nor codified into a set of rules, regulations, or codes. Good moral judgment is developed and refined through contextual learning with good models and by ongoing communal critical reflection on the practice of moral judgment. Support for this process of apprenticeship with mentors and peers must be concretely institutionalized in organizations.

Moral leadership is a project which we can all share. We all already inhabit organizations and share relationships which provide us with the opportunities for this sort of careful mutuality.

Notes

1. Thanks to Blaine Garvin for the phrase "careful mutuality."
2. Clarence Walton, *Moral Manager* (New York: Harper Business, 1990).
3. Manuel Velasquez, *Business Ethics: Concepts and Cases* (Englewood Cliffs, N.J.: Prentice Hall, 1988), 116-118.
4. Stephen Hudson, *Human Character and Morality* (Boston: Routledge & Kegan Paul, 1986), 85-86.
5. Edmund Pincoffs, *Quandries and Virtues: Against Reductivism in Ethics* (Lawrence, Kansas: University Press of Kansas, 1986), 31-32.
6. See especially Pincoffs, *Quandries and Virtues*; Alasdaire MacIntyre, *After Virtue: A Study in Moral Theory* (Notre Dame, IN: University of Notre Dame Press, 1981); James Wallace, *Virtues and Vices* (Ithaca, NY: Cornell University, 1978); and Stephen Toulmin, "The Recovery of Practical Philosophy," *The American Scholar* 57 (Summer, 1988): 337-352.
7. See especially Carol Gilligan, *In A Different Voice: Psychological Theory and Women's Development* (Cambridge, MA: Harvard University Press, 1982); Sara Ruddick, *Maternal Thinking: Toward a Politics of Peace* (Boston: Beacon

Press, 1989); and Claudia Card, ed. *Feminist Ethics* (Lawrence, Kansas: University Press of Kansas, 1991).

8. Janice Castro, "Condition: Critical," *Time* (November 25, 1991): 36.

9. "The Crisis in Health Insurance," *Consumer Reports* (August 1990), 533-34.

10. *Time*, 33-34.

11. *Consumer Reports*, 534.

12. "Ouch! The Squeeze on Your Health Benefits," *Business Week* (November 20, 1989), 110-116.

13. Gonzaga University, *Faculty Handbook* (1989), 302.12.

14. Cahn, *Saints and Scamps: Ethics in Academia* (New York: Rowman & Littlefield, 1986), 52.

15. Jon Moline, "Professionals and Professions: A Philosophical Examination of An Ideal," *Social Science and Medicine*, 22 (1986): 501-508.

16. Wallace, *Virtues and Vices*, 230.

17. See especially Marilyn Friedman, "Friendship and Moral Growth," *Journal of Value Inquiry* 33 (1989): 3-13, and Elizabeth Spelman, "The Virtue of Feeling and the Feeling of Virtue," in *Feminist Ethics*, 213-232.

18. For a discussion of the difficulties and benefits of crossing boundaries of color, class, culture, sexual preference, disability, and age to make friends, see Letty Cottin Progrebin, *Among Friends: Who We Like, Why We Like Them, and What We Do With Them* (New York: McGraw-Hill Book Company, 1987), 132-226.

19. See Rose Mary Volbrecht, "Friendship: Mutual Apprenticeship in Moral Development," *Journal of Value Inquiry*, 24 (1990).

20. Robert Jackall notes that this would require organizations to institutionalize a tracking system to trace responsibility. See *Moral Mazes: The World of Corporate Managers* (New York: Oxford University Press, 1988), 87.

21. *Moral Mazes*, 199.

22. *Moral Mazes*, 38-39.

23. Rosabeth Kanter provides an insightful discussion of how managers carefully guard power and privilege for those who fit in, for those they see as "their kind." Trust is based upon external manifestations of social similarity to determine who is the "right sort of person," rather than on personal knowledge of one another and mutual commitments/shared values. See her *Men and Women of the Corporation* (New York: Basic Books, 1977), 47-68.

24. George Eliot, *The Mill on the Floss* (New York: Modern Library, 1940).

25. In her book *Maternal Thinking*, Sara Ruddick explores how the daily practice of raising children and the patience, flexibility, and peacemaking which this entails offers us a model for the kind of work that needs to be done to promote world peace. This is but one example of how these virtues could be applied outside of the domestic context of childcare.

26. In this volume see Jane Rinehart, "Learning to Lead." Another essay by Rinehart, "Re-visioning Leadership with Feminists," presented at the Northwest Women's Studies Association Conference on "Living in the Margins," April 21, 1991, has helped me a great deal in thinking about this issue.

Chapter 11

We Need Not Be Ruled By Leaders: The Early Town Meetings

Bob Waterman

Introduction

Leaders tend to be viewed as the crucial element for the occurrence of political events; they tend to get most of the praise for them as well. Perhaps that is appropriate. But, as I hope to persuade you in this chapter, the ordinary citizens who support or follow leaders are equally crucial for political life. Furthermore, followers deserve--if not the same amount of praise as received by a leader--at least the quiet assurance that they too have added something unique to the world: either their thoughtful and articulate reasons for supporting a leader's goal or their similarly noteworthy reasons for opposing a leader's project.*

Start from three premises. First, that many Americans when growing up are urged repeatedly to be leaders--or at least often are within earshot of such urging. When young, we are told to be a leader or hear leadership urged on others in a way that suggests that anyone who is going to become a person with a distinct identity will have to have tried successfully for leadership position. I remember this urging most vividly from school, from scouts and from young people's religious organizations. The lasting impression I have is that one is supposed to stand out from the crowd by being a leader within the group. Thus, we are trained from an early

---

* Several other chapters in the book also view political leadership from the perspective of citizens; see especially those by Eloise Buker, Jane Rinehart, and Blaine Garvin.

age to look upon leadership as a favorable status and obligation; becoming a leader is portrayed as desirable.

The second starting assumption is about political life. After being an adult for a while, an American pretty much has to realize that political leaders are both a blessing and a curse. They are a blessing when they do what we want them to do; they are a curse when they do something we oppose. Leaders can get something done, but they also can get the wrong thing done. Political leaders do that for the community as a whole, thus affecting everyone, sometimes for good, sometimes for ill.

Since everyone has to live in some political community, each person does have to bear the burdens of wrong direction as well as enjoy the benefits of the good, so one learns to be wary of political leaders. The very qualities stereotypically associated with political leadership--the ability to chart a course, to persuade others to it, and to stick resourcefully with a goal until completion---are precisely the reasons for fearing leaders. Leaders are inherently demanding, unsettling, and even dangerous because they can be effective.

Although the safeguards established in American political institutions were designed to prevent misuse of power, they were not designed to ensure that everyone always will be in the majority. As you probably know, majority opinion has to work its way through the moderating channels of the legislative, executive, and judicial branches of the government before it can become policy. Even if our checks, balances, and provisions for careful deliberation were perfect, which they are not, one's views would not necessarily prevail. No one always wins the political disputes in which they are involved. In this situation, victorious political leaders sometimes will be against what we want to see happen and for something else which we do not want. At those times political leadership will be an especially difficult burden. Prudence counsels that we face up to the reality that leadership may thwart us as much as it may help us. So our second starting point is that leadership probably is an inescapable part of our human surroundings--an always potentially troublesome part of that reality.

Sum up these two beginning propositions about leadership from a slightly different angle. The term leadership elicits contrary emotions: one part of our hearts moves us to hear in the term our desire to be a leader, to stand out as someone distinctive and to be praised for it. But equally passionately, another part of our hearts tells us to fear political leaders, since all of us at times will be affected by leaders who gain widespread support for policies which we do not want enacted. For me at least, leadership is a human activity about which I have very strong mixed feelings. Almost inevitably I am likely to be under someone else's political leadership through much of my life; and, if the leader is worth his or her salt, we will disagree upon goals a substantial part of the time.

The central factor for dealing with the mixed emotions about political leadership is the connection between leaders and ordinary citizens. Human ingenuity can help us put citizens together with leaders in a way which would at least make the inevitable relationship sensible and endurable. The best version of this relationship that I know about took place most dramatically and most attractively in American town-meeting government at the time of the revolution against England and the creation of the Constitution. For our purposes the great virtue of this early leadership arrangement was ongoing political contact between the followers themselves, so that ordinary citizens already felt powerful at the local level when they delegated power to representatives to lead them at the state and national levels. Town government at its best did simultaneously a version of the two things associated above with leadership: (1) it provided the opportunity for everyone to try to gain public recognition of their viewpoint, hence to be known as someone who counts in the world; (2) it also established a two-way relationship between the ordinary citizens and leaders which could withstand their disagreements with each other.

In the rest of the essay I will describe the major elements of this early American arrangement whose remnants also can be found among us today.

I want to explain why today's citizen has the right to expect that her or his political opinions be taken seriously; what habits are needed by the self-respecting ordinary citizen in order to assert that right; and why one might want to do so. Since we are going to consult the American past for perspective, most of this essay will be about American town-meeting citizens before 1850, when their form of local government began to disappear. While the essay ventures back into political history for a benchmark, it is about ordinary citizens, people like you and me. And it is written for us today, whether we like politics or not. The overall point I wish to make is that Americans historically have had a variety of ways to stay politically independent as individuals while putting up with the leaders elected by the majority. We do not have to be passively ruled.

The third premise of the essay concerns the historical fact that only free, white, adult males participated in American town-meeting government. Today we no longer publicly believe that people born either with other skin colors or with the other gender are ineligible for politics. As well, there was no reason within the logic of the town-meeting political arrangement to exclude these human beings from its activities when, through substantial effort and bloodshed, citizenship was extended to all adults. However, for the sake of historical accuracy, this essay will talk about those politically active in towns as males. That accuracy is not meant to imply that the rest of the population should be barred from citizenship.

I

Many people are familiar with the term "town meeting" from American history; fewer know the major details; hardly anyone has experienced that kind of politics. A description of town-meeting government will help us understand the essence of the town's distinctive leadership arrangement.

Town-meeting government started in North America almost with the beginning of English settlement. The first agreement among citizens to establish temporarily what became the town-meeting form of government was the Mayflower Compact of 1620. The first historical records we have for a town government which was separate from a colony government are for the town of Dorchester which, in 1635, was granted the right by the Massachusetts Bay Colony to take care of its own affairs with a town-meeting government. Thereafter, for about three hundred of the next four hundred years, most Americans' experience with politics began with the towns. New towns were established repeatedly everywhere in the colonies. Town-meeting government with its distinctive feature of direct democracy--which, in effect, made the final decisions for local life both before and after Independence--was present only in the north, where it flourished until the period from 1850-1900, when government by elected representatives replaced it. In the South, representative government began earlier because county government by representatives elected from rural areas was the decisive local political arena. But in the north, town-meeting government was the local political organization from which revolution was declared, fought, and won; from which the new state and national governments were erected; and within which local political life was done for the century after the revolution. The towns were rudimentary arrangements. They usually held few inhabitants by today's standards: often several handfuls of eligible citizens and their families; at most, a couple of thousand people. Their political issues were closely connected to necessity: roads, fences, fire protection, the school, security. Town-meeting government was relatively simple in form and operation.

All political offices were part-time positions filled by citizens who earned a living at some other activity, usually farming. All of a town's major political decisions were made at the town meeting which was the law-making body of the town. Problems and proposals were debated; laws were passed by common agreement. All property owners had a seat or position in this legislature by virtue of permanent residence in the town. So, by moving into a town and acquiring property there, a person also acquired direct law-making power. No elections were held for the town legislature since citizens automatically had legislative seats.

However, the executive part of town government was separate from the legislative part and these offices were filled by election. The most general elective office was an executive committee, usually called the Selectmen. This group oversaw the day-to-day operation of town government. These officers did make minor decisions on their own in order to implement laws and in order to deal with matters that arose during the year between regular town meetings; but, for any major new situation or dispute, they usually called a special town meeting. As well, a petition by a small number of citizens, most often ten, could require the Selectmen to call a special legislative session. Thus the executive council really was the servant of the town meeting; a member was expected to "employ his judgment and integrity on his neighbors' behalf."[1] The executives were not an independent power, not even a checking and balancing power, as are the present state and national executive branches of government, since the people holding town executive offices already held lifetime legislative seats from which to express their judgments directly in the law-making deliberations. More specialized town executive offices were important also. There were tax assessors and tax collectors, a fence viewer to help ensure that livestock did not stray into neighboring gardens and fields, a sheriff, a clerk, and several other positions.

Election for these executive offices took place at an annual town meeting. All citizens were eligible. Because of the rudimentary nature of executive duties and because of the ease with which any citizen could be aware of the issues within the small sphere of the town, most citizens were able to carry out most offices. Especially after the Revolution, executive offices turned over often enough that a year or two of service usually was required during a citizen's lifetime. Presumably people would be picked for offices for which they had an inclination and some ability. Hence, the quality of executive service usually was adequate; at times, it could be very high, such as during the revolutionary era, but it occasionally could be mediocre or worse.

The towns also participated in a court system. This was organized at the county level outside the town. The county court system applied town and, when appropriate, higher governmental unit law to individual cases, attempting to ensure impartial justice when someone was accused of wrongdoing. While occasionally a court case might be used to settle a town dispute, the townspeople usually settled their political matters in the town meeting. And unlike today, when state and national laws determine so many aspects of an individual's local life, the townsperson's life most of the time was lived according to the laws of the town meeting. However, the county court system did regularly scrutinize the performance of town executive officers to check on the handling of money and fulfillment of other responsibilities.

II

While by no means perfect, town meeting government was a remarkable arrangement for human beings. According to the famous French observer Alexis de Tocqueville in the 1830's, while the towns are "composed of [the] coarser elements" of society and prone to "numerous blunders," they "teach" ordinary citizens to "appreciate...peaceful enjoyment" of liberty and "accustom them to make use of it."[2] The towns were crude but lively and an admirable model for local government, in his opinion. Since town-meeting government made every citizen a legislator, every citizen could have a definite, direct say in the decisions by which they told each other what they should and should not do in their lives together. Each citizen could speak his mind before a decision was made and each person had the opportunity to agree voluntarily to the decision. Subsequent law enforcement, if it was done well, was enforcement of what had been accepted ahead of time as commonly agreeable. Humans jointly were telling themselves what to do, rather than being told or commanded by someone else.

These features--a place to give a viewpoint, the expectation that it would be heard and weighed, and the opportunity to voluntarily agree to outcomes--were inherent in the way the town was set up politically. They meant that its citizens were politically free in the fullest sense of the word. Note that people had to take account of others and find decisions with which others could agree also, not merely make up their own minds in isolation, removed from the difficulties and joys of getting along with other people. But since the town's citizens directly governed themselves, the term self-government received its fullest American expression in this kind of arrangement.

Since it is almost impossible to overcome the politically misleading habit of thinking that self-government means doing only what one wants to do, as decided by oneself, apart from others, the operation of town-meeting government is especially instructive to us. We are assuming here that an individual cannot live completely on his or her own simply because one wants public sidewalks, roads, and schools as well as more complicated common arrangements which require some degree of cooperation. To be sure, there are other ways to decide cooperation, but none of them can be more direct or explicit than that of the town meeting, except perhaps case-by-case informal negotiations.

Another way to state the political freedom of the towns is to emphasize that no adult citizen had to put up with being told by someone else what he had to do. No citizen within the jurisdiction of the town was under the command of another, except in the town militia. As well, since state and national political officials at that time rarely intervened in local matters, townsmen were the most politically free Americans that we know about.

Indeed the freedom to make up one's mind and not be under the command of others is remarkable in the history of the world. The eras in which ordinary citizens were not ruled by others deemed to be their political superiors can be counted on the fingers of one hand. So, under town conditions of self-government, it could easily become a habit to believe that ordinary citizens were supposed to think for themselves, even within politics. Ordinary people, not just a political elite, considered, made, and were responsible for decisions--or at least they had a guaranteed right to do so, if they took advantage of the opportunity presented by their legislative position at the town meeting. From this perspective, a person's self-respect and feeling of dignity as a human being--what differentiated an adult politically from a child--rested on the conviction that one should govern with others. This belief was set forth boldly and solidly in the elementary political structure of the town; in other words, the town meeting conditioned ordinary citizens to believe in themselves politically and to act as though their opinions counted.

Some historians argue that a handful of a town's citizens often took a more prominent role in debate and deliberation, so that their voices were more decisive than those of their fellow citizens. In this interpretation, the handful provided direction, fashioned compromise, and either persuaded others to it or forced it upon them; in sum, the towns supposedly had a political elite who more or less monopolized political life. The main evidence for the elite interpretation is that executive committee office sometimes was held for long periods of time, though through yearly election, by the same few people and sometimes their descendants. The interpretation then supplies the assumption that such Selectmen naturally would prevail in debate. While the assumption certainly is plausible, the historical records of the actual debate in meetings are so scanty that one cannot possibly tell whether an elite monopolized the legislative arrangement.

The decisive points for our purposes are whether the meetings were genuinely open to every citizen and whether the citizens had an incentive to raise their viewpoints. The historical records do show that attendance at town meetings was high, especially when controversial matters were treated. The incentive for stating one's opinion was that one would be bound by the outcome of the deliberations. Self-interest and self-protection are fairly dependable goads to speaking out. In addition, since most townsmen owned and worked farms, they were economically independent of the political wishes of an employer. As for the supposed monopoly of executive offices specifically, the number of yearly turnovers which has been recorded is at least as high as the number of reelections, especially after the revolution.[3]

III

One further major detail of town self-government needs examination because it forces upon us a seemingly insurmountable problem. Ideally, from the interpretation we have made so far, town government would pass a law only when everyone would be in complete and full agreement on it. Debate and deliberation would have continued until a resolution could have been found to which every citizen could have wholeheartedly and voluntarily agreed. With unanimous decisions everyone truly would have been living by agreements which really were his decisions. Self-respect and human dignity based on voluntary agreements would have been perfect.

But in practical terms unanimous decisions usually would be too time-consuming, even if they always were possible among a fairly large number of people, each with a different viewpoint. And, in fact, townsfolk usually didn't agree unanimously. Some disputes festered for lifetimes. For example, intense rivalry between the three geographical sections in the Massachusetts town of Concord persisted from 1725 to 1771 when the number of Selectmen was reduced from five to three, one from each area.[4] Even more importantly, the town operating procedures required decisions by majority vote rather than by unanimous agreement. So what happened to the citizens who were left out of the majority on a particular issue, those who disagreed with the outcome of a deliberation? Weren't they ruled by the others, instead of governing themselves, thus robbed of their self-respect?

In practical terms, town politics could work successfully only when self-respect rested primarily upon acknowledgment of an individual's viewpoint during deliberations, rather than on complete agreement by all citizens about all decisions. The specific value of the town meeting arrangement was that its institutional structure approximated a guarantee of acknowledgment for each individual's viewpoint by putting each person in the decision-making body where he could make a viewpoint known and where the purpose of deliberation was to reach voluntary agreement among the varying viewpoints. Thus citizens in the town-meeting situation showed respect for each other, even regardless of whether they fully felt it in their hearts, when they talked and listened to each other in order to get their public business done together.

For this respect to happen, the decision-making actually had to take place in public at the town meeting. The talking and listening had to be about something and not play-acting about a previously and privately agreed upon outcome among a power clique. Without a decision at stake, no incentive existed for the real talk and listening which simultaneously was the respect for viewpoints. And the deliberations had to be open to all citizens so that they could feel and see that their viewpoints were acknowledged.

As mentioned above, we are assuming here that complete agreement among varying viewpoints is too unlikely and maybe not even desirable. We are assuming that differing viewpoints always will exist and that politics is living together constructively with differing opinions rather than trying to eliminate them. Hence, the specifically political problem is to cooperate genuinely while preserving the variety of individual viewpoints which inevitably arise among us, when we are free to have a say about matters of mutual concern. So one crucial factor for enabling self-respect had to be the respect of others, had to be whether one's viewpoint genuinely was taken account of somehow during deliberations, rather than whether one was in total agreement with others on decisions.

IV

Despite these qualifications, the difficulty remains for our interpretation that citizens who lost to the majority on the outcome of a debate naturally suspect that their viewpoints were overlooked or were not quite as seriously weighed as they should have been. Outcomes which are majority compromises surely will fail to fully encompass some of the viewpoints which were aired in the deliberative process, even when the majority very carefully and conscientiously weighed all factors before deciding. How did the town citizens deal with this inevitability? We know little for sure; yet we can create a set of answers, based on the political structure of the town and the well-established fact that most people loved their towns and stayed in them for their lifetimes. Using these factors, we can imagine five most obvious ways a townsman might have preserved his dignity in response to an undesirable decision. The essence of the five alternatives is that one can continue to think for oneself politically and retain self-respect as a citizen by finding an independent reason from one's viewpoint for either enduring or rejecting a disagreeable outcome.

The most general reason which can be invoked genuinely by an individual for abiding by a disagreeable policy result is respect for the judgment of the majority. Political issues seldom have entirely right or wrong answers; they are matters of judgment, not of absolutely certain knowledge. Political decisions usually are matters of weighing the contingencies of a situation, possible actions, and projected results about which no one has a monopoly of truth. As well, political decisions are about the wise way to live together, given a variety of viewpoints on how to do it. While the majority usually does not have all the wisdom, one person's viewpoint seldom encompasses all the wisdom either. So, the first path to self-respect is deference to the majority, in a particular situation, because it has as likely a chance for prudence as one's own position. Townsmen no doubt were familiar with this line of thinking.

A second alternative path is that, even from one's differing viewpoint, the majority's considered opinion often will add some partial good to the world when implemented. If so, one can support the disagreeable outcome hesitantly, with reservation, because it will at least do something salutary, from one's viewpoint. While outvoted, one still is governing oneself instead of being ruled by others on this issues, because one still is thinking for oneself rather than going along blindly or in utter defeat.

Deference to the majority and the garnering of a partial good are two general ways to abide by decisions, two ways helpful for seeing how self-respect could work out on disagreeable outcomes. Other alternatives would have been needed also. Occasionally, some citizens would not be at all able to support an outcome. These are the hardest cases to deal with. Take a gradation of responses for examples: critic, dissenter, and democratic revolutionary.

The critic loses on the outcome of a political dispute but persistently raises a viewpoint which he believes nonetheless is essential in the deliberations and their results. This townsman's voice is heard and he believes the outcome would have been even less attractive, if not for the presence of his viewpoint. While this citizen cannot enlist enthusiastically and voluntarily in an outcome, he also is not willing to undermine the community's considered opinion. The critic still disagrees after really searching for a reason to support, wants to participate in future debate, hopes to be on a winning side eventually. But, even if a future victory never occurs, the critic may take part in future deliberations out of the above mentioned belief that his opinions alter but do not accord with outcomes. The critic purposefully accepts community rulership on an outcome in order to keep intact personal integrity, since he feels more self-respect as a person ruled by an undesirable decision than he would have felt if he had agreed to it. Since the critic believes the debate acknowledges his viewpoint, he has a genuine and ongoing, although somewhat attenuated, connection to the community.

The danger inherent in the critic's response arises from its habitual use and is twofold. First, rulership by others on an accumulating number of decisions can become onerous, especially in the town situation where so many freely follow their own considered opinions. The critic's resulting frustration might drive him to an increasingly contentious viewpoint which few will take seriously. Second, even if the habitual critic does not become contentious, other citizens may tire of listening to one never able to bend enough for cooperation on decisions. Either way, the habitual critic can become a perennial outsider without respect for his viewpoint during deliberations, whereas the occasional critic is outside only on a handful of outcomes.

Dissenters on specific policies must also have been present among a town's citizens. The dissenter characteristically refuses to be bound by an undesirable majority outcome, hence to be ruled by others on it. Non-violent civil disobedience is the most dramatic way by which dissenters enact their resistance. Somewhat later in American political history, Thoreau is given credit for founding our tradition of civil disobedience. This honor perhaps would have been awarded to the townsmen who, in the years immediately preceding independence, resisted the string of English policies reasserting imperial control over the colonies, had they not finally become revolutionaries.

Civil disobedients do planned actions which break another law, such as trespassing on property or refusing to pay taxes, in order to publicize their dissent and to make it difficult for the community to operate in normal fashion. But they also accept punishment for their infractions, thereby acknowledging that they respect law and the way it is made, even though they have chosen to break one. In this specific sense, civil disobedients are not ordinary criminal law-breakers who try to escape enforcement, but citizens active in full public view. So they simultaneously demonstrate dissent on the undesirable decision and consent to the need for majority decisions in general.

In the short term, civil disobedients seem to have achieved the impossible. They lost to the majority deliberations in which their viewpoint presumably was acknowledged; yet, afterwards, they also managed to avoid putting up with the resulting decision, so are neither deprived of their ability to continue to think for themselves nor ruled by others on the outcome. Their self-respect is perfectly intact. However, in the longer term the civilly disobedient dissenter seriously risks his political standing within the community. During future town meetings, other citizens will be sorely tempted to dismiss his viewpoint purely because of his refusal to abide by previous deliberations during which his opinion was aired, considered, but set aside. This risk is worth taking only on the gravest issues because dissent may so readily undermine the effectiveness of the town citizen's legislative seat.

The democratic revolutionary also is active, also cannot find reasons to join the outcomes of the community, but differs decisively from the critic and dissenter because he believes the citizens' political structure itself is endangered. In his opinion, an outcome or a series of them purporting to be democratically made policy have begun to interfere with the town's guaranteed legislative seat for every citizen. If acting responsibly, the revolutionary believes that the community has begun to operate in such a way that his viewpoint and those of others are not and cannot be respected. Tyranny has begun; only the tyrant's viewpoint counts. Hence, the revolutionary tries to persuade others to overthrow the existing, allegedly corrupted or inadequate political arrangement. In the town meeting situation, the rebellion would be oriented toward return to the proper way that the town is supposed to operate. On the other hand, a revolutionary could believe that a new arrangement other than the town-meeting type would be even more respectful of individuals' viewpoints while also fostering cooperation. Either motive would be a reason for revolution on the town-meeting arrangement's own grounds, respect for viewpoints. Like the other citizens who one way or another can deal with an outcome with their integrity intact, the revolutionary clearly is not being told what to do politically by someone else.

From the town perspective, the revolutionary response to outcomes is the most risky. The political revolutionary seeks respect for viewpoints while also being willing to take up arms in order to kill some holders of opinions, thus eliminating their viewpoints. Revolutionary action directly risks the goal of politics: getting along with people with whom we disagree. In the chaos of civil upheaval, it is exceptionally difficult to distinguish between revolutionary enemies whom one will kill because they make respect impossible and tough-minded political adversaries whose viewpoints one ought to respect, even though they are troublesome. The excesses of the French Revolution exemplify this point compellingly. Only dire circumstances warrant taking such a risk. However, genuinely revolutionary circumstances can occur, as many American townsmen believed in 1776, after the mother country began interfering in town government.

In sum, the town citizen who lost on a majority decision had five typical responses: deference to the majority, acceptance of a partial good, criticism, dissent, and rebellion. While we have treated each of the five separately, they might better be viewed as a single repertoire from which an outvoted citizen could draw the response appropriate to his circumstances. During a lifetime, the typical citizen was likely to disagree with a number of policies. While his viewpoint presumably would have been acknowledged during the town-meeting deliberations, he also would have wanted one or another of the responses in order to avoid being forced into rulership by the majority on each of the objectionable decisions. The purpose of the responses was to enhance his self-respect by enabling him to continue to think for himself while also admitting a majority's prerogative to decide issues. Taken together these responses are as good an array as one is liable to find. And, in conjunction with respect for viewpoints during deliberation, the responses may very well be the best part of our heritage as ordinary citizens.

V

Turn now expressly to the topic of political leadership. Recall from the opening paragraphs of the essay that the most troublesome feature of leadership was that leaders try to take us in some direction--perhaps one in which we do not want to go. Our question was how to arrange politics so that disagreeable directions could be endured. The town meeting had an excellent answer. The town really did not designate political offices for leaders. The Selectmen executive offices were subordinate to the town-meeting legislature, hence would not give their holders unusual power in the community. The legislature gave potential leaders a place to advocate their goals; but, since every citizen had a seat, the position did not necessarily give leaders more power than followers.

Town decisions were made and authority for them was created in the town meeting, so potential leaders had to work through it in order to gain supporters. Because of their legislative seats, the potential followers could scrutinize each leadership proposal, speak their minds about it, try to shape and alter proposed goals and the means to them. So, first of all, there were as many checks, before a decision was made, against an undesirable leadership direction as there were citizens in the town.

Furthermore, since the town-meeting worked through the majority, a leader had to be flexible enough about goals to gain a following among fellow citizens. This also meant that any leadership direction came to the citizens as a decision of the majority, not as the command of a leader. Any leadership goals which a citizen might deem undesirable could be handled with the same array of responses as were any unattractive majority decisions. So one supporter would accept an objectionable leadership goal as the wisdom of the majority, another would accept it as the addition of a partial good to the world from his viewpoint; other citizens would be critics who object but endure a leader because their voice was heard in deliberations; still others as dissenters would attempt to thwart the leader with civil disobedience; on occasion, some would be rebels set upon protecting the community from a potential tyrant. Therefore enduring with dignity a successful leader's undesirable goal was completely within the habits of a politically active townsman.

As a result of the town's protection for followers from leaders, the relationship between leaders and followers can be understood as an "interdependence" of people doing different activities rather than as a hierarchy between two kinds of people, one politically superior to the other. Leaders are essential for originating goals, for advocating common endeavors, and for proposing ways to deal with issues and problems. Not everyone is able or willing to take this leadership role, especially to do it well. So leadership ability is an unusual talent. Nevertheless, leaders need the assistance of followers for doing projects as much as followers need leaders for suggesting plans. Thus, leaders stand out within the community but also are dependent upon the rest of the members of the community in order to be of actual value.

Followers also are both dependent and independent. While followers depend upon leaders for direction, followers also can think for themselves. They can choose between alternative, competing leadership proposals. Much more importantly, as we already have seen, town citizens were essential actors in deliberations. They stated the variety of viewpoints which preceded the majority decision, hence, gave reasons of their own for what the decision should be, and so were on record as joint participants with leaders in decisions. They could have joined with a leader on a project for reasons of their own, independent of a leader's reasons. This latter ability is the special provenance of the followers. By finding independent reasons for joining or opposing a leader in a common endeavor, followers establish their own basis for thinking which will enable them to check whether and how they wish to continue to respond to a leader, throughout a series of events, as a situation changes. As well, when followers do not have to submit passively to the commands of another, they are joint actors with a dignity of their own, though still dependent upon leaders. Thus, ideally, leaders and followers both have a measure of independence in their relationship and also a measure of dependence. The term "interdependence" sums up this mixture.[5] In a democratic setting, instead of leaders doing all the thinking and deciding, then telling others what to do, it was better for the human dignity of both leaders and followers if they recognized their mutual interdependence.

At its best, town-meeting government practiced interdependence between leaders and followers in either of two ways. First we know that citizens alternated the leader and follower tasks. The same person would be a leader on one issue, a follower on another, for instance, depending upon the persuasiveness of his viewpoint. Second, we also know instances when the same people stood out as leaders on consecutive issues, maybe for their lifetime. Then the guaranteed legislative seat for a follower's viewpoint and his independent reason about a leader gave him an equally active place in the relationship. So, a nearly perfect democratic relationship between leaders and followers could be very much alive in the town situation.

Stated another way, while the town-meeting political arrangement protected a follower from a leader, it also gave both a structural incentive to respect each other. Human institutions are limited in what they can accomplish. They cannot make a leader offer direction or a follower respect a leader's ability to do so. Neither can institutions make a follower find reasons of his or her own for joining or rejecting a decision; nor can they make a leader actually respect a follower's reasons for joining. Yet an institution such as the town meeting can bring together both potential leaders and followers in positions as political peers whose attention to each other is the most likely way to gain a great political reward--the power which comes from voluntary cooperation. The structure of joint decision-making encourages habits of listening and talking to each other, of respecting differing viewpoints and judgments, of responding to objectionable decisions, as we have claimed in the earlier sections of the essay. Thus town leaders, whether potential trouble for citizens or potential originators of mutually engaging, inherently worthwhile things to do, did not rob fellow citizens of the self-respect which arises from thinking for themselves politically. In retrospect at least, that is a way to say what our political forbears accomplished by creating town-meeting government.

VI

If we judge contemporary political arrangements for the ordinary citizen by the benchmark of town-meeting government, they are woefully inadequate on one point but immediately useful on another. As you know, we lack town-meeting legislative seats for direct exercise of political power. Towns exist today, but most are governed by representatives, albeit ones elected by the ordinary citizen. As admirable as is representative democracy, it lacks the distinctive guarantee for each citizen of a legislative seat from which to say his or her viewpoint and to decide what will be law. Another contemporary difference from early America is that towns have been overshadowed by cities as the governmental unit in which most Americans live. The creators of American cities possibly might have redesigned town-meeting government for the urban context, but they did not. As early as 1822, the city of Boston was granted an exemption from the town-meeting requirement in order to establish only representative local government for its numerous citizens, rather than some sort of mixed direct and representative democracy. Every other American city also has adopted solely indirect democracy, so the town-meeting forum virtually has disappeared. Today any connection for the ordinary citizen with political decision-making has to be indirect--either through representatives, political parties, and interest groups--or as a more or less isolated spectator.[6]

Because contemporary political life does not offer direct local level legislative seats to ordinary citizens, the most important immediately useful legacy the townspeople left to us is their set of citizenship habits. Sum them up in a list: the expectation of being heard individually on political issues; the ability to raise one's voice publicly, to talk with others in order to arrive at an improved individual judgment and at a group compromise; practice with whether one's viewpoint has been acknowledged on issues lost; and experience with finding ways to take responsibility for disagreeable policy by responding as a qualified supporter, critic, dissenter, or maybe even as a revolutionary, so that one is living by one's own decisions. Since these habits are relatively general, they are intrinsic to the life of many public associations which are not a formal part of government. Finding contemporary alternative ways to acquire similar public habits is more possible than the absence of town-meeting government might lead us to believe. My experience is that opportunities inevitably have appeared in front of me during my life, but that I did not always recognize them as such.

The opportunities lie in the various community groups which exist in one's immediate surroundings. (1) We all live in an apartment or a house somewhere; a neighborhood association, planning council, blockwatch, or other kind of public group almost always is active there or about to form. They welcome new members and do not require previous experience. (2) Schools will be nearby. They always are looking for residents who will join a group to do something likely to be worthwhile. This possibility is perhaps especially attractive to anyone who has or will have children attending the school, but is not necessarily limited to them. (3) Cities invariably have community-wide public groups that address timely issues such as civic improvement, crime, an environmental hazard, or a controversial governmental policy. These groups seek members from the city's various neighborhood areas or residential sectors in order to broaden their base of support. In short, finding and joining an organization in which to be publicly active at the local level is hardly more difficult than signing up for a video store rental membership.[7]

When one wants to learn town-meeting habits, probably the most important distinction to keep in mind about community groups is between those seeking a broader public interest from which all citizens benefit and those typically associated with special interests driven by a narrow agenda. For example, an interest group striving for benefits for its membership--such as the many business, professional, and labor groups--are less likely to encompass a broad range of viewpoints then are those groups which count among their members people from all those kinds of occupations--such as groups with names like *Citizens For a Crime-free Neighborhood, For Improved Schools*, or *For a Fairer Tax Policy*. Contemporary citizens will want to be involved with a range of viewpoints similar to those which the town meeting would have offered them. Acquisition of the town's public habits is the general reason for joining a community group, when we lack a legislative seat. More specifically, we know from the town-meeting benchmark why the effort and frustration of public activity is worthwhile: one's viewpoint and actions will count in the community, however modestly, and one will gain the additional self-respect which comes from thinking for oneself in response to desirable and undesirable community outcomes. An active community member with good public habits also learns that he or she can be powerful with others about a segment of public life, even without a place for direct political power. The list of town-meeting habits and the description of their operation will help one judge whether participation has been fruitful.

My most recent experience with a citizen group is six years of monthly meetings at the West Central Community Center. The organization decides general policy for the building rented from the city of Spokane, Washington, which houses the neighborhood's cluster of programs. The programs range from after-school recreation for children to nutrition and health assistance for low-income families, ballet classes, adult karate, a gardening club, and a political forum. In dollar terms the neighborhood center yearly involves about $350,000 of projects, so the responsibility is grave enough to require serious public talk. On the other hand, the people in the organization during my time with it were ordinary citizens from a relatively wide variety of backgrounds who usually wished simply to be of service in return for the company of their peers. A handful were senior citizens, some retired from jobs as various as minister, secretary, engineer, and civil servant. One ran a tavern in the neighborhood, another a small building construction company, a third a flower and gift shop. A doctor, architect, utility middle manager, a mother returning to college, and a full time housewife also served with us.

A few were veterans of neighborhood or other organizations. Many were novices, some of whom were a bit hesitant at first about how to participate in meetings. The newcomers usually quickly learned their versions of the general meeting habits discussed earlier in the chapter. Almost all turned out to be disposed to like as well as be liked, treated each other with respect, and manifested a substantial amount of goodwill in trying to discover the public interest according to their own viewpoints. A number listened well; a few did not. At times any one of them could be admirably contentious or stubbornly resolute.

Arguably the most important discovery I made was about whether people realized that their viewpoints had been acknowledged by others in the deliberations, even when a person's preferred outcome had not been incorporated into a final decision. One of the major advantages of participation in a community organization is the opportunity to speak more informally with people after a meeting. Not especially surprising in retrospect, I suppose, is the discovery that a few people never believe they have been taken seriously unless they win on an issue. Probably any group will have some such members; they are difficult human beings with whom to get along. Yet most people with whom I spoke after meetings had a pretty realistic sense that they had made a difference, even when on the losing side. This was the core of my most important discovery. Furthermore, the occasional opportunity to explain to someone the specific way their viewpoint had made a difference in my thinking was a pleasure. In turn, mention of how another's viewpoint counted prompted me to imagine that my viewpoint probably had counted more than I had realized when I had lost on a decision. So, talk after meetings can be as crucial for forming habits as talk during deliberations.

Overall, the most enduring part of my experience at West Central is the memories I have of the unique identities I saw in action in meeting situations, in the heat of debate, when none of us were directly conscious of projecting an image of ourselves. I will never meet another person exactly like each one of those individuals; and I was happy to be in their public company. As well, I felt a modicum of mutual power together with them in our corner of the world. These memories are among the most compelling reasons that I have had for trying to set out in this chapter a part of our political heritage as citizens and suggestions for its contemporary continuation. The memories assure me that I live in a community of unique people who know how to cooperate rather than in a world of leaders supported by anonymous masses.

Yet, the early townsmen probably did not have to figure out reasons for taking up an opportunity to learn public habits. They were conditioned by the structure of the town. They took it for granted that one would be pulled into town political life by the plain self-interest of having a voice in the laws by which one was going to live, if not by the sheer attraction of being in on the decisions. Since direct exercise of political power was a regular feature of their fathers' and grandfathers' lives, townsmen did not have to wonder much about whether to do politics. Since we often do wonder, public life seems more difficult to want, more formidable to try, and easier to put off. Nevertheless, thanks to the townsmen of the seventeenth, eighteenth, and nineteenth centuries, contemporary citizens have a historical right, not only the privilege, to expect that their individual voices should be heard in public, so long as they also are willing to accept the responsibility of finding public reasons for the outcomes. Following the town citizen example, any contemporary exercise of their habits will demonstrate that the right is alive for the next generation, too.

Furthermore, the more widely that public habits are spread throughout our large population, the more likely we are to have the political wherewithal as ordinary citizens to deal with leaders, regardless of the directions they want to take us, because people will have the habitual reflex of raising their voices and taking responsibility for policy. We do not have to be passively ruled by others.

Notes

1. Robert A. Gross, *The Minutemen and Their World* (New York: Hill and Wang, 1976), 34.
2. Alexis de Tocqueville, *Democracy in America*, ed., J.P. Mayer (Garden City, N.J.: Anchor Doubleday, 1969), 62-63.
3. Stanley Elkins and Eric McKitrick, "A Meaning For Turner's Frontier," *Political Science Quarterly* 69 (1954): 321-353; 565-602, especially 591 n. 54; 598.
4. Gross, *Minutemen*, 15-17.
5. The theoretical alternative of interdependence to the traditional hierarchy between leaders and followers is substantiated ably by Hannah Arendt, *The Human Condition* (Chicago: University of Chicago Press, 1958), especially 189-190; 220-30.
6. One need not necessarily take the eclipse of direct democracy as an unchangeable fact. For example, I teach a course which does not and a number of activists throughout the country are organizing citizens to assert this traditional heritage. For an instructive account of an ongoing, though not altogether successful, mixed arrangement in a California city, see Mark E. Kann, *Middle Class Radicalism in Santa Monica* (Philadelphia: Temple University Press, 1986).
7. Any of the recent books by Harry C. Boyte reports the successes and failures of community groups. Perhaps the variety is best surveyed in *The Backyard Revolution: Understanding the New Citizen Movement* (Philadelphia: Temple University Press, 1980).

Chapter 12

A Lesson for Citizens

Blaine Garvin

I.

Years ago I had a friend named Steve--Steve, a short, orangebearded, barrel-chested, ex-gymnast turned behavioral psychologist, now long gone to Kansas City and another college. In those days Steve and I both worked on the third floor of Gonzaga's old, imposing Administration Building (north side, view of the mountain, a cozy hole for an academic). A late afternoon habit brought him down the hall to my office to joke for half an hour. A favorite of his was to pick a book from my shelf to make fun of its author and title. One day it might be Cochrane's *Christianity and Classical Culture*: "A few things Cochrane thinks he knows about Greeks and Romans in church," Steve would say, giggling. Or Tarn's *Alexander the Great*: "Old Alex, who Tarn happens to think was pretty neat." Or John Stuart Mill's classic essay *On Liberty*: "Pontifications by a stuffy Victorian who wouldn't know how to loosen his shirt collar." By now Steve would be laughing loudly. Once in a while I would puff up in mock outrage to defend a book. Hanna Pitkin said everything important about *The Concept of Representation*, I'd fume, and said it well.[1] But Steve's laugh was infectious and soon I'd be laughing with him.

The point of Steve's joke? Book titles make big promises the books seldom keep. To use a fancy word, the titles are pretentious, pretending to more worth than the books really have. To be even blunter, you may sag with disappointment when you put the book down, that is, if you really had high hopes about learning everything there was to learn. The books I just mentioned are great books, but they don't--they can't--tell you everything. You'd be a fool to think otherwise, Steve seemed to say.

So I've been well warned about one kind of ambition. There's no way I was going to let my title make you think I was going to tell you everything about political education (or even something like "Political Education in Late 20th Century America"). I didn't want you to catch me raising inflated expectations. Now a writer should aim high. Spread those handsome wings, try something new, explore the unknown--people give you this advice. It is good advice: without a spirit of adventure, learning would go nowhere fast and the trip wouldn't be much fun. But this advice is not the only good advice. Narrow the scope, focus in, concentrate--these are various ways of saying, "Learn the lesson behind Steve's joke." Having learned it, I intend to tell you only one or two things I know and care about.

On the other hand, I suffer from a different sort of ambition which may be even harder for you to accept. My big ambition concerns you. You, me, and our country. Our country cannot work well, cannot be what it is supposed to be, without you. You have to take an active part in its public affairs--you and others--or our public life will go stale, grow corrupt, decay. You have a heavy responsibility. Fortunately, you are an able person. You have nearly every piece of equipment you need to do the job already. The rest is a matter of attitude and I can help with that. I can help make you a better citizen of our country.

Putting it one way, I am concerned--now don't feel insulted--about your *followership*, which must be just as good a word as leadership although we don't hear it much. Let's face it--we can't all be leaders, at least not all the time. Then, too, don't we all know this truth, that leaders need good followers? Some people eventually become great leaders who have to wander around until their followers catch up. Winston Churchill in the 1930s is an example. But if the British had never followed Churchill, what kind of a "leader" could he possibly have been? When the voters did abandon him in 1945 for the Labour Party and Clement Atlee (that "sheep in sheep's clothing," as Churchill once called him) the great Prime Minister ceased to be the leader he was, although he went on guiding the Conservative Party in opposition and later regained the mandate.

No followers, no leaders! Moreover, it takes a good follower to make a good leader; a stupid follower, by contrast, will trail a bad or even crazy leader down the path to national self-destruction, and reminisce later about what a pleasant journey it was. History praises or blames leaders, but the ordinary people who follow along bear responsibility as well. And it doesn't just happen in the movies. My part of the country has been bedeviled by crazy white supremacists who go around preaching hatred. People have been killed--in one recent instance, a federal agent. Nothing funny about that.

Before, I said that I wanted to help you be a better citizen. Just now I have been talking about followers. I mean roughly the same thing. I just said that most of us will be ordinary citizens ("followers") rather than leaders for most of our lives. When I say that I want to prepare you for citizenship I mean that I want to help you be a good follower: a smart follower, not a stupid one; a responsible citizen, not one who recklessly attacks his fellow citizens or refuses to work to improve her country. Calling you a follower, assuming that you will be an ordinary citizen, doesn't mean that I think you will never lead. Of course you will. At your work, in the groups you join, in your own town, you will often lead. You may even get yourself elected to office. In any case, as the philosopher Aristotle reminded people a long time ago, even leaders have to learn to follow first.

Who am I to tell you what kind of citizen to be? It's a fair question. Being a college professor of political science isn't credential enough by itself. It helps, though. I have spent twenty years reading what some great minds have thought about democratic citizenship. The question of democratic citizenship was on my mind when I wrote my Ph.D. dissertation, and it has often guided my teaching since. I can claim at least minor league credentials in practical politics--I once ran for office, which less than 1% of all Americans do. True, I lost badly. Still, I hope I learned a little along the way.

In the end, though, I believe my credentials matter less than the force of my words, whatever that turns out to be. Thomas Hobbes, a seventeenth century English political philosopher, once wrote that in political science, unlike mathematics, the reader must find reason to be persuaded from within, "this kind of doctrine admitteth no other demonstration."[2] In other words, I can't *prove* to you that I am right. But I do invite you to listen. I'm going to be upbeat about citizenship and about politics in general. That may seems strange these days. We have a good politics, as I will try to show you later. We will always need new citizens to carry our good politics into the future. These new citizens will need to learn how to act. If you are ready to learn, then I am here to help.

I know people who would think this was a downright goofy thing to say. Take another friend of mine still at Gonzaga, Professor Jane Rinehart, who is a co-editor of this volume and has her own chapter. We've known each other for years, like each other enormously, and have had good times teaching together. (Ten years ago we taught a seminar called The American Experience--can't you hear Steve laughing about that title?) Lately Jane and I have been at odds over this question: Is it better to help students find a place to stand where they can criticize the world they live in, feel empowered, and perhaps restructure the world altogether? Or is it better to help students appreciate and enter into their world's way of doing things, presuming that these ways are pretty good and will already lead to some kind of empowerment? A detached person, not caught up in the argument, might say that it is important to do both things and dangerous to neglect one for the other. But what if you had to choose?

Nobody is forcing a choice on me, but if somebody did, I would be for "going along." No country is perfect, and surely there are things wrong with ours that need fixing. A citizen myself, I want these problems solved, too. I call myself liberal because I do see the need for reform and change. On the other hand, I have a conservative's respect for a politics that has proved itself over time, that has held out rich resources to discontented people who want to work changes. Not that change is easy. To those who take the lead, it must seem like killing work. Unfortunately, for Martin Luther King it was killing work. But profound change does happen, as the history of the civil rights movement shows; this profound change can happen, moreover, without a radical shuffling of our basic practices and institutions. It's sometimes hard to remember in these frustrating times when bitter words fill the political airways, when we seem so stuck, but I believe it's true. Jane would choose the other answer and tell a different story.

There is danger in the habit of criticizing, although a lot depends on how you do it. A person who criticizes everything all the time is a cynic. My friend Steve, although funny, was something of a cynic. Sometimes he seemed so cynical that he couldn't *do* anything. I wouldn't mind your laughing with Steve, but I have to tell you that I wouldn't want you to be like him. My friend Jane is another matter; she would talk in strong language about the need to criticize in order to empower those living at the margins of society. It would be a different lesson than mine and an instructive one. I don't mind her kind of criticism, at least if it's not done to death. Right now, though, I want you to see the good side of America. And I want you to learn how to be a part of America.

II.

Some strong-minded people don't think I should be talking with you about citizenship at all. They don't complain about you and me in particular--they don't know you and me--but they do complain about the general idea of citizenship training. Their complaints are serious. Among the people who complain are scholars, teachers, and administrators, the people who determine what college education will be about.

In this quarrel, I confess to you, I am not the one with novelty on my side. Universities since their founding have initiated students into positions of power and prestige. (In connection with this point, see Julie Tammivaara's chapter.) American colleges and universities have included citizenship training, the path to power and responsibility for us, among their goals for a long time. My university's mission statement, for example, speaks of the need to prepare students for public service, another way of talking about citizenship.[3]

You could call what I argue for an "established truth," one taken for granted so long that it seems refreshing to hear it challenged. There is nothing wrong with challenging established truths. Even if an old truth does stand up, it should get battered around from time to time; after the challenge, we understand better what we believe and why.

Don't give up on a truth, though, just because you have heard it many times. People have been telling you to be a good citizen since you were in day care. You may be bored hearing it, but it is still true. Let me take as my motto for this section of my paper some words from an English writer I admire, Bernard Crick. "Boredom with established truths," Crick says, "is a great enemy of free men."[4] Free women, too.

In our free country, power is supposed to belong to the people. Or, to put it more modestly, we are supposed to have a share in power. Teaching you about citizenship is really just giving you advice about what to do with your share of the power, advice about what kind of person you should be in order to use power well. It's just a case of one citizen trying to help out another. Who could object?

The list is long, but I will only tell you about two objectors. One kind of person who objects is the educational purist. This person loves ideas more than practical experience; or at least he or she doesn't see what the "world out there" has to do with "the life of the mind." Although old itself, the lure of "ideas for their own sake" always has a fresh feel about it.[5] I, at least, feel moved when I read the words of the well-known educator Jacques Barzun, as he defends reading and thinking and warns against subordinating these activities to an indiscriminate list of practical skills.

> Instead of trying to develop native intelligence and give it good techniques in the basic arts of man, we profess *to make ideal citizens*, super-tolerant neighbors, agents of world peace, and happy family folks, at once sexually adept and flawless drivers of cars.[6]

Barzun, I guess, assumes that you and I will find time for friendship, sex, and love on our own. Politics, too. But it seems to me that the practical life, including politics, also has just claims to make on us. So do our cars. Once you admit we should pay attention to practicalities, you must admit that it is o.k. to try to teach people to do these activities well. If the end is o.k., so are the appropriate means.

There is another kind of person who objects to citizenship training of the sort I have in mind. This person doesn't believe it is wrong to use education to help people act, but does think that my version of this education is too conservative. Scientific curiosity does not move the social critic as much as certain passions do--an angry resentment at the way things are, a love of justice that demands they act for radical change. To the critic socialization seems like and may have felt like a sort of brainwashing meant to quiet protest. Socialization makes us (or is supposed to make us) into well-behaved subjects who do not question existing power arrangements. Directly or indirectly, many of these critics have learned from Karl Marx's powerful insights about ideology and indoctrination.[7] From this point of view, citizenship training is a means of social control, cheaper than violence, and maybe even more effective. To the critic, not to drop your oar, not to stand up to rock the boat, is to continue as a passive slave in the galley.

This way of thinking has an appeal for some articulate people who come from and try to represent the least powerful people in our country. It also appeals to some who don't feel good about being reared in wealth and want to speak out for those who haven't any. (This can cause trouble when the less well-off want to speak for themselves.) In either case, the critic thinks the social building we live in is out of whack down to its foundation, like some of the flimsily constructed buildings that blew down in the recent Florida hurricane. As long as the building stands, however precariously, those who get the best rooms won't want to rebuild; but the rest of us should be ready to call in the bulldozers (bright, shiny yellow Caterpillars), get out new plans, and start over.

Having been in college as a student or a teacher since I was eighteen, I have heard this talk all my adult life.[8] This language spoken or written well--as it was by Marx himself-- appeals to me. It forcefully condemns injustice--which is an important thing to do. At first foreign and difficult, moreover, Marx's language gets easy with a little practice. It can be a powerful political tool in the right hands.

Overuse of this powerful tool, however, dulls the senses. Slipping into Marx's language becomes as easy as slipping into your baggy Sunday afternoon outfit--which may be a danger sign. When words come very easily, it may be because you are thinking especially clearly; or it may be because you have learned enough words in prepared clumps so that you don't have to think at all. George Orwell, the famous English novelist and social critic, makes this point about Marxist writing in particular and modern writing in general:

> [M]odern writing at its worst does not consist in picking out words for the sake of their meaning and inventing images in order to make the meaning clearer. It consists in gumming together long strips of words which have already been set in order by someone else, and making the results presentable by sheer humbug.[9]

I'm afraid that this is what much of the writing by social critics has come to be: sheer humbug. No one is likely to be moved to serious action by humbug. Contrast how you feel when you hear a Martin Luther King speech, with its biblical concreteness and preacher's passion, with how you feel after reading a dry, abstract article on a subject you're not sure you care about. You will see what I mean. Or think about a book you've read that makes you see and feel what you're reading about, contrasted with one whose words you have to plow through like heavy, dense snow as occasional tree branches slap you sharply in the face.

The language of social critique has begun to sound pretty old-fashioned. I remember the early 1960s when the voices of protest were strong, immediate, telling.[10] Stultifying jargon crept into radical talk over the course of the 1960s and 70s, in my view helping to dampen the enthusiasm for change and to quell the exhilaration of the times. When I talk about citizenship, I try to recapture some of the enlivening sense that participation *can* be an important part of our lives, without falling prey to the critic's way of talking. I think it matters, too, that the critics--by their own admission--haven't really helped change the country as much as it should be changed.

I have always found our country lovely. a place worth becoming a part of. I mean its people and its geography but also its politics. Since I was eight years old the politics of our country has tugged at me, for reasons I can't fully explain. Now past fifty I am not ready to admit disenchantment. Like a person in love, I want you to see how beautiful my love is. I am anxious to help you be a citizen--to be an active, participating American, not just an American the way the Census Bureau thinks you're an American. This will seem like a good idea to you only if we can see eye to eye on the answers to these questions: Is our country lovely? Is its public life worth attending to? Can its politics be good and honorable? Tough questions in the aftermath of the rugged 1992 presidential election. Tough questions as we watch President Clinton and the Congress struggle with one another. Tough questions even for those in love with the country--for we know that the country isn't always at its best. Let's see about some answers to these questions.

III.

Our country is free and democratic. It needs good citizens, citizens who know what they are doing and care about what happens to the country. This is why political or civic education is important. Besides enabling you to do your part, such an education may also increase your power.

It may sound pedantic and professorial to say this, but our starting point needs to be a clearer set of terms. Over the next few pages I want to: (1) define democracy, freedom, politics, and political education; (2) show you how these four terms are connected; and (3) argue that America meets the standard for a free and democratic country, one suitable for your participation. These are three separate tasks: the first task is one of sensible definition, the second of interlacing ideas, the third of presenting a few pertinent facts about the country.

Let's start with the definition of democracy. Rather than make up a meaning of my own, Humpty-Dumpty style, I will go back to the first appearance of the word.[11]

Democracy existed in the world before people had a name for it. I am thinking of the democracy created by Kleisthenes, an Athenian statesman of the sixth century b.c.e., the democracy which came to its greatest glory under another statesman, Pericles, in the fifth century b.c.e.

This is the famous democracy of the ancient Greeks written about in the schoolbooks. It is also the democracy criticized by Plato.

It would be wrong not to point out right away that this was democracy for the few: only native, adult, male Athenians need apply; aliens, women, and slaves need not. But compared to any other place in the world, then and for a long time after, it was an astonishing sharing of power.

Today we would call it a *direct* democracy. Making laws, deciding whether to go to war or make peace, rendering judicial decisions--these were all things done by ordinary citizens. Instead of electing representatives to a legislature, all citizens were invited to attend, indeed required to attend meetings of the *ekklesia*, or assembly. Some juries, like the one that condemned the philosopher Socrates, had several hundred members. The head of the executive council--the nearest equivalent to the Speaker of the House, I guess, or maybe the President--was chosen daily by lot. (Think about that: Your name is drawn from a jar and--bingo!--you're president of the country for a day.) As Alfred Zimmern, an English classical scholar, once wrote, "with us, however democratic our constitution, the few do the work for the many, [but] in Greece the many did it for themselves."[12]

Plato wasn't the only one who didn't like this new form of government. Many of the words written about democracy at the time were unfriendly. As one history book says, "almost without exception our sources are unsympathetic or actively hostile toward the Athenian democracy."[13] These critics gave the new form of government its name, a name meant to sound ugly and implausible. The name was *demokratia*, the ruling power (*kratos*) of the people (*demos*, meaning not *all* the people, but the unimpressive majority, as opposed to the very best people, the *aristoi*). As often happens when people start calling each other insulting names, the insulted soon took on the label as a badge of honor. Someday I hope you get a chance to read Thucydides's history of the great war between Sparta and Athens. I hope you will read the words he gives to Pericles as Pericles praises the virtues of democracy, by the 420s a word said with great pride. (Too much pride, Thucydides thought, but that's another story.)[14]

Since the days of Pericles democracy has had many enemies and a few friends, a growing number of friends. Over the centuries many questions have been asked about democracy: Is another democracy like Athens possible? Is it only possible in a small country? Or could it happen in a large country (like ours)? Could America, as Tom Paine suggested, be in the large what Athens was in miniature?[15] Does having representatives help or hurt democracy? What is the best way to make the power of the people effectual?

Through all the debate, however, there has been little disagreement about what democracy means. It means rule by the people.

What about freedom?

Freedom and a closely related term, liberty, seem to have been given hundreds of shades of meaning--moreover, the word freedom is used in every field from physics to theology. Help is at hand in sorting out *political* meanings, however, help from yet another English writer (they are very good at this sort of thing). Isaiah Berlin suggests that people speak of political freedom "negatively" and "positively." In other words, some talk about the absence of something, while others talk about the presence of something.

Freedom or liberty defined negatively, as it has been by liberal writers from Hobbes to Mill, from John Locke to Thomas Jefferson to you, has to do with the absence of impediments, interferences, and obstacles. Negative liberty involves that space or area

> within which a man can act unobstructed by others. If I am prevented by others from doing what I could otherwise do, I am to that degree unfree ... I can be described as being coerced, or, it may be, enslaved.[16]

You could enjoy negative liberty in a state of complete enervation; no one pokes or prods you, so you don't even twitch; but you are, in a sense, free.

There is another side to freedom, an opposite side to liberty. It has to do with the presence of power or capacity, the presence of an ability to do what you regard as important to do. Thinking about your positive liberty, I see you in motion, acting, doing, accomplishing. After you enjoy the peace and serenity of being left alone, you crave the feeling of power and self-direction. Berlin says,

> The 'positive' sense of the word 'liberty' derives from the wish on the part of the individual to be his own master. I wish, above all, to be conscious of myself as a thinking, willing, active being, bearing responsibility for my choices and able to explain them by reference to my own ideas and purposes.[17]

In reality, nobody experiences positive liberty unadulterated. There are always obstacles. These obstacles include other people with *their* ideas and purposes. Knowing how truly limited we are, some people think we must find positive liberty through surrendering to our weakness or in the strength of another (or Another). In a sense, Tom Jeannot's chapter is about liberty of this kind.

This idea of finding freedom through giving up may seem paradoxical. But there is something to the idea. In politics, too, there is a certain "giving up," --in Part VI of this paper I will show how crucial to freedom it is to be willing to give up some of what we want in order to accommodate others.

Over the years Americans have treasured freedom or liberty in both the negative and the positive sense. Americans love negative liberty. Don't tread on me! Don't fence me in! Give me space! We (like Greta

Garbo) have wanted to be left alone, even by the government we supposedly control--hence our Bill of Rights. But we also have wanted to govern ourselves, to make our own choices--hence, our frequently commented-upon gift for involvement and association, our instinctive interest in joining.

Since we cling to both negative and positive liberty, it is important to know if there is potential conflict between them. It turns out there is. The more we attach ourselves to negative liberty, the less interesting positive liberty becomes to us. The more we like to be alone--or to be with just our family or closest friends--the more we resist getting out to be with other people. We need to resist this urge in ourselves. On the other hand, the more we are used to getting out, the more likely we are not to succumb to merely negative liberty. My favorite political writer, who turns out to be French, not English, explained this well in 1856. Alexis de Tocqueville, who had observed American freedom in person twenty-five years before, told French readers how positive freedom could overcome too much privacy and isolation:

> [O]nly freedom can deliver the members of a community from that isolation which is the lot of the individual left to his own devices and, compelling them to get in touch with each other, promote an active sense of fellowship. In a community of free citizens every man is daily reminded of the need of meeting his fellow men, of hearing what they have to say, of exchanging ideas, and coming to an agreement as to the conduct of their common interests. Freedom alone is capable of lifting men's minds above mere mammon worship and the petty personal worries which crop up in the course of everyday life, and of making them aware at every moment that they belong ... to a vast entity, above and around them--their native land. It alone replaces at certain critical moments their natural love of material welfare by a loftier, more virile ideal; offers other objectives than that of getting rich; and sheds a light enabling all to see and appraise men's vices and their virtues as they truly are.[18]

Bob Waterman's chapter tells you more about the American townships which inspired this appreciation.

Now let's turn to the meaning of politics. And let's turn again to that helpful Englishman, Bernard Crick, the biographer of George Orwell and himself a powerful political writer. "Politics," Crick writes, "can be simply defined as the activity by which different interests within a given unit of rule are conciliated by giving them a share in power in proportion to their importance to the welfare and survival of the whole community."[19] Politics is an activity. The activity is aimed at conciliation; its aim is to keep different interests talking to one another, to keep them living together with at least some minimal harmony. The activity of politics accomplishes this aim (or more properly, the people who do politics accomplish it) by giving important interests a share in power.

If you matter, then you should get your share of power. Any systematic exclusion of important elements of society tarnishes the political character of that society, turning it into a society which to that degree is ruled by force or some other non-political means.

You notice that I am not bashful about suggesting that politics is good and more politics is better. I am a democrat. We have already seen that democracy promotes a lot of politics. A democrat believes that all people matter and that all adults at least should share in power. No one small segment of society should get to play this game while others have to stand on the sidelines.

The ideas I have been discussing come together, they are interconnected or interlaced, in this way: Democracy is rule by the people. Freedom involves, among other things, self-government or self-rule. Although it is possible in some settings for self-rule to exist only for the few, this is not possible in a true democracy. Democracy, at its best, extends freedom to practically everybody, all citizens being equally entitled to enjoy its benefits. A free democracy is not the only possible kind: the people can rule coercively, as writers from Plato to Tocqueville have said. Many Americans with unpopular political views or "suspect" backgrounds could tell you about the "tyranny of the majority," as Tocqueville called it.[20] While tyrannical democracies may exist, a free democracy is the best kind. And politics is the best manner of rule for a free democracy, although coercion and the threat of coercion never completely vanish even in a free democracy. To rule politically requires skill. Such skill must be learned. So must the willingness to use it. Hence the need for political education.

I have defined my terms and shown their interconnection. The next point? It is to show that America does measure up to the standards of a free, democratic, politically run country. Tocqueville said that our country was born free, even if not all its inhabitants were. He meant that Americans were lucky to have achieved democracy without undergoing an extraordinarily violent class war, like the one France experienced after 1789. Americans fought a bloody war to free themselves from British rule. Even so, while some British Loyalists suffered dearly, the winners didn't have to chop the heads off fifteen thousand of their fellow countrymen. By 1783 America was free, but making everybody in America free was another matter. Among other things, this required a bloody, terrible, but probably entirely necessary Civil War that Tocqueville dreaded but did not live to see.[21]

Some of this needs brief elaboration. At least I think it does and I hope you'll stick with me.

First, America was a free country even before it was an independent one. Before the 1760s, Britain left America alone. Being left alone, the colonies, although not independent or even desiring to be independent, were for internal purposes self-governing. Not only that, the colonists enjoyed the various rights and protection that belonged to all British subjects under the British Constitution. The mixed form of government-- later to be emulated in the American Constitution, and known among us as the separation of powers with checks and balances--together with rugged, self-reliant British character produced happy effects. As the historian Bernard Bailyn explains:

> The colonists' attitude to the whole world of politics and government was fundamentally shaped by the root assumption that they, as Britishers, shared in an unique inheritance of liberty. ... The word 'constitution' and the concept behind it was of central importance to the colonists' political thought... For if the ostensible purpose of all government was the good of the people, the particular goal of the English constitution--'its end, its use, its designation, drift and scope'--was known to all, and declared by all, to be the attainment of liberty.[22]

After 1763 British policy seemed to change. To many Americans it appeared that their countrymen in England had grown lax and corrupt; worse yet, they had begun to corrupt the constitution. Liberty was slipping away in Britain, leaving the British in America as its only defenders. In his great pamphlet of 1776, *Common Sense*, Thomas Paine showed what was needed:

> O ye that love mankind: Ye that dare oppose not only the tyranny but the tyrant, stand forth: Every spot of the old world is overrun with oppression. Freedom hath been hunted round the globe. Asia and Africa have long expelled her. Europe regards her like a stranger, and England hath given her warning to depart. O receive the fugitive, and prepare in time an asylum for mankind.[23]

And so they did, those revolutionary Americans. Their belief in liberty led them to risk all for its sake. The American Revolution was fought to preserve liberty, not to create it.

Black slavery was an awful exception to the reign of American liberty, one that reminded the free how fortunate they were. As Bailyn says, "The degradation of chattel slavery--painfully visible and unambiguously established in law--was only the final realization of what the loss of freedom could mean everywhere."[24] Free Americans felt lucky, but the more they thought about slavery the guiltier they felt as well. It is no coincidence that the era of the American Revolution saw the first serious anti-slavery agitation. It would be over three-quarters of a century before the Thirteenth Amendment of 1865 abolished slavery. Then the Fourteenth Amendment made former slaves citizens in 1868. It would take another hundred years, until the Voting Rights Act of 1965, before it could reasonably be claimed that African-Americans enjoyed essentially the same *political* rights as the white population. To this day there is no equality of political and economic power.

Black Americans eventually received political rights. Native Americans, who were not covered by the Fourteenth Amendment, were made citizens by an act of Congress in 1887. Women received the most visible symbol of full citizenship, the vote, by means of the Nineteenth Amendment to the Constitution in 1920.[25] By these acts citizenship, and the political freedom it brings to Americans, ceased to be exclusive.

Our country began free, but not democratic. Or to put it Tocqueville's way: the colonies in America "contained the germ, if not the full growth, of a complete democracy." The American soil and climate were suitable: "All, from the beginning, seemed destined to let freedom grow, not the aristocratic freedom of the motherland, but a middle-class and democratic freedom" not previously seen in the world.[26]

When the American Revolution broke out, democracy was not a popular idea. The men who wrote the Constitution didn't hold democracy in high regard. They did not set out to create a democracy, but our country became a democracy of free white males within a single lifetime. James Madison's lifetime.

Known among historians as the Father of the Constitution, James Madison began his political career with a deep distrust of the people. Like others of the revolutionary generation, he worried that the people could not use power well or unselfishly; they would invariably serve themselves rather than look out for the rights of others or concern themselves with the long-term interests of the country. In his most famous essay, *Federalist Paper #10*, written in defense of the new Constitution in 1788, Madison argued that democracy

> can admit of no cure for the mischiefs of faction. A common passion or interest will, in almost every case, be felt by a majority of the whole; a communication and concert results from the form of government itself; and there is nothing to check the inducements to sacrifice the weaker party or an obnoxious individual. Hence it is that such democracies have ever been the spectacle of turbulence and contention; have ever been found incompatible with personal security or the right of property; and in general have been as short in their lives as they have been violent in their deaths.[27]

Madison's solution was twofold: Instead of local democracy, a larger, extended, federal republic, relying on representation, would make pernicious majority rule difficult or impossible; and a complicated scheme of mixed powers within the national government--the famous separation of powers derived from the British constitution--would prevent the representatives of the people, or any other part of government, from ruling arbitrarily or tyrannically.[28] The new government would rest on consent and it would contain a popular element--the House of Representatives--but it would not be a democracy.

Our politics became democratic in spite of Madison. (To be fair, you might also say because of him, since he helped his friend Thomas Jefferson form the first democratic political party.) Madison died in 1836, a week short of ten years after Jefferson. (Another interruption: Did you know that both Jefferson and John Adams died on July 4, 1826, the fiftieth anniversary of the Declaration of Independence? I always thought that was spooky.) By 1836 America was well into the era of Jacksonian

Democracy, the time of triumph for democratic culture and spirit. No longer a disreputable word, democracy was as welcome in America as it had been in Periclean Athens. Andrew Jackson was in his third year as president when Tocqueville visited America in 1831. Looking around in awe at the power of ordinary people, Tocqueville concluded, "The people reign over the American political world as God rules over the universe."[29]

Democratic we remain today, even though late nineteenth century industrialization made our society less egalitarian and money far more important in politics. The new power of rich people did create problems, but it didn't change the form of government, or even the political culture. Even Karl Marx thought industrial America was the freest and most democratic country in the world, a model in the short run, until eventually communist revolution destroyed monied power forever.[30] Without being Marxist, many American progressives have tried over the years to use democracy in order to remedy the worst abuses of economic inequality. May this work continue. May we become even more democratic than we are now. May our country become even lovelier.

IV.

You may receive this word with some relief--the preliminaries are out of the way. It is time to give you my advice about political education. It's time for me to teach you what I know abut becoming a better citizen.

Anticlimax time? Maybe it will seem that way, for my advice turns out to be pretty simple.

Let me proceed by silly indirection and analogy. You didn't know this about me until now, because these words aren't in a book with my picture on the dust jacket, but I could use to lose a few pounds. Now that I am into middle age, I could use to lose thirty pounds to be exact. Imagine the actor Richard Dreyfuss with that much excess baggage and you have a person who looks a lot like me.

I know how to do the job. A diet book in my possession has proven useful to thousands and, on one occasion, for a short time, to me.

The book sums up its sage advice in a single, short phrase: "Walk more, eat less fat."[31] The advice, the book says, is simple. Simple, but hard to follow.

My advice to you is the same: simple, but maybe very hard to follow.

My advice to you on how to be a good citizen is this: Avoid cynicism, be civil. Somehow I need to say it louder: AVOID CYNICISM, BE CIVIL!

In the next section I want to show that I know it is hard to avoid cynicism, that it takes a large dose of self-overcoming. In the section after that, I want to spell out what I think being civil means.

These two sections together are my attempt to give you the right attitude and point you toward the skills you need to be an effective participant in our democratic politics. They are my attempt to help you be free.

V.

A simple point begins this section on resisting cynicism. The simple point is that most of us like honesty. We can have fun watching clever cons in a movie, but most of us wouldn't want to know them or call them friends.

A lot of people seem to think that politicians are like cons who are too clever for their own good and, besides, they're not even funny. Politics has a bad reputation, in part, because many people just don't think politicians are honest.

I want to tell you straight out that I don't think politicians are as dishonest as they are made out to be. True, we find out about some real prizes, like the Arizona legislators who took bribes from an undercover F.B.I. agent, or the Congressman caught in the ABSCAM sting a few years ago who told the hidden microphone he had larceny in his blood.[32] The temptations in politics are big and some folks, even some well-meaning folks, fall by the wayside. There are thousands of men and women in politics, though, whose ethics are able to stand scrutiny. My own Congressman, Speaker Thomas Foley, seems to be an upright and honest man, although he has drawn criticism for the House bank and post office scandals and his personal financial dealings have been questioned.

However honest they are, politicians don't always *sound* honest. There is something about political speech which makes it sound as if politicians are lying when they really aren't. There is a class of political speech which might be labelled "waffling," "obfuscating," or even "misleading with half-truths" which is not quite the same as lying. Artfully done, this kind of speech serves more than one important purpose in politics. Yes, it may protect the self-serving politician from being pinned down in an uncomfortable position. But it also may fuzz the edges of political debate in a way that serves the common good. Hostile groups being blunt with each other is sometimes a recipe for disaster. Take the blunt edge off with some fuzzy but appealing language and perhaps you've raised the possibility of peaceful co-existence. Fuzzy speech may prevent the pollution of the political atmosphere by acrimonious and recriminating words, making it possible for people to work together.

I'm not saying that lying is good. I'm not saying that a weasel shouldn't be called a weasel. I am saying that we should open our minds to the possibility that untruthfulness might not always be bad. Understanding the differences between private and political speech is a step toward healthy citizenship. A fault in a friend might not always be a fault in a politician. It might--but it might not.

Politics is not the search for truth. It is not religion, philosophy, or science. The first obligation of the politician is not to seek and speak truth at all costs. Politics is rule by persuasion and conciliation. Sometimes the whole truth is the most persuasive and conciliating thing to speak. Hearing the truth, followers fall readily into line behind the morally blameless leader. It could happen. It is a pipe dream of a certain kind of political philosopher (Plato, Rousseau, Marx) to think that it could all the time, if only the right people with the purest hearts were put in charge.

Politics is not the search for truth, and truth in politics is not always clear to see. More often than not, it is in dispute. Frequently in politics, truth is not really the issue. Many political fights are about reconciling conflicting desires felt by diverse groups of people. I want this, you want that. Worse, we both want the same thing and there is not enough of it to go around. The politician's task is not to find the right answer--if by right you mean the only true answer. His or her task is to find the attractive and workable answer. The workable answer is the one that both attracts a following and proves its effectiveness in practice.

Politicians put together coalitions of people who don't rush to put themselves together. Run-of-the-mill politicians put together temporary coalitions of this kind all the time. Great politicians sometimes put together a new coalition that moves the country decisively forward, solving longstanding, apparently intractable problems, giving the country a new look. This is what Abraham Lincoln did. (You can see this in Michael Leiserson's chapter.) This is what Franklin Roosevelt did. In a certain way, even though he never held elective office, this is what Martin Luther King did. There are negative examples, too. Demagogues are the bad version of the same thing, men or women who put together coalitions based on envy, hatred, or the desire for revenge.[33]

It is an easy step now to the next higher plateau, where we can see that democratic politicians, although friendly to us, cannot be our friends. The politicians we elect to lead us generally want at least two things. First, they want to lead us in the right direction. They want to do the right thing. Second, they also want to please us so that we will re-elect them, so that they can go on leading. Politicians accomplish this second task with surpassing skill, often far greater skill than they bring to bear on the first task. Their success should be traced, in part, to their skillful self-presentation. (They have numerous other advantages, too: the right party label for their district, more money from PACs, free mailing privileges to keep up name recognition, etc.) They are wonderfully adept at telling us what we want to hear. This is true even if what you want to hear is not the same as what I want to hear--they will find a way to please us both. The results are plain and well known: almost all Congressmen, for example, are re-elected if they choose to run. This success is striking in the face of the overwhelmingly poor performance ratings the public gives Congress as a whole.[34] In the absence of other cues prejudicing us against what we hear, we end up liking the particular politician speaking to us, even though we despise the class of people he or she comes from.

In fact, nothing would please most politicians more than to say the right thing to all people. They want with deep sincerity to be friend to all the people. They are inherently, unabashedly, incurably promiscuous.

Promiscuity is likely to be incompatible with friendship. The point, though, is not to reject the politician because he or she is fickle or in love with too many people at once. After all, we are choosing servants here, not friends. If they do their job well, then politicians should be supported--even if they seem to be too many things to too many people. Understanding politics and politicians, we should put up with behavior we wouldn't want to see in a friend.

Now the last step.

Cynicism is rooted in disappointment. Disappointment and hurt. We are not born cynical, although early abuse will make even children withdrawn and cynical. Happier childhoods leave the development of cynicism to a later date, where it is kin to the development of judgment. We learn to make distinctions, to see behind appearances, to call one thing more genuine than another. As our world and our judgment become more complex we run the risk of disillusionment. Something we thought was genuine turns out to be fake and we are disappointed. Too much of this and we lose the capacity to regard anything as serious or genuine.

There are, however, two reasons to be disappointed which are quite different from one another. We can be disappointed when people or things fail to perform as they should. We cherish the grace and beauty of an athlete who turns out to be lazy, so we feel cheated by the loss of greatness. The product we bought with high hopes turns out to made of pot metal, not stainless steel as advertised. Or we can be disappointed when our expectations are set too high, when we hold somebody or something up to an unreasonable standard of excellence. "Son, you've got to do better than that. You're acting like an eight year old." "But, Dad, I am an eight year old." This time the fault is ours. We are asking for more than we should ask, so we have guaranteed our disappointment.

True enough, politicians engage in a little false advertising. In politics there is a lot of pot metal trying to pass for stainless steel. We must learn to live with this state of affairs. In any case, we are bound to be disappointed if we judge politicians by too high a standard, say, the standard of friendship. They are not necessarily capable of it and we mustn't expect it.

To finish this section I offer an example of a politician who disappointed me. The lesson is the same: the disappointment was as much or more my fault as his. I shouldn't have held him to such a high standard and I shouldn't have put so much stock in him when he asked me to trust him.

My example is James Earl Carter, President from 1977 to 1981.

In the summer of 1979 President Carter was more than halfway through his term in office; and he was in deep political trouble. Fair or not, presidents get the blame when the economy is not good, and it wasn't in 1979. The consumer price index had risen 11.3% in a year; prices were almost 20% higher than they had been when Carter took office. The unemployment figures were better than they had been under President Ford, but they were still high; the 1979 figure would be 5.8%. The prime interest rate fluctuated during the year, but was at historic levels.[35] The other yardstick for presidential performance, foreign policy, was not in shambles, as it was later in the year after Iranian militants took American embassy personnel hostage in Tehran, but it was irksome enough. OPEC was causing difficulties, for example. So the public blamed the president. In 1979 President Carter's public approval rate hovered near the 30% mark, a low point rarely reached or exceeded by modern presidents.[36]

Carter had raised expectations about new directions. Planning to speak on the technicalities of the "energy crisis," but in the mood of an Old Testament prophet, he had retreated to the mountain-top at Camp David to prepare. He consulted with other national leaders--politicians, educators, and religious leaders all had their say. As the date of the speech grew nearer, Carter shifted its theme to the condition of public morality in America, the state of our public-spiritedness. Carter's diary entry for July 4 notes the "remarkable sense of relief and renewed confidence" he felt at the change; he would shake the public, up until now "completely immune to warnings about the future," from its lethargy and self-absorption like an Old Testament prophet.[37]

President Carter delivered his speech on July 15 with his usual earnestness. He announced his belief that the country was in a crisis of fundamental importance. It wasn't just bad economic times that plagued us, but a spiritual malady as well. "Our people are losing faith," he said, "not only in government itself, but in their ability as citizens to serve as the ultimate rulers of our democracy." He urged Americans to return to that faith and promised "I will lead our fight." His last words were part warning, part plea for help: "I will not do it alone. Let your voice be heard."[38]

I was livid. Nor was I alone in my reaction.

Why did Carter's speech disappoint and anger me?

What bothered me was what I took to be Carter's smug self-righteousness, and the feeling that suddenly I was being blamed. The president seemed to say, "The country is in a hell of a fix. Maybe I'm a little bit to blame but mostly it's your fault. You've lost faith in yourself." Well, I hadn't and I didn't appreciate his telling me I had. Moreover, his promise to lead the fight seemed very hollow, since he had done precious little leading up until then. He offended me. Here he had asked to be trusted, and we had trusted him, and now he had turned on us. Some leader! Some friend!

I voted for Carter in November, 1980, just as I had in November, 1976, although this time with far less enthusiasm. My wife Susan canceled my vote by going with John Anderson, the third-party candidate. In 1980 voting seemed a chore performed from duty, not a happy affirmation of my connection to the political system. I danced on the edge of the inviting galley of cynicism.

What did Carter do that was so awful? Not much, in retrospect. He was clearly the wrong man for the job, but then the country elected him with its eyes open. He was doing his best to do what politicians must do--rally the people behind a program and get them to like him so he could go on leading. Of course his words were a little misleading and quite self-serving. To think badly of him for this is to forget what he was--a democratic politician. And his message was not so bad. After all, it was a call to virtuous participation, very like the plea I am making in this essay. In the end, it seems the problem was not so much Carter as it was my unreasonable expectations.

Instead of wallowing in our disappointment at frail leaders, perhaps we should spend more time making sure we are prepared to be the "ultimate rulers of our democracy."

Which brings me to civility.

VI.

In Part IV I told you that the political education I have to offer could be summarized as "Avoid cynicism, be civil." In Part V you fought alongside me against cynicism. Now we come to civility. First I want to say that civility, whose component parts I will describe, is neither the same as nor a substitute for either political passion or material interest. People are often drawn into politics by some passion or interest which almost compels them to act. They defiantly protest the state highway department's plan to put a freeway through their neighborhood.[39] They are outraged that their taxes are too high and determine to do something about it. They can't stand the injustice of racial discrimination any longer and so they join a sit-in to protest. They can't believe that their country would make immoral war on a small nation, so they march. And so on. There are many interests and many high causes. They are not the same as civility, though they should be pursued with civility.

People who are drawn into politics solely by passion or interest are often political shooting stars; their passion expended, their interest protected, they disappear, lights flickering out, not to be seen again. Others sustain their involvement for years. I saw a film the other night of the civil rights march at Selma, Alabama, in 1965. There was John Lewis, first across the bridge and first to be beaten by police. It made me happy to think that he sits now in the House of Representatives as a Congressman from Georgia and a Deputy Whip of the Democratic Party.

There are, however, always more shooting stars than there are John Lewises.

Passions or interest can get us started in politics, but they can't be counted on to prod citizens toward the daily exertions that are needed to make a free democratic politics work. Something closer to "chosen duty" is needed, a willingness to work born of the realization that this is how we will preserve our way of governing.

In a well-known essay on political leadership, *Politics as a Vocation*, the German sociologist Max Weber wrote that "Politics is a strong and slow boring of hard boards."[40] To keep going, a political leader needs both passion and perspective, the kind of perspective that enables a leader to see that one day's work is never the whole job. Richard Neustadt, an expert on the American presidency, makes a similar point in citing President Franklin Roosevelt's comment on Abraham Lincoln: "Lincoln was a sad man because he couldn't get it all at once. And nobody can."[41] Political leaders must learn to live with disappointment and frustration and then get on with business. It is the same for citizens. We are boring our own hard boards. We need the strength of character to keep at the job.

This is what civility is--that collection of habits of heart and mind that enables us to sustain political involvement. They are the habits that make us free.

I have prepared a partial list:

Public-spiritedness. You need to care about the common good. Press your claims, yes, but see that they are not the only worthwhile ones. You can't care about the common good if you deny there is such a thing. Resist Karl Marx who tells you there is no common interest, only class interest. Resist Jeremy Bentham who tells you that, since society is only a fictional term for a collection of individuals, the common good is nothing more than all the individual goods added up, subtracted, canceled out.[42] In some commonsense fashion (or doesn't that exist either?), don't we know that we share interests with all or most of the other people living in our country? It may be the common defense, a prosperous economy, a system of good laws well obeyed, a liveable planet. These are the big-picture goals politicians aim to achieve, even while conciliating opposing interest. You need to think along the same lines: in your own situation can you find a way to serve the common good?

No politician but a good American, I go to a lot of committee meetings, mostly at work. I've been in some meetings where a problem is to be solved but, at the outset, there is no clear solution in view. One or two proposals are tried out, but found wanting. As the talk goes on, with seriousness and good will, the group inches its way toward a solution that not only is acceptable to all, but pleases them. In effect, the participants in the meeting have discovered the common interest.

Look for this sort of possibility in your own groups. Recognize, also, that discovering the common good is not a matter of easy and thoughtless surrender to somebody else's view--rather it is the hard work of finding what really is shared. Spinelessness is a handicap, not a help. In short, pursuing the common good, being public-spirited, is compatible with remaining an individual, with being yourself.

Self-sacrifice. My wife Susan, a counselor by profession, warns me to look out for co-dependence. It is not healthy, she says, to take on too much responsibility for other people's happiness. Her advice is sound, as always, so let me clarify. What is wanted in politics is not a surrender of autonomy so much as a recognition of mutual commitment. As fellow citizens, we should acknowledge our interdependence and pledge to care for what we share in common, our political life. We must be prepared to sacrifice self, in the sense of sacrificing interest. Since we are inclined to be self-interested, this is a difficult sacrifice for us to make. It is easier in the context of a bargain: "I'll give you some of what you want, if you'll give me some of what I want." Much of politics is conducted this way. Free people, though, must get used to the idea of a self-sacrifice that brings no immediate tangible reward. Knowing the unwillingness of hard-nosed yankees to give without return, Tocqueville conjured up an "American" moral teaching, the doctrine of self-interest properly understood. Americans, he said, refused to put much stock in virtue, but they brought themselves around to habits of virtue indirectly, by practicing self-interest properly understood. One American helps another out with no thought of return--now. The generous American earns the right to similar generous treatment when it is needed some time later on. Once this habit is widespread, people act virtuously from motives that are purely self-interested, though Tocqueville concluded that Americans were instinctively more generous than they liked to let on.[43]

However it is done, free people need to be able not to insist on winning the day for their interest every time. Maintaining political rule over time means that diverse interests must be conciliated. Moreover, new interests will, from time to time, be admitted to the political arena. Their entrance cannot be resisted without a sort of shrinking of political space, without a protective closing in by those already inside. Prior occupants must give up a share of power to newcomers; or at least they must be willing to operate in a more crowded space which makes the task of self-government more complicated.

Ultimately, maintaining freedom and democracy may involve even greater sacrifices of substance, energy, and time. At the extreme, maintaining freedom may involve risking one's life. I am talking about fighting wars in defense of freedom (thus disappointing another college roommate, a Quaker pacifist). People my age are often made uncomfortable by such talk because we have seen so many lives lost in dubious "freedom fights" in our time. Nevertheless, there are genuine freedom fights that must be fought, World War Two, for example. Recognizing the need for an ultimate sacrifice does not mean that you have to approve every stupid war that comes along. You can be a patriot without approving of Vietnam or even the Gulf War.

Patience. This is an easy virtue for those who are content but a hard one for the discontent. The need for patience should be clear if what I have previously said about politics is convincing. People who are struggling to get into the political arena--blacks in the 1950s and 60s, many women now--are caught in a particularly painful bind. Impatience, a refusal to put up with injustice, fuels their political engines; but to assure success in the longrun it is necessary to rest content temporarily with partial victories, or even to take a step back, absorbing a defeat without crumbling. A minority, without positions of power, in particular, has to curb anger effectively enough so that allies are not turned away and so that it is still possible to talk to powerholders. The alternative is to be defeated, to retreat to an enclave, if that is possible. If you are in this position, work hard not to close your ears automatically when somebody preaches "go slow" to you. Do this, mind you, without for a moment reconciling yourself to subordination.

Tolerance, and beyond tolerance to empathy. A free and political country is peopled by diverse human beings. Human diversity is to be treasured, but it also can be scary. One group's customs, behavior, and beliefs are bound to appear strange or distasteful to another group. What is true of groups is also true of the people who speak for them. Try this mental experiment: form an image right now of the person in public life who seems to you to be the most odious, unbelievably wrong person in creation. Make sure it is an American. (Since I am not keeping secrets from you, I'll tell you that my spontaneously formed image is of a certain senator from North Carolina.) A person who expresses views so obnoxious (read: so different from yours) must come from another planet, you think. If you are human like the rest of us, you might even fantasize about what you would do to this person in the right circumstances. In unfree countries, people with power act out their fantasies. In a free country, in a political regime, no such maltreatment is allowed nor should it even be contemplated. In politics you are not asked to love your enemies, but you are asked to let them live, and to live with them.

You are less likely to be tolerant of people you know nothing about. So start learning.

Daily contact with people who are different from you can either induce tolerance, if your experiences are good ones, or make it nearly impossible, if your experiences are bad ones. People who are too content with the way things are may misinterpret a "new" group's demands for recognition and dignity. They may feel pushed. The proper response, the political response, is not resistance, but understanding and acceptance. You and I are different. I don't understand you--yet--but I know that you and I are going to have to live together. So I will not try to interfere with your life. And I will try to work with you on matters of common concern. Most of all, I will listen to you, doing my best to find out who you are and what you want. I will try to put myself in your place. Please do the same for me. In the end we may understand each other. Although it is not strictly necessary, we may end up liking each other a lot.

The ability to listen and to speak. My last remarks show the need. Although always valuable abilities, good speaking and good listening are essential in politics. Neither ability is easily won.

We learn to speak by copying other speakers. Having grown up in a closed-mouthed family, exposed daily to the true Colorado accent (a sort of slow mumble), I consider myself lucky to be able to speak at all. I didn't receive real training in the art until I became a teacher and had to practice on my students, bless their patience. You have your story about learning to speak, too.

We learn political speech from politicians. I have already done my best to disagree with the notion that such political speech is a pack of lies, although it does not always have the virtues of candor and eloquence, I admit. Think not just about the speech of candidates running for office, but also about the speech of ordinary citizens working with each other in a variety of settings--workplace, public meeting, and so on. To put your case effectively, to say the words that point the way toward common ground, to encapsulate a solution in a brief statement--these achievements are attainable through practice. Think about what you are doing as you act politically, form your speech to accomplish a political aim, and you are well on your way. You will make more progress if you are self-consciously political than if you are merely blowing off steam or filling the air with noise.

Listening is the greater problem. Much of the political speech we hear is now indistinguishable from ordinary advertising, and you know how that deadens the ear. Also, our habits of listening to contending interests in politics can be pretty thoughtless. Our friends say what we like to hear and we rush to agree and applaud. Our enemies upset us and we rush to talk over whatever they say. Unfortunately, it is also hard to listen and hear when we are among our fellow citizens. The art of listening requires focused concentration, the ability to repeat or paraphrase what has just been said, and skill at asking just the right probing question. Like speaking, listening requires self-conscious practice.

Conciliation and compromise. All that I have said so far about the habits of civility culminate in this section. Indeed, I am very near the end of the political education I have to offer you and, I believe, you are by now able to anticipate what I will say here.

The abilities to conciliate and compromise are at the heart of politics. Good citizens engage in mutually acceptable compromises to further their interests, but also to ensure the greater common good. They conciliate because they know that diverse people living in the same country need to go on living together peacefully, that politics is better than force. A compromising nature seems inborn in some people; others seem to learn the art as they grow and mature. I am quite convinced that the necessary skills can be cultivated, or I wouldn't be telling you all that I've told you.

The ability to compromise involves recognition of your own interests, recognition of what others have at stake, and willingness to look beyond the present bargain to think about how others not in the room are likely to be affected. The ability to conciliate involves the generous acceptance of newly heard claims as well as the repetition of old deals. A mature exercise of the habits of civility enhances our ability to act in the world as autonomous, self-governing individuals. This "chosen duty" is a small burden to bear for the sake of freedom.

VII.

Freedom can also be loved.

Apparently, Americans of an earlier generation loved their political freedom so much that participating in the public life of their country was a joy, not a duty or burden. At least, this is what Tocqueville said, although he admitted to exaggeration from time to time to make a point. Here are his words from *Democracy in America*:

> No sooner do you set foot on American soil than you find yourself in a sort of tumult; a confused clamor rises on every side, and a thousand voices are heard at once, each expressing some social requirement. All around you everything is on the move: here the people of a district are assembled to discuss the possibility of building a church; there they are busy choosing a representative; further on, the delegates of a district are hurrying to town to consult about some local improvement; elsewhere it's the village farmers who have left their furrows to discuss the plan for a road or a school.

So busy, these self-governing Americans:

> It is hard to explain the place filled by political concerns in the life of an American. To take a hand in the governance of society and to talk about it is his most important business and, so to say, the only pleasure he knows.[44]

Without denying ourselves our other pleasures, let's make it so again. Let's restore politics to a central place in our lives. Let's prove that Tocqueville was right when he said that our love of freedom would be nearly unconquerable.

VIII.

There are several things I would like for you to do for me, if you would, over the next ten to twelve months. If you've already done them, pat yourself on the back. Here's my list:

(1) Vote. Vote in more than one election, if possible.

(2) Meet three people who represent you in Congress, the state legislature, the city council, or a county or special district board of commissioners.

(3) Once a month, write a one-page argument on a major issue of the day that agitates you. Then write an argument for the other side.

(4) Befriend someone of a different race or ethnic background. Sound out their picture of America.

(5) Read a history of racism in America.

(6) Listen to feminists. Take a class if it will help.

(7) Form a small group whose purpose is to encourage its members to talk with and listen to each other closely. Engage in self-revelation. Make sure the group contains both men and women.

(8) Speak in a public meeting.

(9) After study and reflection, and for good reason, change your mind about something important.

On top of this list, upon its completion, please do me one more favor. Write me a letter, telling me how it all turned out. I won't leave here until I hear from you. I am easy to find: Blaine Garvin, Gonzaga University, Spokane, WA 99258.

Notes

1. Charles Norris Cochran, *Christianity and Classical Culture* (New York: Oxford University Press, 1957); W. W. Tarn, *Alexander the Great* (Boston: Beacon Press, 1956); John Stuart Mill, *On Liberty*, Currin V. Shields, ed. (Indianapolis: The Bobbs-Merrill Company, 1956); Hanna Fenichel Pitkin, *The Concept of Representation* (Berkeley: The University of California Press, 1972). There is no particular significance to this choice of texts. I reached for books on my shelf, just the way Steve would have.

2. Thomas Hobbes, *Leviathan*, selections by Richard S. Peters, Michael Oakeshott, ed. (London: Collier-MacMillan, 1962), 20.

3. *Gonzaga University Catalogue, 1991-93* (Spokane: Gonzaga University, 1991), 2. The words appear in this context: "We hope that the integration of liberal, humanistic learning and skills with a specialized competence will enable our graduates to enter creatively, intelligently, and with deep moral conviction into a variety of endeavors, and provide leadership in the arts, the professions, business, and public service." It seems that in America public service always comes after business.

4. Bernard Crick, *In Defense of Politics*, 2nd ed. (Chicago: University of Chicago Press, 1972), 15.

5. The stance is as old, at least, as politics and political education. For a discussion of the tension between thought and action, see Hannah Arendt, *The Human Condition* (Chicago: The University of Chicago Press, 1958).

6. Jacques Barzun, *The Forgotten Conditions of Teaching and Learning* (Chicago: The University of Chicago Press, 1991). Quoted by reviewer David Alexander, "Begin Here," The New York Times Book Review, April 21, 1991, 16. Emphasis added. Perhaps it proves Barzun's concern well founded that I culled his quotation from a review rather than read his collection of essays.

7. See Karl Marx and Friendrich Engels, "The German Ideology" and "The Communist Manifesto," *The Marx-Engels Reader*, 2nd ed., Robert C. Tucker, ed. (New York: W.W. Norton, 1978), 146-200, 469-500.

8. I went to Swarthmore College and to the University of California at Berkeley. Those who know these two schools will agree, I think, on their ability to awaken the critical mind.

9. George Orwell, "Politics and the English Language," in *A Collection of Essays by George Orwell* (New York: Harcourt Brace Janovich, 1946), 164.

10. Take, for example, the words of the 1962 "Port Huron Statement," a founding document of the Students for a Democratic Society: "We would replace power rooted in possession, privilege, or circumstances by power and uniqueness rooted in love, reflectiveness, reason and creativity." Cited in Tom Hayden, *Reunion* (New York: Random House, 1988), ix.

11. The reference is to Lewis Carroll's story of Alice's adventures. Arguing with Humpty Dumpty, a large egg with hands, feet, and a face, Alice said words mean what they mean. No, Humpty Dumpty replied, it is a question of mastery: who is to control meaning, the word or the person using it? They both may be right. Words ought to mean what they mean, but we all give a special twist to the terms we use. Right now, though, I am going with Alice's view. Lewis Carroll, "Through the Looking Glass" in *The Annotated Alice*, Martin Gardner, ed. (New York: Bramhall House, 1960), 268.

12. Alfred Zimmern, *The Greek Commonwealth*, rev. ed., (New York: Oxford University Press, 1961), 160. For further description see Donald Kagan, *Pericles of Athens and the Birth of Democracy* (New York: The Free Press, 1991).

13. Joint Association of Classical Teachers' Greek Course Background Book, *The World of Athens* (Cambridge: The Cambridge University Press, 1984), 199.

14. *The Complete Writings of Thucydides: The Peloponnesian War* translated by John H. Findlay, Jr. (New York: The Modern Library, 1951), 102-109.

15. Thomas Paine, *The Rights of Man*, Harry Hayden Clark, ed. (New York: Hill and Wang, 1961), 193.

16. Isaiah Berlin, "Two Concepts of Liberty," *Four Essays on Liberty* (London: Oxford University Press, 1969), 122.

17. Ibid., 131.

18. Alexis de Tocqueville, *The Old Regime and The French Revolution*, trans. Stuart Gilbert (Garden City, NY: Doubleday & Co., 1955), xiv.

19. Crick, *In Defense of Politics*, 22. (See note 4 above.)

20. Alexis de Tocqueville, *Democracy in America*, J.P. Mayer, ed., trans. George Lawrence (Garden City, NY: Doubleday & Co., 1969), 250.

21. Ibid., 363. Tocqueville feared that slavery could not be ended without great violence. Nevertheless, he was clearly opposed to slavery as these words from *Democracy in America* show: "all my hatred is concentrated against those who, after a thousand years of equality, introduced slavery into the world again ... slavery, amidst the democratic liberty and enlightenment of our age, is not an institution that can last. Either the slave or the master will put an end to it. In either case great misfortunes are to be anticipated." I can see no way a political solution abolishing slavery could have been arrived at.

22. Bernard Bailyn, *The Ideological Origins of the American Revolution* (Cambridge, MA: The Belknap Press of Harvard University Press, 1967), 66-9.

23. Paine, *Common Sense*, 34.

24. Bailyn, *Ideological Origins*, 234.

25. The history of the franchise is recounted in Patterson, *The American Democracy* (New York: McGraw-Hill, 1990), 203-204.

26. Tocqueville, *Democracy in America*, 33.

27. James Madison, "Federalist Paper #10," in Alexander Hamilton, James Madison, and John Jay, *The Federalist Papers*, Clinton Rossiter, ed. (New York: New American Library, 1961), 81.

28. Professor Leiserson, one of the editors of this volume, and I have written a short piece in explanation: "The Separation of Powers," *Today's Constitution and You* (Seattle: Metrocenter YMCA, 1986). This piece is not widely available but perhaps we could send you a copy.

29. Tocqueville, *Democracy in America*, 60.

30. One of the most complete collection of Marx's writings on America is *Marx and Engels on the United States* (Moscow: Progress Publishers, 1979). Subsidized writings from the former Soviet Union are not generally well known for their veracity, but as far as I can tell the accounts given here are accurate.

31. Martin Katahn, *The Rotation Diet* (Toronto: Bantam Books, 1987), 147.

32. See "Arizona Lawmakers Resign, One Ousted," *State Legislatures* 17 (May 1991), 6. The Congressman in question was John Jenrette of South Carolina. See *1980 Congressional Quarterly Almanac*, XXXVI (Washington: Congressional Quarterly Press, 1981), 516.

33. My appreciation for good democratic politicians comes partly from watching America, partly from reading about Greece. A graduate school teacher of mine was especially helpful in persuading me that politics was more about seeking accommodations than seeking truth. "Even in the hostile pages of Plato, [the democratic politician] emerges as the true 'political' man, the leader whose problems are defined by the ever-changing patterns of 'politics' and whose knowledge is pragmatic and empirical, because he aims not at pursuing an absolute principle but at discovering a policy whose duration depends on the alignment of political forces at any moment." Sheldon Wolin, *Politics and Vision* (Boston: Little, Brown, 1960), 45-50.

34. In part, incumbents succeed because they run against Congress. One of the best analyses, although now several years old, is Richard Fenno, *Home Style: House Members in their Districts* (Boston: Little, Brown, 1978). Surveys reveal the unpopularity of Congress. See *Congressional Quarterly Weekly Report*, November 2, 1991, Vol. 49, No. 44, 3719, for a survey showing that Congress stacks up unfavorably to other institutions. The survey, done by the Gallup

organization, is reported alongside a picture of a Congressman with a paper bag covering his head.

35. For these and related data see Harold W. Stanley and Richard G. Niemi, *Vital Statistics on American Politics* (Washington: Congressional Quarterly Press, 1988), 346-363.

36. James Q. Wilson, *American Government: Institutions and Practices*, (Lexington, MA: D.C. Heath, 1986), 340-341, shows a clear graph of presidential popularity dating back to the Truman administration.

37. Jimmy Carter, *Keeping Faith* (New York, Bantam, 1981), 114-115.

38. *1979 Congressional Quarterly Almanac*, XXXV (Washington: Congressional Quarterly Press, 1980), 46-47E.

39. Tocqueville, *Democracy in America*, uses a similar example: a farmer drawn into local politics because the town plans to build a road across his land. (See note 29 above.)

40. Max Weber, "Politics as a Vocation," *From Max Weber: Essays in Sociology*, H.H. Gerth and C. Wright Mills, trans. and ed. (New York: Oxford University Press, 1958), 128.

41. Richard E. Neustadt, *Presidential Power and the Modern Presidents* (New York: MacMillan, 1990), 153.

42. See Marx, "Communist Manifesto," and Jeremy Bentham, *The Principles of Morals and Legislation* (New York: Hafner, 1948), 3.

43. Tocqueville, *Democracy in America*, 525-528.

44. Ibid., 243.

About the Authors

Mary Jo Bona: I was hired at Gonzaga to teach nineteenth-century American Literature in the English Department. My interest in marginal women writers has allowed me to design new courses, one of which is Women and American Literature. When I was teaching this course for the first time, I was also thinking about how women typically lead one another in non-traditional ways. Out of this reflection came my paper on how Italian/American women writers represent the family functioning as leaders in Italian/American communities in the earlier decades of the twentieth century.

Eloise A. Buker: I am an associate professor of political science at the University of Utah and have a joint appointment in Women's Studies. I have directed Women's Studies Programs at the University of Utah and Denison University, and served as Director of the International Studies Program at Gonzaga University. My work in directing these programs inspired my interest in leadership. I struggle with finding ways of governance that enable full participation, wise decisions, and ease. My previous work includes a book about storytelling and politics. My current major project is a study of the rhetoric in American feminist theory, showing how that rhetoric opens up new possibilities for political practices and public policy. I teach courses in political theory, feminist theory, methodologies, and American political life.

Frank B. Costello, S.J.: My career-long experience of teaching courses on the American presidency (I am now professor emeritus in the Department of Political Science at Gonzaga) led to the investigation of what made the historians rate five presidents as great leaders. Was it the crisis in American history they encountered, or their response to the crises that made them great chief executives? My essay attempts to answer those questions. I have previously written a volume on *The Political Philosophy of Luis de Molina, S.J.*

Peter B. Ely, S.J.: Several years ago I saw Eric Rhomer's movie version of *Perceval*. The film started a train of reflection about the crisis which occurred in the life of Perceval when he failed to ask a simple question. When a group of Gonzaga University professors--the authors of this book--began talking about leadership, I realized the story of Perceval is about the education of a leader. My background as a priest and theologian naturally leads me to a view of leadership that is religious and moral. I am pleased to be a piece of the mosaic formed by the chapters of this book.

Blaine Garvin: Born in Denver in 1943, I grew up in nearby Golden, Colorado. I was a political science major at Swarthmore College, graduating in 1965, and at the University of California at Berkeley, where I received an M.A. in 1966 and a Ph.D. in 1973. While at Berkeley I was a teaching assistant for Professor Leiserson and a classmate of Professor Waterman. Preceding them to Gonzaga in 1971, I began a career teaching American politics and classical, medieval, and modern political philosophy. I was briefly a congressional press secretary for a Colorado congressman in 1966, and have been an eager if ultimately disappointed office-seeker in Washington, running for the state legislature in 1974 and for "freeholder" in 1992.

Tom Jeannot: I am an assistant professor of philosophy at Gonzaga University. My academic interest in leadership studies began with a course I teach on organizational ethics in G.U.'s Organizational Leadership program. The style of leadership practiced in Alcoholics Anonymous has contributed to its remarkable success, and I believe there are lessons within its spirituality that all of us can learn.

Mike Leiserson: My main qualification for writing about practical wisdom is a profound awareness of wanting it. In its place I earned a Ph.D. in Political Science (Yale, 1966), and did field research and published on Japanese politics, mathematical and experimental studies of politics, and *The End of Politics in America*. When I was fired from Governor Ronald Reagan's University of California at Berkeley in 1971, the students hired me to continue teaching for two years. Then I learned Buddhism with priests from Tibet, and came to Gonzaga to learn Christianity with priests from Europe and America. Other relevant information is in my chapter, which owes much to teaching with Garvin and Waterman, and to an invitation to lecture on Ethics and Politics to the "Life on a Star" Conference of the Unitarian-Universalist Association, Isles of Shoals, NH, August 1986.

Patrick B. O'Leary: Though my doctoral studies at the Gregorian University in Rome were in Systematic Theology, my focus of interest during the last half of my 45 years as a Jesuit has been Ignatian Spirituality and its implications within the wide variety of activities that Jesuits engage in. When I became the religious superior of the Jesuits at Gonzaga in 1986, I involved myself in fostering serious reflection among all segments of the University concerning the implications of the spirituality of St. Ignatius Loyola, the founder of the Jesuits, to the educational vision of Gonzaga. At present I am pursuing the same efforts at the other Jesuit university in the Pacific Northwest, Seattle University, in the Puget Sound area where I grew up.

Jane Rinehart: I have been teaching sociology for more than twenty years. My special fields are the sociology of gender, feminist social theory, and sociology of family life. I have also relished the opportunity to teach the introductory course to students with a wide variety of majors and backgrounds. It is this course that has challenged me to define ways that a sociological perspective can be a valuable tool for people who do not intend to become professional social analysts. My interest in relating this perspective to leadership was sparked by a series of discussions with faculty colleagues about establishing a leadership institute. During these conversations, I discovered that I had been brewing ideas about leadership while thinking about many other things. I tested some of these ideas as one of the organizers of an effort to establish a women's studies program at Gonzaga University. The experience of that project gave me the courage to present my version of what learning to lead entails. I'm still learning.

Julie Tammivaara: My enduring interest is human communities: what brings people together, what alienates them from one another. I have learned something of five languages in addition to English (French, Italian, Spanish, German and Hebrew), and have studied amongst a variety of peoples both ethnically (African Americans, Hispanics, and Native Americans) and religiously (Catholics and Jews). I am currently a field researcher for the Council for Initiatives in Jewish Education in Baltimore, MD. I like to learn of people's roots and assist them in recovering and adapting traditional practices for use in the modern world.

Rose Mary Volbrecht: I am an associate professor of philosophy and co-director of a new Women's Studies program at Gonzaga. My essay grows out of teaching courses in applied ethics, as well as presenting numerous workshops for nurses, respiratory therapists, hospital chaplains, personnel directors, business managers, city employees, engineers, professional women, and others. My graduate studies taught me to think of the role of philosophy professor as someone engaged with ideas and arguments. It did not prepare me to think of a philosophy professor as a member of an organization. My greatest challenge as a teacher has been trying to understand how these two roles are related and how to make a difference in my organization.

Bob Waterman: I teach politics at Gonzaga University. During the 1960's when participatory democracy sometimes worked at its best in the United States, it fascinated me. So did subsequent work at a democratically run restaurant in Oakland, California. More recently, as a teacher and scholar, I have tried to find old-fashioned American reasons for reviving direct democracy while studying its contemporary manifestations.